WHAT THE VICTORIANS MADE
OF ROMANTICISM

What the Victorians Made of Romanticism

MATERIAL ARTIFACTS, CULTURAL PRACTICES, AND RECEPTION HISTORY

TOM MOLE

PRINCETON UNIVERSITY PRESS

PRINCETON & OXFORD

Published by Princeton University Press,
41 William Street, Princeton, New Jersey 08540

In the United Kingdom: Princeton University Press,
6 Oxford Street, Woodstock, Oxfordshire OX20 1TR

press.princeton.edu

Jacket image: Cigarette card showing the Scott Monument, Cope Bros., c. 1900.
Courtesy of the author.

Library of Congress Cataloging-in-Publication Data

Names: Mole, Tom, 1976- author.
Title: What the Victorians made of romanticism : material artifacts, cultural
practices, and reception history / Tom Mole.
Description: Princeton : Princeton University Press, 2017. | Includes bibliographical
references and index.
Identifiers: LCCN 2017007679 | ISBN 9780691175362 (hardcover : alk. paper)
Subjects: LCSH: English literature--19th century--History and criticism. |
Romanticism--Great Britain--19th century.
Classification: LCC PR461 .M55 2017 | DDC 820.9/007--dc23 LC record available at
https://lccn.loc.gov/2017007679

British Library Cataloging-in-Publication Data is available

This book has been composed in Arno Pro

Printed on acid-free paper. ∞

Printed in the United States of America

10 9 8 7 6 5 4 3 2 1

For Heather

CONTENTS

Illustrations

Tables

THIS BOOK was begun in Montreal, developed in Durham, and completed in Edinburgh. Along the way I have incurred many debts. In Montreal I would like to thank Michael Van Dussen, Wes Folkerth, Thomas Heise, Monique Morgan, Derek Nystrom, Monica Popescu, Fiona Ritchie, Ned Schantz, and Tabitha Sparks, who taught me what an intellectual community could be; Dorothy Bray, Nathalie Cooke, Miranda Hickman, Maggie Kilgour, Peter Sabor, Brian Trehearne, and Paul Yachnin, who all offered valuable advice and mentoring; and Susan Dalton, Andrew Piper, Jonathan Sachs, Michael Sinatra, Nicola von Merveldt, and the Interacting with Print collective, who are excellent Romanticists, innovative book historians, and true friends. I was a fellow at the Institute of Advanced Study at Durham University in autumn 2013, and I am very grateful to Elizabeth Archibald, Barbara Graziosi, Michael O'Neill, and Veronica Strang for making my time there so enjoyable and productive. Research for this book was funded in part by grants from the Social Sciences and Humanities Research Council of Canada and the Fonds de Recherche du Québec: Société et Culture, and I am pleased to acknowledge their support.

Many people have helped with particular parts of this book. I gratefully acknowledge Craig Kubic and his staff at Midwestern Baptist Theological Seminary in Kansas City, Missouri, and Judy Powles at Spurgeon College in London for their help researching the library of C. H. Spurgeon; Catherine Bradley at McGill University for information on costume history; local historian Alan Smith for information on the Bowder Stone; Emma Hambly for help researching postcards and other ephemera; Kaiwen Zhang and Samuel Schmidt for database development and support; Brenna Baggs, Danielle Barkley, Susan Civale, Melissa Dickson, Amy Fox, Matthew Ingleby, Christine Lai, Tara MacDonald, Tara Murphy, Lauren Welsh, and above all Mark Algee-Hewitt for their help with compiling the database of nineteenth-century anthologies for part 5; Michel Pharand and Ellen Hawman of the Disraeli Archive at Queen's University in Kingston, Ontario; Andrew Burkett for information on Fox Talbot; Elizabeth James and James Sutton of the Victoria and Albert Museum; Jeff Cowton and Rebecca Turner of the Wordsworth Trust; Jack Wasserman; and Marsha M. Manns. I am grateful to the staff of

McGill University Library, the National Library of Scotland, the National Library of Scotland Maps Library, the Scottish Record Office, the Centre for Research Collections at the University of Edinburgh, the University of Glasgow Library Special Collections, the National Archives, the Courtauld Collection, Abbotsford House, Drew University Special Collections, and the British Library. Thanks also to Anne Savarese and the anonymous readers at Princeton University Press, and to Louise McCray for help preparing the book for publication. Earlier versions of parts of the book appeared in *Romanticism and Victorianism on the Net* 58; *Romanticism: Criticism and Debates*, edited by Mark Canuel; and *BRANCH: Britain, Representation and Nineteenth-Century History*, edited by Dino Felluga. Full details are in the bibliography. I am grateful to the editors and publishers for permission to reprint this material here.

My greatest debts are to Heather and Freya, my wife and daughter. Heather has lived with this book from its beginnings and Freya has lived with it from *her* beginnings. I am immensely grateful to you both.

WHAT THE VICTORIANS MADE
OF ROMANTICISM

Introduction

Don Juan in the Pub

I am for an art that embroils itself with the everyday crap and still comes out
on top.

—CLAES OLDENBURG[1]

ONE NIGHT, Dandy Mick saw Don Juan in The Cat and Fiddle. He'd been
drinking gin twist, but he wasn't seeing things: Juan was a fixture in this particular gin palace. Benjamin Disraeli described the encounter in his novel *Sybil*
(1845), basing his fictional scene on a tavern of the same name in Stockport,
or perhaps one he saw during his 1844 visit to Manchester.[2] Dandy Mick took
two factory girls, Caroline and Harriet, to the pub that night. They made their
way to an upper room named "The Temple of the Muses."[3] "[I]f I had called
it the Saloon," the proprietor "Chaffing Jack" explained, "it never would have
filled, and perhaps the magistrates never have granted a licence." The room's
décor suited its name:

> The ceiling was even richly decorated; the walls were painted, and by a
> brush of considerable power. Each panel represented some well-known
> scene from Shakespeare, Byron, or Scott: King Richard, Mazeppa, the
> Lady of the Lake were easily recognized: in one panel, Hubert menaced
> Arthur; here Haidee rescued Juan; and there Jeanie Deans curtsied before
> the Queen.[4]

Caroline was delighted ("Oh! I love the Temple! 'Tis so genteel!") and Harriet
was dazzled ("It's just what I thought the Queen lived in"). Mick looked
around "with a careless *nil admirari* glance," and showed Harriet the murals.
"'You never were here before; it's the only place. That's the Lady of the Lake,'
he added, pointing to a picture; 'I've seen her at the Circus, with real water.' "[5]
He might have been remembering one of several spectacular adaptations of

1

Walter Scott's 1810 poem that appeared in Victorian theaters and circuses, where he could also have seen staged versions of Byron's *Mazeppa* (1819), which was one of the period's most popular hippodramas.[6] Though he had little time for reading poetry, Mick encountered the works of Byron and Scott through other channels.

This book is about those kinds of encounters. In it, I study the material artifacts and cultural practices that shaped the reputations of Romantic authors in Victorian Britain and recirculated some of their works, often in fragmented or modified forms. I show how Romantic authors and their works were naturalized in a new media ecology and recruited to address new cultural concerns. Dandy Mick's encounter with characters from Romantic literature in his local tavern would be overlooked by most reception histories, but it is just the kind of reception that interests me here. Mick encounters Scott and Byron through a new material artifact, a painting on a tavern wall by an unknown artist. It remediates its source material, shifting it from writing to painting, and so reminds us that the reception of literature is not itself always literary or literary-critical but happens across several media. Indeed, it offers a second-order remediation: Mick sees a painting of a staging of a poem. It is popular and commercial: Chaffing Jack puts up the mural to attract customers, not because he loves literature. It is historically fugitive: the mural apparently disappears when the Temple is "newly painted, and re-burnished" at the end of the novel.[7] And Mick's encounter is embedded in social practices such as dating (or "treating") and cultural institutions such as the tavern.

The mural in "The Temple of the Muses," like every artifact I examine in this book, both implied a reading of an author or a work and recruited them to serve some present purpose. On one hand, painting scenes from Byron and Scott alongside scenes from Shakespeare helped to canonize the recently deceased poets, and selecting the episode in which Haidee rescues Juan indicated a preference for the early, romantic cantos of *Don Juan* over the more outspoken later cantos, a preference shared by Victorian anthologies. On the other hand, Byron and Scott were recruited by Chaffing Jack to lend a genteel tone to his establishment, by Dandy Mick to impress his date, and by Benjamin Disraeli to provide a documentary account of lower-class life with a comic inflection.

Dandy Mick may not have been much of a reader, but he still took his place in a dark web of reception made up of many strands. This web of reception, I argue, is not incidental but essential to the continued vitality of literature. It is the matrix in which literature exists, if it exists at all for people beyond the time and place in which it was written. Authors' reputations never simply endure, and their works never simply find readers unaided. The web's different strands weave together stewardship, which is attentive to the meaning and integrity of an author's works, and appropriation, which conscripts authors and their works for its own purposes. But authors and their works do not simply survive: either they are renewed or they are forgotten. For this reason, the cultural work of reception is never finished, although it may be abandoned. The web of reception is still being woven in the present. This book, too, is part of it.

Most reception histories illuminate only one or two strands of the web. They uncover genealogies of poetic influence, or assemble narratives of the critical heritage. These strands are familiar to modern critics because they structure our own place in the web. But the web extends in other directions, through other media. As well as poetry and criticism, it weaves in sermons, statues, engravings, anthologies, postcards, photographs, cigarette cards, memorial plaques, and much else besides. Things and people, objects and practices, have their place. The web is rhizomatic: it has no center, no one strand from which all others branch, and there is no Archimedean point outside the web from which to see and judge all strands. It is intermedial: the reception of literary works often involves their remediation into other media, both "old" and "new," and requires us to think in terms of a media ecology. Its operations often appear chaotic or stochastic: the chains of contingency that cause a line of poetry to be reprinted in an anthology, read by a clergyman, quoted in a sermon, and remembered by a congregant are inscrutable. But the web is also disciplined by traditions: multiple, intersecting, temporally extended discourse communities that share usually unarticulated assumptions about how literature should be approached. It is, no doubt, traversed by flows of power: different interests woven into the web contest the reputations of authors and the readings of their works. And therefore it is usually presentist: the actors in the web turn back to the literature of the past as a way to engage with pressing contemporary concerns.

This book unpicks some strands of the web of reception in visual, verbal, plastic, and print media. It focuses primarily on the reception of five Romantic writers: Lord Byron, Felicia Hemans, Walter Scott, Percy Shelley, and William Wordsworth. Canonical Victorians who discussed these writers feature in the following pages, but I'm mainly interested in what the Victorians made of Romanticism rather than what they wrote about it. By that, I mean how they renovated Romanticism for a new generation by producing material artifacts such as illustrations, anthologies, statues, photographs, and postcards and how those material objects, in turn, remade their understanding of Romantic writers and their works.

In part 1, I identify underlying conditions for this renovation project in shifting concepts of history, memory, and media. I examine developments in the media ecology between the Romantic and Victorian periods, suggest reasons why the Romantics seemed in danger of being forgotten, and argue that their works had to be naturalized in the changed media ecology if they were to reach new readers (chapter 1). I suggest that their reception is structured by multiple traditions operating in different media. Critics have either neglected reception history altogether, because they have tended to value the context of composition and first publication above all others—a tendency I call "punctual historicism"—or else they have focused on the tradition they inhabit themselves (chapter 2). Victorian commentators thought that a generation gap separated them from the Romantics, so that the writing of even the recent past no longer spoke to their concerns. This meant that Romantic writing needed to be renovated for a new generation if it was not to be forgotten (chapter 3).

I then turn to four different strands of the web of reception, in sections on illustrations, sermons, statues, and anthologies. In each section, I identify a problem and describe efforts to solve it. In part 2, the problem the Victorians faced was how to update the material forms in which Romantic writing circulated in a period of rapid change in book manufacture (chapter 4). Retrofitted illustrations—that is, new illustrations produced for works that initially appeared without illustrations—thematized this process of renovation (chapter 5), while illustrated frontmatter allowed readers to imagine bridging the generation gap (chapter 6). In part 3, I examine a distinctively religious reception tradition for Romantic writing, which had trouble accommodating apparently irreligious poets such as Byron and Shelley (chapter 7). I show how Victorian sermons first minimized Shelley's atheism and then dispensed with it altogether (chapter 8), and examine how one preacher read Byron's works in a variety of books and mediated them to his congregation in complex and inconsistent ways (chapter 9).

In part 4, I suggest that there was a pressing need to foster new forms of cultural consensus in the age of Reform. Pantheons of past heroes offered one version of the desired consensus, but existing pantheons were felt to be inadequate. Commemorating Romantic writers, I argue, played a key role in reimagining the pantheon. At first, this involved looking for new pantheonic structures (chapter 10), but the pantheon rapidly spread across the cityscapes of London and Edinburgh, and eventually the whole country (chapter 11). This allowed for new local, regional, national, and even international constellations of monuments to create new networks of significance (chapter 12). Finally, in part 5, I turn to anthologies. Here the problem was a mismatch between the format in which much Romantic poetry originally appeared, as stand-alone volumes, and the format in which it often circulated to Victorian readers, in anthologies (chapter 13). I show how Victorian anthologies privileged Romantic short poems (chapter 14) and scanned long poems for detachable sections that could be treated like short poems, creating them through editorial intervention where they did not exist (chapter 15). In the process, Victorian anthologies not only made Romantic poems conform to Victorian media of cultural transmission but also eliminated parts of those poems that seemed alien or threatening to Victorian sensibilities.

Each part of the book, then, identifies a large-scale historical change and situates the reception of Romantic writing in relation to it. Part 1 concerns the shift into full-blown modernity, with its attendant sense of acceleration and dislocation from the past, its distinctive kind of historical consciousness and crisis of cultural memory, and its shifting media ecology. Part 2 concerns the sense that the cultural products of the past needed to be made new once again or disappear from consciousness. Part 3 concerns the process of secularization, which throws religious faith into sharp relief and makes religious ways of reading newly distinctive. Part 4 concerns the prolonged uncertainty about national identity produced by the Reform movement, and the sense that new histories were needed to renew social cohesion. And Part 5 concerns a period of media change, as the modern, mass-produced anthology emerged alongside universal state-supported education and became the material form in which many people encountered poetry for the first time. In thinking across the boundaries of periods, disciplines, and media, *What the Victorians Made of Romanticism* necessarily cultivates a variety of methods. Throughout, I draw on literary history, book history, cultural history, and media archaeology, as well as a range of theoretical and historiographical models. Part 1 outlines my approach in detail. I also employ some quantitative methodologies in part 5, which are described in more detail in chapter 13. These different methods allow me to triangulate my object of inquiry by approaching it from different angles. The object of inquiry itself is twofold: the reputations of Romantic authors in Victorian Britain, and the circulation and reception of their works in multiple media.

Unpicking the web of reception reveals new histories of appropriation, remediation, and renewal, showing how the Romantics were naturalized in the Victorian media ecology and recruited to address new cultural concerns. Understanding how this happened in the past should also model how it could happen again, indeed—as I suggest in the coda—how it is still happening. Like the Victorians, we find ourselves living through a moment of media change in which the cultural products of the past often seem in danger of being forgotten if they are not remade for the new media ecology. Those of us who assume responsibility for curating those cultural products, critiquing them, and introducing new generations to them are often asked to justify our work's relevance. This demand is itself a modern one, predicated on the idea that the present is detached from the past. Our critical tendency to stitch literary texts tightly into the context of their composition or first publication sometimes makes it harder to respond to such demands. The first response might be to reject "relevance" altogether, or to historicize the demand for relevance, but paying attention to the dark and densely woven web of reception also offers a way to explain literature's continuing vitality. It reminds us that a literary text is not a singular historical event but something that is repeatedly renewed in different contexts and media, in ways beyond the imagination of its author or its first readers. This web of remaking extends into the present, and not only in the academy but also—as Dandy Mick discovered—in the pub.

PART I

The Web of Reception

1

Romantic Writers in the Victorian Media Ecology

FOR A WHILE, it seemed that the Romantics would not be remembered at all. Many early-Victorian commentators worried that the writing of the recent past no longer compelled readers' interest, and that it would soon be forgotten. The predictions began polemically. *Blackwood's Magazine* claimed in 1820 that John Keats had ruined his talent by imitating Leigh Hunt, that "he must be content to share his fate, and be like him forgotten," and Coleridge wrote in 1825 that he "dare[d] predict, that in less than a century" Byron's and Scott's poems would "lie on the same Shelf of Oblivion."[1] John Todd felt sure in 1835 that Byron would "quickly pass from notice."[2] Predictions soon became warnings. The *Quarterly Review* asserted that Scott was "in danger of passing—we cannot conceive why—out of the knowledge of the rising generation," and Thomas Carlyle cautioned in 1829 that "Byron [...] with all his wild siren charming, already begins to be disregarded and forgotten."[3] And the warnings became simple statements of fact. Orestes Brownson asserted in 1841 that Shelley was "seldom spoken of and much more seldom read." *The Graphic* cattily remarked in 1873 that Hemans was "almost as much neglected now, as she was overrated formerly," while another journalist in 1886 thought that she was "a writer too little read by our young people of the present day." Stopford Brooke declared simply in 1893 that Byron was "not much read now."[4]

If anyone read the Romantics, some claimed, it was only those people who scarcely counted, like adolescents or the uneducated. Selections of Wordsworth's poetry "chiefly for the use of schools and young persons" appeared from as early as 1831, while in 1848 *Readings for the Young, from the Works of Sir Walter Scott* inaugurated a tradition of excerpting or retelling Scott's works for children.[5] Walter Bagehot wrote that "a stray schoolboy may still be detected in a wild admiration for *The Giaour* or *The Corsair* [...], but the *real* posterity—the quiet students of past literature—never read them or think of them."[6] T. S. Eliot followed this line when he recalled taking "the usual

9

adolescent course with Byron, Shelley, [and] Keats," dismissed enthusiasm for Shelley as "an affair of adolescence," and described some of Byron's *Don Juan* as "not too good for the school magazine."[7]

This chapter explains why so many Victorians thought that Romantic writing was starting to seem irrelevant and in danger of being forgotten. The underlying causes, I argue, lay in shifting concepts of history, new anxieties about cultural memory, and a rapidly changing media ecology. When these elements came together, sometime between roughly 1750 and 1850, they created the cultural conditions of modernity, which defined itself as distinctly and self-consciously different from what had gone before. When self-consciously modern people looked back from the nineteenth century to the poets and novelists of their parents' generation, those writers seemed unfitted for addressing modern concerns. The Romantics began to look perilously outdated and uninteresting to new readers. They were liable to gather dust on the "Shelf of Oblivion" if no one took pains to make their works relevant once again. But if the modern nexus of history, memory, and media that I trace here made the Romantics seem old-fashioned, it also created the conditions in which they could be fashioned anew. Changing configurations of history, memory, and media produced the problem and the materials for solving it. Even as they made literature from the recent past seem obsolescent, they created new possibilities for renovating, memorializing, and remediating it. The web of reception would be woven on the conceptual frames that modern understandings of history, memory, and media constructed.

Concerns about who would be remembered and by whom especially clustered around those writers who had been celebrities in their lifetimes. As I have argued elsewhere, a distinctly modern culture of celebrity took shape at the end of the eighteenth century.[8] It emerged in response to the industrialization of print culture and the growth of an audience that was large, anonymous, socially diverse and geographically distributed, and it was bound up with shifting conceptions of subjectivity. In these conditions, celebrity emerged as a cultural apparatus with both material and discursive aspects. Celebrity was often understood, then as now, to be an inferior kind of recognition, opposed to true, worthwhile, and lasting fame. Celebrity was thought of as something ascribed rather than earned, here today and gone tomorrow, a meteor that burned itself out too soon. True fame, in contrast, was slow to arrive and usually posthumous, but it lasted forever because it was deserved. Celebrity and true fame each operated in its own timeframe, and they seldom overlapped. Once celebrity and true fame had come to be understood as mutually exclusive, it became easy to assume that those like Byron and Scott who had been celebrities in their lifetimes would soon be forgotten after their deaths. For some individuals, that proved to be the case. Mary Robinson's celebrity was already deserting her by the end of her life (only two people came to her funeral), and after her memoirs and an edition of her works were published posthumously she disappeared from view almost entirely for the rest of the century.[9] When celebrated authors were not in fact forgotten, we can usually discern a variety of efforts that helped to move them across the bar from life-time celebrity to posthumous fame. This book, then, is partly a sequel to my earlier work; in it, I pursue the story of celebrity beyond the grave to discover what happens to celebrity authors after their deaths. But celebrity is not the whole story here: the web of reception weaves in some other threads as well.

Predictions that Romantic authors would be forgotten were part of a wider set of complaints about the ignorance and presentism of the "rising generation." As early as 1827, William Hazlitt argued that as the reading public grew in size, it began to ignore the literature of the past. "When a whole generation read," he claimed, "they will read none but contemporary productions. The taste for literature becomes superficial, as it becomes universal and is spread over a larger space." "Many people would as soon think of putting on old armour, as of taking up a book not published within the last month, or year at the utmost," Hazlitt asserted.[10] Facing the challenge of raising funds for a statue of Byron (a project I describe in chapter 12), Benjamin Disraeli complained in an 1876 letter that "unfortunately, we have to appeal to a generation, which never read Byron, or, perhaps, anything else."[11] The *Quarterly Review* grumbled in 1868 that "the instances are rare, we suspect, in which, even among educated per-sons, young men or young women under five-and-twenty know anything at all either of what Scott wrote or of what he did."[12] Thomas Carlyle began "Signs of the Times" by affirming that his age preferred to "deal much in vaticination" and look to the future at the expense of the past.[13] The writing of the recent past seemed in danger of dropping out of the stock of common knowledge, as the concerns of the present became ever more urgent. Even people who had read the Romantics seemed unlikely to return to their works. In 1860, Francis Turner Palgrave claimed that what distinguished contemporary read-ers from those of a century before was that now, "everything is to be read, and *everything only once*" (a tendency Palgrave tried to correct when he published *The Golden Treasury* the following year).[14] These commentators anticipated Walter Benjamin's fear that "every image of the past that is not recognised by the present as one of its own concerns threatens to disappear irretrievably."[15] They shared a sense that Romantic writers were beginning to slip into history and anticipated the desuetude of their works. If no one found new ways to reconnect them to the present, they would soon be forgotten altogether.

These anxieties reflect an underlying concept of history that was still fairly new. It emerged, as several historians argue, around 1800. Before then, the passing of time could be understood in a variety of ways, each of which has its own complex historical backstory. Time might be thought of and experienced in terms of seasonal cycles, or in terms of durable continuities that reasserted themselves despite occasional disruptions, or in mythical terms as having a beginning, middle, and end, or in terms of slow but steady teleological progress.[16] Beginning with Thucydides in the fifth century BCE, as Bernard Williams has argued, a conception of historical time emerged that made it possible to ask questions about the truth or falsity of historical accounts.[17] With the rise of Christianity in the first five centuries CE, as François Hartog and others have described, a new conception of salvation history gestates, coming to fruition in Augustine.[18] This understanding orients historical time, first, in relation to the interval between the saving action of Christ's passion and its fulfillment in his Second Coming, when history itself will be gathered into God's Kingdom, and, second, in relation to the Divine "fullness of time" that exists beyond human temporality. As modernity begins to take shape, as Charles Taylor has explained, a new kind of "secular time" begins to appear that can operate "horizontally" in purely human terms without reference to any concept of "higher time."[19] This way of understanding and experiencing historicity makes it possible to conceive of progressively perfecting society and promoting human flourishing over time, first in terms of Providential Deism and later in terms of exclusive humanism. In secular time, as in Thucydides's historical time, the present is essentially continuous with the past. Time flows smoothly from past to present, making the present just the latest moment in what Reinhart Koselleck calls "a purely additive chronology."[20]

By contrast, the French Revolution fostered a radically new historical understanding, in which history itself ruptured and restarted with the revolutionary "Year One." The Revolution should be understood not only as an event *in* history, but as the starting gun for what Hartog calls a modern "regime of historicity," which he dates schematically from 1789 to 1989. Peter Fritzsche argues that the Revolution offered a model for conceiving other kinds of historical change as drastic and discontinuous, which was shared by both Revolutionary sympathizers and conservatives. The "Industrial Revolution," for example, was understood as a technological revolution by analogy with the political revolution that preceded it.[21] In these conditions, what Koselleck calls the "concept of history" emerged.[22] It became possible, even necessary, to think and speak of modernity as radically distinct from the past. The German word *Neuzeit* (modernity) was coined in the nineteenth century, and the English word "modernity" took on a new usage. (As we shall see in chapter 3, Henry James was still putting the word in inverted commas in 1884.)[23] Modernity defines itself by its self-aware historicity and its sense of being fundamentally different to what has gone before.

The new sense of a sharp disjunction between present and past produced a number of effects. It was tied to a new understanding of temporality. An experience of time grounded in nature was gradually replaced by one measured by the clock. A temporality that was natural, cyclical, locally variable, and imprecise gave way to one that was mechanical, linear, uniform, and measurable.[24] It encouraged contemporaries to think of themselves *as* contemporaries, "differently situated subjects who nonetheless shared the same time and place," and introduced a new sense of historicity into individual lives, making people feel that their experiences were different local manifestations of large historical forces that were producing a general, rapid, and unpredictable transformation.[25] As a result, people increasingly thought of themselves as inhabiting a distinct historical period, unlike any that had gone before. They looked for the key characteristics of this period, its spirit, producing what James Chandler calls "the age of the spirit of the age."[26] And when moderns looked back to the past, they increasingly saw it, too, in terms of distinctive, self-contained epochs, which replaced each other with accelerating rapidity. Historians divided history into periods that got shorter the closer they were to the present.[27]

The period covered by this book, then, was arguably the first in which most people expected their lives to be shaped by forces and circumstances that had been unknown a generation or two before. As a result, Victorians felt alienated from even the immediate past, perhaps more acutely than ever before. While the future seemed to be open and uncertain, both promising and worrying, the past started to seem strange, disconnected from the present and removed from its new concerns. In 1886, one journalist could look back and claim that the world of "just sixty-two years ago was almost as unlike the world of to-day as the reign of George I."[28] But even as they mourned their historical alienation from the past, Victorians were also impelled to reconstruct and reinterpret it from the historical standpoint of the present. (The concept of a "historical standpoint" is itself a modern one.) In Fritzsche's phrase, "new time did not always flow steadily into a progressive sea, but pooled and puddled around the wreckage of the past."[29] Perhaps this is why so much intellectual history has been written about the Victorians' engagement with earlier periods.[30] When the present felt unprecedented and the future unforeseeable, the past demanded to be recovered and remade for present purposes. In thinking about the Victorian reception of Romanticism, then, I'm concerned not just with how the Victorians remodeled Romanticism to suit their own concerns but also with the historical conditions that made this renovation project necessary.

The modern sense that time was accelerating, opening a crevasse between present and past, produced a crisis of memory. When people faced "[a]n increasingly rapid slippage of the present into a historical past that [was] gone for good," they made new efforts to remember the past precisely because it was in danger of being lost.[31] The "natural" space of cultural memory, considered as the sum of individual memories passed from one generation to another, was no longer adequate for modernity. Instead, cultural memory increasingly took mediated forms and required self-conscious interventions. The premodern world was imagined as a place in which cultural memory was pervasive and mundane, experienced in the everyday lives of individuals through a comparatively stable sense of belonging and continuity with the past. In this premodern world, people "were able to live within memory."[32] In the modern world, by contrast, this kind of immersion in cultural memory was no longer available, and so cultural memory had to be crystallized in what Pierre Nora calls *lieux de mémoire*. Cultural memory, as Raphael Samuel insists, is not a passive storage system but a dynamic, historically conditioned force, "changing colour and shape according to the emergencies of the moment."[33] When cultural memory ceased to be everywhere, it became newly visible *somewhere*, located in specific sites and often mediated in new ways.

The artifacts and practices that I examine in the following chapters responded to the fear that the Romantics would be forgotten, even when their producers argued that great literature endured without any help. In doing so, they participated in the broader feeling that memory itself was in peril and needed to be shored up in particular sites and through newly vital forms of cultural work. Unveiling a memorial plaque for Felicia Hemans in 1899, the mayor of Liverpool worried that Hemans was in danger of being forgotten in the rush of modern life. Although he had read her poems with pleasure in his youth, he said, "time and changes in the mental condition of the people had contributed somewhat to place her works in shadow." He looked ahead, only half hopefully, to less harried days "when in times of less feverishness of competition and less urgency in life's battle these quieter muses would reappear on the mental horizon."[34] Hemans's works had been read in the past, and they might be read again in the future, but in the present a memorial plaque marked her place of birth until people had time to turn back to her poems. "There are *lieux de mémoire*, sites of memory," Nora asserts, "because there are no longer *milieux de mémoire*, real environments of memory."[35] The existence of *lieux de mémoire* is in fact symptomatic of a fear of forgetting. "The moment of *lieux de mémoire* occurs at the same time that an immense and intimate fund of memory disappears, surviving only as a reconstituted object beneath the gaze of critical history."[36] If the nineteenth-century web of reception was densely woven, it was because those who wove it were acutely conscious of how much was slipping through the net.

But while the memory cultures of modernity responded to a fear of forgetting, they also entailed active efforts to forget. What memory "contrives symptomatically to forget," Samuel writes, "is as important as what it remembers."[37] Studies of cultural memory are useful here only if we understand that memorials and other efforts to commemorate the past are as much about suppressing some elements of past culture as they are about conserving others. While the Victorians were keen to save some aspects of Romantic writing from the forgetfulness of history, they were just as eager that other aspects should be consigned to oblivion, and the sooner the better. Political commitments, religious opinions, and sexual dissidence all had to be soft-pedaled in the Victorians' efforts to remake Romantic writers' reputations and recirculate their works. This was true not only of radicals, freethinkers, and advocates of free love such as Shelley, but also of a Tory like Scott, whose close association with a particular political context threatened to limit his appeal in the age of Reform. The web of reception highlighted certain facets of the Romantics' reputations and certain parts of their oeuvres, but it also cast others into shade.

The Victorian fascination with the past was therefore a distinctly modern one. Turning back to even the recent past required efforts of recovery. Romantic writers and their works seemed to be slipping into history by the middle of the nineteenth century, and they needed to be renovated for the present. Some of the Victorians' efforts to remake Romanticism are best understood as creating *lieux de mémoire* (an idea I return to in part 4), but even when they took place under the sign of memorialization they often entailed kinds of renovation: efforts not so much to remember the Romantics and their works as to revitalize them, to make them produce new effects in the present. In some respects, the distance between Victorians and Romantics was more troubling than the distance between the Victorians and earlier periods, because it pointed to the acceleration of modern life and the possibility of an indifferent posterity. The fear that Romantic writers were being forgotten in the present was also a fear that Victorian writers would be forgotten in the future.

In these conditions, remembering required remediating. And so, along with "history" and "memory," the third keyword for understanding the web of reception is "media." I use the word here as Clifford Siskin and William Warner do, "as a shorthand for [. . .] everything that intervenes, enables, supplements, or is simply in between."[38] In my vocabulary, sermons and anthologies are media insofar as they mediate Romantic writers and their works to new audiences, just as photography or chromolithography is a medium. Media are best understood as combining technologies and practices. They are at once particular material configurations of available technology and sets of socially embedded protocols that govern its use. And, following Bruno Latour, "mediators"—whether they are things or people—always "transform, translate, distort and modify the meaning" of what they mediate.[39] The concept of mediation provides a way to read artifacts and practices alongside one another in ways that illuminate reception history. A history of mediation finds room for artifacts, such as statues, and practices, such as citing or reciting poetry. And it shows that there can be no history of artifacts without a history of their use. The artifact of a published sermon cannot be understood apart from the practice of preaching, and the artifact of a postcard cannot be understood apart from the historically situated practice of sending postcards.

Effectively mediating old works to new audiences was key to renovating Romanticism in Victorian Britain. For the Victorians, as often for us, media were the index of the new.[40] One sign of Romanticism's obsolescence was that Romantic writing seemed unsuited to the Victorian media ecology. Both the material forms in which Romantic writing first appeared and the infrastructure that initially disseminated it began to look outdated from the 1830s on, as new media and technologies for the production and distribution of cultural products took hold. But media, even—perhaps especially—new media, were also "functionally integral to a sense of pastness."[41] They offered new windows onto history, while also clarifying its status *as* history. Nothing more clearly signaled for the Victorians their difference from earlier periods than the new communications infrastructure they developed, but one of the things they did in this new media ecology was to remediate the writers and works of earlier periods.

I'm not claiming that this process of mediation was new, or that Romantic writing had ever been unmediated, or that Romantic authors were in any way naïve about the process of mediation. Sophisticated awareness of mediation was common even before the Romantic period. Eighteenth-century novels displayed this kind of awareness when they innovated in their graphic design as well as their textual content and mobilized their bibliographic codes to create new kinds of books as well as new kinds of writing.[42] And novels are only one example: as eighteenth-century readers became adept at navigating the burgeoning marketplace for print, they often encountered books that drew attention to the material forms of their circulation and their status as fashionable objects or fungible commodities.[43] Clifford Siskin and William Warner make this history of mediation crucial to their revisionist account of Enlightenment. Romantic poets and theorists were likewise impelled to reflect on the conditions of their work's mediation. They tried to reimagine poetry itself as a medium, rather than the content of another medium.[44] Tracing the history of mediation back to the Romantic period or the eighteenth century (and beyond) gives a longer chronological reach to a historical archaeology of media that was initially focused on so-called technological media such as the telegraph, the phonograph, the radio, and the cinema.[45]

But while media change and the self-consciousness about mediation that it fosters extend before and after the period examined here, the long nineteenth century witnessed a number of innovations with far-reaching consequences.[46]

They significantly altered how literary works circulated, as well as offering new vehicles for authorial images. The exponential growth in the total output of printed matter, from 1770 onward, was the beginning of a "long revolution" in media, extending throughout the following century. Whether they locate the causes in legal decisions that deregulated the reprint market, increased literacy creating higher demand, technological innovation enabling greater supply, or some other factor, book historians often make their accounts of print culture and the print trade hinge on the year 1800.[47] Broadly speaking, people after 1800 experienced print culture differently—and often more self-consciously—than their parents or grandparents had, and the pace of change accelerated as the century went on.

Technological innovations changed book production. The steam press—first introduced in 1814 but initially used primarily for printing newspapers—was used increasingly for printing books.[48] Stereotypy made it possible to reprint books more easily as demand required, eliminated the need to reset type for new editions, and so reduced the financial risks of publication.[49] The shift from paper made of cotton or linen rags to paper made of wood pulp reduced costs, as did the elimination in 1861 of taxes on paper.[50] Wove paper increasingly took the place of laid paper. Technologies of image reproduction also changed.[51] Steel-plate etching allowed for more copies of an image to be printed without deterioration, compared to copper plates; its adoption played a role in the commercial success of giftbooks and annuals from the 1830s.[52] Wood engraving increased the number and quality of printed images in circulation, especially when combined with electrotype; it was used both in books and in newspapers such as *Punch* and the *Illustrated London News*.[53] Lithography made it possible to print images and text on the same page cheaply and in large print runs, while chromolithography allowed printers to include color more easily.[54] Photographically illustrated books, from the 1840s onward, introduced an entirely new technology, while the halftone process, patented in England in 1882 and widely used from the 1890s, allowed photographs to be printed in books and newspapers. The printed matter produced by these new technologies circulated along radically improved distribution networks of roads, canals, and railways.[55] As a result, the books that were being offered for sale in the 1860s looked different in many respects to books printed in the 1790s.

Changes in printed matter were just one aspect of a changed media ecology. I use the term "media ecology" to suggest an understanding of culture as a space in which several media interact with one another. Changes in any one medium produce changes in all the others. The introduction of a new medium, or its rapid growth, produces changes in all the others. And any medium can be properly understood only in relation to the others, and to the material networks of circulation on which they rely. The idea of a media ecology foregrounds the relations among media, the ways in which each medium is shaped by the others, and the ways in which those relations change over time. I take the term from Neil Postman, who suggests that "[t]echnological change is neither additive nor subtractive. It is ecological. [...] One significant change generates total change."[56] But I use it not to deplore the effects of new communications technologies on public discourse, as Postman does, but to model the historical complexity of media change. Thinking in terms of a media ecology provides an alternative to the rhetoric of supersession that often characterizes accounts of media change, "the idea that each new technological type vanquishes or subsumes its predecessors," as Paul Duguid puts it.[57] Instead, it allows us to think of new media, as does Lisa Gitelman, less as "points of epistemic rupture" than as "socially embedded sites for the ongoing negotiation of meaning as such."[58] Speaking in terms of a media ecology makes visible the interplay of media, and draws attention to the porous boundaries between them.

In the new Victorian media ecology, existing media could also appear new, or take on new meanings. Illustrated books (part 2) had existed since before the invention of printing; but steel etching, wood engraving, lithography, and photomechanical reproduction changed their physical appearance, their means of production, and their cultural significance. Sermons (part 3) were delivered in a wider variety of venues and remediated by print to an unprecedented extent. Statues (part 4) took on new meanings, as part of the "statuemania" that swept Europe in the nineteenth century. There were more working sculptors; more people seemed to deserve statues (including, for example, engineers); and the resulting works of art were installed in changed urban spaces and newly constructed pantheons. The statues I examine were then remediated in new media such as photography and the picture postcard. Anthologies of literature (part 5) had a long history, but they appeared in unprecedented numbers in Victorian Britain, where they reached new audiences and became entrenched in drastically changed educational contexts. "Old" media survive the introduction of "new" media: television didn't kill radio, and CDs (and then mp3s) didn't kill the vinyl record. But "old" media signify differently in changed media ecologies.

Victorian new media and technologies also made media more visible as such. New media made people think about what a medium was. The story of media in the long nineteenth century, then, is not only about media change but also about changes in the concept of mediation. In rethinking poetry as a medium, Celeste Langan and Maureen McLane argue, "Romantic poets and theorists established a horizon for thinking the conditions of mediality."[59] As those conditions changed in the following decades, John Guillory claims, a fully elaborated "media concept" was "absent but *wanted.*" Only in the later nineteenth century, according to Guillory, did the proliferation of new media render existing vocabularies inadequate and necessitate a newly elaborated concept of media that was then retrospectively applied to existing forms of communication such as print.[60] Whether they used "old" media such as print, or "new" media such as photography, the people and products that made up the web of reception were becoming more acutely self-conscious about their place in the media ecology. Tracing the web of reception makes visible the range of media operating in the nineteenth century, the omnivorous ways in which cultural consumers moved among them, and the sophisticated strategies cultural producers developed for negotiating between them.

If Romantic authors and their works were not to be forgotten, they needed to be naturalized in this new media ecology. This happened when their works were published in new editions, produced with new printing technologies, and often newly illustrated. But their images and writings were also remediated in sermons, frontispieces, photographs, anthologies, primers and books of quotations, statues, figurines, collectable artifacts, and postcards. I analyze these remediations both in J. David Bolter and Richard Grusin's narrow sense of that term and in a more general sense. Bolter and Grusin call it remediation when one medium represents or refashions another: for example, when William Henry Fox Talbot photographed a manuscript in Byron's hand (as I discuss in chapter 11), photography remediated handwriting.[61] More generally, when admirers of Scott and Byron raised statues of them, they shifted their reception from the medium of print to that of sculpture. In the cases I examine in part 4, the sculptors drew attention to this remediation by depicting the authors holding books. Both kinds of remediation, I argue, made Romantic authors and their works seem at home in the new media ecology, and therefore renovated them for Victorian audiences. "The medium through which works of art continue to influence later ages," Walter Benjamin generalized, "is always different from the one in which they affect their own age."[62]

The remediations I examine displayed two linked tendencies: to canonize Romantic writers and their works, and to commodify them. On one hand, self-appointed stewards of Romantic writers' reputations eased them into the canon of English literature, and more generally into the ranks of British worthies, by publishing their works alongside established writers from earlier periods, placing them on syllabi (for the Civil Service exams, for example), putting up monuments to them, and arranging for their images to feature in places like the new National Portrait Gallery (founded in 1856). These efforts aimed to insulate the writers from political controversy, distance them from commerce, and make clear that their works belonged not to an age but to all time. On the other hand, entrepreneurs keen to profit from the Romantics and their works, especially as they came out of copyright, published cheap editions, circulated engravings and affordable miniature busts, and included Romantic writers and their characters on cigarette cards. These efforts aimed to make money by associating a variety of products with the names, images, and works of Romantic writers. Canonizing and commodifying were sometimes rhetorically opposed, but actually they went hand in hand.[63] When Matthew Arnold wrote a preface to Wordsworth that aimed to make his place in the canon clear, it appeared not in a literary journal but in a cheap, mass-market selected edition. When Scott was immortalized in marble in his Edinburgh monument, his statue was quickly reproduced by manufacturers of ephemeral picture postcards who recognized it as a commercial opportunity and a stimulus to the tourist trade. Tendencies of canonization and commodification were locked into an uneasy relationship in which each benefited from the other.

History, memory, and media. Each concept took on its modern form between roughly 1750 and 1900, taking shape as durable intellectual and affective structures of modernity. These shifting concepts allow us to see the frames on which the web of reception is woven. As they transformed, they created the conditions of possibility for the reception histories I trace in the following chapters. The modern concept of history made the Romantics seem historically distant from the Victorians, fostered the anxiety that they might soon be forgotten, and created the felt need for their works to be renovated. The perception that premodern foundations of cultural memory were crumbling made it seem necessary to memorialize past individuals and their achievements in novel sites, products, and practices, and ensured that the work of memory was always fragile and never finished. The changing media ecology provided a range of means—both new and newly inflected—to remediate Romantic writers and their works, while bringing mediation itself into view. In these conditions, Romantic writers reached new audiences in new ways, and their reputations and writings were remade in the process. This book aims to show how that happened.

2

Reception Traditions and Punctual Historicism

AS THE moment when the Romantics wrote retreated into history, assorted practices of appropriation and redeployment remediated Romantic writers and their works to Victorian audiences. Examining this web of reception brings us face to face with what Frank Kermode called the "strategies of accommodation" or "the temporal agencies of survival" that sustain and remake literature over time.[1] Many critics of Romantic writing tend to overlook this history, because they think the most important context for understanding literature is the context of its composition or first publication. I call this tendency "punctual historicism." Of course, there are many good reception histories of Romanticism, but even they tend to neglect the ground covered in this book, because they understand reception history as primarily literary or discursive, rather than approaching it through book history or material culture. I suggest that their approach reflects their place in a tradition of literature or literary criticism, and their tendency to think back through that tradition. By contrast, this book aims to decenter that tradition and put it back into dialogue with other traditions, which it intersected with historically. In order to do that, toward the end of this chapter I outline an approach that sees traditions as plural, relational, and inescapable.

Historicists may start to bristle at this point and accuse me of tilting against straw men, so let me be clear. I don't mean to oppose historicism *tout court*. I don't want to suggest that historicism excludes an account of reception history—on the contrary, I think it demands one. And I don't claim that historicist critics are always blind to reception history in practice. But I want to distinguish my approach here from the punctual historicism that criticism of Romantic literature often displays. Historicist criticism rightly insists that texts are made meaningful in specific contexts. In doing so, it recovers the extent of writers' political engagements or evasions and restores a sense of the social embeddedness of their texts.[2] A historicist approach can be brought to bear not only on the context of the text's production but also on any subsequent context of reception. Some historicist critics acknowledge this. Leah Marcus notes that authors can be "localized" in a specific milieu, without "the implication that such activity restricts them within these 'local' limits."[3] Jerome McGann affirms that "any current interpretation of a work of poetry issues from the previous history of the work's meanings."[4] But—not always but often—historicist critics concentrate on one particular context to the exclusion of all others: the context in which a work was written and/or published. This is what makes this kind of historicism "punctual."

Punctual historicism is often a tendency to prefer one context and one kind of evidence to another, rather than an explicitly argued position. Marjorie Levinson invokes the Wye Valley in 1798 as a context for "Tintern Abbey." Nicholas Roe and Jerome McGann invoke the post-Peterloo periodical press as a context for "To Autumn." Alan Liu invokes Welsh nationalism in the 1790s as a context for parts of *The Prelude*. Marilyn Butler invokes anti-Jacobin Tory politics as a context for Jane Austen's novels. They all agree that the relevant interpretive context is the context in which a work was written and published (or withheld from the press).[5] Reimagining this moment of production and first reception was a hallmark of the new historicism from at least as early as Stephen Greenblatt's *Shakespearean Negotiations* (1988). Greenblatt left behind his "dreams of finding an originary moment" and recovered instead "a network of trades and trade-offs, a jostling of competing representations, a negotiation between joint-stock companies," but he remained concerned with the historical context of literary production. Whether it argues that literary works emerge, in Greenblatt's terms, from the "circulation of social energy," or, in McGann's, from "a theoretically endless series of stochastically generated feedback loops," this kind of historicism tends to keep its gaze firmly fixed on the moment of writing.[6] In concentrating on the context of writing and first reading, punctual historicism restricts itself to what Thomas Pfau has criticized as "a merely topical and occasional model of politics," and so limits the work's effects to those that occur punctually.[7]

This critical preoccupation with the context of composition or first publication has been twinned with a movement in textual scholarship that tends to privilege earlier texts of a work. The massive editorial labors of the twenty-one-volume Cornell edition of Wordsworth and the thirty-volume Edinburgh edition of Scott's Waverley novels are now complete. Both editions document in detail in their critical apparatuses the extensive revisions Wordsworth and Scott made to their works after first publication. But both print reading texts based on manuscripts, giving readers "what Scott originally wrote and intended his public to read" or "a clean reading text based on the earliest finished holograph version of each work" by Wordsworth.[8] In this respect, they depart from the previously orthodox view that editors should aim to reflect the author's "final intentions."[9] Stephen Parrish, general editor of the Cornell Wordsworth, criticized this doctrine as the "Whig Interpretation of Literature" and made an aesthetic case for earlier versions of Wordsworth's major poems.[10] Jerome McGann made a different argument for valuing the early printed texts of a work, based on his understanding of texts as socially embedded cultural products.[11] I do not wish to intervene in this debate here, but only to note that the preference in textual scholarship for earlier texts of a work (labeled "textual primitivism" by its detractors) often shares punctual historicism's assumption that the primary context in which literature functions is the context of its composition or first publication.[12]

Accordingly, a central aim of punctual historicism, and its editorial cousin "textual primitivism," is to help us read a text like its first readers. It aims to reveal what Nicholas Roe calls "aspects of [. . .] poems apparent to [their] first readers," and Marilyn Butler calls "the probable meaning for the informed first reader."[13] Editorially, as in Jerome McGann's *New Oxford Book of Romantic Period Verse*, it aims "to print the texts that had been made available to the poets' original audiences," or, as in Donald Reiman and Neil Fraistat's *Complete Poetry of Percy Bysshe Shelley*, "the texts that PBS intended his first reader(s) to see."[14] Privileging the first reader in this way can give the impression that literary works are events that happen once only. It can make it harder to see how they function in later contexts for other readers. In this way, punctual historicism neglects the important historicist insight that all present readings of a text are shaped by the history of past readings. In this respect, punctual historicism is not historicist enough.

The tendency to stitch texts so tightly to their context of writing ignores part of the special power of literary texts, which can speak to periods beyond their own in ways that are not determined by the context(s) of their production and first reception. Rita Felski explains that "[h]istorical criticism enriches our understanding of the provenance of a work of art, but it can also inspire a stunted view of texts as governed entirely by the conditions of their origin, leaving us hard-pressed to explain the continuing timeliness of texts, their potential ability to speak across centuries."[15] To make that claim is not to slip back into a naïve, idealist investment in literature's power to transcend history, nor to repeat unquestioningly the compensatory rhetoric of what Andrew Bennett has called Romanticism's "culture of posterity."[16] Instead, it is to acknowledge that texts can be revitalized in historically specific ways at later moments. Understanding these practices of redeployment requires us to think of literary texts as repeatedly reactivated by later readers—and even nonreaders—in contexts and media beyond the imaginations of their authors. It requires us to acknowledge that texts never simply endure but always need to be reimagined. And it requires us to consider that they may make their most important impacts when they are reenergized in later cultural, political, and media contexts.

Redeploying texts from the past in this fashion almost always involves new mediations, and often means producing new material artifacts, from editions and anthologies to memorials and illustrations. Any mediator of reception, whether it is a person, a monument, an edition, or an artifact of some other kind, can be located in the web of reception in relation to one or more reception traditions. This is as true of contemporary academic reception histories, which constitute their own reception tradition, as it is of Victorian editions, anthologies, and monuments. Until quite recently, many reception histories of Romantic literature tended to concentrate on two reception traditions in particular. The first is a literary tradition, which critics have traced by constructing genealogies of influence. George Ford and James Najarian mapped Keats's influence on Matthew Arnold, Dante Gabriel Rossetti, and Gerard Manley Hopkins; Stephen Gill traced Wordsworth's effect on George Eliot and Elizabeth Gaskell; and Andrew Elfenbein examined Byron's impact on Alfred Tennyson, Bulwer Lytton, and Oscar Wilde.[17] A second, related approach has been to trace the "critical heritage" from early reviews through readings of Romantic poetry by Algernon Charles Swinburne, Thomas Carlyle, John Stuart Mill, and others.[18] Since many Victorian poets were also critics (or vice versa), these approaches overlap. In books on Romantic writers "and the Victorians" (and others on Dante, Shakespeare, or Milton, "and the Victorians"), the Victorians we hear about mostly come from a limited group of canonical writers.[19] Whether they think of the Romantics as provoking admiration or anxiety in their Victorian successors, these studies approach reception history for the most part through a narrowly literary tradition.

Recently, a more book-historical kind of reception history has illuminated the textual transmission of Romantic literature. It has shown how invested the Romantics were in collecting and reprinting their own works, and how the collected edition cemented the cultural capital of both past and present writers in the period. Publishers rushed out posthumous volumes of "poetical remains," and reprinted Romantic poetry in both Britain and America, while Victorian editors often amended the texts of Romantic writing in significant ways.[20] The production of new editions was tied to the emergence of new cultural practices such as literary tourism and poetry memorization and recitation, as well as a huge range of nonliterary uses to which books could be put.[21] In some cases, reception histories of Romanticism have extended their purview to include other media. In recent years, we've heard about illustrated editions of Wordsworth and film adaptations of Jane Austen, about Keats's influence on painting, Byron's reappearances in films, television programs, and graphic novels, and Blake's internet afterlife.[22]

Building on this tendency, I look beyond the traditions of literary influence or the critical heritage; instead of starting with a reading list of eminent Victorians, I begin with material objects such as books of quotations, photographs, anthologies, statues, and postcards, in order to consider how they mediated Romantic writers and their works to Victorian audiences.

Reception histories have often been grounded in literary and critical traditions because their authors occupy those traditions. Modern academic critics inherit a reception tradition that shapes their thinking, and when they write reception histories they tend to "think back" through that tradition.[23] I don't mean that contemporary critics agree with their Victorian predecessors, but that their position in the web of reception disposes them to think of reception history from an intellectual standpoint that reflects their own tradition(s). Moreover, as academic critics of literature, our readings stand in a tradition of reading that took on its modern form in the Victorian period, when academic protocols for the study of vernacular literature were first formulated, as English became a university discipline.[24] Expanding our horizons to include popular, commodified, remediated, and material forms of reception brings us into contact with other traditions of reception, which may be alien to our own historically and institutionally constructed protocols of reading. Understanding these different strands of reception history and the relations among them, then, requires us to think about what a tradition is, how multiple traditions intersect, and where we stand among them.

For a long time, literary historians saw it as part of their job to map the contours of a relatively unitary literary tradition. The titles of classic studies reflect this concern: Cleanth Brooks's *Modern Poetry and the Tradition* (1939), F. R. Leavis's *The Great Tradition* (1948), and M. H. Abrams's *Natural Supernaturalism: Tradition and Revolution in Romantic Literature* (1971).[25] T. S. Eliot gave this understanding of tradition its classic formulation in his essay "Tradition and the Individual Talent" (1919). Writing in the immediate aftermath of the First World War, Eliot sought to reassert the claims of an imperiled tradition of European high culture. For Eliot, tradition is unitary but subject to constant, self-regulating modification:

> The existing monuments form an ideal order among themselves, which is modified by the introduction of the new (the really new) work of art among them. The existing order is complete before the new work arrives; for order to persist after the supervention of novelty, the *whole* existing order must be, if ever so slightly, altered[.][26]

The underlying metaphor here is apparently that of a museum or gallery, in which the existing collection has to be rearranged to make room for new acquisitions. The spatial image suggests that the works in the tradition are not located in time but coexist beyond time. Eliot claims that "the historical sense involves a perception, not only of the pastness of the past, but of its presence."[27] The whole tradition, then, remains available to the educated reader in the present; it "has a simultaneous existence and composes a simultaneous order."[28] Tracing that tradition (or elements of it) became a preoccupation for literary criticism, and certainly for those literary histories organized around genealogies of poetic influence or the critical heritage.

To some, Eliot's museum of tradition seemed much too stuffy, its entry fees far too high. Raymond Williams reacted strongly against this concept of tradition, and the understanding of culture it implied. He cited Eliot's *Notes Towards the Definition of Culture* (1948)—"a book I grasped but could not accept"—as one of the targets of his book *Keywords* (1976).[29] There, he called "tradition" a "particularly difficult word" and defined it like this:

> Tradition [...] came into English [...] from rw [related word] *tradere*, L[atin]—to hand over or deliver. The Latin noun [*traditionem*] had the senses of (i) delivery, (ii) handing down knowledge, (iii) passing on a doctrine, (iv) surrender or betrayal. [...] It is easy to see how a general word for matters handed down from father to son could become specialized, within one form of thought, to the idea of necessary respect or duty. Tradition survives in English as a description of a general process of handing down, but there is a very strong and often predominant sense of this entailing respect and duty. When [...] we realize that there are traditions (real plural, as distinct from the "plural singular" present also in *values* and *standards* [...]) and that only some of them or parts of them have been selected for our respect and duty, we can see how difficult Tradition really is [...] this, in its own way, is both a betrayal and a surrender.[30]

For Williams, as for many others since, Eliot's understanding of tradition contains an ideological sleight of hand, in which the traditions of a particular class are reified as "tradition" itself, while other traditions are marginalized and denied respect.[31] A reception history that took Williams's point into account, then, could not restrict itself to a single tradition of poetic influence or the critical heritage on the unitary model outlined by Eliot, though it would continue to include that tradition as part of the story. Instead, it would have to open itself up to other traditions of reception and attend to the intersections between traditions.

Even while Eliot the critic was writing "Tradition and the Individual Talent," however, Eliot the poet entertained a different conception of tradition. *The Waste Land* (1922) presents not a single unitary tradition but a cacophony of traditions. Materials from a wide assortment of traditions—from European high culture to Pali scripture, from Jacobean drama to Buddhist teachings, from music hall songs to fertility myths—are broken into "fragments I have shored against my ruins" (430).[32] From hearing lectures at Harvard by Gilbert Murray to reading James Frazer's *The Golden Bough* and Jessie L. Weston's *From Ritual to Romance*, Eliot had been drawn to a fusion of anthropology and literary history that offered to reveal fundamental patterns underlying disparate cultural traditions. But in *The Waste Land*, traditions are not just diverse but also incommensurable. If reading *The Waste Land* is a disorienting experience at first, this is not only because it contains so much that's unfamiliar, but also because it seems impossible to imagine that everything it contains could ever cohere into a comprehensible whole. The poet "can connect/Nothing with nothing," which is both a complaint and, ambiguously, his highest aspiration (301–2). The way different traditions jostle together might suggest that one can stand outside of any tradition whatsoever, in order to compare and assess traditions and to choose the tradition that will best alleviate the barrenness of modern life. Eliot himself may have felt this way when he began studying Sanskrit and Eastern religions at Harvard in 1911, where he first encountered the Fire Sermon and wrote the earliest lines that would be incorporated in revised form, a decade later, in *The Waste Land*. He considered converting to Buddhism around this time.[33]

What *The Waste Land* finally offers, however, is not an array of traditions from which one might choose, nor the possibility of synthesizing many traditions into a more complete vision, but a world in which the variety of traditions reminds us of the limits of any tradition as a matrix for understanding.[34] At the end of the poem, "each in his prison/Thinking of the key, each confirms a prison" (413–14). The key would open the door of one's own tradition-circumscribed consciousness, allowing one to escape its confines, but it is also, perhaps, the key to all mythologies that Casaubon dreamed of in *Middlemarch*, allowing one to escape the confines of any tradition and master them all. Neither kind of key is available in *The Waste Land*. By the 1930s, Eliot would recognize the extent to which his subjectivity was bound by the traditions he inherited but did not choose, so that "my only hope of really penetrating to the heart of [Eastern philosophy] would lie in forgetting how to think and feel as an American or a European: which, for practical as well as sentimental reasons, I did not wish to do."[35]

Rather than finding an Archimedean point outside of any tradition, then, we need to learn how to negotiate between traditions from an intellectual standpoint that is itself constituted in relation to one or more traditions. To address this problem, I turn to Alasdair MacIntyre, who makes a plural understanding of traditions central to his thought. MacIntyre is primarily concerned with moral philosophy, but I employ his ideas about tradition to illuminate cultural history. According to MacIntyre, traditions are nonoptional, internally conflicted, and self-referential. Being a rational individual means inheriting one or more traditions. Each of us is "one of the bearers of a tradition."[36] For MacIntyre rationality is constituted by tradition and the history of rational inquiry constitutes traditions in turn.[37] Traditions are nonoptional. You cannot choose the traditions you inherit, nor can you simply opt out of them, because they constitute your identity as a reasoning individual. In the case of literary criticism, the critical heritage is the tradition that underlies critical reading today, and the readings critics produce constitute the continued vitality of the tradition. Our readings are not simply prescribed by the tradition, however, and we are not compelled to repeat the readings of the past, because traditions "embody continuities of conflict."[38] Traditions are internally conflicted. A tradition is "an historically extended, socially embodied argument."[39] This is an argument about the "contents" of the tradition—about what Wordsworth's Lucy Poems mean, for example—but it is also always at some level an argument about the nature of the tradition itself.[40] Traditions are self-referential. So the tradition of literary criticism is constituted in part by an argument about what counts as good literary criticism. Both the methods of study and the object of study are subject to continual questioning and reflection.

On MacIntyre's account, traditions are also plural, incommensurable, and frequently in conflict with one another. A modern individual will find herself the bearer of several traditions, and will be confronted by others of which she is not the bearer. When I examine Romanticism's web of reception, I see it structured by several reception traditions. I encounter a critical heritage, which partly constitutes the discipline of literary criticism as I was trained to practice it. But I am also confronted by other traditions—such as traditions of preaching, illustration, sculpture, or education—with their own preoccupations and their own continuities of conflict. These traditions may be incommensurable. That is, what constitutes a valid response to Byron, or Scott, or Shelley in one tradition may be different from what constitutes a valid response in another and there may be no objective or mutually agreeable standards against which responses from different traditions can be judged. The disagreements between traditions, in fact, may be disagreements about those standards themselves. And because rationality itself is constituted in relation to traditions, for MacIntyre, there is no position outside of any tradition whatsoever from which to assess the claims of different traditions.[41] One Victorian reader, for example, might employ a poem by Hemans for private devotion; another reader might employ it for public recitation; a third might employ it as evidence when writing literary history. These uses of the same poem are embedded in different traditions that are divergent or incommensurable: from within each tradition the ways in which the other traditions employ the poem may appear eccentric or wrongheaded, but there is no good reason to establish any one tradition as normative.

Mediators in different traditions valued Romantic authors and their works differently and for different reasons. *What the Victorians Made of Romanticism* looks beyond traditions of literature, criticism, and high art to other traditions with their own regimes of value. I don't, however, aim simply to invert established hierarchies by asserting the value of "low," "popular," or "mass" culture against "high," "elite," or "minority" culture. Instead, thinking across reception traditions allows us to see those traditions as the matrices in which understandings of value itself are organized. Different reception traditions embed literary works and their authors in different regimes of value, which are not reducible to a single scale. And, as Rita Felski points out, "evaluation is not optional" but integral to reception.[42] Some artifacts exist to ascribe value (such as statues), while others draw on cultural capital already invested (such as cigarette cards). Statements about value, then, reflect neither objective, inherent qualities of an author or work nor idiosyncratic personal preferences that will not bear scrutiny. Instead, they are functions of particular, contingent traditions, and are contested within tradition-bound debates.[43]

Negotiating between traditions requires efforts of translation. MacIntyre compares traditions to languages. Just as one cannot speak without speaking a language, one cannot sustain a project of rational inquiry without doing so in a tradition. One can speak many languages, and engage with many traditions, but most people will have one mother tongue, one tradition in which they are most comfortable.[44] Since the Romantic period, our intellectual mother tongues, at least within the academy, have been academic disciplines, which emerged in the nineteenth century when the structure of knowledge was reimagined as a number of narrow but deep traditions of inquiry. In this book, however, I'm trying not only to be interdisciplinary—that is, to think across current academic disciplines—but also to engage with traditions of reception that did not become institutionalized as academic disciplines. Engaging another tradition requires learning to think within that tradition, rather than translating its concepts into the terms of your native tradition (an effort that will always involve distorting or misrecognizing them).[45] And the effort to think across traditions has its own tradition, bound up with the disciplinary division of knowledge and dating from the Romantic period's encounter with oriental, colonial, mystical, folkloric, and other traditions of thought, and its rejection of the Enlightenment's confidence in a form of rationality that was syncretic and not tradition-bound.[46] MacIntyre calls someone who recognizes the contingency of his or her own tradition a "post-Enlightenment person."[47] Others prefer to speak in terms of identity categories of race, class, gender, and sexual orientation, and the intersections between them; but speaking in terms of traditions has the advantage of taking into account the ways in which the experience and meaning of those identity categories at any moment is itself the product of historically extended processes of construction.

Since conflicts occur both within and between traditions, and traditions may encounter and inform one another, it can be difficult to locate the borders between traditions precisely. Nonetheless, traditions of reception are not simply a heuristic fiction mapped onto the past to make it easier to understand. The material artifacts and cultural practices that I examine in this book were formed into traditions by those who produced, consumed, or performed them. These traditions were self-referential. Sermons, which I discuss in part 3, were self-consciously located in a tradition of previous sermons, with its own specialized metadiscourse of homiletics and its own reference works. Statues, which I discuss in part 4, were sculpted with reference to previous statues; as I argue there, the statue of Byron in London echoes the statue of Scott in Edinburgh. Anthologies, which I discuss in part 5, were compiled with reference to previous anthologies and showed a high degree of consensus in their selections.

These traditions contained internal disagreements and metadiscussions, as MacIntyre would lead us to expect: those commissioning a statue of a Romantic writer, for example, were compelled to consider what makes a good statue. At the same time, reception traditions also referred to one another and cross-pollinated. For example, depictions of a poet in frontispieces and in statues may have influenced one another, even while operating in discrete traditions of book illustration and sculpture. Some Victorians contributed to or encountered more than one tradition. Benjamin Disraeli contributed to the tradition of novels including Byronic characters but also helped commission a statue of Byron. John Ruskin contributed to the critical heritage but also read and heard C. H. Spurgeon's sermons, which often mentioned Romantic poets.

Understanding the web of reception that has historically shaped understandings of Romantic authors and their works, then, means engaging with a variety of reception traditions, without framing them as deviations from the familiar traditions of literary history and criticism. The familiar tradition will then appear as one among others, and its claims to a monopoly on the fullest or most correct understanding of Romantic writing will be relativized. Charles Martindale (who also draws on MacIntyre's understanding of traditions) writes that there is "no Archimedean point from which we can arrive at a final, correct meaning for any text": the tradition in which we stand will not provide one, and there is no place to stand outside of any tradition.[48] *What the Victorians Made of Romanticism* aims to think among and across traditions, in an effort to show how the reception history of Romantic writing was enmeshed in multiple traditions of reading and nonreading. In the process, the familiar ways of understanding Romanticism fostered by our own tradition(s) may be rendered strange.

3

Minding the Generation Gap

TO CONTEMPORARY as well as later commentators, nineteenth-century literary culture often seemed to fall into two distinct generations with different sensibilities, preoccupations, and problems. In this chapter, I show how Victorians constructed the break between themselves and the Romantics as a generation gap, and in doing so helped to create the modern understanding of what it means to be part of a generation. When Matthew Arnold hailed his generation as "we, brought forth and reared in hours / Of change, alarm, surprise," he signaled a self-conscious modernity, a sense of living in what Marshall Berman has called "a maelstrom of perpetual disintegration and renewal."[1] In this accelerated and uncertain time, the literature of even the recent past began to seem alien or obsolescent. "Too fast we live, too much are tried, / Too harrass'd, to attain / Wordsworth's sweet calm," Arnold wrote.[2] Poetry of the recent past no longer seemed suited to addressing the present's most pressing concerns. Echoing Byron's Manfred, who found that "the wisdom of the world [. . .] avail'd not," Arnold turned Manfred's conclusion into a question and made it a matter of generational difference: "what availed it, all the noise / And outcry of the former men?"[3] For Arnold—whom Henry James called "Above all [. . .] the poet of his age, of the moment in which we live, of our 'modernity' "—this was literally a generation gap between himself and his father (elegized in "Rugby Chapel"), and more abstractly (in "Stanzas from the Grand Chartreuse") a generational shift "between two worlds, one dead, / The other powerless to be born."[4] John Stuart Mill shared Arnold's sense that the immediate past was becoming obsolete: "Mankind have outgrown old institutions and old doctrines," he wrote in 1831, "and have not yet acquired new ones."[5] Introducing an edition of Byron's poems in 1866, Algernon Charles Swinburne reiterated Arnold's sense of a generational shift, and framed it ironically in the religious language that Arnold would use earnestly in "Dover Beach" the following year. "Men born when this century was getting into its forties were baptised into another church than [Byron's] with the rites of another creed. [. . .] No man under twenty," he asserted, "can now be expected to appreciate" Byron or Wordsworth.[6] Arnold, Swinburne, and Mill were convinced that the present generation could not rely on the "former men" to address their new concerns.

Both Arnold and Swinburne used proper names metonymically to represent this generational shift as a changing of the guard. Swinburne named Coleridge, Keats, and Shelley as "chief among the past heroes of the younger century" along with "the two great opposing figures of Byron and Wordsworth."[7] Arnold yoked together Goethe, Byron, and Wordsworth as representatives of the passing generation in "Memorial Verses," and Byron, Shelley, and Senancour in "Stanzas from the Grand Chartreuse."[8] And both writers made Tennyson stand metonymically for the rising generation. "Upon their ears, first after the cadences of the older poets, fell the faultless and fervent melodies of Tennyson," according to Swinburne, while Arnold noted that "Mr. Tennyson drew to himself, and away from Wordsworth, the poetry-reading public, and the new generations."[9] To speak of Wordsworth or Byron as poets of a different generation from that of Arnold, Swinburne, or Tennyson, then, is not to impose a period break for the convenience of modern academics "carving up the nineteenth century" (in the terms of a recent set of essays in *PMLA*) but to employ a vocabulary current in the period.[10] As the avant-garde replaced the old guard, Romantic poets increasingly seemed to be in need of renovation if they were to continue to find Victorian readers.

A number of literary works grapple with this bracing but unsettling sense of their own modernity by representing the distance between Romantic and Victorian as a generation gap. I briefly examine four examples. Matthew Arnold's "Empedocles on Etna" (1852) has long been understood as a major product of Arnold's sustained and ambivalent attempt to grapple with the Romantic inheritance. It splits that inheritance between two characters of different generations: the older Empedocles, whose dedication to his Romantic poetic vocation has led him into despair, and the younger Callicles, whose immature, euphonious enthusiasm for Romantic poetics remains undimmed. Frank Kermode, who identified Arnold as "a very influential transmitter of Romantic thought," asserted that "Empedocles is the Romantic poet who knows enough; Callicles the Romantic poet who does not know enough."[11] Arnold's division of Romanticism between two characters of different generations does not follow the chronological generations familiar from twentieth-century criticism of Romanticism. Rather, Arnold "dissociates" (Kermode's word) a Wordsworthian or Coleridgean Romanticism between his characters.[12] Empedocles mixes a Wordsworthian desire to "share the fruitful stir / Down in our mother earth's miraculous womb" (II.i.339–40) with a Coleridgean dejection that "I alone / Am dead to life and joy, therefore I read / In all things my own deadness" (II.i.320–22).[13] Callicles, not yet having ascended to Empedocles's disillusioned elevation, embraces a Romantic joy in nature.

As a representative of Romanticism, Empedocles has outlived his hour of triumph. Having survived to see a new generation of thinkers rise to prominence—the Sophists—he describes himself as one "who has outlived his prosperous days [. . .] whose youth fell on a different world / From that on which his exiled age is thrown— / Whose mind was fed on other food, was trained / By other rules than are in vogue to-day" (II.i.261–65). Empedocles, as Kermode notes, "belonged to a great age of poetry," when the poet served a therapeutic function in society.[14] That age is over. His pursuit of Romantic ideals has left him disconnected from the world. This sense of generational dislocation, as Arnold explained, is part of what makes Empedocles's situation share "much that we are accustomed to consider as exclusively modern."[15] "With men thou canst not live," Callicles tells him, "Their thoughts, their ways, their wishes are not thine" (II.i.19). The only logical end for Empedocles, and the destiny of Romantic art in modernity, Arnold's poem suggests, is isolation and self-destruction. Even in the guise of reunifying him with nature, Empedocles's death suggests that Romanticism can no longer function in the world. Callicles ends "Empedocles on Etna" singing a Wordsworthian song of consolation in nature on the lower slopes of the mountain, but by the end of the poem no one is listening to him. He can neither remain among the society at the foot of the volcano nor (yet) ascend like Empedocles and his precursor Manfred to the isolation of the summit and the embrace of self-destruction it requires.

Arnold himself came to disavow and suppress the poem; he felt it failed to "inspirit and rejoice the reader," because it showed a mental state in which "suffering finds no vent in action."[16] This judgment reflected both his ambivalent relationship with Romanticism and his sense that it had outlived its usefulness for a rising generation that made new demands on its poets, just as Empedocles has outlived the cultural moment that endowed his poetry with significance. The superannuation of Romantic ideas, as Arnold conceived it, was partly a matter of working out tensions within Romanticism itself, but it was also simply a matter of generational change. Empedocles's generation gave way to that of the Sophists just as Wordsworth's gave way to Arnold's.

Benjamin Disraeli's novel *Venetia* (1837) dramatizes this generational shift in the relationships of its three main characters. Disraeli wrote that he had "attempted to shadow forth, though as 'in a glass darkly,' two of the most renowned and refined spirits that have adorned these our latter days."[17] But rather than offer simple portraits of Byron and Shelley, Disraeli splits aspects of both men between the characters of Marmion Herbert and Plantagenet Carducis; and rather than make those two characters near contemporaries, born four years apart as Byron and Shelley were, he separates them by a generation, making Herbert old enough to be Carducis's father. This allows him to make Herbert an amalgam of the Romantic inheritance, rather than a portrait of an individual Romantic poet. The fact that his Christian name invokes one of Scott's most popular poems adds to his composite nature. Two characters of the younger generation then dramatize two ways of relating to the Romantic inheritance Herbert represents: his daughter Venetia and his would-be son-in-law Carducis.

Disraeli represents Romanticism as superannuated in a number of ways. By the beginning of the novel, Herbert is middle-aged, estranged from his family, exiled from his country, a traitor to his king. His principled love of liberty led him to raise a regiment and fight for George Washington in the American Revolution, in a chronologically displaced and dramatically heightened version of Byron's involvement in the Greek War of Independence. As a result, he is a figure of shame in his own country. Venetia is brought up in ignorance of her father's identity, and in this respect she is a dramatized version of Byron's daughter Ada.[18] Disraeli's characterization of Herbert blends Shelleyan ideas with elements of biography from both Byron and Shelley, but significantly, when depicting Herbert he draws only on Byron's later life, after the moment of his most intense celebrity. Episodes from Byron's early life are given to Carducis instead. By the time he appears in volume 2, Herbert has long retired from active involvement in literature and politics; like Arnold's Empedocles, he has outlived his moment of cultural significance. In these ways, Disraeli depicts the Romantic inheritance as a source of fascination for the younger generation, but no longer a potent force in Britain's cultural or political life. (A decade earlier, Mary Shelley took the opposite approach in *The Last Man* [1826], where she imagined an alternative Britain in which characters based on Shelley and Byron became intellectual and political leaders.) Disraeli also projects the action of *Venetia* backward historically by a generation, so that the story begins when Venetia and Carducis are children in 1765 and ends with the deaths of Herbert and Carducis just a few months before the birth of Byron in 1788.[19] Romanticism therefore seems less like a pressing concern and more like a historical event—interesting, but distant.

Carducis embodies a response to Romanticism that is passionate yet wrongheaded, and metaphorically fatal. Despite initially sharing the widespread disapproval of Herbert, Carducis becomes enamored of his ideas well before he encounters him in person. When they meet, Herbert rapidly becomes a surrogate father to the orphaned Carducis. They spend their time in passionate conversation, based in part on Shelley's own fictionalization of his relationship with Byron in "Julian and Maddalo." The novel can be read as the story of the powerful homosocial bond shared by Herbert and Carducis, and its triangulation through Venetia.[20] Homosocial desire mediated by female relations is a feature of Disraeli's novels, for example, in *Coningsby* (1844), where Henry Coningsby's powerful, sexually ambivalent attraction to Oswald Milbank is safely contained when he marries Oswald's sister Edith. In *Venetia*, however, Carducis dies before he can marry Venetia. By this time, the characters of Herbert and Carducis have almost merged into one another, so complete is their mutual sympathy, and they both drown in a boating accident based on Shelley's death. Carducis's deep attraction to the Romantic inheritance of the previous generation, represented by Herbert, ultimately proves to be self-destructive.

Venetia also falls in love with the Romanticism of Herbert and Carducis. But whereas Carducis reacts to the Romantic inheritance with self-destructive abandon, Disraeli gives Venetia a more measured response. In some respects, her situation resembles that of Carducis, with incestuous rather than homosocial desire being contained by triangulation. While Carducis's illicit desire for Herbert is transferred to Venetia, her illicit desire for Herbert is transferred to Carducis. But, although she accepts Carducis's proposal, Disraeli does not allow them to marry. Carducis's death prevents her espousing his Romantic ideas, and the novel ends with her happy marriage to his less Romantic and more respectable brother George.

Many readers have noticed that, alongside its celebration of Byron and Shelley, *Venetia* also provides an allegory for Disraeli's rejection of their influence, as a condition of his full entry into Victorian political life (he took his seat in Parliament the year *Venetia* was published).[21] Ann Hawkins argues that throughout the novel's composition, Disraeli was engaged in a "process of decision-making, considering different approaches to and departures from the Byronic myth."[22] Here, I want to stress that his reluctant but final rejection of Romanticism is presented as the correct response to the inheritance of an earlier generation. *Venetia* offers two ways of responding to the Romantic inheritance represented by Herbert. Carducis responds adoringly, and the result is that his distinctive identity, and finally his life, is forfeited. To identify uncritically with Romanticism is to share the errors of the previous generation.[23] Venetia also experiences a deep attraction to Romanticism, but she turns away from it at the novel's close toward a more forward-looking and productive union with her quasi-Victorian husband. He takes his seat in the House of Lords while she restores the house of her ancestors to its former glory, in a metaphor for Disraeli's Tory political program.

The sound of shifting generations can also be heard in Tennyson's dedicatory poem "To the Queen," even though layers of modesty and courtesy muffle it.[24] This dedication was Tennyson's first new publication as poet laureate, and appeared in every edition of his *Poems* after the seventh in 1851.

In the second stanza, Tennyson styles himself "one of less desert" to whom the queen has granted "This laurel greener from the brows / Of him that uttered nothing base" (6–8). The praise of Wordsworth here is cagey, since Wordsworth only accepted the laureateship on the understanding that he would not be expected to write any laureate poems.[25] He uttered nothing base because by that time he hardly uttered anything at all. When Tennyson revised this poem in 1853, he rewrote the third stanza, marking more clearly the generational shift between himself and the previous laureate. He imagined Victoria "mak[ing] demand of modern rhyme / If aught of ancient worth be there" (11–12). "Ancient" is ambiguous: its primary meaning may be "classical," but, so close to the reference to Wordsworth, it could also mean "former," or even "old-fashioned"—in which case these lines oppose Tennyson's specifically modern poetry to Wordsworth's outdated merits.

"To the Queen" mobilized poetically the widespread tendency to make Tennyson stand metonymically for the rising generation. It began with Tennyson's friends: in 1829 Arthur Henry Hallam was already telling William Gladstone that he "consider[ed] Tennyson as promising fair to be the greatest poet of our generation,"[26] and George Venables told Tennyson he could become "*the* artist of modern times."[27] Gladstone felt that "[o]ver the fresh hearts and understandings of the young [. . .] he had established an extraordinary sway."[28] The Bishop of Ripon described how Tennyson "had drawn the younger generation to his side," and made enthusiasm for his poetry a litmus test distinguishing one generation from another. "When I went up to Cambridge in 1860," he reported, "Tennyson was the oracle poet among the younger men; but the feeling of doubt still remained among the older men."[29] The same was true at Oxford University, where Frederick Robertson reported, "a choice selection of the most brilliant among the rising men, have pronounced him to be the first poet of the day."[30] As "the rising men" breathlessly invoked by Robertson replaced "the former men" gloomily invoked by Arnold in "Stanzas from the Grand Chartreuse," Tennyson was identified as their spokesman; "and herein lay the promise of his poetry" according to Sir Alfred Lyall, "for to the departing generation the coming man can say little or nothing."[31] Tennyson's poetry was routinely associated with the concerns shared by the young men of the rising generation, in a rhetorical move that divided the century into two distinct generations, each with their own concerns.

My final example of a work that depicts the distance between Victorian and Romantic as a generation gap is *The Aspern Papers* (1888). Henry James found the seed of this story in the same sense of a generational shift. In James's tale, a poetry enthusiast seeks the acquaintance of Juliana Bordereau, one of the last living relics of the Romantic generation, and her niece, Miss Tina, hoping to gain access to the relics of the poet Jeffrey Aspern that they guard. The story is loosely based on an anecdote James heard in Florence about Captain Silsbee, who sought lodgings with Claire Clairmont, Byron's former lover, in order to get at letters by Byron and Shelley that she treasured. On 12 January 1887, when James wrote this anecdote in his notebook, he immediately responded to the tensions and dislocations between the Romantic generation(s) and his own that it illuminated. "Certainly there is a little subject there," he noted, "the picture of the two faded, queer, poor and discredited old English women— living on into a strange generation."[32]

The sense of generational dislocation is introduced right at the story's opening, where the narrator recounts his surprise at discovering that anyone of Aspern's generation is still living. "The strange thing had been for me to discover in England that she was still alive," he notes; "it was as if I had been told Mrs Siddons was, or Queen Caroline, or the famous Lady Hamilton, for it seemed to me that she belonged to a generation as extinct."[33] Juliana Bordereau appears as a woman who has survived beyond her time, just as Empedocles or Marmion Herbert, in their very different ways, have outlived theirs. James returned to this point at a climactic moment, when Juliana shows the narrator a miniature portrait of Jeffrey Aspern. "I'm afraid to mention his name," she claims disingenuously, "lest you never should have heard of him [...] I know the world goes fast and one generation forgets another. He was all the fashion when I was young."[34] The narrator instantly recognizes Aspern, but he too dissembles, saying at first only that the painting's subject is "clearly a man of a past age."[35] Jeffrey Aspern is thus presented as a figure from a former generation, detached from the current generation, even if he still fascinates some of them.

When he came to write the preface for the story in the New York edition of his works, in 1908, James reflected that part of the appeal of the Romantic period lay in its having recently slipped into the past. "[T]he case had the air of the past just in the degree in which that air, I confess, most appeals to me," he wrote, "when the region over which it hangs is far enough away without being too far."[36] The Romantic generation was, for him, just on the cusp between memory and history, "a world we may reach over to as by making a long arm we grasp an object at the other end of our own table."[37] If *The Aspern Papers* offered "a final scene of the rich dim Shelley drama played out in the very theatre of our own 'modernity,' ," the attraction of the story lay in both its historical distance and its continuing interest.[38] "We are divided," James asserted, "between liking to feel the past strange and liking to feel it familiar; the difficulty is, for intensity, to catch it at the moment when the scales of the balance hang with the right evenness."[39] As the last individuals to have known the Romantics personally passed away, Arnold, Disraeli, Tennyson, and James all reflected on the sense that a generational shift divided Romantic writers from the present.

When Arnold, Swinburne, Mill, Disraeli, Tennyson, and James thought of their distance from Romanticism in terms of generational change, they also helped to construct the modern concept of a "generation" as a historical object or agent.[40] At the beginning of the nineteenth century, the word could still be used for any group. Calling a group a "generation" didn't necessarily imply that its members were born or came of age at around the same time, or that their shared attitudes and concerns distinguished them from their parents and offspring. When Scott puts the word into the mouths of characters in *Rob Roy* (1817), it often has this loose and slightly outdated sense (especially but not exclusively when the characters speak in dialect). The gardener Andrew Fairservice describes the bees that he keeps as "a contumacious generation," Baillie Nicol Jarvie complains about "that play-acting and play-ganging generation," and Christopher Nielson, a doctor and apothecary, says that "we surgeons are a secret generation."[41] In each case, "generation" describes a group of people (or bees), but with no sense of a chronological or biological unit. Keats's "No hungry generations tread thee down" represents history as a series of generations, each displacing its predecessor, from which his nightingale has escaped.[42] But Keats's usage still lacks what Raymond Williams calls "the full modern sense" of the word to signify "a distinctive kind of people or attitudes." This sense, he asserts, "only fully develops" from the middle of the nineteenth century. "One of the earliest uses," he notes, "is that of Sainte-Beuve: 'Romantic generation.'"[43] Scott's narrator uses the word in this modern sense in *Waverley* (1814), a novel whose subtitle ("'Tis Sixty Years Since") implicitly points to the generation as a historical marker. In the opening chapter, he notes that his task of blending instruction and amusement is "not quite so easy in this critical generation as it was," and in the final chapter he hopes that "to the rising generation the tale may present some idea of the manners of their forefathers."[44] Both these instances carry the sense of a decisive shift between the ideas and concerns of an older generation and those of a younger one. Although the term "generation gap" belongs to the second half of the twentieth century, the idea of a break between two generations with different attitudes and concerns emerges in the first half of the nineteenth century, and the first historical shift to be described in those terms is the shift from Romantic to Victorian generations.

Karl Mannheim's classic essay "The Problem of Generations" suggests that rather than existing as biological units, generations crystallize in response to the social "trigger" of a "dynamic de-stabilization."[45] Franco Moretti observes that "this cannot possibly explain the *regularity* of generational replacement," but speculates that "a particularly significant 'destabilization'" could structure a series of generations, with later ones replacing the earlier ones as they aged biologically, without new "triggers" for each generation.[46] This makes sense if we think of the French Revolution not only as crystallizing the identity of a generation but also as helping to create Williams's "full modern sense" of the word "generation" itself. The shift that these Victorian writers comment on, then, would be the shift between the second and third generations after the French Revolution, using a vocabulary of "generations" that invoked the word's new connotations.[47] This emergent sense of generations as historical agents or units of time received support from several sources. Thomas Malthus's *Essay on the Principal of Population* (1798) made generations the basic units in calculations of population growth. Charles Darwin's *On the Origin of Species* (1859) made generations the key unit of evolutionary change. In nineteenth-century discussions of historical time, then, the generation was emerging as a marker of increased importance.

This importance only grew in the following century, when generations were widely identified as important historical groups. From the "lost generation" who came of age during the First World War to the "dying generations" Yeats invoked in "Sailing to Byzantium" (1928), the sense that generations were a "natural" historical unit became widespread.[48] T. S. Eliot had interrogated the concept of a "Romantic Generation" in a 1919 essay, but the word was sufficiently pervasive for Eliot to disdain it in 1931, when he commented, "I dislike the word 'generation,' which has been a talisman for the last ten years."[49] Allen Ginsberg paid no heed to Eliot's dislike when he wrote in *Howl* (1955) about "the best minds of my generation destroyed," ten years before the British rock group The Who started talking about "My Generation" (1965). But the sense that history was structured into a succession of generations, each with shared attitudes or concerns that differed from those of its predecessors and successors, first emerged in the nineteenth century, and the reception history of Romantic writing was one important arena in which this understanding took shape.

To speak in terms of generations, rather than periods, offers a more flexible way of discussing cultural change, because, unlike periods, generations need not start and finish on specified dates. Generations are fuzzy around the edges. A vocabulary of generational change thus brings us closer to the experience of the individuals who lived through the cultural shift from Romantic to Victorian. For them, the same break with the past seemed to happen twice. Its first iteration was in the 1820s and '30s, when many of the most prominent writers of the previous twenty years died, several of them prematurely. Keats, Shelley, Byron, Blake, and Bloomfield all died in the '20s; Hazlitt, Scott, Lamb, Coleridge, Hemans, and Landon in the '30s. But thirty years later, in the 1850s and '60s, a second iteration of the same generational shift occurred. Other prominent writers from the beginning of the century died, including Wordsworth, Moore, De Quincey, Hunt, and Peacock. But these decades also witnessed the deaths of many of those who had been closest to the Romantics, and had been stewards of their memories, including some who were important writers or editors themselves: Dorothy Wordsworth, Mary Wordsworth, Sara Coleridge, Lady Byron, Augusta Leigh, John Cam Hobhouse, Mary Shelley, and Fanny Brawne. In the years between these two iterations, we might think of Romantic writers as "semidetached" from their Victorian audience. With the second iteration of the generational shift the detachment became complete, as the last living connections to the Romantic generation(s) were severed. By 1874, a correspondent to *The Times* asserted that "of the great number of persons mentioned by name or referred to in Byron's poetry there is no man now living."[50] A few of the earlier cohort lived into advanced old age, such as Joseph Severn (d. 1879), Claire Clairmont (d. 1879), and Edward John Trelawny (d. 1881). But for the most part the Romantics slipped in the 1850s and '60s from the realm of personal memory into that of history. When Henry Taylor, Southey's literary executor, died in 1886, at the age of eighty-five, his obituary noted that "another link with the literary world of Byron, Rogers, Wordsworth, Scott, and the whole galaxy of poetical genius which adorned the first quarter of the nineteenth century, has been removed from among us—we believe we may almost say the last link."[51] William Graham collected his interviews with Claire Clairmont and Joseph Severn under the title *Last Links with Byron, Shelley, and Keats* (1898).[52] The generational shift from Romantics to Victorians—begun in the 1820s and '30s and reiterated in the 1850s and '60s—produced an increasingly acute sense that Romantic authors were historically detached from the present.

This produced a corresponding need for their images, lives, and works to be mediated to nineteenth-century readers in new ways. Even as they insisted on their difference from the past, later nineteenth-century writers, artists, and commentators were also fascinated by the possibility of reviving it. The widely different forms of fascination with the premodern, preindustrial, or pre-Reformation past shared by the Pre-Raphaelites, the Arts and Crafts Movement, and the Oxford Movement respectively reflected this interest in historical revival. The rapid coining of neologisms prefixed with "neo-" suggested that both the distant and the recent past could return in new and altered forms in the present: the words "neo-Catholic" (1842), "neo-Hellenic" (1869), "neo-medieval" (1879), "neo-Kantian" (1881), "neo-Christian" (1882), "neo-Gothic" (1892), and "neo-Darwinian" (1895) all entered the language in this period.[53] The prefix "neo-," which is not used in this way before this period, could mark the return of styles or ideas from the distant past (e.g., "neo-Gothic"), the revival of enduring ideas that were in danger of becoming moribund (e.g., "neo-Christian"), or the need to give even fairly recent ideas a new twist to keep them up to date (e.g., "neo-Darwinian"). In any case, the prefix "neo-" marked both a connection to the past and a difference from it: when the past returned in the present, it did so in altered forms. To address the specific concerns of the present, the culture of previous generations had to be renovated, regenerated, remediated, made anew.

Robert Browning's poem "Memorabilia" (1855) registers both the sense that a generation gap was opening between Romantic writers and Victorian readers, and the corresponding need for Romantic writing to be newly mediated.[54] It hinges on the difference between memory and memorabilia, between a kind of knowledge based on direct experience and a kind mediated by commemorative artifacts. The difference measures the distance separating its Victorian speaker from the Romantic poet of a previous generation who fascinates him. The poem's addressee once met Shelley, but he (or she) only draws attention to the generation gap, and does not bridge it. The addressee's experience of Shelley was immediate and sensory—he could "see Shelley plain" and hear his voice—while the speaker's can only be mediated by images of Shelley and writings by and about him (1). The speaker's haltingly phrased question "And did he stop and speak to you / And did you speak to him again?" (2–3) expresses his wonderment at the interactive nature of their encounter. His own experience of Shelley, by contrast, is necessarily asymmetrical: mediated by books that won't answer back. Meeting someone who once met Shelley seems "strange" and "new" (4) precisely because the speaker (like the narrator of *The Aspern Papers*) has grown used to thinking of Shelley and his contemporaries as old. The addressee's memory of Shelley, by contrast, is embedded in his lived experience. The speaker says, "you were living before that, / And also you are living after" as though he finds it hard to believe (5–6). It seems strange that this encounter with Shelley was not a life-changing one. But it also seems strange that it survives as a memory, because for the speaker, living with a modern sense that history is accelerating and the present is detached from the past, the Romantics have already become history. To discover that one of them is still a "memory" for a living individual dislocates the speaker's sense of his own historicity (7). The addressee seems to have outlived his generation.

While the addressee's encounter with Shelley was direct and interpersonal, the speaker can only encounter Shelley indirectly through *lieux de mémoire*. As the poem pivots from the first half, dominated by the addressee's experience, to the second, dominated by the speaker's, the distinction is clear. While the addressee encountered Shelley socially, the speaker can only connect with him by turning away from society to a desolate moor. The moor, as in "Childe Roland to the Dark Tower Came," is a place to encounter poetic predecessors. It has "a name of its own / And a certain use in the world, no doubt" (9–10), but to experience it as a literary *lieu de mémoire* means turning aside from its modern, worldly utility, whatever that may be. The molted feather the speaker picks up on the moor crystallizes the poet from the past into a material memento in the present. The speaker grasps it as a talisman of authenticity, a guarantee that the eagle really was there. He puts it "inside [his] breast" in a metaphor for how poetry from the past can be internalized in memory and integrated in subjectivity (14). But as an artifact of memory, the feather is selective—a feather is a poor substitute for an eagle, and a molted feather is inessential to the bird that sheds it. It is contingent—the speaker happens upon the feather on the moor apparently by accident. And it may be misleading—although the speaker insists he has picked up an eagle feather, the poem seems knowingly to hint that it could belong to some lesser bird: perhaps a skylark or a nightingale, Shelley's preferred emblems for poets and poetry.

Reception mediated by material artifacts—even relics like a molted feather—invites us to "forget the rest" (16): the rest of the eagle, the rest of the moor, and the rest of the poem Browning's speaker intended to write. But as the last living links of memory were severed by death, a mediated experience of Romantic writers was the only kind available. The poem "Memorabilia," appearing in Browning's 1855 collection *Men and Women*, becomes itself an artifact of mediation like the eagle's feather it contains. It offers to remediate Shelley to a new generation of readers, but it ends with a sense of the losses inherent in that process. For my purposes, the feather could be pressed into service as an image for the lines of Byron or Shelley broken off from their contexts and quoted in Victorian sermons (part 3), or the sections from long poems by Byron, Hemans, and Shelley reprinted in Victorian anthologies (part 5); or it could appear as an image for the Victorian statues and memorials of Scott and Byron that commemorated them (part 4), or the Victorian illustrations of Wordsworth, Byron, and Hemans that mediated their writings to new readers (part 2). All these things responded to the feeling that Romantic writing was slipping from the living repository of memory into the mediated realm of history, and that as a result it needed to be remediated to a new generation if it was not to be forgotten altogether.

PART II
Illustrations

4

Illustration as Renovation

WHEN VICTORIANS read Romantic-period writings, they were not usually reading Romantic-period books. Instead, they mostly encountered Romantic writing in new editions, which supplied existing works with a new bibliographical format. These new editions often included illustrations. In this part of the book, I focus on what I call retrofitted illustrations: that is, new illustrations produced for works that initially appeared without illustrations. Since very few canonical Romantic works were published with illustrations on their first appearance, this term covers most of the illustrations to Romantic works that appeared in Victorian Britain. In this chapter, I show how often Victorians described illustration as a distinctively modern bibliographical feature and a decisive advance in book production. Reprint editions with retrofitted illustrations circulated alongside the increasing number of Victorian works that were published with illustrations from their first editions, making illustrated books a prominent element in the Victorian media ecology. Retrofitting Romantic works with illustrations therefore offered a way to naturalize them in the new media ecology and renovate them for a new generation of cultural consumers.

In 1846, the aging Wordsworth expressed his dismay at the proliferation of illustrated books in a sonnet:

> Discourse was deemed Man's noblest attribute,
> And written words the glory of his hand;
> Then followed Printing with enlarged command
> For thought—dominion vast and absolute
> For spreading truth, and making love expand.
> Now prose and verse sunk into disrepute
> Must lacquey a dumb Art that best can suit
> The taste of this once-intellectual Land.
> A backward movement surely have we here,
> From manhood—back to childhood; for the age—
> Back towards caverned life's first rude career.

Avaunt this vile abuse of pictured page!
Must eyes be all in all, the tongue and ear
Nothing? Heaven keep us from a lower stage![1]

This sonnet's "scanty plot of ground" contains a kind of miniaturized media history of the world.[2] The first five lines move with stadialist optimism from speech to writing to printing, before reaching the pivotal epoch of the present day in the last three lines of the octave. Here this formally conservative poem makes its Petrarchan volte, and starts to unravel in the sestet, as time seems to move backward, away from the universal enlightenment promised by the printing press and toward illiterate cave dwellers. This macrohistory of media, in which speech is superseded by writing and then print, is superimposed on the microhistory of an individual's maturation, in which childish prattling is replaced by accomplished handwriting, which in turn raises the possibility of published work. When the different media are not ordered sequentially as part of individual growth or historical progress, then they appear antagonistically. Images and text jostle for dominance on the printed page, and appeals to different senses vie for prominence in an economy of attention where one sense can be engaged only at the cost of the others. The "vile abuse" that sends history into reverse is the inversion of the social hierarchy of media: now words must "lacquey" images, and not the other way round. Illustrated books are both newfangled signs of technological modernity and symptoms of cultural regression. On the leading edge of contemporary innovations in book production, they nonetheless create a "backward movement" toward the past. For Wordsworth, illustrations are guilty of bringing back into the present things that a properly maturing individual, or a properly advancing society, should have left behind.

The rising importance of illustration seemed to Wordsworth to be distorting the "natural" relations among media. In this respect, at least, he shared the "fear of [. . .] visual images" that William Galperin identifies as "endemic to romantic poetics."[3] Several critics have argued that Romantic writers tended to think of illustration as an imposition, something that interfered with literature's ability to stand on its own merits, interposed in the relationship of writer and reader, and usurped imaginative work, and pleasure, that properly belonged to the reader. While landscape illustrations might be acceptable for their documentary value, illustrations of characters and events in the narrative seemed to trespass on the collaborative imaginative construction of the author and the reader. "[P]erhaps nothing is more difficult than for a painter to adapt the author's ideas of an imaginary character," Scott wrote in 1804, "I should like at least to be at his elbow when at work."[4] The relationship between the literary and the visual was an important fault-line in Romantic culture. Gillen D'Arcy

Wood has argued that one of the Romantic period's defining antagonisms was the conflict between an elite literary class that sought to enforce the distinction between literary and visual culture, and a popular audience that omnivorously consumed literary and visual media alongside one another.[5] For those committed to literary culture, illustrations deadened the works they were intended to embellish, because "the pictorial or graphic image," in W.J.T. Mitchell's formulation, was "a lower form—external, mechanical, dead" and opposed to the imagination's "'higher' image which is internal, organic, and living."[6]

However, Wordsworth's general suspicion of illustrations coexisted with his tolerance, and even encouragement, of certain illustrators and visual artists. He sat for many portraits, including several by up-and-coming painters, he encouraged landscape artists working in the Lake District, and he paid careful attention to the visual appearance of his later editions, including their frontispieces.[7] The concern Wordsworth expresses in his sonnet "Illustrated Books and Newspapers" is not about the visual per se, so much as it is about the heterogeneity and transient interest of illustrated newspapers, which seem to deny the mind any fixed point of contemplation or lasting interest.[8] What worries Wordsworth is the coming shift in the relations among media. Despite enjoying increasing recognition as he grew older, Wordsworth was still strongly invested in the idea that great poets received the reputations they deserved only posthumously, an idea he had articulated as early as the *Essay Supplementary to the Preface* in 1815. As illustrated books became ubiquitous, he worried that the emerging media ecology would be a hostile environment for his poetry, not one conducive to the lasting reputation he anticipated.

Wordsworth's concern was prescient, even if his fears turned out not to be fully justified. As illustrated books proliferated from the 1830s onward, some degree of illustration increasingly became the norm for new publications. Publishers featured illustration conspicuously in genres such as literary annuals, giftbooks, and luxury editions, before expanding it throughout the century to the whole range of books, from the most expensive to the cheapest. Over fifteen hundred illustrations of works by Scott alone have been identified in the nineteenth century.[9] This proliferation was driven in part by new techniques, processes, and materials, which changed the production of illustrated books. The revival of wood engraving led by Thomas Bewick made it possible to include detailed images on the same page as letterpress text. The widespread adoption of steel-plate engraving made high-quality images available in larger print runs. Lithography made illustrations available in cheaper books alongside letterpress. As high-art standards were increasingly applied to illustration, the art of printmaking entered a "golden age" in the 1860s. Book illustration, in turn, drove developments in other kinds of printmaking.[10]

New books that appeared with illustrations from their first publication became more common in the Victorian period, produced either by a single artist working in two media, such as William Thackeray, Edward Lear, or Beatrix Potter, or by collaborators such as Charles Dickens and Hablot K. Browne (Phiz), or Lewis Carroll and John Tenniel. Serial publication (as in the case of Dickens) also lent itself to illustration, with one or two images appearing with each number, which were then reprinted when the numbers were reissued as a volume. Of course, the Romantic period had illustrated books too. William Blake, Henry Fuseli, J.M.W. Turner, and other artists produced many illustrations for others' works, while projects like Boydell's Shakespeare Gallery and Fuseli's Milton Gallery combined gallery exhibitions of paintings with the sale of engraved prints and the subscription publication of illustrated editions.[11] However, very few canonical Romantic works appeared with illustrations when first published, with the obvious exception of Blake's illuminated books. Even the Waverley novels, which were illustrated in reprint editions, including the Magnum Opus edition, all appeared without illustrations on their first publication.

In the Victorian period, not only were there more illustrated books in circulation than ever before, but they were also more profusely illustrated and more extensively ornamented. Publishers multiplied the numbers of head- and tailpieces, decorative dividers, and printers' ornaments they used, so that in some Victorian books almost every page is embellished with some kind of visual ornament. Colored ink was also more commonly used for initials and borders. This level of ornamentation extended to the trade bindings that were growing in popularity in this period, so that books were increasingly offered for sale in bindings decorated with blind or gilt tooling rather than in the plain paper wrappers common in the early decades of the century. All these features made books from the middle of the nineteenth century look noticeably different from those of the 1810s and '20s. Today, any well-informed librarian, book historian, or antiquarian bookseller could tell which of the two periods a shelf of books came from without crossing the room to examine the volumes individually.

The use of the word "illustration" itself shifted to reflect the growing popularity of illustrated books. At the beginning of the nineteenth century, it was used primarily to mean an example or instance that served to elucidate something. Johnson had defined "illustration" as "explanation, elucidation, exposition," without mentioning pictorial embellishments. An abstract argument could be "illustrated" with specific cases. When Walter Scott published his edition of John Dryden's works in 1808, the publisher described it as "illustrated with notes, historical, critical, and explanatory."[12] The book was "illustrated" with notes, not with pictures (its eighteen volumes contained only one image: a frontispiece portrait of Dryden). Although "illustrations" in this sense could be pictures, the word did not imply a visual supplement to the verbal. John Cam Hobhouse's *Historical Illustrations to the Fourth Canto of Childe Harold's Pilgrimage* (1818) similarly offers notes rather than pictures to "illustrate" Byron's poem. In 1822, William Wordsworth used "illustration" in a sense that illuminates the transition to a more specifically pictorial meaning. When he reprinted his sonnet on the Rhinefall in *Ecclesiastical Sonnets* (it had first appeared in *Memorials of a Tour of the Continent* earlier that year), he retitled it "Illustration: The Jungfrau and the Fall of the Rhine near Schaffhausen." The new title indicated that the word-picture of the turbulent river provided an elucidation for the volume's other poems about civil and ecclesiastical discord. The imagery in this case was poetic rather than pictorial. As books embellished with prints became more common, however, the word "illustration" was increasingly used in the limited sense to refer to pictures accompanying a text. It is only from 1813 that *OED* records a new sense of the word that limits it to pictorial embellishments. One of the earliest citations it gives concerns Richard Westall's illustrations to Scott's poems. By the middle of the century, when Wordsworth was writing "Illustrated Books and Newspapers," this would become the word's primary meaning, reflecting and reinforcing the prevalence of illustrated publications in the period.

Victorian commentators often identified illustrated books as a characteristically modern phenomenon. When the publisher Robert Cadell claimed in 1844 that his was "the age of graphically illustrated Books," he reflected a widespread understanding among publishers and booksellers that the new popularity of book illustration had recently made illustrations a virtual necessity for commercial success. (The fact that "graphically illustrated" was not a tautology in 1844 also reflects the fact that "illustration" was still not confined to its pictorial meaning.) The sense that the Victorian period was an age of illustrated books extended beyond the book trade. The *London Review*, in 1859, called illustrated books "a distinctive feature of the age," and *The Times*, in 1868, averred that "[t]he age in which we live is as much distinguished by its illustrated books as the Middle Ages were by their illuminated manuscripts."[13] To the Victorians, illustrated books appeared distinctively modern.

Many Victorians thought that the progress of book illustration was another manifestation of the generational shift that separated them from the Romantic period. They insisted not only that illustrated books were characteristic of the current moment but also that their quality was one of the things that set that moment apart from the preceding age. To be illustrated was to be up to date. The *Journal of the Society of Arts* declared, in 1864, that "[t]he art of illustration, as applied to poetical and other works, shows marked progress."[14] Describing the recent history of book illustration often involved describing how a new generation of illustrators had surpassed an old one. *The Graphic* claimed that "there has been an advance in Art-taste during the last few years which makes it impossible for us to tolerate the illustrations which satisfied our fathers," and the *Daily News* asserted "the superiority [...] of the present generation of book illustrators over that which immediately preceded it."[15] Invoking a generation shift allowed commentators to minimize the vitality of Romantic-era illustration and depict illustrations as a mark of modernity in book production.

Illustrations were not confined to new works. Older works that had initially appeared without images were republished in new editions that had been ret-rofitted with illustrations. Newly illustrated editions of Romantic poetry, from artistic landmarks like Gustave Doré's *Ancient Mariner* (1876) to cheap, mass-market part-works like Henry Vizetelly's *Illustrated Byron* (1854–55), began to appear frequently in Victorian Britain, especially after Romantic works started to come out of copyright.[16] By the middle of the century, when the *Illustrated London News* noted that "the public taste and fashion of the day are running strongly in favour of illustrated books of poetry," canny publishers understood that reprint editions needed to be embellished in order to compete in the marketplace.[17] In 1860, the *Morning Post* traced this genealogy of illustration:

> The old annuals, with their watered silk covers, *olla-podrida* contents, and the steel engravings that never had anything to do with the matter they were supposed to illustrate [...] have been deposed by illustrated works, in which some favourite poet or prose author is bravely decked out with the fancies and conceits of the artist of the brush[.][18]

The highest point in the evolution of illustrated books, on this account, was the retro-illustrated volume, where "some favourite poet or prose author," who was already known from his or her unillustrated publications, was "bravely decked out" with new illustrations. By 1866, the *Pall Mall Gazette* could complain about the "Illustration Nuisance": "there seems to us just now to exist a sort of stupid rage of illustration—a passion for getting up woodcuts to every-thing readable—which in its results is a source of very imperfect pleasure to cultivated book-buyers."[19] Whether they endorsed or disdained illustrated volumes, these commentators focused on new illustrations produced for pre-viously published poems, either issued in new illustrated editions of poetry or as stand-alone volumes of illustrations designed to be viewed alongside poetry volumes or bound into collected editions as extra-illustrations. These, then, are the "retrofitted illustrations" I examine in the next two chapters.

Without this kind of embellishment, some commentators suggested, works from the past would not be bought and read at all. The *Morning Chronicle* claimed in 1853 that "[t]he public taste, palled by novelties" would neglect the works of the past without new illustrations. The public needed "to be aroused to interest in old themes" by "superadding to all that is classical and beautiful in literature all that is gorgeous, graceful, and captivating in the arts of the painter and engraver."[20] In comments like this one, the sister arts were united to compel the attention of cultural consumers by making them both readers and viewers at once. But visual art was imagined as the younger, more "gorgeous," and vibrant sibling who came to the aid of her "classical" older sister. Illustrations could not only promote the sale of a new book; they could also renew interest in a work that was going out of fashion, by "superadding" their attractions to its inherent qualities. In this way, illustrated editions promised to renovate writing from the past, making it fit for consumption in the present. Illustrated editions of Romantic writing therefore aligned with the concern, outlined in part 1, that the literature of even the recent past was becoming outdated and uninteresting to a new generation. They addressed this concern by producing a new and modern form of embellishment that would allow Romantic works to circulate in updated forms. David Blewett, in his study of illustrated editions of *Robinson Crusoe*, compares the effect to the way in which new productions can renew a play or an opera.[21] Retrofitted illustrated editions turned old texts into new books and therefore helped to bridge the generation gap emerging between Romantics and Victorians.

While Scott shared Wordsworth's misgivings about illustrations, he expressed his concern in a simile that reflected illustration's capacity for renovating texts. He compared an illustrated book to "a faded beauty [who] dresses and lays on a prudent touch of rouge to compensate for her want of her juvenile graces."[22] Scott's image of today's woman of a certain age aping yesterday's debutante reveals his anxiety that the charms of a literary work, like those of an aging woman, may fade over time and need some cosmetic assistance. Retrofitted illustrations could make aging texts newly attractive to readers by adding "prudent" embellishment, renovating them when they threatened to seem past their prime. In doing so they tackled the sense—sometimes anxiously backward-looking, sometimes optimistically forward-looking—that the century fell into two distinct generations with little to say to one another.

When they renovated Romantic works for Victorian audiences, illustrated editions helped them to reach new readers across the social spectrum. William St. Clair has described the process of "tranching down" by which Romantic-period works reached large audiences over several years.[23] Initially published in expensive editions with large profit margins but limited print runs, new works were then republished in progressively cheaper editions, in smaller formats, with slimmer profit margins but larger print runs. A high-margin, low-volume business model in the short term was thus supplemented by a low-margin, high-volume one in the long term. This approach made it possible to sell a work all the way down the market, from upper-class readers who would pay a premium for new works, to a mass readership content to wait for cheaper editions. Illustrated editions could extend this process. Vizetelly's *Illustrated Byron*, for example, was aimed at the bottom of the market. It appeared in parts costing only a few pence, with advertisements on the wrappers. A single poem could extend across several parts, creating an incentive to keep buying them. The complete set contained over two hundred illustrations. Cheap, illustrated collected editions like Vizetelly's, then, helped to make the whole of Byron's works accessible to the whole of the reading public.

At the same time, illustrated editions could initiate a new process of "tranching up." By the time Doré's *Ancient Mariner* appeared, Coleridge's poem had been in print in various editions for decades and had been "tranched down" to a mass readership. But by producing an expensive, large-format edition embellished with high-quality illustrations, the publishers targeted the upper end of the market once again. Many of the people who bought the book must already have had copies of the poem in their libraries, but the illustrations created a new attraction that reopened the high end of the market for the poem. Tranching down was supported by long copyright terms, which prevented wide reprinting. Once Romantic poetry came out of copyright, however, it became more important for publishers to distinguish their edition of a Romantic poet from other competing editions in the marketplace. Prefaces, notes, biographical sketches, and other paratexts provided added value. But illustrations offered a conspicuous tool for publishers wanting to boost sales of their editions while distinguishing them from other reprints on the market.

The modernity of the illustrated book was especially pronounced when the illustrations were produced in the new medium of photography. Carol Armstrong has argued for the importance of studying photographically illustrated books. She notes the need "to reinscribe the nineteenth-century photograph in its textual surround, and if art history and the art museum have removed it from its album series or book pages, to reinsert it there."[24] In the first decades of photography's existence, it entered into complex intermedial negotiations with the codex form. The new medium of photography gained cultural legitimacy by associating itself with the established medium of the printed codex. Having described his inventions in scientific papers, William Henry Fox Talbot demonstrated them to a wider public in *The Pencil of Nature* (1844–46), a printed book with an elaborately decorated title page, issued in parts. Talbot's book imitated contemporary illustrated volumes so closely that in the second part he added a note explaining that readers were seeing "the sun-pictures themselves, and not, as some persons have imagined, engravings in imitation."[25] As photography became more familiar, however, the printed codex in turn gained from its association with the photograph, as photographically illustrated books positioned themselves on the cutting edge of technological developments in publishing.

To some extent, *all* new editions, illustrated or not, participate in the process of renovation I am describing by providing an updated "bibliographic code" to accompany the work's "linguistic code" (to use Jerome McGann's terms for the "double helix of perceptual codes" deployed by "[e]very literary work that descends to us").[26] But I suggest that retrofitted illustrated editions provide an exceptionally rich example of this process of renovation, because adding illustrations to a previously unillustrated text makes the bibliographic code especially conspicuous. Adding illustrations means incorporating the medium of engraving or photography into the book, and producing new intermedial negotiations. An intermedial or multisensory dimension is never absent from the printed codex, which is always experienced as a visual, verbal, tactile, and even olfactory medium, but it is especially noticeable in illustrated books, and particularly in photographically illustrated books at this period, which, like digital editions today, were sufficiently new to encourage consumers to reflect on the meanings of the medium. Moreover, illustrations could make a book seem modern even if the pictures themselves were old-fashioned. When Gall and Inglis published a retrofitted illustrated edition of Wordsworth that depicted some of his characters in quasi-medieval costumes, the form of the illustrated book still connoted modernity, even if the content of the illustrations did not.[27]

In some cases, the process of renovation was thematized by the retrofitted illustrated books in which it was accomplished. In the examples I discuss below, the interplay of existing texts and new images in the material object of the book allowed cultural consumers to imagine the work floating free of its original context of production, or, alternatively, to imagine themselves floating free of their own context of reception. My argument, therefore, has both specific and general forms. Specifically, I contend that the books I examine in the next two chapters offered implicit ways to address the sense of a generational shift between Romantic texts and Victorian audiences. More generally, I suggest that—even when the process is not thematized—newly illustrated editions of dead authors can productively be understood as both registering the passing of time and seeking to efface it, in order to renovate earlier texts for later readers.

These effects were not necessarily intended by any individual—whether illustrator, publisher, or engraver. Instead, they appear when the books are considered as material objects, or what Thomas Tanselle would call "artifacts."[28] As J. Hillis Miller observes, "what is needed" in studies of illustrations "is the ability to read not just pictures and words separately, but the meanings and forces generated by their adjacency."[29] Reading the retrofitted illustrated book prompts us to reappraise the reception history of literature. Reception history appears in these books not only as an encounter with texts from previous historical periods, nor even as an engagement with the discursive construction of their authors' reputations. Instead, we recognize reception history as a process mediated by the creation of new material artifacts, incorporating different media and reflecting the efforts of several individuals divided by time and space.

This approach rethinks the critical tendency—common from Lessing's *Laocoön* (1766) onward—to understand encounters between word and image as competitive or "paragonal."[30] Morris Eaves asserts that "[a]wesome combinations of failure, difference, distance, lag, divergence, and conflict establish the relations of texts and images in the Romantic period," and Julia Thomas notes that "[t]he Victorian illustrated text has frequently been seen as a divided genre, in which image and word fail to coincide."[31] Critics who think in these terms typically approach images as synchronic, or atemporal, and words as diachronic, or inherently in motion. James Heffernan, in his study of ekphrasis, opposes the "driving force of the narrating word" to the "stubborn resistance of the fixed image."[32] In the case of retrofitted illustrated books, however, this position could be reversed. Here it is the words that risk becoming static, stranded in the past, and the images that dynamically engage with them, allowing them to move between past and present. In 1842, the *Illustrated London News* championed the progress of illustration in just these terms:

> At one plunge it was in the depth of the stream of poetry—working with its every current—partaking of the glow, and adding to the sparkles of the glorious waters—and so refreshing the soul of genius, that even Shakespeare came to us clothed with a new beauty, while other kindred poets of our language seemed as it were to have put on festive garments to crown the marriage of their muses to the arts.[33]

The watery metaphors of this sentence subtly make the point. At first poetry is figured as fluid, like an ever-rolling stream, and illustration dives in; but three dashes later poetry seems in danger of stagnating or drying up, and now it's illustration that is fluid, like a refreshing drink of water. Illustration is here depicted as fundamentally dynamic, active, and temporal. It replaces the old-fashioned or threadbare clothes of the classics with new "festive garments" and "refresh[es] the soul of genius" when it threatens to flag or stumble. The paper's commercial interests obliged it to depict the relation between word and image as a happy marriage rather than a sibling rivalry. But, here as elsewhere, illustration was troped as renovation. Rather than reducing the temporal extension of the poetic line to stasis, illustration rescues it from the threat of a static existence in the past and restores to it the possibility of a renewed energy in the present.

5

Renovating Romantic Poetry

RETROFITTED ILLUSTRATIONS

IN THE PREVIOUS chapter, I argued that retrofitted illustrations—that is, new illustrations added to works that previously appeared without illustrations— renovated Romantic writing for Victorian book-buyers, and thus symbolically bridged the generation gap that seemed to be opening up between Romantics and Victorians. In this chapter, I examine some books that prompted their purchasers to reflect on that process. These volumes effectively thematized illustration's potential for renewal by including Victorian people and updated landscapes in illustrations to Romantic poems. With this artistic choice, they insisted that Romantic poetry could be made newly appealing to readers of the new generation, if it were recirculated in new bibliographical forms and fitted with new embellishments.

Charles Daly's 1852 edition of *Don Juan* almost literalized the *Illustrated London News*'s metaphor of "cloth[ing]" a classic "with a new beauty."[1] The book included fifteen illustrations, by an unknown artist, in which Don Juan's appearance is extraordinarily mutable. In a visual correlative to Byronic mobility, his age, dress, hairstyle, facial hair, and even his facial features shift between illustrations. As the narrative requires, Juan is unmoored from any particular location, appearing in different surroundings as his picaresque story unfolds. But he is also unmoored from culture; he appears in these illustrations not as a Spaniard abroad but as a cipher who adopts the customs and the costume of the country in which he finds himself. On Haidee's island in canto 4 he adopts a version of traditional Greek dress, which he is still wearing in the slave market in canto 5.[2] When Juan reaches Russia and meets Catherine the Great, Byron gives a full account of his military uniform, with "scarlet coat, black facings [. . .] brilliant breeches [. . .] of yellow casimire [and] [. . .] White stockings" (9.43). But the artist does not follow this description closely. Instead, Juan is depicted as a civilian, in historically specific dress. He wears a full-skirted coat, with large cuffs and pocket flaps, knee breeches, and dark stockings. He carries a tricorn hat and appears to be wearing a wig (fig. 1). Catherine's gown has a scooped neck and tight-fitting bodice, and may have been copied from Fedor Rokotov's 1763 portrait, completed shortly after the beginning of Catherine's reign in 1762. Since Juan brings news of the Siege of

FIGURE 1. Engraving of Don Juan at the Court of Catherine the Great, from
*Lord Byron's Don Juan: with Life and Original Notes by A. Cunningham Esq.
and Many Illustrations on Steel* (London: Charles Daly, 1852), facing p. 262.
© The British Library Board, shelfmark 11656h38.

Ismail (1790), this is one of the few episodes in the poem that can be precisely dated, and this image aims, at least approximately, for historical accuracy.

But if Juan looks the part of an eighteenth-century gentleman in canto 9, he soon changes his outfit. Dating the action of the English cantos is more complex: although the story is continuous with the Russian episode, many of the descriptive details are drawn from the Regency, and the narrator continually refers to the period of the poem's composition. An illustrator could therefore set these scenes at any time from 1790 to 1824 with good reason. But to do that in 1852 would be to anchor the poem in the previous generation, which is not what this illustrator chose to do. In two illustrations to the English cantos, Juan wears a dark tailcoat, a waistcoat with scooped neck and shawl collar, and dark trousers with narrow legs. He has short hair and, for the first time in the poem, a mustache and sideburns (fig. 2). These details date his appearance to 1835 at the earliest, after the beginning of the so-called great masculine renunciation that, in John Harvey's words, saw "colour die, garment by garment, in a very few years."[3] The ladies pictured with Juan confirm this dating. Both wear gowns with low, wide necklines showing bare shoulders and throats, unadorned with jewelry, in a style popular from the 1840s.[4] The ladies' gowns reach the floor, in a fashion popular after 1835, and both wear their hair parted in the middle and smoothed back to either side of the face, in a Victorian style.[5] In a third illustration, Juan wears either a morning coat or a sack coat (a short lounge jacket without waist seam), both of which date to the 1850s, with the black cravat and turn-down collar that were starting to appear at that time.[6] This image therefore shows a scene that is more or less contemporaneous with the book's 1852 publication date.

In these images, Juan has migrated not just to England but to *Victorian* England. Following his habit, he has adopted the costume of a Victorian gentleman. These illustrations allow him to drift not only across cultures and continents but all the way into the mid-nineteenth century. This adds a further layer of complexity to *Don Juan*'s already complex handling of time. By depicting Juan in mid-nineteenth-century clothes, the images add a fourth temporal layer, closer to the moment of the edition's publication. Bringing Juan up to date invites readers to consider the English cantos not as historically specific or temporally bounded—a topical satire from thirty years ago, aimed at the vices of the 1820s or even the 1790s—but as a poem of continuing relevance for England in the 1850s.[7] The book therefore invited readers mentally to shift *Don Juan* onto their side of the generational gap that was increasingly perceived between Romantic and Victorian writers. Just at the moment when Byron's works were starting to seem historically distant, these illustrations inserted Juan into the modern age.

My second example also includes apparently modern individuals, dressed in Victorian clothes and taking part in a newly fashionable activity. It comes

FIGURE 2. Engraving of Don Juan in London, from *Lord Byron's Don Juan: with Life and Original Notes by A. Cunningham Esq. and Many Illustrations on Steel* (London: Charles Daly, 1852), facing p. 292. © The British Library Board, shelfmark 11656h38.

from Thomas Ogle's photographically illustrated book *Our English Lakes, Mountains and Waterfalls, as Seen by William Wordsworth* (1864, 1866).[8] Thomas Ogle provided A. W. Bennett, the publisher of *Our English Lakes,*

Mountains and Waterfalls, with thirteen photographs of locations associated with Wordsworth and his poems, probably drawn from Ogle's existing collection of stereoscope photographs, since stereoscopy was his primary medium and source of income.[9] Ogle's photograph of Brougham Castle illustrates Wordsworth's "Song, at the Feast of Brougham Castle" (1807), which tells the story of how Lord Clifford spent his youth incognito as a shepherd in order to avoid the Wars of the Roses, and how he declined to take revenge on his persecutors when restored to his estates (fig. 3). Presented as a framed minstrel's song, it draws its structure and some of its themes from Scott, who admired the poem.[10] Wordsworth represented a feudal past, but one in which the "savage virtue" (165) of the aristocracy had been "softened into feeling, soothed, and tamed" (160) by communion with nature and life among the

FIGURE 3. Photograph of Brougham Castle, from *Our English Lakes, Mountains and Waterfalls, as Seen by William Wordsworth, photographically illustrated* [by Thomas Ogle] (London: A. W. Bennett, 1864; 2nd ed. 1866). Reproduced by permission of The Wordsworth Trust.

peasantry. Through adversity, Clifford had learned to prefer stability, humility, and forbearance to the aristocratic virtues of martial valor, strong leadership, and dynastic succession. In his life as a shepherd, he had become a steward of the land and its people rather than a conqueror of them, earning the sobriquet "The Good Lord Clifford" from his vassals.

Ogle's photograph provided a self-consciously updated vision of the poem's self-consciously outdated setting. The poem operates on three distinct temporal layers: the time of its composition and publication, the time when its minstrel tells his story, and the time when the events of that story take place. Wordsworth draws attention to this temporal displacement in the first lines of the poem: "The words of ancient time I thus translate, / A festal strain that hath been silent long" (3–4). By illustrating it using the new technology of photography, Ogle superimposed a fourth temporal layer on the poem: the time when his photograph was taken. The image used a thirty-year-old medium to illustrate a sixty-year-old poem about a six-hundred-year-old castle.

Photographs can capture their subjects only at the instant the shutter opens and so they always present a scene exactly contemporaneous with the moment of exposure. In some cases, such as Julia Margaret Cameron's photographic illustrations to Tennyson's *Idylls of the King* (1875), early photographers resisted this feature of their new medium, using costume and setting to present an image of the distant or mythical past. But a connection to the present moment was hard-wired into the medium of photography. And, as Susan Sontag points out, photography's inescapable contemporaneity is always also an index of temporality. "Precisely by slicing out this moment and freezing it, all photographs testify to time's relentless melt."[11] The *Edinburgh Review* had already noticed this quality of photography in 1843, when it described how the landscape that "self-delineated" in a photograph was "seized at one epoch of time."[12] By illustrating this poem in a medium that was unknown at the time of its composition, then, Ogle's image drew attention to the time that had elapsed since the poem was written and first published. The sense that the poem was a survivor of a past age was reinforced by the volume's typography, which used the long "s" that had been almost abandoned in book design since the beginning of the century. If the photograph could speak its own caption, then, it might say of the poem what the poem's speaker says of the minstrel's song: "The words of ancient time I thus translate, / A festal strain that hath been silent long" (3–4).

While the medium of photography connoted modernity, the composition of this photograph pressed the point home by including modern figures engaged in a modern practice. Ogle included two spectators in the foreground, likely a tourist and a guide, with their backs to the camera; one of them wears a top hat and tailcoat that mark him as modern and middle class. The inclusion of figures in the foreground, as Bruce Graver has shown, was a convention that stereoscope photographers such as Ogle inherited from the picturesque tradition and used to emphasize the three-dimensional illusions and virtual-reality effects made possible by stereoscopy.[13] But these modern, touristic foreground figures, standing in a location that had only recently become accessible to large numbers of middle-class tourists, were not simply conventional. The fashionable top hat worn by one of them—a Barthesian *punctum*—pricks the viewer's attention because it is contemporary, modish, and connected to a temporal horizon far shorter than the *longue durée* of the castle's feudal past and slow deterioration.[14] The past invoked in the poem is represented here for the appreciation of modern tourists and the consumption of modern book-purchasers. The middle classes, who were necessarily absent from the poem's feudal setting, are prominent in the photograph. One of the "numerous and noble feudal Edifices," which Wordsworth described as "so great an ornament to that interesting country," was thus repackaged in Ogle's photograph as a contemporary tourist destination—one of those that sustained Ogle's livelihood as a stereoscopic photographer. The book's introduction noted that it offered "the Tourist the additional pleasure of identifying with his own favourite spot any of the poet's verses which refer especially to it."[15]

In both its medium and its composition, then, this image at once asserted its distance in time from the poem's first appearance and affirmed the poem's continued vitality. Looking at this photograph, we might see only the nostalgia that Helen Groth identifies in Victorian photographic illustrations to literary texts.[16] Ogle's image might seem to be wistfully mourning the loss of Wordsworthian nature, of Wordsworth himself, and of the consolations his poetry once offered, which no longer seem to help the modern, alienated generation. Wordsworth's poetry would then seem like Brougham Castle: a once glorious edifice now fallen into disuse. But I want to resist this nostalgic reading and see in this image a testament to the poetry's potential, not for endurance, but for renovation in the present. If Brougham Castle no longer signified as it once did, it nonetheless continued to dominate the landscape around it, and was now being reimagined as a heritage monument and repurposed as a tourist destination. Wordsworth's poetry remained an intellectual landmark, and with the right embellishments it could still draw new readers and prompt reflection. In Ogle's photographic illustration of "Song, at the Feast of Brougham Castle," a poem from almost sixty years before was shown to be still capable not only of kindling a reader's imagination but also of shaping a tourist's itinerary in the new pastime of middle-class sightseeing, influencing an artist's practice in the new medium of photography, and structuring a publisher's output in the new mass market for illustrated books.

My third example also introduces modern figures into a landscape associated with a Romantic poet, but it does so under the guise of tradition. In 1839, four years after Felicia Hemans's death, William Blackwood published a seven-volume edition of her works with a memoir by her sister. The volumes were produced to a high standard, in an effort to memorialize Hemans and canonize her writing. The title page featured a picture of "Gwrych near Abergele, Denbyshire" that Hemans had drawn herself, engraved by J. H. Kernot (fig. 4). Hemans lived in this part of Wales from the age of seven to sixteen, in a house her biographer Henry Chorley described as "a solitary, old, and spacious mansion—lying close to the sea shore, and in front shut in by a chain of rocky hills."[17] This house appears to the right of her drawing, with the sea visible beyond it. A smaller cottage appears in the foreground on the left, with low cliffs behind it.

Although Hemans sketched occasionally throughout her life, this appears to be the first time one of her drawings was engraved and published. By reproducing Hemans's drawing, Blackwood was not trying to suggest that she was the kind of multitalented individual who could turn her hand to anything. Rather, the juvenile drawing reconnected her poetry to a reassuringly domestic

FIGURE 4. Title-page picture of "Gwrych near Abergele, Denbyshire" drawn by Felicia Hemans, engraved by J. H. Kernot, *The Works of Mrs Hemans, with a Memoir by her Sister*, 7 vols. (Edinburgh: William Blackwood, 1839). Reproduced by permission of the University of Edinburgh Centre for Research Collections.

context of female accomplishment from which it threatened to escape. Chorley had already mentioned Hemans's accomplishments in drawing and music. In both arts, he said, "she would have signally excelled, could she have bestowed the time and patient labour requisite for obtaining mastery."[18] Her sister's memoir repeated the point:

> She had a taste for drawing, which, with time and opportunity for its cultivation, would, doubtless, have led to excellence; but having so many other pursuits requiring her attention, she seldom attempted anything beyond slight sketches in pencil or Indian ink.[19]

The gendered vocabulary of these quotations intimates that Hemans was too busy with her responsibilities as a daughter and a mother to pursue her "taste" for drawing, and too unsuited, as a woman, for the "patient labour" required for "mastery" of the art. As Susan Wolfson and Paula Feldman have pointed out, Hemans was a highly professionalized writer, who negotiated large payments for her poems, and this professionalization threatened to disrupt Victorian ideas of proper female conduct.[20] Even as Blackwood's seven-volume posthumous edition positioned her as a major author, its use of her own amateur drawing on the title page reinscribed her in the domestic sphere, where accomplished women might make sketches, music, or verses but could not aspire to the sphere of professional cultural production.

The image also located her geographically, suggesting that her biographical connection to Wales was important for understanding her poetry. Hemans in the Welsh mountains, it suggested, was like Scott in the Scottish Borders or Wordsworth in the English Lakes. (Hemans visited both these writers at home and drew a picture of Wordsworth's house at Rydal Mount that she described as having "no other merit than that of fidelity."[21]) This local connection was reinforced by Chorley when he described the house at Gwrych as "precisely such an [sic] one as from its situation and character would encourage the developement [sic] of her poetic fancies." Her sister also mentioned "that warm attachment for the 'green land of Wales'" that Hemans "cherished to the last hours of her existence."[22] But Hemans had lived in England and Ireland as well as Wales, and had not always been associated with Wales in her lifetime. John Wilson, for example, claimed in 1819 that "Scotland has her Baillie—Ireland her Tighe—England her Hemans."[23] If Hemans was recurrently concerned with the idea of home (in poems such as "The Homes of England"), she was also a poet of polyglot learning and cosmopolitan interests, who published a series of poems called "Lays of Many Lands" and drew inspiration from Spain, Egypt, America, Italy, Greece, and elsewhere. She wrote about exile (in *The Forest Sanctuary*) and sought to rearticulate the idea of home for an imperial, increasingly globalized world in "The Graves of a Household." Localizing

Hemans in rural North Wales muted these aspects of her writing and helped to reinforce the dominant Victorian image of her as a poet of more limited, local, and domestic concerns. Tricia Lootens argues that nineteenth-century women writers were marginalized from literary history not because they were ignored, suppressed, or forgotten but because the gendered attributes for which they were valued were not their most characteristic or important.[24] Even while Blackwood's 1839 edition of her poetry commemorated Hemans, then, its illustrated title page also circumscribed her achievements.

In 1865, Blackwood published another edition of Hemans's poems, which reused her drawing of Gwrych on its title page (fig. 5).[25] For this book, he had it redrawn and embellished by H. Warren and reengraved by Edward Finden. Warren added trees in the foreground, framing the image. As a whole, the picture

FIGURE 5. Title-page picture of "Gwrych near Abergele, Denbyshire" drawn by Felicia Hemans, redrawn and embellished by H. Warren, engraved by Edward Finden, *Poems of Felicia Hemans* (Edinburgh: William Blackwood, 1865). Private collection.

is technically a vignette—an engraving with no clearly defined border, whose edges shade away into the whiteness of the page. But adding the trees twists the conventions of the vignette by creating an inner border. Warren also added three figures to the foreground of the image, between the trees. Two women in traditional Welsh dress, one of whom rides a donkey, have stopped to speak to a man who's reclining by the side of the path. This renovated and embellished image from 1865 carries the same connotations as the earlier version from 1839 but adds new layers of significance for a new generation of readers.

Adding figures in traditional Welsh dress to Hemans's drawing might seem to be a very different choice from including a Victorian Don Juan in an edition of Byron or a modern tourist in an edition of Wordsworth. In fact, however, the traditional costumes these women wore were every bit as modern, in their way, as Juan's black suit or the top hat worn by Ogle's tourist. The "traditional" Welsh costume depicted here was actually a recent invention. Eric Hobsbawm defined invented traditions as "responses to novel situations which take the form of reference to old situations." Invented traditions react to the modern sense of acceleration and dislocation by defining some elements of social life as unchanging.[26] In response to the growing sense that "authentic" Welsh culture and language were at risk of disappearing, Prys Morgan claims, an invented tradition of Welshness was constructed in the nineteenth century.[27] It included efforts to document and promote the Welsh language, to collect and perform traditional songs, to revive interest in the druids and Celts of the Welsh past, to promote a newly codified set of heraldic motifs including the leek, the daffodil, and the red dragon, and to revive and formalize eisteddfodau. The elements of this invented tradition were not conjured out of thin air. Instead, they were existing components of life in Wales that were researched, compiled, and rede-scribed as "traditional" elements of a distinctly Welsh national identity.

Welsh costume was part of this invented tradition. Augusta Hall, Lady Llanover (1802–1896) is usually credited with "creating" the traditional Welsh costume as it appears in Warren's picture.[28] She won a prize at the Cardiff Royal Eisteddfod in 1834 for her essay on Welsh language and costume, and shortly after commissioned a set of costume prints to document traditional dress and encourage its adoption. She led by example, dressing her servants in Welsh costume and wearing it herself on social occasions and in an 1862 portrait. As with other elements of the invented tradition, Welsh national costume did not appear from nowhere and Lady Llanover did not invent it single-handedly. Drawing on existing forms of dress, she codified it, identified it as a national symbol, and fostered the idea that wearing it was an expression of national heritage and pride. By promoting indigenous materials and styles, Lady Llanover hoped to support the Welsh textile industry, which faced com-petition from imports. She also helped to shape the nascent Welsh tourist trade, as commercial tourism began to reach further into the north and west of Wales, sped along by the relatively late arrival of the railway in the 1860s. In the thirty years between Hemans's death in 1835 and Warren's drawing in 1865, Welsh traditional costume took on its modern form as an expression of national identity, a way to bolster domestic production, and an image for export to attract tourists.

The foreground figures Warren added to Hemans's drawing, then, were as modern in their fashion as the top-hatted tourist Ogle featured in the foreground of his photograph of Brougham Castle. While he was there to look, they were there to be looked at. While he was a surrogate for the touristic viewer, they were ambassadors from the unspoiled scenes of the picturesque. Adding these figures to Hemans's drawing—and then adding the embellished drawing to a new edition of her poems—located her as a poet in a rural community that was apparently governed by tradition but in fact dressed up for modernity, ready to market its supposedly antique charms to a new generation of increasingly mobile consumers. In the same way, Hemans's poetry was implicitly identified both as a repository of long-established values of faith, family, and femininity and as a stimulus of continuing interest for contemporary readers and continuing profits for publishers.

In the editions of Byron, Wordsworth, and Hemans examined here, illustrations included recognizably modern figures as a form of updating, like producing Shakespeare's plays in modern dress. Doing so acknowledged the widening generation gap between Romantic writers and Victorian readers, but suggested that illustrations could help Romantic poems across that gap. Adding illustrations renovated poetry that was in danger of seeming out of date and embellished books of poems for consumers who were increasingly accustomed to purchasing illustrated volumes. In the case of Blackwood's Hemans editions, the title-page illustration from the 1839 book was itself retrofitted with new embellishments for the 1865 edition, introducing apparently traditional figures that in fact reflected modern developments. In all three cases, adding illustrations that featured Victorian people helped to assert the continuing interest and relevance of Romantic poetry.

Illustrators did not need to introduce figures in modern dress to produce this renovating effect; landmarks could be modernized in a similar fashion, as my next two examples show. First, consider Ogle's photograph of the Bowder Stone, a massive boulder, probably a glacial erratic, thirty feet high and fifty feet wide, in Borrowdale (fig. 6). Ogle represented the stone as a modern attraction, modified and managed for the convenience of tourists. His photograph's foreground is dominated by the set of stairs that allowed tourists to ascend the stone from the east side and survey the views from the top. The stairs had been installed earlier in the century, when Joseph Pocklington

FIGURE 6. Photograph of the Bowder
Stone, from *Our English Lakes,
Mountains and Waterfalls, as Seen by
William Wordsworth, photographically
illustrated* [by Thomas Ogle] (London:
A. W. Bennett, 1864; 2nd ed. 1866).
Reproduced by permission of
The Wordsworth Trust.

bought the land around the stone and began exploiting it as a tourist sight.[29] Some contemporaneous depictions of the stone hid or omitted the stairs—the lithograph in J. B. Pyne's 1859 book, *Lake Scenery of England*, for example, concealed evidence of the landscape's exploitation by the fledgling tourist industry—but other stereoscope photographs of the sight, like Ogle's, showed the stairs prominently.[30] Including the stairs meant representing the Bowder Stone as part of a managed landscape. Like the top hat in his photograph of Brougham Castle, the stairs in Ogle's photograph of the Bowder Stone prick the viewer into consciousness of the photograph's modernity.

The Bowder Stone made two brief appearances in Wordsworth's poetry, although he never mentioned it by name. He might have been thinking of it when he compared the leech gatherer in "Resolution and Independence" to "a huge stone [...] Couch'd on the bald top of an eminence" (64–65). It features briefly in *The Excursion* as "A mass of rock, resembling, as it lay / Right at the foot of that moist precipice, / A stranded ship, with keel upturned, that rests / Fearless of winds and waves" (3.52–55). But the only time he mentions the stone explicitly is in his *Guide to the Lakes*.[31] Wordsworth split the body of the *Guide* into three parts: "View of the Country as Formed by Nature," "Aspect of the Country, as Affected by Its Inhabitants," and "Changes, and Rules of Taste for Preventing Their Bad Effects." These parts were loosely connected to three historical epochs, in a scheme comparable to that of his sonnet on illustrated books, discussed in the previous chapter. Beginning by describing the landscape in an originary epoch untouched by human interference, Wordsworth went on to detail the effects of farming and husbandry on the country, before deploring the modern epoch's "introduction of discordant objects, disturbing that peaceful harmony of form and colour, which had been through a long lapse of ages most happily preserved."[32] Aiming to educate cultivated observers into a proper appreciation of the scenes before them, the *Guide* fought a rearguard action against the influx of tourists it ostensibly helped to facilitate.

Ogle didn't share Wordsworth's distaste for the "introduction of discordant objects," whether convenient stairs or modern visitors, but made those objects prominent; his photographs show a landscape that was not only stewarded for agriculture and husbandry but also administered for middle-class tourism. "To possess such a volume is the next good thing to going for an autumn's tour in Cumberland and Westmoreland themselves," the *Daily News* noted in its review.[33] Romantic Nature—itself arguably a defensive construction conceived in response to the threats of industrialization and urbanization rather than a historical reality—was here shown not as something enduring from time immemorial but as something to be staged or packaged by entrepreneurs for new generations of visitors. Wordsworth wanted to stop the clock before the Lakes were overrun by tourists (in the *Guide*) or to turn it back to a stable and idealized past (in "Song"). But this tendency threatened to confirm his poetry's affiliation with a previous generation's concerns. Ogle's photographs bridged the generation gap and connected the poems to a modern, administered landscape.[34]

The engraving of the Rialto that appeared in Edward and William Finden's *Illustrations of the Life and Works of Lord Byron* (1833–34) similarly updated a landmark.[35] *Findens' Illustrations* was one of the most substantial retrofitted illustration projects devoted to any Romantic author in this period. It was initially advertised as fourteen parts, to appear monthly from January 1832.[36] But, in fact, the Findens issued twenty-four parts, each of which contained five engravings, which could be used to extra-illustrate editions of Byron's works. The prints were subsequently published in three volumes with accompanying text, in quarto and large octavo size, the first two appearing in 1833 and the third in 1834. The Findens added a frontispiece and a title-page vignette to each volume, and included in the quarto edition thirty-five additional engravings that had first appeared as illustrations to one of John Murray's editions of Byron's life and works. As a whole, therefore, the *Illustrations* consists of 161 engravings, based on the work of several artists, including a number of landscape drawings contributed by J.M.W. Turner.[37]

The first volume began with an advertisement that took pains to position the book, materially and ideologically, within the domestic space of the cultured middle class:

It has been thought desirable in making up the first Eight Numbers of these Landscape and Portrait Illustrations of LORD BYRON into a Volume, to arrange them in a manner less desultory than was the unavoidable order of their publication, and to accompany the Plates with accounts of the subjects of the Engravings, from authors of eminence and from original sources. The First Volume is thus presented to the Public in a complete

form; and the succeeding Eight Numbers of the Work will, upon their publication, be adapted in the same way, and form an elegant accession to the
drawing-room table and to the library of illustrated works.[38]

Destined not for the masculine study but for the feminine drawing room, the book
was marketed as a desirable ornament for middle-class interiors. The Findens had
initially approached Byron's friend John Cam Hobhouse to solicit his help with
the project, and his encouraging response had left them with the impression that
he would supply them with notes to accompany each illustration. But, as work
proceeded, Hobhouse became more cautious about Byron's memory and he withdrew his cooperation (which, he claimed, he had never promised in any case).[39]
The Findens then approached William Brockedon, who had already written the
letterpress to accompany their engravings of *Passes of the Alps*. He supplied notes to
accompany each picture, usually quoting some relevant lines from Byron's poetry
and drawing heavily on Thomas Moore's biography of Byron.

The Findens' engraving of the Rialto (fig. 7) seems designed neither to illustrate specifically any of the occasions on which Byron mentions the bridge in
his poetry nor to allow the reader to assess the accuracy of his descriptions,
since he never describes the bridge in detail. The gondolas that pass under the
bridge in Edward Finden's engraving may recall Byron's description in *Beppo*

FIGURE 7. Engraving of the Rialto, from Edward Finden and William Finden,
Findens' Illustrations of the Life and Works of Lord Byron, with notes by William
Brockedon, 3 vols. (London: John Murray and Charles Tilt, 1833–34).
Reproduced by permission of McGill University Library.

("Didst ever see a Gondola? For fear / You should not, I'll describe it you exactly" [19]) of the Venetian boats that "under the Rialto shoot along" (20). The strong shadow on the right-hand side of the Rialto in the illustration may recall Lioni's remark in *Marino Faliero* about "Some dusky shadow checkering the Rialto," but Lioni is describing a moonlit scene (*Marino Faliero* IV.i.101). Or it may recall Byron's letter of June 1818, published by Thomas Moore in 1831, which concludes, "Good night—or, rather, morning. It is four, and the dawn gleams over the Grand Canal, and unshadows the Rialto."[40] This passage would later be singled out by Ruskin in *Praeterita* as an example of Byron's "noble [. . .] *perfect*" writing, "with choice of terms which, each in its place, will convey far more than they mean in the dictionary."[41] The picture as a whole may also recall the mention of this landmark as part of the invocation of Venice at the opening of *Childe Harold* canto 4, where Byron asserts that the city's immortality in literature is "a trophy that will not decay / With the Rialto" (4).[42] If you bought this image to extra-illustrate an edition of Byron's works, then, there were at least four places where you could have it bound in.

But William Brockedon's caption, published with the engraving, did not pick up any of these possible references. Instead of evoking a moment from Byron's life or work, he described the sight's effect on "most travellers":

> The magnificent situation of the Ponte Rialto, spanning the Great Canal, will be remembered by most travellers who have taken up their residence in the Leone Bianca, or the adjoining albergo. From every window in the front of either of these hotels this interesting view is seen.[43]

The ambiguous construction "will be remembered" suggests the doubleness of Brockedon's aim. On one hand, he addressed himself to a traveled and cultured upper middle class, for whom the engraving acted as an aide-mémoire stimulating pleasant memories of a previous visit to Venice. On the other hand, he addressed an aspirational lower middle class that would have liked to make the trip, but had yet to do so. He even offered advice on which hotel to stay in for the best views. For members of this group, Findens' *Illustrations* were souvenirs of tours they had never made. The volumes offered a fantasy of travel, made glamorous by Byronic associations and yet rendered affordable and accessible at home. The illustration and its caption remediated the aristocratic grand tour for a middle-class audience to whom European travel was newly accessible. By associating Byron with the rise of European cultural tourism for the middling classes—an association massively reinforced by the tourist guidebooks produced by John Murray III, which were studded with quotations from Byron—publications such as this helped to rehabilitate Byron's works for the respectable readers who had largely turned their backs (at least in public) on his post-1816 poetry.[44]

When illustrators of Hemans, Wordsworth, or Byron depicted modern individuals or landmarks, they helped to ease Romantic poems into the Victorian period and to palliate the increasingly acute sense that they belonged to a previous generation, whose most pressing concerns were now outmoded or obsolete. Including recognizably contemporary people—whether they were characters in the poem (as in Daly's *Don Juan*), surrogates for the reader/ viewer (as in Ogle's photograph of Brougham Castle), or objects of the touristic gaze (as in Warren's women in "traditional" Welsh costume)—these images offered points of connection for a new generation of readers. Depicting landmarks, such as the Bowder Stone or the Rialto, not as things that endured unchanged, but as sites administered for the convenience of modern tourists, emphasized both the passage of time and the efforts to conserve or exploit sites from the past for the consumers of the present. By implication, Romantic poetry itself needed conserving or updating, fitting out with new embellishments to make it more readily accessible, or reclothing to make it fashionable once again. The illustrated book offered a modern medium in which this renovation could take place.

Rather than introducing new readers to the pleasures that these poems had always offered, illustrated editions supplemented them in order to produce what one of the books called an "additional pleasure." Adding illustrations to previously published poems, like adding a set of steps to the Bowder Stone, made a new approach to them possible, rendering them accessible to new people in new ways. But, once the steps had been installed on the Bowder Stone, it could no longer be experienced as it had been before their installation. Illustrated poems could not easily be experienced as though they were unillustrated. The pleasures and satisfactions they offered to earlier readers were not just added to by their new embellishments but supplemented and even supplanted by them. Illustrated editions thus helped to create the sense that Romantic poems could not speak to new readers without embellishment, even as they renovated them for new readers by offering such embellishment.

6

Turning the Page

ILLUSTRATED FRONTMATTER

IN THE PREVIOUS chapter, I discussed retrofitted illustrated editions of Romantic poetry that featured updated people and places, and in doing so suggested that illustrated books could renovate Romantic poems for a new generation of book-buyers and readers. But illustrations also helped to nego-tiate the generation gap between Romantics and Victorians in another way. As well as drawing poems from the past forward in time to meet the concerns of the present, illustrated editions invited readers to turn back time, and to expe-rience poetry from the past as though it were fresh and new. In this chapter, I examine three books whose frontmatter produced this effect. I argue that these books combined images in a way that made the hinge of the book into the fulcrum between present and past. When the reader opened the book, he or she saw a portrait frontispiece on the verso and an engraved title page on the facing recto, separated by a tissue guard. Viewed together, these images both commemorated and renovated the books' authors.

The books produced this double effect by drawing on three elements of visual culture that were familiar to their Victorian purchasers. First, they used narrative images, which relied on viewers whose ability to read narrative cues in static images had been cultivated by a popular tradition of narrative painting and printmaking stretching from William Hogarth (1697–1764) and David Wilkie (1785–1841) to George Cruikshank (1792–1878), Augustus Leopold Egg (1816–1863), and William Frederick Yeames (1835–1918). Kate Flint has shown how pervasively the vocabulary of narrative and visual effects intertwined in art criticism of this period.[1] The title-page prints I examine here represented scenes but also told stories, making those scenes meaningful as episodes in the poet's career, and therefore drawing attention to that career as something extended in time, as well as separated from the present by the passage of time.

Second, the opening pages of these books presented diptychs, in which two adjacent images became meaningful in ways that neither would have been alone. Although different artists created the frontispieces and title pages, probably working in ignorance of each other's intentions, the images addressed the generational shift between Romantic writers and Victorian readers most powerfully when combined in illustrated codices. Gazing at either image meant confronting the generation gap; turning from one to another meant imagining how to cross it. The narratives they invited their viewers to imagine, then, took place not only within images but also between images. As the viewer's attention moved from one image to the other, the first picture remained as a kind of afterimage imposing itself on his or her perception of the second.

Third, and relatedly, these books participated in the Victorian fascination with optical toys.[2] The zoetrope, thaumatrope, and phenakistiscope, which all employed afterimages to produce their effects, were contrivances that relied on viewers looking at two or more images in rapid succession. The stereoscope and some versions of the magic lantern were contrivances that offered two images for simultaneous viewing. The illustrated editions that I examine in this chapter made the book into just such a contrivance—call it the bibliotrope—in which turning the tissue guard between the frontispiece and the illustrated title page produced the trope or turn from one image to the other, and viewing the images simultaneously or in succession produced effects that neither would have produced alone. As Jonathan Crary argues, widespread understanding of the persistence of vision, the phenomenon on which many optical toys relied, resulted in "the introduction of temporality as an inescapable component of observation."[3] Viewers bringing this awareness to illustrated books might have been sensitized to the ways in which one image of the pair was implicated in the viewing of the other, as well as the time that had elapsed between the poet's life and the moment of viewing his or her portrait. While they didn't produce optical illusions or protocinematic effects, the books I examine here stitched together images of commemoration and renovation. The visual effect, as one image took the place of the other like the dissolving views of the magic lantern, was to dissolve the differences between generations. In this sense, the books weren't just informed by the habits of viewing cultivated by optical toys: they were optical toys.

While the frontmatter of these books affiliated them with contemporary visual culture, the portraits on their frontispieces connected them to a tradition of book design even older than print. Chaucer appears in a painted frontispiece to an early fifteenth-century manuscript of *Troilus and Criseyde*, which shows him reading the poem from a pulpit to the King, Queen, and nobles.[4] Whether or not such a reading ever took place, Chaucer is depicted as the originator of the poem, with an authority comparable to that of a preacher or teacher (whose iconography is borrowed in this depiction) and a connection to the highest echelon of society. The engraved portrait of Shakespeare by Martin Droeshout that appeared on the title page of the First Folio in 1623 helped to reposition Shakespeare as an author of books, not just a writer of plays, and to construct a Shakespearean oeuvre unified around its creator.[5] In both cases, the frontispiece elevated the author and functioned as a paratextual "threshold of interpretation" (in Gérard Genette's phrase) shaping the reader's approach to the book.[6] As frontispieces became more common in the seventeenth and early eighteenth centuries, the meaning of "frontispiece" itself shifted from its original architectural sense, meaning the façade of a building, to refer instead to the front matter of a book. By the mid-eighteenth century, "frontispiece" came to mean specifically an illustration placed before the title page, typically on the facing verso. As author portraits became more commonly used in frontispieces, the word extended figuratively, by the second half of the century, to refer to an individual's face. The inclusion of a frontispiece significantly raised the price of the book, at least until the end of the eighteenth century, and it therefore functioned as what Janine Barchas calls a "caste label" reserved for prestigious publications.[7] William St. Clair notes that the "old canon" of out-of-copyright texts usually appeared with an author portrait in the frontispiece.[8] By the late eighteenth century, then, the portrait frontispiece was an essential element for fashioning an authorial reputation in the burgeoning print marketplace. By placing the head of the author at the head of the book, and conferring prestige on both, portrait frontispieces offered material support to Romantic conceptions of poetry as self-expression. As Roger Chartier puts it, the function of the portrait frontispiece was "to reinforce the notion that the writing is an expression of an individuality that gives authenticity to the work."[9] Critics have argued that frontispiece portraits of Romantic poets in collected editions built "moral authority" and helped to "secure a secular afterlife" for their subjects.[10]

But the connections between the author, the author's picture, and the author's works were never straightforward. The portrait frontispiece ostensibly guaranteed the continuity of the writing subject with the artist's depiction and the texts that followed, but it could also raise the possibility of discontinuities among all three. In Andrew Piper's phrase, "the vogue for authorial portraits as frontispieces disclosed an important tension between person and personality as the frame of writing, between the individual and the simulacrum of individuality that the book promoted."[11] By the eighteenth century, the use of authorial portraits as frontispieces was sufficiently common to be satirized. There was no guarantee that the person in the frontispiece portrait was even the author of the text: as Barchas shows, frontispiece portraits to books by Defoe and Swift—including representations of Lemuel Gulliver as the "author" of *Gulliver's Travels*—"query the authority that they have come to represent in contemporary print culture."[12] Frontispiece portraits allowed the reader to think about how the literal picture of the author in the frontispiece might differ from the imaginative picture of him or her that the reader constructed, and how both might differ from the historical individual who wrote the works.

Frontispieces, then, could follow a Derridean logic of the supplement, undermining the authority they were supposed to reinforce. Ben Jonson's poem "To the Reader," printed opposite the frontispiece in the First Folio, emphasized not the mutually supporting authority of frontispiece and text but the discontinuity between them. He noted that it was impossible for the engraver to "have drawn [Shakespeare's] wit / As well in brass, as he hath hit / His face" (5–7) and so counseled the reader to "look / Not on his picture, but his book" (9–10).[13] The arts of portraiture, engraving, and book design were recruited to help Shakespeare's writing endure, but their contributions were disavowed because they suggested that his works were not self-sustaining. Ostensibly, the frontispiece supplemented the poetry, which was already complete and sufficient in itself; it was "a plenitude enriching another plenitude," in Derrida's words.[14] But the frontispiece was also a reminder of absence or insufficiency—the absence of the dead author, the inability of his works to endure without support. The frontispieces I examine here portrayed Hemans, Byron, and Wordsworth in idealized memorial images. As the last works published in their lifetimes came out of copyright, this helped to assimilate them to the old canon of the previous generation. But it also, inevitably, raised questions about whether their work would continue to find new generations of readers and what kinds of support it would need in order to do so.

The frontispiece to Blackwood's 1865 edition of Felicia Hemans's poems, whose illustrated title page was discussed in the previous chapter, brought these issues sharply into focus. A publisher looking for an image of Hemans to use as a frontispiece engraving had a limited number of options. In his memoir, Henry Chorley claimed that "few celebrated authors have caused so little spoliation of canvas or marble as Mrs Hemans. She never sat for her picture willingly and the play of her features was so quick and changeful as to render the artist's task difficult almost to impossibility."[15] Hemans was depicted only three times in her life—twice by painters and once by a sculptor—a fact that reflects gendered expectations of women's self-effacement, rather than any lack of opportunity for artists to depict her, or any special difficulties in doing so. The earliest image of Hemans was the painting by William West from 1827, owned by her sister Harriet Hughes. The second available image was a miniature by Edward Robertson, painted in Dublin soon after Hemans moved there in 1831. The final option was the bust by Angus Fletcher from 1829.[16] Hemans said the bust was "so very graceful that I cannot but accuse the artist of flattery, the only fault he has given me any reason to find."[17] All three likenesses had been published as engravings by the time Blackwood's published

FIGURE 8. Frontispiece from *Poems
of Felicia Hemans* (Edinburgh:
William Blackwood, 1865).
Private collection.

its 1865 edition. This edition used
the bust as its frontispiece, in a new
engraving by Edward Finden (fig. 8).

Of the three images available to
him, Blackwood picked the one that
did most to classicize, memorialize, and canonize Hemans. The bust
offered the most cultural capital, as
well as the most idealized depiction
of Hemans available, with generic
clothes, no surroundings, and no jewelry. Comparing Fletcher's bust with
West's painting, one of Hemans's children commented, "the bust is poetess
but the picture is *all mother*."[18] This
comment captures how Blackwood's
choice to replace the West portrait
from the 1839 edition with the bust
used in 1865 reflected a shift toward
framing Hemans as a poet of historical significance and lasting achievement. This move eased her away to
some extent from the interpretative framework that emphasized her feminine
virtues and domestic attachments and toward a set of classicizing, memorializing, and idealizing conventions deployed both in sculpture and in book design
to celebrate famous individuals and canonize worthy writers. The Hemans on
the frontispiece deserved all the trappings of poetic success.

Turning from the frontispiece to the engraved title page meant turning to
a rather different vision of Hemans. The reader's eyes moved from the bust's
marmoreal solidity on the verso to Hemans's juvenile drawing of her childhood home on the recto, discussed in the previous chapter. While the frontispiece on the verso showed Hemans as the author of a lifetime's poetic works,
originally published in nineteen volumes and now ranged over hundreds of
pages in this edition, the title-page illustration on the recto reminded readers
of Hemans the precocious teenager, who had drawn this sketch around the
same time she published her first volume of poems, at age fifteen. (Readers
unfamiliar with these facts could have learned them from the chronology
included in this volume.) While the frontispiece bust suggested that Hemans
had taken her place among the English poets after her death, the title-page
sketch suggested that her place was in a remote corner of North Wales, far
from any cultural center. The title-page image called to mind a Hemans who

had yet to achieve the poetic success the frontispiece celebrated, and therefore held out the possibility of encountering her poetry without preconceptions. It was an invitation to imagine oneself into the position of a reader encountering not the well-known and respected Mrs. Hemans of the frontispiece but the unknown Felicia Dorothea Browne.

By putting these two images in apposition, on facing pages of the book's frontmatter, this volume both commemorated Hemans and invited readers to turn away from that commemoration. It reassured its purchasers that Hemans was the kind of esteemed author who sat for her bust, and whose collected works appeared in high-quality volumes with the "caste label" of a frontispiece. But it also encouraged them to turn away from that version of Hemans, turning the tissue guard to reveal an image on the title page that recalled a time when Hemans was young and unknown. On one hand, the frontispiece bust drew attention to the distance between Hemans's lifetime and the publication of this edition, and the judgment of time it represented. On the other hand, the book invited readers to turn back across the generation gap and experience her earliest poetry afresh.

My second example is the edition of Byron's poems edited by William Michael Rossetti in 1870 and illustrated by Ford Madox Brown.[19] This was the first volume in Moxon's Popular Poets, "a cheap series of poets" that Rossetti told Swinburne he had agreed to edit in a "rather cursory way."[20] Volumes in the series typically included eight illustrations plus a portrait frontispiece. The publisher "wishe[d] to get these good," Rossetti noted in his diary, "but not from a man of such position as to demand a heavy price."[21] From 1870 onward, this series published the collected poems of Byron, Longfellow, Wordsworth, Scott, Shelley, Keats, Coleridge, and others, as the copyrights on their poems started to lapse, making this an important publishing vehicle for conveying Romantic poetry to mid-Victorian audiences.

William Michael Rossetti had already written the preface to his edition of Byron when Harriet Beecher Stowe's article accusing Byron of incest appeared in September 1869. He acknowledged in a letter to his brother Dante Gabriel that "[t]he question is a practical one to me, as I must make *some* modification in the notice of Byron I wrote lately."[22] Rossetti could not ignore the accusation, and yet he could not indulge it. He inserted an extra paragraph in his preface, which concluded, "I feel it right to eliminate this gross and ghastly story from the materials of Byron's life: not to reject it, for it may yet prove to be true, but to exclude it as hitherto unverified."[23] Despite his obvious discomfort, Rossetti could neither "eliminate" nor "exclude" the accusation that he had felt compelled to include and incorporate. As his preface rose to its peroration, signs of strain began to show. He insisted that Byron was "emphatically" a genius, and that his poetry was "as imperishable as genius itself," which "knows no vicissitude, and acknowledges no fleeting jurisdiction."[24] This should have been a ringing endorsement, ascribing to Byron a quasi-juridical power to compel readers. But Rossetti's negative formulation reminded his readers of the vicissitudes Byron's reputation was experiencing and the risk that interest in his poetry would after all be fleeting. Moreover, Rossetti found himself caught between the content of his assertion and the venue in which it was made. Great poetry, he claimed, simply endured; but the existence of his annotated, prefaced, and illustrated edition implied that great poems needed careful stewardship. Rossetti's avowal that Byron's poems were inherently meritorious obscured his own efforts to invest them with cultural capital. And not only his own efforts: an important part of the edition's significance lay in the illustrations by Ford Madox Brown and the anonymous frontispiece. These elements combined to form a print artifact that invited readers to acknowledge Byron as a poet of great and lasting achievement, and yet also to set their knowledge of that achievement aside in order to experience his poetry anew.

When a reader opened this edition, he or she faced a frontispiece on the verso, opposite an engraved title page and vignette on the recto, with a tissue guard separating the two (fig. 9).[25] Assuming that the reader's attention moved from left to right, he or she would examine the frontispiece first. It is a medallion portrait of Byron, depicting him in profile facing left, with the word "Byron" in Greek script alongside his head. Byron's hair is arranged in regular, classical curls and his one visible eye is blank, like the unincised eyes of a bust. This image was not by Madox Brown, and it had already appeared as the frontispiece to the first edition of Swinburne's selected edition in 1866 (although it would be omitted from the smaller-format 1885 edition of that book).[26] The medallion showed Byron as a mature man, whose achievements were worthy of commemoration. Its classical depiction and use of Greek letters associated him with Greece and the cause of liberty, recalling his death in the Greek War of Independence. Appearing as if stamped on bronze, he was represented as canonical, solid, and inert, his reputation deserved and enduring. If the reader glanced to the right, the outlines of another image, but not its details, were visible through the tissue guard on the engraved title page that formed the facing recto. At the center of this other image is a circle almost identical in its size and position on the page to the medallion on the frontispiece. When the book is closed, the two circles are pressed together. Turning over the tissue guard veils the medallion portrait and reveals an image that is materially and thematically opposed to it.

The engraved title page is composed of several elements. At the top, the words "Byron's Poetical Works" appear in an exuberantly decorative, contemporary style. At the bottom, the publisher's imprint appears in a plainer engraver's hand. In the center of the page is an image consisting of two distinct

FIGURE 9. Frontispiece and engraved title page from *The Poetical Works of Lord Byron*, ed. William Michael Rossetti, illus. Ford Madox Brown (London: E. Moxon, Son and Co, 1870). Private collection.

parts, one inside the other. The outer part shows a grave on the edge of the sea. The inner part, which is contained within a circular border, shows a youth and a young woman, sitting on the ground under a tree. A horse and rider are visible in the distance behind them to the left. The border of the circle breaks the horizon of the sea in the outer picture, but is itself broken by the gravestone in the foreground and the long grass that grows on the grave. Underneath the whole image is an uncredited (and slightly misquoted) caption from *Don Juan*: "The grass upon my grave will grow as long, / And sigh to midnight wind tho' not to song" (4.99).[27]

The inner image does not illustrate this quotation; it depicts a passage from Byron's poem "The Dream," in which the speaker sees "a maiden and a youth" on a hill. The boy gazes lovingly on the maiden, but she loves another, and gazes into the distance in the hope of seeing him returning on horseback (27–74). This poem was often understood as having been motivated by memories of Byron's early love for Mary Chaworth. Nineteenth-century illustrations of the poem did not always pick up the connection—in the 1849 edition illustrated by Mrs. Lees, for example, the youth appeared in generic Renaissance costume, without any Byronic features—but in this edition the autobiographical association was reinforced.[28] The poem was grouped under the heading "Domestic Pieces," and Rossetti drew attention to the biographical episode in his preface:

> Byron, from the time when he first met Miss Chaworth, fell deeply in love with her, nor was the passion a transitory one: it darkened many an after year with vain longing and yearning protest.[29]

In Brown's image, the youth is recognizably Byron, but a different Byron from the medallion print on the frontispiece. This Byron is young and diminutive; the poem says that the youth "had fewer summers" than the maiden, and here he is significantly smaller than her (46). His ankles and feet are covered by a piece of plaid, which draws attention to his deformed leg even as it conceals it, and refers to his Scottish upbringing. He is unlucky in love, ignored by the maiden. This is a portrait of Byron before he became a great poet or a hero of liberty, before he had achieved anything worth commemorating. The book's frontmatter, then, invites the reader to turn—literally by turning the tissue guard—from a Byron whose fame is lasting and assured to a Byron who has yet to achieve his fame. It invites us to place Byron's legacy symbolically under occlusion, behind tissue, and to experience his poetry as though it were fresh (like the boy in the picture) and modern (like the curlicued lettering).

The turn from an accomplished, canonical Byron on the frontispiece to a fresh-faced, potential Byron in the center of the title page is also played out in the title-page engraving as a whole. The grave in the foreground of the outer picture illustrates in part the caption from *Don Juan*: "the grass upon my grave will grow as long." This grave is indeed neglected; although mourners have laid wreaths on it, it is now overgrown with long grass. But the headstone seems designed to illustrate another poem entirely. With its carving of a helmeted soldier, complete with sword and shield, it recalls the closing lines of what, at that time, was thought to be Byron's final poem, "On This Day I Complete My Thirty-Sixth Year":

> Seek out—less often sought than found—
>   A soldier's grave, for thee the best;
> Then look around, and choose thy ground,
>   And take thy rest. (37–40)

This reference takes the viewer back to the martial, civic, Grecian Byron of the medallion. The poem, however, was not printed in this volume. Although it entered circulation almost immediately after Byron's death, it was not officially published until 1831 and so, according to the terms of the 1842 Copyright Act, remained under copyright to Murray until 1873. Rossetti reported to Swinburne, "the Byron volume *does* contain everything, save some few copyright scraps."[30] In this way, the illustration serves to supply the volume's deficiencies. The title-page image, then, relegates Byron's later life to its margins, and centralizes a youthful, romantic, and idealized version of the poet. Rossetti's preface seconds this focus on a youthful Byron by claiming that he had "a great deal of boyishness in his character from first to last."[31]

The following year, when Rossetti's edition of Wordsworth appeared in the same series with illustrations by Edwin Edwards, the book's frontmatter followed a similar pattern, suitably adapted for the older poet. This book appeared in an earlier state, with illustrations by Henry Dell; in this version a letterpress title page appeared between the frontispiece and the illustrated title page.[32] In its second state, with illustrations by Edwards, the frontmatter was rearranged into the same order as the Byron edition, with the frontispiece on the verso facing the illustrated title on the recto, with a tissue guard separating the two (fig. 10). The frontispiece—which had already been used in the earlier version—shows Wordsworth almost in full profile, facing left, with a high forehead and aquiline nose. His neck is bare, with no visible collar or clothing of any kind. His hair is short and combed forward in a classical style, unlike any depiction of Wordsworth from life. Like the bust of Hemans discussed above, this vignette presents a mature, classicized, and idealized Wordsworth, divested of such historically specific markers as clothes or a hairstyle. In his preface, Rossetti archly described Wordsworth as having "a face in which one could discern intellect if one attended to it, but which one was not much tempted towards attending to. Casual inspection would have set him down as

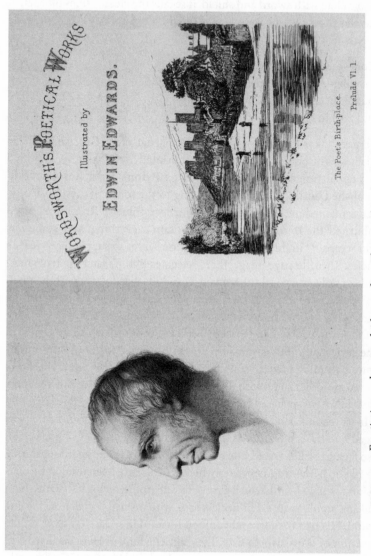

FIGURE 10. Frontispiece and engraved title page from *The Poetical Works of William Wordsworth*, ed. William Michael Rossetti, illus. Edwin Edwards (London: Edward Moxon, Son and Co., 1871). Reproduced by permission of The Wordsworth Trust.

an ordinary prosaic-looking person enough."[33] The frontispiece begs to differ: it gives Wordsworth the appearance of a man of high achievement, depicted in a highly finished style of engraving.[34]

Depicting Wordsworth in middle age, rather than as the aged poet laureate, also contributed to the sense that he was a poet of the past. This was an early endorsement of the view that, by the time he reached his forties or fifties, Wordsworth's best work was already behind him. Rossetti regretted in his preface that "a certain crust of 'Respectability,' perceptible even in the youthful Wordsworth, continued to increase upon him unpleasantly, and to clog and warp the clear and pure contours of his mind."[35] Matthew Arnold would give this view its lasting formulation in 1879 when he claimed that Wordsworth's poetic powers were concentrated into "one single decade [...] between 1798 and 1808, [when] almost all his really first-rate work was produced." Arnold's own edition of Wordsworth sought to clear away "[a] mass of inferior work [...] done before and after this golden prime, imbedding the first-rate work and clogging it, obstructing our approach to it, chilling, not unfrequently, the high-wrought mood with which we leave it."[36] This frontispiece probably doesn't show Wordsworth as early as the end of Arnold's great decade. But it nonetheless anticipates his point by a decade, freezing Wordsworth before the supposedly long decline that "clogged" his oeuvre (the word Arnold and Rossetti both use). The image pushes him back in time, away from his Victorian readers and into the historical distance. Showing him not twenty years previously, at the time of his death, but perhaps fifty years previously, at the time of his greatest poetry, makes Wordsworth appear as a poet of the previous generation.

As with the Byron and Hemans volumes, by turning over the tissue guard that separated the frontispiece from the illustrated title page, readers were invited to veil an image of the mature poet and turn to an image of his early life. For the title page, Edwards supplied a vignette entitled "The Poet's Birthplace," which shows two figures on the banks of the River Derwent, one of whom is fishing. The village of Cockermouth is visible behind the figures, with Cockermouth Castle in the background. This image draws on the celebration of childhood in Wordsworth's poems, and his conviction that he was "Much favoured in my birth-place," because the landscapes among which he grew up endowed and sustained his creative powers.[37] It also promotes the increasing nineteenth-century interest in visiting writers' birthplaces, discussed by Nicola Watson.[38] Like the editions of Byron and Hemans already examined, then, the frontmatter of this volume invites readers to turn away from the later Wordsworth and to experience the earlier Wordsworth afresh.

The caption beneath the image on the title page points not, as one might expect, to the first book of *The Prelude*, where Wordsworth mentions his birthplace, including specific references to Cockermouth Castle ("a shattered

monument / Of feudal sway" [1.284–85]) and the River Derwent ("A tempt-
ing playmate whom we dearly loved" [1.287]), but to *"Prelude* VI.I." This passage speaks fondly of these scenes but is primarily concerned with narrating
Wordsworth's departure from them to return to his studies in Cambridge.
Wordsworth repeatedly says that he didn't regret leaving: he went "gay and
undepressed" (6.7), "Without repining" (10), "not loth" (12), and "in light-
some mood" (18). Like *The Prelude* in general, or "Tintern Abbey" and the
"Intimations" ode in particular, then, this passage is concerned with a process of maturation (not without frequent backward glances) in which the loss
of early, emotionally direct experiences of nature brings with it "abundant
recompense" in the form of growing imaginative power.[39] By returning to
Cambridge, Wordsworth lost his daily commerce with nature for a time, but
gained the chance to lay up stores of inspiration from his wide reading: "many
books / Were skimmed, devoured, or studiously perused, / But with no settled
plan" (6.23–25). As a result, he felt his poetical ambitions stirring and was "first
emboldened [. . .] to trust" that he might "leave / Some monument behind
me which pure hearts / Should reverence" (6.52–57). Taken together, then, the
title-page image and its caption direct the book's readers to Wordsworth's early
life, but also situate the early Wordsworth within a narrative of maturation
toward the fully developed poet depicted in the frontispiece. This narrative of
maturation is mirrored in the organization of the volume's contents, which follows Wordsworth's arrangement of his poems, beginning with "Poems Written
in Youth" and "Poems Referring to the Period of Childhood," progressing
through a number of thematic or biographical categories, and ending with
"Poems Referring to the Period of Old Age," "Epitaphs and Elegaic Pieces,"
and the capstone achievements of *The Prelude* and *The Excursion*.

All three of the posthumous illustrated editions examined here used
illustrations from several artists, some of them recycled from other books,
to negotiate the sense of a generational shift between Romantic writers and
Victorian readers. They included frontispieces that presented their subjects
as mature writers of genuine achievement, who were worthy of commemoration. By depicting their subjects in an idealized, classicized, memorial mode,
these frontispieces situated them as writers of an earlier generation, whose
achievements had already withstood the test of time. The books also included
illustrated title pages that evoked early moments of their subjects' lives or
(supposedly) autobiographical moments in their poetry, while simultaneously
locating these moments in relation to later developments. By foregrounding
these early episodes, the title pages invited readers to experience them afresh,
suggesting that poems by Romantic authors could still live anew for later readers. Moreover, these books arranged their frontmatter to invite readers to turn
from one depiction to the other, veiling the frontispiece with the tissue guard

and turning their attention to the title-page vignette. In doing so, readers symbolically turned back across the generation gap, away from a memorial of the poet and toward a fresh experience of his or her poetry, away from the stasis of the frontispiece and toward the dynamism of the title-page illustrations, away from a dead icon and toward a living presence. The generation gap was not elided in these editions: the format actually insisted on it by presenting two different versions of each poet. Instead, it was bridged: turning the pages of the illustrated book became a way of turning back the clock.

In opposition to the rhetoric of endurance that nineteenth-century critics often applied to Romantic poets, then, illustrated editions embedded an alternative model of cultural transmission in their bibliographic codes. In that model, the transmission of literary texts to later audiences relied on the creation of new material artifacts, rather than the persistence of cultural memory, the durability of poetic language, or the stability of aesthetic categories. Those artifacts were works of bricolage assembling elements produced or controlled by artists, engravers, editors, publishers, and poets. Some of these elements were not designed to be combined, some initially appeared elsewhere, and some went on to appear in other books or in stand-alone versions. But when they came together to make a new illustrated edition of a Romantic poet's work, they offered a way of negotiating the generational shift between Romantic writers and Victorian audiences. The retrofitted illustrated editions of dead poets so popular in the nineteenth century implied that the work of those poets would reach a new audience not so much because its inherent merit allowed it to offer the same satisfactions to successive generations of readers (despite what the prefaces to these editions often said) but rather because it could be embellished in a way that allowed it to offer new satisfactions, including some that were previously unforeseen and unintended.

While these particular works thematized the interplay of memorializing and renovating, that dialectic was already implicit in their form. The examples I discuss, therefore, point to a logic of embellishment that was at work in all newly illustrated editions of Romantic poetry published in the second half of the nineteenth century. Adding illustrations to the work of a dead author, like supplying it with a preface or editorial notes, simultaneously suggested that the poetry still deserved to be read and that it might not in fact be read if it were not for the careful stewardship of publishers, editors, and illustrators. Illustrations performed a work of renovation that supplemented and repackaged the poetry of the previous generation, giving it a bibliographic format consistent with that of new books, which were often published with illustrations from their first editions. At the moment when the Romantic generation seemed about to slip into the twilight of history, the illustrated edition offered new ways to connect it to the current generation of Victorian readers.

PART III

Sermons

7

A Religious Reception Tradition

IN DECEMBER 1821, Lord Byron, who was living in Pisa, received a letter from someone in England whom he had never met. This was not an unusual occurrence for the celebrity poet, but Reverend John Sheppard's letter particularly piqued attention and prompted reflection. Sheppard reported that his wife, who had died in 1814, had left a prayer of intercession for Byron among her papers. When he came across the prayer, Sheppard forwarded it to Byron. Byron wrote a sensitive, courteous reply, in which he reflected:

> Indisputably, the firm believers in the gospel have a great advantage over all others—for this simple reason—that if true—they will have their reward hereafter, and if there be no hereafter—they can be but with the infidel in his eternal sleep—having had the assistance of an exalted hope—through life—without subsequent disappointment—since (at the worst for them) "nothing out of nothing can arise"—not even Sorrow.[1]

Sheppard might have recognized this as a version of Pascal's Wager, the classic argument for the rationality of religious belief that first appeared in his *Pensées* (1670). (Byron discussed Pascal's ideas with James Kennedy in 1823.)[2] But he might also have noticed that Byron did not profess any religious belief of his own in the letter. This passage was cited and reprinted many times in the nineteenth century by religious writers. The fact that the thought within it is usually associated with another writer makes it especially revealing that Byron's expression of the idea was repeated so often, not only by biographers and critics interested in Byron's thought, but by religious writers interested in arguments for belief.

This letter provides a window onto the specifically religious reception tradition I examine in this part of the book. This tradition played an important role in shaping how Victorians understood Romantic writers and their works, but it has tended to receive scant attention in existing reception histories. This is partly because its operating protocols were drastically different from those of Romanticism's modern academic critics. Commentators in the religious reception tradition read differently from us, and for different reasons. They read in different contexts, and wrote (and spoke) in different genres. Their tradition certainly intersected with the more familiar critical, literary, and artistic traditions traced in existing reception histories, and indeed helped to shape the emergence of English literature as an academic discipline. Sometimes the vicars and lay preachers I consider in this part of the book turned away from the genre they were most familiar with—the sermon—and wrote or spoke in genres that we are more familiar with—the lecture, the critical essay, or the textbook. But superficial similarities should not conceal significant differences in aim and approach. In this chapter, I trace the outlines of this tradition, discuss what makes it distinctive, and situate it in context. I argue, perhaps counterintuitively, that secularization is the relevant context in which to understand the religious reception tradition. Religious commentators turned to Romantic writing partly in response to their perception that they inhabited an increasingly secular society.

Byron's letter entered the religious reception tradition almost immediately after his death, when Sheppard published it in his book *Thoughts Chiefly Designed as a Preparative or Persuasive to Private Devotion*.[3] This volume was part of a pervasive Victorian culture of sermons and religious publications. Most Victorians heard a sermon every week, some heard more than one, and many also read sermons. The "religious census" carried out on 30 March 1851 found that 58 percent of those estimated to be able to attend religious services in England and Wales that day had done so, and a similar census in Scotland found that 61 percent of the population attended worship. That means more than nine million people in Britain heard a sermon that day— and contemporaries thought these figures were shockingly low. The number of sermons preached increased throughout the period, as more churches were built and more clergy employed. Hundreds of new Anglican churches were built in every decade of the century, peaking at 1,409 new churches in the 1840s.[4] The number of dissenting congregations also grew. Those churches and chapels needed ministers: the number of Anglican clergy in England and Wales rose by nearly 40 percent between 1851 and 1891. Other denominations grew even faster in some cases, although the overall number of their ministers was smaller.[5] To some extent, these statistics reflect the rising population, but Church membership per capita also increased, although one could be a member without attending regularly.[6] Members came from a variety of social classes, with the working classes well represented.[7] Preaching and listening to sermons, then, was extremely common in Victorian Britain. In the 1880s an estimated two million sermons were preached in Britain each year.[8]

Sermons could be read as well as heard. Religious publishing supported and extended the robust preaching culture. In the first half of the century, roughly one-fifth of all new books published were on religious subjects. The religious publishing sector expanded significantly until the 1880s: more new religious books appeared in the 1870s (7,653) than during the thirty-two years from 1814 to 1846 (7,268), and the number published in the 1880s was even higher (8,640). "Religion" slowly lost market share to "literature," especially after the 1880s, but these figures still represent a large and growing market for religious books.[9] These books encompassed mass-produced bibles and a variety of tracts, including some self-reflexive it-narratives in which bibles and tracts themselves became the protagonists.[10] They also included large numbers of published sermons. Joseph Meisel argues that the printed sermon shifted its audience in this period. From being aimed primarily at other clergymen who found themselves short of time or ideas when writing their own sermons, they were increasingly directed at general religious readers who used them as a supplement to (or a substitute for) the sermons they heard on Sundays.[11] The printed page became an extension of the pulpit, offering some preachers a way to reach a wider audience and earn a higher income. Byron's correspondent John Sheppard certainly saw it this way: he published nineteen books, including travels, hymns, sermons, and devotional works.

This matrix of religious speech and writing interests me because it sustained a distinctive reception tradition for literature. Many of the men (and much smaller numbers of women) who delivered sermons were also enthusiastic readers of literature, with sufficient education and leisure to read widely. Their literary reading provided a resource to enliven their sermons, while literary lectures and essays offered an alternative outlet for their interests. There was, indeed, a whole metadiscourse (to which some of the preachers discussed in the next two chapters contributed) about how to find and select "illustrations" for sermons from literature or everyday life that would make theological points easy to understand through familiar or entertaining comparisons. When they referred to Romantic poems in their sermons, or in their literary essays and lectures, religious commentators elaborated distinctive readings of Romantic literature.[12] But they also recruited the Romantics for the task at hand, which was usually not reading literature but preaching the gospel.

Some writers were easier to recruit than others. Wordsworth, for example, was readily accommodated by the religious reception tradition. Stephen Gill has shown how readers from a variety of denominations hailed Wordsworth as "a source of spiritual power." The strategic vagueness of some of Wordsworth's poetry—the sense it offered of access to "something far more deeply interfused" without specifying what that "something" was—made it a source of "consolation, spiritual counsel, and imaginative succour unattached to doctrine or sect."[13] Wordsworth offered a kind of spiritual uplift that was compatible with Christianity, without demanding assent to any detailed creed, doctrine, or article of faith. "Much of the religion by which Wordsworth lives is very indefinite," Hale White noted, but "it is not therefore the less supporting."[14] For some, this was not enough. The lack of specificity, they worried, opened the door to deism or worse. They sought to clarify Wordsworth's orthodoxy by showing that his oeuvre (and not just his later, more obviously religious poetry) was not only congruent with Christian belief but expressive of it. Charles Kingsley, for example, claimed that Wordsworth was "not only poet, but preacher and prophet of God's new and divine philosophy."[15] Others tried to involve the aging Wordsworth in doctrinal debates by claiming him as a supporter of the Oxford Movement. These different efforts reveal that Wordsworth was readily assimilated to the religious reception tradition, and even more readily because his works didn't consistently occupy any well-defined position within it.

But, as the next two chapters show, the religious reception tradition could also address writers such as Byron and Shelley whose religious beliefs (or lack thereof) were much more problematic for Christian readers than Wordsworth's. Once it had been published in Sheppard's devotional book, Byron's letter quickly began to appear in other religious texts, which mediated it to people who—whether through lack of interest or opportunity or out of moral choice—would not otherwise have encountered Byron's works. Within a few years of its first appearance, the letter had been quoted in numerous sermons and reprinted in several religious tracts. It didn't always appear in discussions of Byron's religious opinions. Rather, it was used to exemplify the argument that religious belief was a good that could be rationally embraced, or to show that even a habitual sinner could be moved by true piety. The exchange of letters was reprinted as an appendix in Thomas Dick's *The Philosophy of a Future State* (1831), where it counterbalanced Dick's use of Byron as an example of immorality in the body of his book.[16] David Bristow Baker quoted the crucial passage in the preface to his *Treatise on the Nature and Causes of Doubt, in Religious Questions* (1831) and reprinted the letters in an appendix, where he exclaims: "[i]nteresting! unhappy Byron! how does this letter, written in some calm reflecting hour, amidst that sensual, degrading life you then were leading, unfold to us, a prospect of better things."[17] The following year, John Morison made a familiar Pascalian argument in his *Portraiture of Modern Scepticism* (1832). "Does it never occur to you, that if Christianity be true, you are undone?" he wrote, "that if it be false, he who believes it can suffer no injury?" And he drove his point home by quoting Byron's letter in a footnote.[18] These authors, among others, established this passage as a familiar citation in sermons and works of popular theology.[19] As early as 1832, a journalist could say that Byron's letter had been "extensively circulated in the religious world."[20]

At the same time, Byron's letter was being quoted in the more familiar "literary" reception tradition. After Sheppard published it, the letter was promptly reprinted in the *English Monthly Repository*. From there, it was picked up by the memoirs, biographies, and critical discussions of Byron that were published in large numbers after his death, from Matthew Iley's *Life, Writings, Opinions and Times of [...] Lord Byron* (1825) to Thomas Moore's *Letters and Journals of Lord Byron with Notices of His Life* (1830–31).[21] The letter continued to appear in biographies of Byron and collections of his writing throughout the nineteenth century. For example, it featured in John Nichol's short life of Byron (1880) and Rowland E. Prothero's edition of his letters (1898–1904).[22] These biographical and critical books form part of the critical heritage of Byron studies, from which modern criticism of the poet descends. This is not to claim that modern critics are directly influenced by these texts but to acknowledge that, as participants in an "intellectual tradition in good working order," they share what Alasdair MacIntyre calls "unarticulated presuppositions which are never themselves the objects of attention and enquiry."[23]

As it circulated in Victorian Britain, then, Byron's letter to John Sheppard began to live a double life. Sometimes it appeared in the company of Christian writers preaching the gospel. At other times it appeared among litterateurs discussing the works of a still somewhat notorious poet. The fact that the letter moved in both circles shouldn't surprise us, because, as William McKelvy has argued, they included many of the same people. The nineteenth-century clergy "was distinguished by its profound involvement with varieties of textual production."[24] The church was the main profession for authors who did not live by the pen, and clergymen had the leisure and education to read literature, the rhetorical training and practice to write about it, and the status and connections to publish what they wrote.[25] Many of those who pioneered English literature as a subject of serious study in its own right were ordained. The position of Oxford Professor of Poetry, for example, was held by an unbroken series of clergymen from its foundation in 1708 until Matthew Arnold became the first layman to occupy the post in 1857. Contrary to claims that literature displaced religion in the nineteenth century, then, McKelvy argues that the "cult" of literature "developed in intimate collusion with religious culture and religious politics."[26]

Proximity, however, is not identity; imbrication did not produce syzygy. Although the religious reception tradition unfolded alongside a more familiar literary tradition, although some of the same people participated in both, and although the traditions touched in many places, they maintained distinct aims and approaches. One index of this separation is the extent to which each tradition became self-referential, so that someone writing in that tradition could refer back to earlier examples from the same tradition, and in time to the tradition's own reference books, rather than referring across traditions. Before long, the crucial passage from Byron's letter to John Sheppard started to appear in large-scale collections of anecdotes intended to enliven sermons. To list only a few examples: it featured in *The Book of Entertaining and Instructive Anecdote, Moral and Religious* (1852), compiled by the Reverend K. Arvine; in a collection of anecdotes for sermons published by the Religious Tract Society; in *Gleanings from the Harvest-Fields of Literature, Science and Art* (1860); in the six-volume reference work *Bible Illustrations*, edited by James Lee (1867); and again in Donald Macleod's *New Cyclopaedia of Illustrative Anecdote, Religious and Moral* (1872).[27] These reference works didn't make arguments of their own but provided a resource for clergy and lay preachers. They made Byron's words available for use as an illustration in sermons. All these books signaled their religious nature in their titles, and many of the preachers who used Byron's letter in their sermons must first have encountered it in this kind of compendium. The religious reception tradition developed its own branches of textual transmission, alongside its own ways of reading the texts transmitted.

From the moment Byron's comments on the "great advantage" of the "firm believers" first appeared in print, then, they were absorbed into two traditions: first, a tradition of biography and criticism; second, a tradition of religious writing. In this case, the second strand of response actually predates the first, with Byron's letter appearing in Sheppard's devotional work before it was reprinted in Iley's biography. The religious tradition continued largely independently of the critical heritage, with later writers referring back to earlier authors within this tradition, and eventually to its specialized reference books, rather than turning to the standard text of the letter provided by Thomas Moore. The aim of this tradition was not primarily hermeneutic; whereas the critical heritage was concerned to understand the poet and his works, the religious tradition was concerned to use Byron's words for its own primarily evangelical or homiletic purposes. Those purposes produced an ambivalent attitude toward Byron's reputation (and, I suggest in the next chapter, toward Shelley's too). In some cases, religious writers wanted to reclaim Byron as a spokesman for Christianity, one who was able to reveal "a prospect of better things."[28] In others, the force of this letter, for the religious, lay in Byron's notoriety. What might otherwise have remained an obscure and rather uncharacteristic passage from one of Byron's letters, read only by those who had got through over a thousand pages of Moore's *Life*, became widely cited and reprinted precisely because it was uncharacteristic, because even such a notoriously sinful man as Byron could eloquently express the reasonableness of religious belief. English vicars looking through books of anecdotes while preparing their sermons must have thought that if even Byron could acknowledge the claims of Christianity, surely their parishioners could too.

The religious reception tradition should be situated in relation to the process of secularization that many historians have identified in this period, and not simply set against it. Secularization is a complex process and there is little consensus about what it entailed, when it happened, how long it took, and whether it is complete and irreversible. Most historians of secularization can agree, at least, on what secularization is not. It should not simply be understood negatively as the widespread loss or rejection of religious belief and neglect of religious practice. Rather, following Charles Taylor, we should think of secularization as a long, slow, multifaceted change from a society in which belief in God is the default position, to one in which, even for the most devout, belief in God is recognized as only one possibility among others.[29] It is not that religious belief becomes impossible in a secular age, but that even a devout believer must understand faith as a distinct construal of experience and acknowledge that other reasonable people, faced with similar circumstances, construe their experience without reference to the divine. This process is, Taylor insists, not simply a "subtraction story," in which religious worldviews are sloughed off to leave a disillusioned account of experience. Rather, it requires the construction of new self-understandings in which human flourishing becomes the highest conceivable goal. Taylor's story is a long one, tracing the origins of secularization in attempts to reform the Church from within beginning in the medieval period. But the nineteenth century is when, on his account, "unbelief comes of age."[30]

Secularization in nineteenth-century Britain was, first, a political process in which the state slowly relinquished its jurisdiction over the religious beliefs of its citizens. The modern secular state typically avoids endorsing any view on spiritual matters, even when its politicians are motivated by their personal religious convictions. At the start of the nineteenth century in England, this was not the case. Those who were unwilling to subscribe to the Church of England's articles of faith faced significant obstacles to education, civic participation, and professional advancement. They could not graduate from or hold teaching positions at Oxford or Cambridge, sit in Parliament, or hold public office. By the end of the century, these obstacles had been removed with the repeal of the Test and Corporation Acts (1828), Catholic Emancipation (1829), the decision to make English state schools nondenominational, and related measures. Without going so far as to disestablish the Church of England and remove its bishops from the House of Lords, successive governments had so limited its power over public life that full disestablishment was a step that few still thought was worth taking. In Scotland, a different but comparable process took place. Secularization in this sense describes how the state realigned its relationship toward religious belief and withdrew from doctrinal disagreements. Religious belief became privatized; it was increasingly seen as a personal affair.

This mode of secularization was compatible with the loss of individual religious belief, although it did not cause it. A number of Victorian people (particularly men) who have been central to our understanding of the period lost or abandoned their religious faith. John Stuart Mill claimed that "[t]he world would be astonished if it knew" how many of the most distinguished Victorians were "complete sceptics in religion."[31] Some, like Matthew Arnold, lamented the "melancholy, long, withdrawing roar" of the "sea of faith";[32] where religious belief had previously offered individual consolation and social cohesion, Arnold sought alternatives in personal relationships or in high culture. Some, like Arthur Hugh Clough, found themselves in two minds and articulated their religious doubts and sense of loss alongside a bracing sense of having shaken off the dead hand of religious propriety. Some, like James Thomson, became fierce atheists, or, like Thomas Henry Huxley, elaborated agnosticism and defended scientific progress against religious orthodoxy. And some, like Mill, could say that they had "not thrown off religious belief, but never had it."[33] In certain literary, scientific, and intellectual circles, then, the secularization of the public sphere went hand in hand with the loss or absence of personal faith.

But elsewhere in Victorian Britain, religious belief persisted or intensified. If the political mode of secularization was compatible with loss of faith, it was also compatible with religious revival. Taylor describes the way religious belief moves from being a dependable part of the background of life to being a contested part of the foreground during the process of secularization in the late eighteenth and nineteenth century. The robust program of church building and growth of the clergy described above testifies to this process; it was accompanied by successive waves of evangelism throughout the century, from the revival associated with Hannah More, William Wilberforce, and the "Clapham Sect" at the beginning of the century, to the missions of Moody and Sankey toward the end. The Salvation Army, founded in 1865, had thirty-six preachers in 1876, the first year for which records exist. By 1897, its preachers numbered over four thousand.[34] It offered a combination of music, street preaching, and social work in a quasi-militaristic campaign against irreligion and social problems. These movements emphasized an experience of salvation through a personal relationship with Christ, and they won many converts. As Boyd Hilton argues, evangelicalism was well adapted to industrial commercial society, and drew on its economic and contractual vocabulary.[35] In one sense, evangelicals testified to the progress of secularization. They felt the need to evangelize precisely because they thought irreligion was so pervasive, especially in the great industrial cities.[36] But the many converts they made, who became religious or who felt their existing religious convictions strengthened and transformed, undermine any naïve account of secularization as the widespread loss of belief.

Even where Christianity gained ground, however, religious belief now existed alongside the awareness that it had become one option among others. While Christianity continued to be a shaping force in the lives of its many adherents and new converts, it no longer seemed so powerfully normative in society. In an earlier period, it had been possible to inhabit belief unreflectively, to swim one's whole life in the sea of faith without ever sighting shore. Now, belief was necessarily shadowed by a sense that it was a conscious choice, and that others living in the same society had chosen differently. Religious belief had been relativized. This happened between Christian denominations once Anglican doctrine was no longer enshrined in legal tests and so lost some of its normative force. And it happened to faith itself once avowed unbelief became a viable option that, on one hand, no longer incurred severe social and professional sanctions and, on the other hand, offered an intellectually satisfying account of human flourishing. This relativization was reflected in landmark comparative studies published at the end of the century. James Frazer's *The Golden Bough* (1890) placed religion into anthropological perspective and controversially suggested that Christianity could be discussed dispassionately as one religion among others, rather than as the revelation against which all other religions should be judged. William James's *Varieties of Religious Experience* (delivered as Gifford Lectures at the University of Edinburgh in 1901-2) treated religion as a topic for psychology or philosophy, and paid little attention to the theological content or legitimacy of religious experience.

Once religious belief was relativized in this way, the professing Christian became visible as a distinctive kind of person. He or she emerged from the undifferentiated mass as someone who inhabited a particular kind of identity as a result of personal choices and beliefs and was affiliated with a distinctive, if diverse, social group. Where in earlier periods people distinguished themselves by their piety or their heterodoxy, in the nineteenth century in the West the Christian *as a Christian* can be distinguished for the first time from the crowd, because the crowd can no longer be assumed to be Christian. Being a member of a congregation was the Christian's first distinctive feature. The notion of church adherence or membership was itself a modern idea.[37] In an earlier period, everyone in the parish was assumed to be under the authority of the parish church, which played an important local role in civic administration. But by the mid-nineteenth century, with different churches effectively competing for members from the same area, the congregation became more like a club of likeminded individuals, and joining it signaled a distinctive identity. The distinctiveness of this identity was continually reiterated by evangelicalism, which drew a sharp line between the "saved" and the "unsaved." Within the church new evidences of piety were required, such as abstaining from drink, while the rise of street preaching made Christianity newly visible in public space. Only once Christianity had ceased to be quasi-compulsory did it become legible as a category of identity.

In this context, a distinctively Christian reception tradition for literature could take shape. It operated in ways that were self-consciously religious and different from other, nonreligious reception traditions unfolding in parallel. The people who produced it spoke or wrote as Christians and for Christians (or those they hoped to convert), and they knew that this set their discourse apart from other kinds of speech or writing. Within this tradition, it makes sense to talk about a religious reading of (say) Wordsworth. Such a reading was motivated by the convictions of the commentator: convictions that he or she knew were not universally shared. It sought religious elements in Wordsworth's poetry or employed it for religious purposes, to illustrate a sermon, support a theological argument, or provide material for *lectio divina*. This reading came to different conclusions about the nature and value of Wordsworth's poetry from readings in other traditions, because it proceeded according to different aims and in a self-consciously different context. Religious commentators sometimes fudged the question of whether they discovered Christian ideas in literary texts or imported them from their own beliefs. As Deidre Lynch notes, "a description of the emotional, imaginative process that a poem's diction, imagery, and rhythm triggered within a particular readerly psyche (the critic's own) might also, in this period, count as a valid description of the poem."[38] But a poet did not have to be religious, or even be claimed as such, for his or her works to be assimilated to the religious reception tradition. As the next two chapters show, poets could be treated as religious in spite of their statements to the contrary, or their impiety could be mobilized as a warning to others.

In this religious reception tradition, Romantic writing is not a neutral topic of discussion. Romanticism, as readers from the nineteenth century onward have asserted, is implicated in secularization. T. E. Hulme in 1910 famously called it "spilt religion." M. H. Abrams conceived Romanticism as transposing traditionally theological concepts into secular versions. More recently, Mark Canuel has explored its engagements with religious toleration, as Romantic-period writers laid the groundwork for a more liberal approach to religious belief, and Daniel White has traced the connections between Romanticism and religious dissent.[39] On these accounts and others, Romanticism is entangled with the process of secularization. When they discussed Romantic literature, then, commentators in the religious reception tradition were also, at some level, necessarily engaging with secularization more generally. This engagement had both defensive and assertive forms. In its defensive form (examples of which I examine in chapter 9), preachers suggested that Romantics had turned aside from the path of salvation, and urged their hearers and readers to view them as a cautionary tale. In its assertive form (examples of which I examine in chapter 8), they claimed that Romantic writers were not really secular at all, but that they gave voice to Christian ideas, even if they didn't do this in obvious ways. The general process of secularization, to which the Romantics contributed, then, unfolds alongside their sacralization within a specific reception tradition, not as an alternative to Christianity but as another expression of it.

The next two chapters examine the reception of Shelley and Byron in this tradition by drawing on the sermons, lectures, and writings of several clergy and lay preachers. They represent a variety of denominations, but the individuals discussed in the chapter on Shelley cluster toward the liberal end of the theological spectrum, while C. H. Spurgeon, discussed in the chapter on Byron, comes from the conservative, evangelical end. Each chapter explores both the reading of Shelley or Byron that emerges from these preachers' comments and the homiletic or rhetorical reasons for turning to Shelley or Byron at a particular moment in their discourses. In chapter 9, I also focus on the process of mediation that conveyed Byron's writings to Spurgeon, drawing on the evidence of Spurgeon's library, which has survived almost intact. As a whole, this part of the book aims to reveal the religious reception tradition as one important strand in the web of reception that remade Romantic writing for Victorian audiences. Like the statues considered in part 4, this is a reception tradition that reaches nonreaders. The preachers considered here mediated Romantic writers in fallible, fragmentary ways to congregations of listeners who might not have encountered their poetry elsewhere. By tracing this process, these chapters show how Romantic writers and their words are remade through contact with discourses, practices, and contexts that they might not have imagined their poems circulating in, and that modern literary critics have largely overlooked.

8

Converting Shelley

WHEN NEWS of Percy Shelley's death reached England in 1822, *The Courier* wrote, "Shelley, the writer of some infidel poetry, has been drowned; *now* he knows whether there is a God or no."[1] Sixty-four years later, in 1886, Stopford Brooke rose to address the first meeting of the Shelley Society. He painted a very different picture of Shelley for his assembled listeners, who included several clergymen like himself. "[T]he world will always be grateful for the religious gravity in [Shelley's] teaching," he claimed, because "the method Shelley laid down for attaining the perfect state is that of Jesus Christ; and is stated by him with strong reiteration."[2] In a generation, Shelley had gone from being an infamous unbeliever, whose "reputation was that of an atheist and rebel who behaved abominably and wrote poetry," to being a Christian teacher, and even a prophet.[3] "I think we have never yet fully realized what religious truth, as we conceive it, owes to Shelley," Brooke said in a later lecture.[4] Brooke's view of Shelley was not eccentric; though he stated it with particular clarity and force, it was widely reiterated by other commentators. The *Courier*'s critic would have found it a willful, perverse misreading. Shelley's modern critics, working in broadly secular academic contexts, would mostly agree. Shelley's atheism no longer embarrasses his readers, and we feel no need to rescue his poetry from his own unbelief. But throughout the nineteenth century, a number of clergy and laypeople conducted an informal campaign not only to make Shelley's poetry acceptable to Christian readers but also to encourage them to see religious truths revealed in it. This chapter traces that tradition of Shelley's reception through four individuals: Clara Lucas Balfour, George Gilfillan, Richard Armstrong, and Stopford Brooke. It shows how these commentators sought first to excuse or minimize Shelley's atheism, then to deny it altogether and reimagine his poetry as fundamentally Christian and himself as a kind of prophet, and so to recruit him as a tool for evangelism and an ally in theological and doctrinal controversies.

The tradition I'm tracing here did not operate in isolation and its attempts to rehabilitate Shelley for Christian readers drew support from other sources.

Leigh Hunt was by no means orthodox in his religious beliefs, but as early as 1822 he claimed that "at the time of the foundation of Christianity, Percy Shelley would have been among the most devoted and disinterested followers of the benevolent Jesus."[5] Thomas Wade —"an advanced liberal in politics and religion"—published a sonnet to Shelley in 1835 that hailed him as "Holy and mighty Poet of the Spirit" who "by a reasoning instinct all divine, [...] feel'st the Soul of things."[6] The "lark's music" of Shelley's poetry, Wade wrote, "Laps us in God's own heart." The accusation of atheism, he concluded, was a slur on Shelley. "Men profane, / Blaspheme thee: I have heard thee *Dreamer* styled—/ I've mused upon their wakefulness—and smiled."[7] By a neat reversal, Wade repositioned Shelley the blasphemer as the one blasphemed. Hunt and Wade, among others, claimed that Christians should not anathematize Shelley but should admire his moral vision. This reading of Shelley, emerging in the 1820s and 1830s, informed the religious reception tradition I'm tracing here, which pushed its claims for Shelley's Christianity much further.

Four people did much to shape Shelley's reputation in religious circles and beyond. Clara Lucas Balfour (1808–1878) had a life story that could easily have featured in one of the evangelical temperance tracts she distributed. She grew up in poverty after her father died when she was nine. (He may have married her mother bigamously.) She married James Balfour when she was not yet sixteen. The following thirteen years were difficult, as the couple lived in London with no reliable income and Clara gave birth to several children, some of whom died in infancy, while James descended further into alcoholism. But in 1837, when Clara was twenty-nine, the Balfours' lives were changed by a temperance lecture. Both signed a temperance pledge, which marked a turning point in their fortunes. Clara Balfour became a Baptist in 1840 and was rebaptized (having been christened in the Church of England). She began to lecture and write in the temperance cause, but also in support of women's advancement and on literary topics. She spoke to large audiences at mechanics' institutes and in churches and community halls across England.[8]

George Gilfillan (1813–1878) studied at the universities of Glasgow and Edinburgh (where John Wilson taught him moral philosophy) and, having been ordained, served as a Presbyterian minister in Dundee for the rest of his life. His elaborate, dramatic style of preaching brought him a wide following, which he extended with published sermons and literary essays in Scottish newspapers, as well as popular devotional books such as *The Bards of the Bible* (1850). Once established in Dundee, Gilfillan maintained an unremitting schedule of preaching and writing; he gave public lectures, wrote dozens of book reviews, and produced biographies of Scott (1870) and Burns (1878) all while carrying out his parish duties. His poetic aspirations were dashed after William Aytoun's satire *Firmilian* (1854) depicted him at the head of the "spasmodic school" and mocked his extravagant style. Among those who came to Gilfillan's defense was the famously terrible poet William McGonagall, a fellow resident of Dundee whose support Gilfillan could probably have done without. McGonagall wrote an "Address" to Gilfillan, which included lines such as "He has also written about the Bards of the Bible, / Which occupied nearly three years in which he was not idle."[9] Gilfillan's biographers estimated that, through a lifetime of preaching and writing, he had "helped to create modern religious thought throughout the English-speaking world."[10]

Richard Armstrong (1843–1905) was born in Bristol, trained in London, and ministered to Unitarian congregations in Ireland, Nottingham, and then at Hope Street Church in Liverpool from 1883 until the end of his life. His father, who died when he was fourteen, was also an ordained minister, who seceded from the Established Church of Ireland and joined the Unitarians in Bristol. Armstrong continued his father's trajectory toward liberal theology and politics, embracing what one contemporary called "Gladstonian Radicalism" and his son called "iconoclastic rationalism."[11] He helped to found a quarterly magazine, *The Modern Review*, dedicated to liberal, Unitarian theology and "scientific" biblical criticism.[12] He published works of popular theology and, like Balfour, was involved in temperance campaigns. Like Gilfillan, Armstrong supplemented his preaching with lectures on literary topics, which he subsequently published. One of his college friends claimed that Armstrong's interest in poetry awakened his talents for writing and oratory. While he was still a student, a clergyman in Stratford asked Armstrong to deliver a paper on poetry to members of his congregation on a weekday evening, and then to come back and preach one Sunday. "In writing these two things," his friend remembered, "Armstrong found, for the first time, a positive delight in the expression of thought."[13]

Stopford Brooke (1832–1916) was born in Ireland, trained at Trinity College, Dublin, and ordained as an Anglican in London. He served as a curate in parishes in Marylebone and Kensington before traveling to Germany as the chaplain to the British embassy in Berlin. Having come to wide notice with his biography of the churchman F. W. Robertson, he became a chaplain to Queen Victoria in 1867 and preached several sermons in Westminster Abbey. He took the lease on a proprietary chapel in St. James, and then at Bedford Chapel in Bloomsbury from 1876, where he positioned himself on the Broad Church wing of Anglicanism. Brooke would break from the Anglican Church in 1880, but he continued to preach at Bedford Chapel. He never formally affiliated himself with Unitarianism, but like the Unitarians, he rejected the doctrine of the Incarnation, and he preached in Unitarian churches on several preaching tours. He pioneered lectures on secular topics in churches and published widely on literary subjects, as well as giving guest lectures on literature at Queen's College (the independent girls' school founded in 1848 by F. D. Maurice). In addition to helping found the Shelley Society, he was a key figure in the campaign to buy Dove Cottage for the Nation and published editions or studies of Shakespeare, Milton, Wordsworth, Shelley, Tennyson, and Browning. A. C. Bradley, the great Shakespeare scholar, was among the signatories of the Congratulatory Address sent to Brooke on his eightieth birthday.[14]

All these people were part of an active Victorian culture of lecturing on moral, literary, and religious topics. In the 1870s and 1880s, a number of clergymen, especially those with more liberal theological views, began giving lectures in their churches on Saturday or Sunday afternoons. Rather than preaching on a text from the Bible, they took questions of general interest as their subjects, and often spoke on literary topics. Brooke pioneered this approach in 1872 with a series of lectures on Cowper, Wordsworth, Coleridge, and Burns, writing that "I had long desired to bring the pulpit on Sunday to bear on subjects other than those commonly called religious."[15] This was a potentially heretical idea among those who thought preaching should focus on biblical exegesis, and Brooke was reportedly almost summoned to explain himself to his bishop.[16] But the lectures were so well received that he repeated the experiment the following year, lecturing on Blake, Shelley, Keats, and Byron. Richard Armstrong followed Brooke's lead with a series of lectures on poetry delivered to his congregation in Liverpool on Sunday evenings, treating Shelley, Wordsworth, Clough, Tennyson, Arnold, and Browning. The lectures aimed to reach people who might not sit through a sermon and to provide a wholesome alternative to other ways of spending Sabbath afternoons and evenings. They were therefore in sympathy with the temperance movement, whose lectures offered an alternative to the alehouse. Clara Lucas Balfour was one of its leading lecturers, regularly speaking on literary topics as well as on the evils of drink.

This was a primarily oral culture, committed to the pulpit and the platform, and many of the sermons and lectures that touched on literary topics must have left no historical trace. But the lecturers also embraced print. The published versions of their lectures reached a much wider audience, as well as supplementing their income (Brooke's first book of literary lectures went through ten editions). At some moments, this tradition intersected with theological controversies. Brooke and Armstrong were both invited to give the annual Essex Hall lecture established by the British and Foreign Unitarian Association in 1892 to "assist in advancing the cause of a truer and more helpful religious faith among men than that which still finds expression in creeds and churches commonly called 'orthodox.'"[17] At other moments, such as when Brooke addressed the Shelley Society, it intersected with the early history of English literature as an academic discipline.[18] Brooke and Balfour both produced primers of English literature, which were used by schoolchildren in their classes, by would-be civil servants cramming for entrance exams, and by many others seeking to divert and improve themselves.

A favorite genre for all these writers was the "sketch" or "portrait": a potted critical biography that drew moral lessons from its subject's life. These sketches could be published either as separate tracts or as part of a compilation. Balfour published a number of collections of exemplary lives before writing *Sketches of English Literature from the Fourteenth to the Present Century* in 1852. Gilfillan published three "galleries" of literary portraits in the 1840s and '50s. Armstrong used sketches of contemporary and recent writers as a form that reached those who might not hear or read a sermon. His *Latter-Day Teachers* (1881) included John Stuart Mill and Matthew Arnold, and was followed by *Faith and Doubt in the Century's Poets* (1898) and *Makers of the Nineteenth Century* (1901). Brooke's lecture series were similarly made up of biocritical accounts of individual poets. Including a sketch or portrait of Shelley in this kind of series helped to assimilate Shelley to the literary canon by presenting him alongside less controversial figures.

But Shelley also threatened to break out of the sketch's limits and skew the proportions of the canon of which it was a part. In the writings of these authors, Shelley doesn't seem to know his place. He looms large in Balfour's slim volume *Sketches of English Literature*, taking up fifteen pages, which is not only more than Balfour allocated to Wordsworth (nine pages), Byron (five), or Keats (four), but also more than she gave Shakespeare (ten), Spenser (nine), or Pope (eight). Only Milton got more space, with twenty-two pages. Gilfillan similarly gave Shelley an important place in his writings. Having written one of his first newspaper articles about Shelley, he reprinted and extended it in his first *Gallery* (1845), then added an essay on *Prometheus Unbound* in the *Third Gallery* (1854), making Shelley the only writer discussed in two "galleries." Brooke often drew on Shelley for illustrations in his sermons.[19] His bestselling primer of English literature compressed seven hundred years of literary history into just 150 pages. He nevertheless found room for four pages on Shelley, which one of his correspondents complained was too much.[20]

These individuals shed light on Shelley's reception among the religious in Victorian Britain from several angles. They come from different parts of the country: Brooke and Balfour from London, Armstrong from Liverpool, and Gilfillan from Dundee. They represent different denominations, from Baptist to Presbyterian to Broad Church Anglican to Unitarian. Their lectures, sermons, and publications span the second half of the century. They thus open different windows onto a reception tradition that was committed—sometimes uneasily—to both religion and poetry. This tradition had its internal disagreements and was home to diverse views about literature and doctrine. But it also shared a set of arguments about Shelley and, I suggest, a set of doctrinal debates to which Shelley was provocatively recruited.

Shelley's atheism was, of course, an embarrassment for the religious, and they deployed several rhetorical strategies to explain it away or intimate that it needn't get in the way of appreciating his poetry. They suggested that Shelley's atheism was a product of specific biographical circumstances: an understandable, if regrettable response to his environment. Bad treatment in early life was to blame. "Persecution from his childhood had seared his mental vision," Balfour claimed, and Gilfillan concurred that "Shelley was far too harshly treated in his speculative boyhood."[21] "Religion was a word ever on the lips of his oppressors—a word rendered odious to him by their conduct," Balfour asserted. It was Shelley's misfortune, she suggested, to have fallen among censorious people against whose proscriptive version of Christianity he was bound to rebel. "He seems never to have seen Christianity really embodied in the life of its professors."[22] This argument presented atheistic views as the product of contingency, adversity, or just bad luck, rather than a reasoned intellectual commitment reached by rational deliberation.

Things could so easily have turned out differently in other conditions. If only Shelley had been blessed with kinder parents and better teachers in his youth, or more lenient tutors at Oxford, he might have held different views in his maturity. Balfour felt that "Love he never could have resisted—persecution made him unyielding."[23] Gilfillan wrote (in a good sample of his overcharged prose) that "had pity and kind-hearted expostulation been tried, instead of reproach and abrupt expulsion, they might have weaned him, ere long, from the dry dugs of atheism, to the milky breast of the faith."[24] Coleridge later claimed that he could have been the good influence that Shelley lacked if the two had met when Shelley was in Keswick in the winter of 1811. "His Atheism would not have scared *me*," Coleridge said, "for *me* it would have been a semi-transparent Larva, soon to be *sloughed*, and, through which, I should have seen the true *Image*; the final metamorphosis."[25] Oppression and mistreatment led Shelley astray, but "truly pious" observers could forgive Shelley's atheism, because (Balfour wrote) "[t]hey always saw that persecution had caused and confirmed all they mourned over as Shelley's speculative errors."[26] These rhetorical moves laid the blame for atheism not with Shelley himself so much as with those who "persecuted" him (the word Balfour and Gilfillan both used) in his youth.

Having identified the causes of Shelley's atheism in his early life, religious commentators tended to dwell on his youth. Armstrong called him "the Eton boy" and "this frenzied youth"; Balfour began her sketch with a reference to his "brief life passed in storms and sorrows"; Gilfillan claimed that Shelley and Keats were both "essentially young poets."[27] Shelley's youth seemed to excuse his religious views, which were presented as immature. "The fact, too, that he was but twenty-nine when his troubled career closed," Balfour concluded, "will ever plead with the thoughtful and the good in extenuation of his opinions."[28] Gilfillan reminded his readers that "we must ever, in merest justice, remember his age. He died ere he had completed his twenty-ninth year!"[29] All of Shelley's poetry was therefore in some sense juvenilia. *Prometheus Unbound*, Gilfillan said, was "written twenty years too soon, ere his views had consolidated, and ere his thought and language were cast in their final mould."[30] At some moments, Shelley's youth seemed not just a biographical fact but an existential one. "There is [. . .] one spirit in Shelley's work which fills and brings into unity all his poems," Brooke wrote. "It is the spirit of youth."[31] Gilfillan saw in Shelley's physiognomy a "spiritual expression: wrinkle there seems none on his brow; it is as if perpetual youth had there dropped its freshness."[32] If Shelley was not just young but essentially, fundamentally immature, then his atheism could be made to seem like a juvenile phase he never got the chance to grow out of.

His religious readers, in contrast, sometimes depicted themselves maturing beyond their youthful enthusiasm for Shelley. In the "Advertisement" for his first *Gallery of Literary Portraits*, which included his first essay on Shelley, Gilfillan described himself as having "garnered up the results of his young love and wonder" in the book. With its publication, "one mental period of his history [was] closing" as he reached maturity and prepared himself for "some other more manlike, more solid, and strenuous achievement."[33] His autobiographical narrative *The History of a Man* (1856) reiterated the impression that he had left Shelley's poetry behind as he grew up. In a reported conversation, Gilfillan's autobiographical narrator "struck in, and ventured to say a word in behalf of my favourite [Shelley]; for he was so then much more than now." Gilfillan acknowledged "what some of the critics called my 'criminal lenity'" toward skeptical writers in his first essays, and claimed that "were I speaking of some of these authors now, I would use language of a very different kind."[34] While Shelley did not live long enough to outgrow his youthful atheism, his Victorian readers sometimes claimed to have outgrown their juvenile enthusiasm for his skeptical poetry.

They also liked to imagine that, had he lived longer, Shelley himself would have outgrown his atheism and embraced Christianity. Indeed, they thought he was already showing signs of improvement toward the end of his short life. Balfour claimed it was "certain that he saw reason to regret" *Queen Mab*, as "maturing judgment modified his opinions."[35] Armstrong felt that Shelley "mellowed and matured" away from the extremity of his early opinions.³⁶ And Gilfillan offered a confident prognosis:

> Ultimately, indeed, he admitted more fully than at first, the existence of a great, pervading though not creative mind, co-eternal with the universe. His tone, too, in reference to Christ, underwent a change. He continued to read the scripture with delight till the last; and there are many grounds for believing that he was emerging from the awful shade of unbelief, when there came down upon him, so suddenly, the deeper darkness of death.³⁷

Comments like this one take their cue from Shelley's sustained engagement with the Bible as a form of wisdom literature, his strategic deployment of scriptural allusion, and the nontheistic spirituality expressed in poems such as "Mont Blanc." Others might see in Shelley's use of the Bible an effort to salvage a secular morality from the ruins of religious belief, and in his nontheistic understanding of the supernatural an attempt to elaborate an alternative spirituality untainted by monarchy. Instead, Shelley's religious commentators read these aspects of his writing as the seeds of Christian belief, which, by God's grace, might have grown in time. Gilfillan thought that Shelley was just one step away from Christianity. "Why did he not just reverse his own first principle, which would have brought him to the first principle—the life and essence of the Christian faith?" Gilfillan asked. "He said, 'Love is God.' Why did he not change it into 'God is Love?'"³⁸ Across the Atlantic, others concurred. Had Shelley lived, Margaret Fuller Ossoli claimed, "he would have become a fervent Christian." Nathaniel Hawthorne playfully imagined a middle-aged Shelley taking holy orders.³⁹

Excusing Shelley's atheism as a youthful error produced by biographical circumstances, and indulging in speculations about how he might have cast it off had he lived, went some way to repairing his reputation. But it still did little to render his poetry acceptable. To do this, his Christian critics claimed that his best poetry was untouched by his religious views. Gilfillan drew a line between the two in his portrait, writing, "[w]e gladly turn from his creed to his poetical character," as though the former had no effect on the latter.⁴⁰ This idea gained support in 1840 when some of Shelley's essays and letters first appeared in print. In that volume, readers found Shelley borrowing Christian phraseology in "A Defence of Poetry" to state his view that the personal conduct of a poet was irrelevant to an appreciation of his poetry. It mattered little if "Homer was a drunkard," he said, because his sins "have been washed in the blood of the mediator and redeemer, time." The same volume published for the first time the 1821 letter in which he asserted that "[t]he Poet & the man are two different natures."⁴¹ The religious views held by Shelley the man, then, did not have to hinder an appreciation of Shelley the poet.

Beyond suggesting that Shelley's poetry was not really concerned with religious ideas, these commentators implied that Shelley was not a poet of ideas at all. Brooke wrote in his primer that for Shelley, "imagination is supreme and the intellect its servant."[42] Shelley was accordingly praised as a poet of sound, who wrote "gorgeous tulip-like language" (Gilfillan), with "voluptuous melody" (Balfour) that had "the quality of great music" (Brooke).[43] If Shelley's true value as a poet lay in the melody of his verse, rather than its sense, then Christian readers could learn to appreciate that melody without fear of the poet's irreligious ideas. These critics therefore limited Shelley's achievement to lyricism and descriptive verse, and praised him for his technical accomplishment in these areas. Brooke asserted in his primer that Shelley was "on his own ground" as a lyric poet, and that his lyrics were "the most sensitive, the most imaginative, and the most musical, but the least tangible lyrical poetry we possess."[44] He later wrote an essay on Shelley's lyrics, which claimed that lyrics, and the lyrical passages in his longer poems, were his most successful works.[45] Gilfillan found the "waste darkness of the metaphysics" in *Queen Mab* to be "sprinkled [with] some clear and picturesque descriptions."[46] In these lyrical or descriptive passages, Shelley showed his virtuosic artistry unencumbered by his religious opinions. "His command of language is not merely great, but tyrannous," Gilfillan wrote, "[o]f versification too, he is a perfect master."[47] The combination of frequent obscurity and technical excellence made Shelley "the poet of poets," in Balfour's words, since "only the highly imaginative could follow him."[48] Brooke wrote of *Epipsychidion*, "[n]o critic can ever comprehend it; it is the artists' poem."[49] By praising Shelley primarily or exclusively in formalist terms, for his sound, versification, and technique, these commentators could turn a blind eye to his atheist ideas.

These rhetorical tactics were primarily negative. They sought to excuse Shelley's atheism, minimize its importance to his poetry, and praise those aspects of his writing that seemed untouched by it. In these respects, they were similar in structure, though not necessarily in content, to some more familiar aspects of Shelley's reception history that reduced him to an "ineffectual angel." Depicting Shelley's poetry as technically accomplished and musically gorgeous, but intellectually vague and nebulous, allowed commentators to overlook a variety of sins. Some wanted to cut the tumor of political radicalism out of the body of his work. Others wanted to cauterize his spiritual errors and prevent their contaminating his oeuvre as a whole. But the same rhetorical solution worked for both problems. Whether they objected to Shelley's political radicalism, his religious freethinking, or some other aspect of his thought, this formalist turn served the same purpose of bracketing content and focusing on style. As a rhetorical tactic, therefore, it functioned just as well to marginalize Shelley's political or his religious opinions, because it detached his poetry from any intellectual content whatsoever.

But Shelley's Christian commentators went far beyond this negative argument. They produced an account of Shelley's poetry that made it appear positively edifying for religious readers. Brooke and Gilfillan especially sought to rehabilitate Shelley as a poet that Christians could not only tolerate or refrain from condemning but actively endorse and value. They found hidden Christian dimensions in Shelley's poems and exhorted their listeners and readers to give his writing serious attention for the moral and spiritual lessons it contained. To do this effectively, they had to overcome a number of obstacles. Shelley explicitly stated his atheist views on many occasions, and the biographical and critical tradition had given those views a central place in accounts of his life and thought. Beyond the attempts to excuse and marginalize Shelley's atheism outlined above, then, a more complex and thoroughgoing rhetorical strategy emerged. It sought to reimagine Shelley as a Christian poet and prophet, and to recruit him for theological and doctrinal debates that passionately concerned his religious interpreters.

The first step was to go beyond claims that Shelley's best poetry was free from religious ideas (or any ideas) and to claim instead that his best poetry was latently Christian in its message. This meant drawing a clear line between Shelley's prose, his statements as reported by others, his biography—all of which showed him to be a conscious and unrepentant atheist—and his poetry, which his religious readers wanted to identify as implicitly Christian. Brooke, in his *Theology in the English Poets*, argued that a poet's theology was to be sought not in his letters or his everyday talk but only in his poetry. "It is plain," he said, "that in ordinary life their intellect would work consciously on the subject, and their prejudices come into play. But in their poetry, their imagination worked unconsciously on the subject."[50] On this view, a poet might say one thing in his prose and mean quite another in his poetry. "Shelley, when the fire of emotion or imagination was burning in him, is very different from the violent denier of God and of Christianity whom we meet in his daily intercourse with men."[51] Brooke recommended to the Shelley Society that they set "Shelley's opinions on religious and social topics as stated in his prose" against "the embodiment of the same opinions in his poetry," commenting that "[t]he contrast itself is curious."[52] In a later lecture, Brooke asserted that "[t]he theology, if I may use the term, of Shelley was far more believing in his poetry than in his prose."[53] One could be an atheist in prose and a Christian in poetry.

Underlying this claim was the idea that poetry was inspired ultimately by God. In the enthusiasm of composition, spiritual truths might be revealed to a poet that he or she did not otherwise acknowledge. Shelley may have professed himself an atheist, Brooke said, but "as a Poet, [he was] carried away beyond" his atheism "by the emotion of the loftier spiritual ideas." Shelley the poet, by God's grace, understood truths that Shelley the man, the prose writer, rejected. "He continually rose out of denial and out of professed ignorance into prophetic cries which imaged forth the truths of which he declared he knew nothing at all."[54] Religious commentators imagined Shelley as a reluctant, unwilling prophet, of whom Jonah was the type. Shelley was an example of what Brooke elsewhere called "the curious spectacle of those who denied Christ teaching the thoughts of Christ."[55] Once they made a distinction between his everyday life and his inspired poetry, his rejection of Christian ideas in one sphere was no longer an obstacle to finding them expressed in the other.

This idea was supported by repeated suggestions that Shelley's atheism was a form of mental derangement, with the implication that he was only fully sane when uttering his "prophetic cries."[56] Gilfillan characterized Shelley's writing "atheist" by his name in the visitors' book at an Alpine hotel as "the climax of his madness" and called him an "ethereal maniac."[57] He doubted whether Shelley had "a healthy or perfectly sane mind."[58] Since Shelley's faculties were deranged, his critics could claim they knew him better than he knew himself. He "was not only misunderstood by others," Balfour claimed, "but it is evident, in some particulars, he misunderstood himself." By nature "the most spiritual and ethereal of modern poets," Shelley "rashly gave in his adhesion to the theories of sceptical philosophers."[59] When he professed atheism, then, Shelley didn't really know his own mind. Shelley thus appeared divided against himself, with a skeptical, slightly unhinged atheist opposed to a naturally religious poet. Gilfillan's autobiography described a visit to Thomas Campbell, where the conversation turned to Shelley. Campbell, Gilfillan reported, "was almost tempted to believe that Shelley was possessed by some extra-mundane power, against whom or which his better nature struggled in vain."[60] Gilfillan found a biblical model for this understanding of Shelley in the story of the man possessed by a demon who was healed by Jesus at Gerasenes; he compared Shelley to the demoniac twice.[61] These repeated references to atheism as a kind of mental derangement reversed the convention of depicting poetic inspiration as a species of madness. Instead, they painted Shelley as least sane when apparently most rational, and only truly sane when carried away by poetic inspiration.

Shelley's poetry, his religious commentators claimed, was fundamentally Christian in spirit, whatever Shelley the man would have said. Shelley was "the mere organ of the message he bore" (in Gilfillan's words) and while the vessel was flawed and sinful, the message was pure and holy.[62] His works could be read as allegories of Christian truths. Drawing on his understanding of biblical typology, Gilfillan saw in Prometheus's triumph through suffering in *Prometheus Unbound* the "outlying and unacknowledged *type* of the Crucified."[63]

Shelley's poetry was a positive influence on more recent Christian poets, because they responded to his latent Christianity. "And of these poets," Balfour maintained, "the more devotional their spirit, the more decidedly Christian their stanzas, the more [Shelley's] influence is manifest."[64] It followed that, whatever Shelley himself said, he *was* a Christian. "In what is understood by the present age as a truly Christian spirit," James Thomson wrote in his 1860 essay on Shelley (written when he was twenty-six and not yet the confirmed atheist of "City of Dreadful Night" [1874]), "he bears comparison with the holiest of Christians."[65] Gilfillan called him "a Christian at heart."[66] Brooke claimed that when he was writing poetry, "his hatred of Christianity [was] lost in enthusiastic but unconscious statement of Christian conceptions."[67] Shelley was depicted as a Christian in spite of himself, the unwitting or unwilling vehicle for a Christian message.

The real target of Shelley's attacks on Christianity, his critics sometimes claimed, was not the true religion itself but the corrupt version of it that prevailed in his lifetime. It was not Christianity that he assailed, James Thomson claimed, but "Priestianity": the errors and venality of the Church.[68] He was not irreligious but only anticlerical. He denounced what Armstrong called "the God of the Church" and in doing so "proclaim[ed] the unknown God of all holiness and verity."[69] Like Jesus condemning the Pharisees or driving the moneychangers from the Temple, Shelley spoke out against a corrupt religious establishment with the voice of the true faith from which it had turned away. Brooke said, "the religion of the day screamed at the man who [...] proclaimed the essentials of Christianity as the foundation of life."[70] Shelley's Victorian critics were confident that the old prejudices had been cast aside by the time they were writing. Brooke said that Shelley's treatment shed "a lurid light on the theology of that day," and Balfour suggested that "less dictation and more inquiry became apparent" after Shelley's death, so that he would not have been so harshly condemned in Victorian England.[71] Shelley attacked the religious establishment of his day, then, not because he was irreligious, but because he was more truly religious than it was.

Pushing this line of argument further, and reacting against a tradition that condemned Shelley's personal conduct as immoral, religious commentators presented him as a paragon and a prophet. Thomson called him "sainted," Brooke asserted that he had "natural piety," and Balfour maintained that "the few who knew him idolised him."[72] Gilfillan (again ventriloquizing Thomas Campbell in his autobiography) suggested that Shelley's inherently but unconsciously religious nature revealed itself in his deportment. "Shelley had [...] a form bending as if, in spite of himself, he were worshipping; his very walk seemed a perpetual prayer."[73] Shelley—the real Shelley—was presented as a morally and spiritually superior being. He was holy by nature, even if a part of him actively struggled against that nature. Armstrong wrote that the evidence for "the sweet innocence and purity of the man's soul [...] is overwhelming." He went so far as to hint that Shelley partook of the divine nature, which, being purely good, could not tolerate evil. "Where Shelley went," he wrote, "wantonness could not be, and what is vile shrank away abashed from his radiant presence."[74] This idea ramified beyond the religious reception tradition. Henry Weekes gave it physical form in his Shelley memorial statue (1853–54) in Christchurch Priory, Dorset, which resembles a *pietà* in which Shelley takes the place of Christ. Edward Silsbee, the Shelley devotee who provided Henry James with the model for the nameless narrator of *The Aspern Papers*, called his idol "the Christ of Literature."[75] Where a generation before Shelley's name had been a byword for atheism and immorality, by the end of the century he was being described as a Christ-like exemplar of virtue, radiant with holiness.

Shelley was also figured as a prophet through biblical allusion. Gilfillan claimed that "Percy Bysshe Shelley, of all the modern poets, with the exception of Coleridge in his youth, reminds us most of Israel's prophets."[76] Armstrong evoked the prophetic calling of Isaiah when he described Shelley as "the singer, whose lips have been touched with the living coal."[77] Brooke represented Shelley as Ezekiel, writing that he called on the ideal of love "as the prophet called on the four winds, and bade it blow over the plains of our country and awake the dead."[78] In these allusions, which would not have been lost on their hearers and readers, Armstrong and Brooke were picking up on Shelley's own representation of the poet as a vatic figure. Shelley himself used a burning coal as an image for poetry in the "Defence of Poetry," and the wind as a metaphor for the poet's inspiration both in that image and in "Ode to the West Wind." For Shelley, these images had both classical and biblical sources, and became part of what Harold Bloom called his "mythmaking."[79] (Brooke also attributed to Shelley "the power of making fresh myths out of nature.")[80] But when Brooke and Armstrong compared Shelley to an Old Testament prophet, they invoked a specifically Christian discourse, familiar to their audience, which bolstered their redefinition of Shelley as a fundamentally religious poet.

So, beyond trying to excuse Shelley's atheism as a youthful phase or a reaction to "persecution," and beyond suggesting that his atheism was not important for understanding his poetry, the religious reception tradition claimed that Shelley was not actually an atheist at all. Certainly he seemed like an atheist, and called himself one, but he was really inherently religious, even if he didn't recognize this fact or if he struggled against it. His virtues were Christian virtues and his attacks on religion were really attacks on the corrupt state of the Church in his lifetime. Shelley was not only someone who Christians could accept; he was claimed as a paragon, a man of exemplary spirituality who shone with the indwelling of divinity. His poetry, moreover, was not only unobjectionable; it was claimed as a form of prophecy, containing a tacitly but powerfully Christian message. Shelley "proclaimed, in all that related to man, the ideas of Jesus Christ."[81] By the beginning of the twentieth century, this view was familiar enough to be satirized. In P. G. Wodehouse's 1917 novel *Piccadilly Jim*, a character in search of some peace and quiet turned away from the door of the morning room after hearing a pretentiously high-minded literary chap inside talking "in a high tenor voice about the essential Christianity of the poet Shelley."[82]

Having been reconceived as an honorary Christian and a prophet, Shelley could then be deployed in theological debates about doctrine and policy that deeply concerned his Christian commentators. Shelley was a valuable ally for evangelism, albeit an unlikely one. His poetry, now understood as essentially religious, spread the gospel more effectively precisely because it was not labeled as Christian. Poetry could be heard where preaching could not. Poets, Brooke said in his Essex Hall lecture, had the power of "commanding the hearts of thousands whom pulpits do not reach."[83] Poetry did this more effectively because its religious message was not crystallized into a logical argument or a set of creedal statements. As a result, a Christian message carried in poetry could "steal with more power [...] into the hearts and lives of men, than [...] any philosophic or argumentative treatment [...] in prose."[84] The "theology of the poets" was "not formulated into propositions, but [was] the natural growth of their own hearts," and this less dogmatic but more emotionally appealing kind of theology could capture the imaginations of many who would never read a religious tract.[85] Shelley in particular served this purpose, Brooke claimed. "Many men [...] who were quite careless of religion, yet cared for poetry, were led, and are still led, to think concerning the grounds of true worship, by the moral enthusiasm which Shelley applied to theology."[86] His Christian commentators believed that Shelley's reputation for irreligion was undeserved, but they also recognized that it could be strategically turned to their advantage if it meant people who couldn't be reached by explicitly religious discourse would hear his implicitly religious message. Poets, Brooke said, "lured the world to believe that God is love."[87]

Progressive theologians welcomed Shelley as an inspiration for liberal theology. Armstrong, Gilfillan, and Brooke were all progressives (albeit of different kinds, in different denominational contexts, and at different stages of their careers) and they saw themselves as engaged in a reforming struggle in favor of religious liberalism. They viewed Shelley as a potential ally in this mission. His poetry had the power "to repeal / Large codes of fraud and woe" that he had attributed to Mont Blanc, so long as those codes were understood as false and outdated religious doctrines, not the grounds of religious belief itself. Having argued that his attacks on religion were really attacks on the corrupt theology of his time, they asserted that he had done much to discredit that false theology and foster a better, more liberal one. "Few in poetry have done more than he to overthrow false conceptions of God, to undo the network of false reverences," Brooke claimed.[88] A poet's theology, as Brooke had argued, belonged in the realm of affect rather than that of logic, and so Shelley's special contribution to undermining the outdated orthodoxy was affective. Others had argued rationally against the old certainties. "But if a veteran theology is to be disarmed and slain," Brooke asserted, "it needs to be brought not only into the arena of thought and argument, but into the arena of poetic emotion. A great part of that latter work was done in England by Shelley."[89] Shelley's impact was not limited to theologians or churchmen but was widespread. "It was necessary, if a nobler theology were to prevail," Brooke wrote, "that the masses should be prepared for it, that what pure human love said was right should be proclaimed to them as the only test of theological truth. This Shelley did for them."[90] In Shelley's lifetime, it would have seemed very strange to claim that his poetry had any positive impact on theological debates, so closely was he associated with atheism. But by 1880 it was possible to think of him as playing an important part in the development of liberal theology.

Religious liberals shared an underlying belief that made it possible for them to recruit Shelley to theological debate in this way. They believed that God progressively revealed his purposes in history, that this revelation was still ongoing, and that it was not (as conservatives argued) limited to scripture. Brooke argued this point in a sermon preached at the University of Oxford in 1873. "Everywhere there is continuity, evolution without a break," he said, "and in revelation it is the same." He urged his hearers to look for God's revelation not only in scripture or Church teaching but in "the ideas which the Spirit of God has evolved in history out of the seeds which Christ sowed."[91] Poetry could therefore be a source of revelation. Brooke's biographer wrote that he was "committed [...] to the way of the poets in the search for truth"; Gilfillan's wrote that he "loved the imaginative intellect as co-witness with conscience for God"; Armstrong said in a sermon that he "placed Jesus in my thought amongst the [...] poets"; Balfour followed her *Women of Scripture* (1847) with *Sketches of English Literature* (1852), moving seamlessly from biblical to literary models.[92] For all four of them, then, scripture was not the only source of religious truth. Instead, scripture could be read alongside poetry, and God could use either to reveal his nature and purposes. This meant, as Gilfillan argued in *Christianity and Our Era* (1857), that Christianity was not static but changing, and that it evolved in relation to changed historical circumstances. If poetry contradicted the established teaching of the Church, then, that was not necessarily a stumbling block, because Christianity had to evolve by absorbing a variety of influences. "I do not think we have yet appreciated how large a

part of that slow liberalizing of theology [...] has been done by the poets,"
Brooke observed.[93]

This belief led religious commentators to blur the distinction between
sacred and secular knowledge. Brooke listed the division of work into sacred
and profane among the obstacles to realizing the universal fatherhood of a
loving God.[94] One reason for lecturing on literary subjects from the pulpit,
he thought, was "to rub out the sharp lines drawn by that false distinction
of sacred and profane." This was necessary because "every sphere of man's
thought and action was [...] a channel through which God thought and
God acted," and therefore "there was no subject which did not in the end
run up into Theology."[95] For Brooke, all discourse was at bottom theological discourse, and theology could be found anywhere, even in the works of
an atheistic poet. Shelley did not simply give expression to theological ideas,
then: he was an important theologian in his own right. Liberal theology was
still catching up with some of his religious insights:

> No modern poet has seen so clearly as Shelley did in what the salvation of
> man consisted, how a Saviour of mankind is to be conceived; and when our
> liberal Theology has fully reached, as it scarcely has yet, the level of Shelley's
> thought, both theologically and socially, we may indeed have a religion
> which will once more regenerate the world, and once more recreate before
> us the proper idea of Jesus of Nazareth.[96]

Brooke could ascribe this kind of theological importance to Shelley because
he thought of theology and poetry as "convertible forms of expression."[97]
Committed as they were to seeking God's revelation wherever it might be
found, Shelley's liberal Christian commentators viewed poetry as a vehicle
for theology, and moved readily between the two.

In the writings of Balfour, Gilfillan, Armstrong, and Brooke, then, we can
trace an unfamiliar reception tradition, which has been neglected in studies
of Shelley's reception history. It should complicate our understanding of
Shelley's reception in at least three ways. First, it draws our attention to the
importance of orality in reception history, because it is a tradition that sustained itself primarily through sermons and lectures. They are available to us in
printed versions, just as they were available to large numbers of contemporary
readers, but they remain grounded in a culture of oratory. Second, it reveals
how complex—and to us how strange—Victorian understandings of Shelley's
religious opinions were. At his death, Shelley was very strongly associated with
atheism, and religious readers were likely to avoid his poetry as a result. But
over the following seventy-five years, his atheism was first downplayed, then
marginalized, and finally explained away altogether to redefine Shelley the
poet as a Christian and a prophet, whatever Shelley the man might have been.

Third, once Shelley was reimagined in this way, liberal religious commentators ascribed a kind of agency to him that is drastically different from Arnold's vision of Shelley as an ineffectual angel. While Arnold and others maintained that Shelley was detached from the world, religious commentators granted him considerable power to change how people thought, felt, and worshipped. They were able to conceive Shelley in this way because of their belief in God's ongoing revelation of his purposes, which meant that the agency was ultimately not Shelley's but God's.

This reception tradition seems alien to Shelley's modern critics, who operate in a mostly secular discourse. But this was the only Shelley many Victorian readers knew. The sermons and lectures discussed in this chapter were deliberately aimed at a popular audience, not highly educated, whose religious beliefs may have made them initially wary of Shelley. One reviewer described Brooke as a "missionary of literature skilled to gain the attention of thousands who, but for him, would have known and cared little about English poetry."[98] For many of his hearers and readers this would have been their first encounter with Shelley's poetry, and perhaps their only one. The religious reception tradition, then, mediated Shelley to new groups of readers—and nonreaders—in specific contexts. This reception tradition seems eccentric to modern academic critics, but rather than characterizing it as a deviation from our normative understanding, we might recognize it as another strand in the complex web of reception that shapes what people made of Romantic poetry in the past, and what they might make of it in the future.

9

Spurgeon, Byron, and the Contingencies of Mediation

ON A DECEMBER day in 1853, Charles Haddon Spurgeon (1834–1892) visited Byron's statue in Cambridge and saw a man divided against himself. The poet commemorated in marble had been dead for almost thirty years, and the nineteen-year-old evangelist who came to gaze on him was at a formative moment in his ministry. Already an accomplished preacher in Cambridgeshire, Spurgeon was about to leave for London, where he would rapidly become the most important dissenting evangelical in Victorian Britain. We don't know whether Spurgeon walked into the library of Trinity College idly or purposefully that day, but we do know that what he saw there made a lasting impression. Spurgeon would invoke his encounter with Byron's statue in sermons and writings throughout his life:

> Before I left Cambridge, to come to London, I went one day into the library of Trinity College, and there I noticed a very fine statue of Lord Byron. The librarian said to me, "Stand here, sir." I did as I was directed, and as I looked at it I said, "What a fine intellectual countenance! What a grand genius he was!" "Come here," said the librarian, "and look at the other side of the statue." I said, "Oh! what a demon! There stands the man who could defy the Deity." He seemed to have such a scowl and such a dreadful leer on his face, as Milton would have painted upon Satan when he said, "Better to reign in hell, than serve in Heaven." I turned away, and asked the librarian, "Do you think the artist designed this?" "Yes," he said, "he wished to picture the two characters,—the great, the grand, the almost-superhuman genius that Byron possessed, and yet the enormous mass of sin that was in his soul."[1]

In Byron's statue, Spurgeon saw an extraordinary genius, but also yet another sinner in need of salvation. Here was a man of contradictory impulses, like his own Manfred, "alike unfit to sink or soar."[2] Brilliance coexisted with vice.

Byron's writing could therefore be a force for good or evil, and his legacy was potent but unstable.

Spurgeon must also have seen in the statue a warning against temptation. He was flattered to have been invited to preach in London (the invitation was extended, and Spurgeon agreed to remain permanently the following April). Poised to leave his congregation in rural Cambridgeshire behind and take his message to a larger and more challenging metropolitan audience, Spurgeon must have been wary of the sin of pride shared by Byron and Lucifer, which he invokes in this passage of his autobiography. Earlier that year, while walking in Cambridge, he had heard "what seemed a loud voice," saying, "seekest thou great things for thyself? Seek them not."[3] He would later credit this moment of revelation with turning him away from academic studies and confirming his vocation for popular preaching. Now, at the first signs of his success, he seemed to need reassurance that he was not Byron: not sinfully proud of his gifts but humbly serving the Lord. At first glance, Spurgeon and Byron seem to be an unlikely pair; no one, to my knowledge, has previously connected the names of the scandalous poet and the revivalist preacher. But this chapter contends that the ways in which Spurgeon read, annotated, remembered, invoked, and quoted Byron form a revealing case study of the contingencies of mediation that structure reception history. While further illuminating the religious reception tradition discussed in this part of the book, Spurgeon stands revealed, in my account, as a node in a contingent and rhizomatic network of mediations, in which each mediator absorbs information through unreliable media before mediating that information to others in turn, also in an unreliable, even aleatory fashion.

C. H. Spurgeon was clearly extraordinary in a variety of ways, but I do not wish to claim that he was an extraordinary reader of Byron; in fact, Spurgeon serves my purposes here precisely because the contingent ways in which he encountered Byron's writings were widely repeated in Victorian Britain, and especially in the religious reception tradition. When Spurgeon cited Byron's name or his poetry, however, he mediated Byron to an extraordinarily large audience, making his citations an important feature of Byron's nineteenth-century reception, particularly among popular, nonacademic audiences. Spurgeon was an exceptionally retentive reader of books of anecdotes and quotations, and when he employed the snippets he found there in his sermons and writings, he reached an especially large audience. Spurgeon regularly preached to five thousand people on Sunday morning and another five thousand on Sunday evening, and once preached to over twenty-three thousand people gathered in Crystal Palace.[4] He had an enormous following among working- and lower-middle-class Christians, as part of the popular religious revival of the mid-nineteenth century, but also attracted the attention of such prominent figures as George Eliot, John Ruskin, William Gladstone, and Matthew Arnold (who mentioned Spurgeon several times in *Culture and Anarchy*).[5] He is therefore both an important mediator within the religious reception tradition and a point of intersection between that tradition and others. After coming to London in 1853, Spurgeon preached at the New Park Street chapel, and in secular halls such as the Surrey Gardens Music Hall. In 1861, the Metropolitan Tabernacle, in Southwark, was built for Spurgeon's congregation and became the headquarters for a range of evangelistic and philanthropic projects. At the height of his ministry, Spurgeon oversaw a Pastors' College, orphanages for boys and girls in Stockwell, a network of twenty-seven Sunday schools, almshouses with quarters for seventeen poor women, and a colportage society of almost one hundred colporteurs, who distributed bibles and tracts (including Spurgeon's own writings) throughout the country.

His enormous congregation was a testament to Spurgeon's lively style, flair for publicity, and extraordinary vocal power ("the finest voice I ever heard," according to the future prime minister, Herbert Henry Asquith).[6] But his impact owed as much to the printed as to the spoken word. Spurgeon spoke from notes rather than reading a prepared text, because he believed that a sermon was an opportunity for the Holy Spirit to speak through the vessel of the preacher in an inspired moment, rather than something that should be composed in advance. But the intensely oral occasions when he preached became the centerpiece in an extensive array of printed matter. From 1855, he published corrected stenographic transcripts of his sermons each week; in this form, his homilies gained a circulation of twenty-five thousand. In 1865, Spurgeon added a monthly magazine, *The Sword and the Trowel*, which rapidly reached a circulation of fifteen thousand. These periodical publications were accompanied by a steady stream of scriptural commentaries, aids to devotion, advice to preachers, and inspirational works. Spurgeon's writings were translated into almost forty languages and were widely distributed in America, Australia, and beyond. Spurgeon's fame thus extended far beyond his own congregation, and his public profile was consolidated in England by preaching tours that allowed his readers to hear him in person. Spurgeon assiduously used the press to supplement his oratorical gifts, since he believed that "God has made the printing press to be a great agent in the world's correction and evangelization" and liked to imagine "a gospellized and purified literature triumphing over and tramping underfoot and crushing out a corrupt literature."[7]

Spurgeon's popularity was bolstered by his canny use of advertising, leading one journalist to describe him as "the very BARNUM of the pulpit."[8] He used multicolored posters to publicize his preaching, making him—in his own words—"a little bit of a celebrity."[9] Spurgeon's sermons were widely reviewed in newspapers and periodicals, and he pasted the reviews into scrapbooks. Images of the preacher, and not simply his message, permeated Victorian culture. An enthusiast could purchase photographs of him, a miniature bust, stereoscopic slides showing him in oratorical poses, or a locket containing his miniature.[10] Spurgeon appeared in cartoons in *Punch*, he was portrayed on the cover of *Vanity Fair*, and his waxwork featured at Madame Tussaud's. His image appeared on packets of tobacco (Spurgeon had a penchant for large cigars) and his name was used to advertise cough syrup. Once he was installed in the imposing neoclassical building of the Metropolitan Tabernacle, Spurgeon became something of a tourist attraction. A writer in the *North American Review* remarked, "we ask our friend who has happened to visit London, 'Did you see the Queen?' and next, 'Did you hear Spurgeon?' There is scarcely any name more familiar than his throughout our land."[11] Bus conductors headed across the Thames toward Southwark reportedly shouted, "Over the water to Charlie!"[12]

Spurgeon was adept at using familiar comparisons to make his points. "A sermon without illustrations," he remarked, "is like a room without windows."[13] He wrote a whole book, *Sermons in Candles* (1890), designed to show that even ordinary objects could offer the inventive preacher plenty of illustrations to help him spread God's Word.[14] Literature was a rich source for Spurgeon, which he ceaselessly mined for useful material, leading one hostile reviewer to call him "a scavenger of the literary world."[15] He read poetry aloud to students in the Pastors' College, and shared with them his early love for Bunyan's *Pilgrim's Progress*, which he claimed to have read over one hundred times.[16] Some books, however, were beyond the pale. "I do not care to read books opposed to the Bible," Spurgeon said, "I never want to wade through mire for the sake of washing myself afterwards."[17] When such books did fall into Spurgeon's hands, he did not scruple to destroy them. According to his wife, "his usual method of dealing with a thoroughly bad book—either morally or doctrinally,—was to tear it into little pieces too small to do harm to anyone, or to commit it bodily to the flames."[18] Spurgeon read voraciously, especially among the Puritan classics, and collected a library of twelve thousand volumes by the end of his life.[19] But whether he was reading Bunyan or Foxe, Dickens or Trollope, Spurgeon was always gathering material that would aid him in his evangelical mission. His understanding of literature was strictly instrumental: "I value books for the good they may do men's souls," he asserted.[20]

Spurgeon had an extraordinary ability to recall what he had read. When he was a boy, his grandmother paid him a penny for every hymn by Isaac Watts that he learned by heart, which helped to train a memory that was "as tenacious as a vice and as copious as a barn," according to his brother.[21] "I have a shelf in my head for everything," Spurgeon claimed, "and whatever I read or hear, I know where to store it away for use at the proper time."[22] He used primers, synopses, and anthologies extensively in his search for new material. On his mental shelf, Spurgeon kept quotations, plot details, and biographical anecdotes that he could call on while preaching extempore, sometimes using the same remembered fragment several times over the course of years in almost identical words. Spurgeon's mental shelf included a surprising number of references to Byron. He mentions Byron or his works on almost forty occasions, which puts Byron on a par with Shakespeare among the authors Spurgeon invoked. While he does not turn to Byron nearly as often as to more obvious choices such as Milton, Cowper, or Bunyan, he invoked Byron more often than Wordsworth, Shelley, and Keats put together.

It is important to distinguish between references to Byron as an individual and citations of his works. When he invoked Byron the man, Spurgeon almost always used him as a cautionary tale, a warning about the wages of sin. But when he cited his poems, his attitude could also be approving. When lines of Byron's poetry were broken off from the body of his oeuvre, they could cast off their association with the sinful man who produced them. When he quoted Byron, Spurgeon encountered the radically fragmentary nature of citation, the way that quoting a text entails what Walter Benjamin called "the interruption of its context."[23] But the violence that citation does to context cuts both ways: the quotation is torn from its original context and leaves it behind, and yet it retains the power to trouble the new context in which it is cited and sited, or recited and resited.

Spurgeon was careful about how he used Byron in his preaching. People who were "deeply read in [. . .] Byronic poetry," he knew, "bec[a]me dissolute and sceptical, and none could wonder. You cannot send the mind up the chimney, and expect it to come down white."[24] Byron therefore needed to be handled with care. In 1876, Spurgeon rehearsed the story of his visit to Byron's statue in order to contrast the flawed nature of humanity with the perfection of Christ: Byron looked beautiful from one side but devilish from the other, whereas Christ was perfect in every aspect (*MTP* 1876, 22:296). Two years later, Spurgeon made the same point, but this time he left Byron out. Where he had previously used Byron's statue as his example, he now said:

> A great many [statues] in London are hideous from all points of view—others are very well if you look at them this way, but if you go over yonder and look from another point the artist appears to have utterly failed. Now, beloved, look at Jesus from any point you like, and he is at his best from each and every corner. (*MTP* 1878, 24:668)

The particular anecdote that suggested the comparison was generalized to refer to "a great many" statues. It is as though Spurgeon felt it was a breach of decorum to put Byron in such discursive proximity to the Savior, even for the purposes of contrasting the two. Spurgeon was well aware of Byron's seductive qualities, noting that "half the youth of England used, at one time, to be infatuated with Lord Byron. The glare of his genius blinded them as to the terrible hue of his character and the atrocity of his conduct" (*MTP* 1916, 62:148). When he deployed Byron as an illustration in his preaching, Spurgeon took care not to encourage those he called "men of the Byron type" to make the poet their idol (*MTP* 1890, 36:421).

But, carefully handled, Byron became a powerful part of Spurgeon's homiletic arsenal. The celebrity poet became his stock example of the gifted but graceless individual whose genius would not avail him before the judgment seat, because it had not been turned to righteous ends:

> I reckon that the meanest Christian that loved his God, though he could only speak stammeringly the profession of his faith, is nobler far than he who possessed the genius of a Byron or the greatness of a Shakespeare, and yet only used his ten talents for himself and for his follow men, but never consecrated them to the great Master to whom the interest of them altogether belonged. (*MTP* 1870, 16:462)

For Spurgeon, literary or intellectual abilities could be an aid to one's own salvation and that of others, but, if misused, they could also be a dangerous distraction from one's impending damnation. In using Byron to illustrate this thought, he drew in part on George Bowen's *Daily Meditations* (1865), which he quoted approvingly in his commentary on the Psalms, *The Treasury of David*:

> The genius of a Voltaire, a Spinoza, a Byron, only makes their folly the more striking. As though a man floating rapidly onwards to the falls of Niagara, should occupy himself in drawing a very admirable picture of the scenery.[25]

Whether linked to a more admirable figure like Shakespeare or a more reprehensible one like Voltaire, Byron helped Spurgeon to make a distinction between gifts and grace, which was crucial to his Protestant soteriology:

> Hast thou, my brother, ever learned to distinguish between grace and gifts? For know that they are marvellously dissimilar. A man may be saved who has not a grain of gifts; but no man can be saved who hath no grace. [...] [O]ne particle of grace is far more precious than all the gifts that a Byron ever had, or that Shakespeare ever possessed within his soul, vast and almost infinite though the gifts of those men certainly were. (*MTP* 1860, 6:200–201)

Whenever he wanted to distinguish between gifts and grace, Spurgeon had only to reach onto his mental shelf for the example of Byron, secure in the knowledge that his congregation would understand the illustration.

These references invoked Byron's reputation rather than citing his works, and therefore relied on the extraordinary panoply of biographies, memoirs, prints, and journalism that mediated Byron's image and reputation to Victorian audiences, rather than the editions, anthologies, and collections of quotations that mediated his works.

Spurgeon returned repeatedly to a small number of Byronic quotations. I will examine four of these, considering in each case the places in which Spurgeon encountered the quotation and the uses to which he put it. Tracing these citations reveals three important properties of the web of reception. First, it is overdetermined and reinforced: in every case, Spurgeon encountered the passages he subsequently quoted in several places. Each of these sources would have been sufficient for the quotation, but the passage stuck in Spurgeon's mind because the memory was reinforced by reading the passage more than once, both in its original context and cited in other books. Second, it is woven from contingencies of mediation: no programmatic intention or intrinsic quality led to the selection and repetition of these passages, or dictated that Spurgeon would read and remember these rather than others. Third, it is selective and unreliable: Spurgeon's sources introduce variants, and his own quotations do not reliably transmit the text, making the process of mediation inevitably transformative.

The preservation of Spurgeon's library in a largely intact condition provides an exceptional opportunity to study this process in detail for an individual who was not himself a major literary figure. Of the approximately twelve thousand volumes he collected, it is still possible to consult the majority. Spurgeon gave away some books during his lifetime and destroyed others (as noted above). After his death, his executors gave some books to the Pastors' College that he had established. These were mostly theological, devotional, and vocational works, and are still available at Spurgeon College in London. Some books went to the Village Preachers' Circulating Library established by his wife and cannot be traced. The remainder—more than six thousand volumes—were sold in 1905 to William Jewell College, in Liberty, Missouri, and subsequently acquired in 2006 by Midwestern Baptist Theological Seminary in Kansas City, Missouri, where I examined the collection in February 2007.[26]

Spurgeon read poetry attributed to Byron in a number of different books. He owned a five-volume reprint edition of Byron's works, published in Leipzig by Bernhard Tauchnitz and imported to England.[27] His library also contained other volumes by Byron, including a first edition of *Childe Harold* canto 4 and two nonce volumes uniformly bound from separate editions of Byron's works.[28] He also encountered Byron in the various anthologies and primers he owned, such as Carey's *Beauties of the Modern Poets in Selections from the Works of Byron, Moore, Scott &c.* (1826) and the volumes of *Beautiful*

Poetry: A Selection of the Choicest of the Present and the Past, issued annually for seven years (1853–59) by the London literary journal *The Critic.*[29] Spurgeon also owned collections of sententiae that quoted Byron's words. The most important book in this category is *Truths Illustrated by Great Authors* (1855), a gilt-edged volume containing "nearly four thousand aids to reflection" drawn from canonical writers and arranged into alphabetical categories such as "Folly," "Fortitude," and "Forbearance."[30] Compiled by its publisher, William White, the book includes quotations in prose and verse from a large number of authors. It contains plenty of references to Byron, including three of the four quotations that I examine. Finally, Spurgeon owned several books that included biographical sketches of Byron, such as *The Civil Service Handbook of English Literature* and Gilfillan's *Galleries of Literary Portraits* (mentioned in the previous chapter).[31] As I will show, in each of these cases Spurgeon could have read the lines he quoted in several different places, all of them unreliable in different ways. Overall, the anthologies, primers, and books of quotations seem to have been more important as media of transmission than the editions of Byron's poetry.

Spurgeon sparingly annotated his books, giving some indication of which Byron poems he read with most care, and what he valued in them. His usual method was to mark lines or stanzas with a line in the margin, although occasionally he also wrote comments. Most of Spurgeon's annotations are what H. J. Jackson calls "mundane marginalia," straightforward evidence of a reader working with a book.[32] Often, Spurgeon simply marks points of high feeling or rhetorical drama in Byron's poetry, such as Conrad's return home to find Medora dead in *The Corsair*, or the two stanzas beginning "I have not loved the world, nor the world me" at the end of *Childe Harold* canto 3. In the left margin alongside the remarkable "lightning" stanza from *Childe Harold* ("Could I embody and unbosom now / That which is most within me" [3.97]), Spurgeon has written, "how extraordinary!" Sometimes, however, Spurgeon engages with or questions Byron, or simply expresses his confusion, in something closer to one of the practices Jackson classes as "socialising with books." Alongside a stanza on Clarens beginning "He who hath loved not, here would learn that lore, / And make his heart a spirit" (3.103), Spurgeon has written, "How can we make the heart a spirit?" There are marks in Spurgeon's copies of *Childe Harold* canto 3, *Childe Harold* canto 4 (both copies), *The Prisoner of Chillon*, *The Giaour*, and *The Corsair*.[33] As I show below, these are *not* the poems to which Spurgeon returned most often in his sermons.

The first quotation I examine in detail comes from Byron's lyric "Euthanasia" and illustrates Spurgeon's repeated claim that, as a gifted but graceless man, "Byron [...] flew through the hell of this world's pleasures" but derived no lasting peace from them (*MTP* 1867, 13:532). Byron became for Spurgeon a type of the unhappy sinner, who does not know the peace of God. Whenever Spurgeon makes this point, he quotes the same lines from "Euthanasia":

Ungodly men at bottom are unhappy men. [...] Their Marah is never dry, but flows with perennial waters of bitterness. What says their great poet Byron:—

> "Count o'er the joys thine hours have seen,
> Count o'er the days from anguish free;
> And know whatever thou hast been,
> 'Tis something better not to be." (*MTP* 1871, 17:187, quoting Byron, "Euthanasia" [33–36])

The line " 'Tis something better not to be" struck Spurgeon as blasphemous, and it became intimately linked in his mind with the nihilistic rejection of spiritual life that he campaigned against. He quoted the line on at least another five occasions, using it on one Sunday in both morning and evening services.[34] "Euthanasia" appeared in the fourth volume of Spurgeon's Tauchnitz edition of Byron's works. We know that Spurgeon also found these lines quoted in Edwin Paxton Hood's *Dark Sayings on a Harp: and Other Sermons on Some of the Dark Questions of Human Life*, because he cited them from that source in his commentary on the Psalms, *The Treasury of David*.[35]

The second quotation comes from a poem called "Farewell to England" ("O land of my fathers and mine"), although Spurgeon never mentions the title. He cites it to support his claim that Byron understood the source of his own unhappiness and confessed it in his most candid poetry. When Spurgeon wanted to make this point, he invariably turned to the same quatrain from this poem:

> I fly like a bird of the air,
> In search of a home and a rest;
> A balm for the sickness of care,
> A bliss for a bosom unblest. (st. 52)

These lines may have stuck in Spurgeon's head because they recalled Psalm 55, verse 6, "O that I had wings like a dove; for then would I fly away and be at rest." In 1855, when he first quoted these lines, Spurgeon included a cautious parenthesis. "Read some of Byron's verses and you will find him (if he was truly picturing himself) to be the very personification of that spirit who 'walked to and fro, seeking rest and finding none'" (*MTP* 1855, 1:350, quoting Luke 11.24). But four years later his certainty had hardened, and he introduced the same quotation with the words "There is a verse which tells you what he felt in his heart. The man had all he wanted of sinful pleasure, but here is his confession" (*MTP* 1859, 5:154). The quotation appeared again in his *Words of Wisdom for Daily Life* and yet again in Spurgeon's autobiography, immediately after the story of his encounter with Byron's statue.[36] Unfortunately for Spurgeon, these lines were not Byron's most heartfelt confession: in fact, Byron didn't write them at all. They came from a spurious volume entitled *Lord Byron's Farewell to England: with Three Other Poems*, written by John Agg and published by James Johnston in 1816.[37] Byron disowned these poems almost immediately ("it is enough to answer for what I have written," he wrote, "but it were too much for Job himself to bear what one has not") and an injunction was granted against the publisher.[38] Spurgeon owned this volume, bound into one of the nonce volumes in his library along with five authentic Byron editions. "Farewell to England" did not appear in any authorized edition of Byron's works nor in Spurgeon's Tauchnitz reprint edition of Byron. The quatrain that Spurgeon quoted was, however, reproduced in *Truths Illustrated from Great Authors*, where it is attributed to Byron and appears under the heading "Mental Anguish."[39]

Byron provided Spurgeon with a readily familiar example of the unhappy sinner whose gifts could not bring him grace, but Spurgeon also valued some of Byron's poetry for the religious sensibility it expressed. Spurgeon's Byron was a soul divided between a gift of genius and a deficit of grace: beautiful and damned. His invocations of Byron and his works reflected this division: Byron was both a sinner who denied God's laws and a poet who could open the way to God in men's hearts. He twice invoked Byron's Ecclesiastean poem "All Is Vanity," and approvingly quoted his moralizing stanzas on William Beckford from *Childe Harold's Pilgrimage* (1.22–23) in *The Treasury of David*.[40] In fact, Spurgeon repeatedly commends Byron as a religious poet, recommending his paraphrase of Psalm 137 ("By the rivers of Babylon"), quoting with approbation "The Destruction of Sennacherib" from *Hebrew Melodies*, and referring with approval to moments in Byron's poetry when the Deity seems to be revealed in nature.[41]

The third quotation that caught Spurgeon's imagination was Byron's address to the ocean, from the end of *Childe Harold* canto 4, as "Thou glorious mirror, where the Almighty's form / Glasses itself in tempests" (st. 183); he recalled these lines imperfectly in two sermons. On one occasion, he said, "Byron speaks of God's face being mirrored in the sea," on the other, " 'The God of nature,' as Byron puts it, 'mirrors himself in tempests as well as in green fields' " (*MTP* 1899, 45:172; *MTP* 1915, 61:450). He could have read this poem in his Tauchnitz edition of Byron, but he also owned a first edition of *Childe Harold* canto 4, bound separately. As I show in part 5, these lines were one of the most anthologized parts of *Childe Harold*. Spurgeon could also have found the lines about the Almighty "glass[ing] himself in tempests" quoted in *Beauties of the*

Modern Poets, which he owned.[42] And the lines appeared in *Truths Illustrated from Great Authors*, attributed to Byron, under the heading "The Sea."[43] The fact that Spurgeon could quote Byron's poetry approvingly, even while he invoked his biography disapprovingly, suggests the extent to which citations become severed from their contexts and even their authors. But the extent to which Spurgeon's citations were mediated by other sources also suggests that this severance did not happen all at once, as a theoretically programmatic "Death of the Author," but was a process of citing and re-citing, mediating and re-mediating, that unfolded in the pages of a variety of printed texts.

The final quotation shows this process at work. When he praised Byron as a poet who saw God revealed in nature in *The Saint and His Saviour*, Spurgeon singled out lines from *Don Juan*, the most notoriously immoral of all his poems:

> There's music in the sighing of a reed
> There's music in the gushing of a rill;
> There's music in all things, if men had ears;
> Their earth is but an echo of the spheres. (15.5)[44]

The choice is especially surprising, since Byron expresses similar thoughts in less objectionable poems (e.g., *Childe Harold* 3.86, 87, or 90; each of these stanzas was marked with a pencil line in the margin in one of the two copies of this poem that Spurgeon owned). The lines from *Don Juan* were, of course, in the Tauchnitz edition of Byron's works. But the crucial lines also appeared in *Truths Illustrated from Great Authors* and in the fifth volume of *Beautiful Poetry*, both of which Spurgeon owned.[45] In these books the lines were credited to Byron, but the poem from which they came was not named. If either of these was his source for this quotation, Spurgeon may not have associated these apparently orthodox lines with the dangerously skeptical and seductive poem in which they appeared.

In each of the four cases I have examined, Byron's writing was mediated to Spurgeon in contingent and thoroughly overdetermined ways. Spurgeon had access to those bits of Byron that became important to him through multiple channels. In the process of mediation, shards of Byron's poetry became detached from their original contexts, other people's poetry was attributed to him, and the practice of calling on Byron's poetry in support of moral arguments was modeled by those who cited him. Spurgeon became another link in the chain of mediation, relaying ideas about Byron and his works to new audiences, including many who never read Byron's works for themselves. This process was inevitably transformative, because Spurgeon had no a priori commitment to fidelity in transmission. Unlike editors concerned to restore texts to an ideal purity, critics aiming to offer accounts of Byron's thought and close readings of his texts, or biographers careful to get their facts straight, Spurgeon was not concerned with the authority of his texts, the validity of his interpretations, or the accuracy of his anecdotes. All that concerned him was the effect he had on his hearers. In a parable, Spurgeon imagined the complaints if the place-names on signposts were substituted by "stanzas from Byron, or stately lines from Milton, or deep thoughts from Cowper or Young." His business, he went on, was not to "indulge in poetical thoughts and express them in high-flown language" but "to set up the hand-posts marking out the way of salvation, and to keep them painted in letters large and plain, so that he who runs may read" (*MTP* 1877, 23:193–94).

When Byron was conscripted into the religious reception tradition to signpost the route to salvation, his oeuvre and his texts both became unstable. Spurgeon claimed that "a spiritually dead man" could "stand, like Byron, under the shadow of Mont Blanc, and write himself '*Atheos*,' without God where God is everywhere" (*MTP* 1914, 60:27). In fact, it was Shelley who wrote "atheist" in Greek next to his name in a hotel register in the Vale of Chamouny, and Byron who scratched the word out.[46] Reception traditions beyond the critical heritage have a high tolerance for inconsistency: at one moment Byron (standing in for Shelley) becomes an example of the sinner's inability to see God revealed in nature; at another (in his image of the ocean as a mirror of divinity), he becomes a witness to exactly that revelation. Spurgeon approvingly noted, "Byron wrote,—'He is a freeman whom the truth makes free, / And all are slaves besides'"; this sentiment is certainly Byronic, but the words are Cowper's.[47] On another occasion, Spurgeon felt "compelled to apply to Israel the language which Byron applied to Rome" and he quoted the following lines:

> What are our griefs and sufferance? Come and see
> Jerusalem in heaps, and plod your way
> O'er steps of broken thrones and temples. (*MTP* 1911, 57:149)

In the original, from *Childe Harold* canto 4, these lines read, "Come and see / The cypress—hear the owl—and plod your way" (4.78). In Spurgeon's copy of the Tauchnitz edition, this stanza is marked with a pencil tick in the margin. When he quoted the lines, however, Spurgeon spliced Byron's poetry with a memory of Psalm 79, verse 1: "they have laid Jerusalem in heaps." The lines were rewritten for the occasion: it was not important to Spurgeon for them to be accurate, as long as they were apposite.

By picking up bits of Byron that were cited in books by religious writers and collections of *sententiae*, Spurgeon was participating in and perpetuating a distinct, populist, religious tradition of responses to the poet. This tradition unfolded alongside the more familiar "critical heritage," but the two traditions also intersected with each other, and Spurgeon himself provided one such point of intersection. John Ruskin, George Eliot, and Matthew Arnold all heard Spurgeon preach. Eliot was not impressed, writing that her "impressions fell below the lowest judgment I ever heard passed upon him," but Ruskin was enthusiastic ("Ruskin is a man of strange whims," remarked Eliot).[48] He returned to Surrey Gardens Music Hall to hear Spurgeon on several occasions in the 1850s, and the two became friends, exchanging a number of letters and visits.[49] Ruskin donated £100 toward the building of the Metropolitan Tabernacle. The multiple traditions that structure the web of reception are not like branches in a stemmatic diagram of textual transmission: they can converge as well as diverge, intersect as well as bisect. While information about Byron was mediated to Spurgeon primarily through a distinct, populist, religious tradition, the possibility of mediation across traditions remained open: Spurgeon may have read the same lines from Byron in an essay by Ruskin and in a book of quotations, while Ruskin may have read the same lines in one of Murray's editions and in one of Spurgeon's sermons.

Spurgeon's practice is radically situational and citational. In his hands, Byron's writing is shattered, and its shards turn up in unexpected places, conscripted for unfamiliar purposes. Spurgeon's use of Byron is not primarily concerned either with borrowing authority from Byron or with conferring authority on Spurgeon. Marjorie Garber writes that quotation "instates an authority elsewhere, and, at the same time, it imparts that authority, temporarily, to the speaker or the writer."[50] For Spurgeon, however, the preacher's authority comes only from God. For him, then, quotation is not the site of authority but the dispersal or deferral of authority, as Derrida observes when he claims that "every sign [. . .] in a small or large unit, can be *cited*, put between quotation marks; in so doing it can break with every given context, engendering an infinity of new contexts in a manner which is absolutely illimitable."[51] Retracing these iterations leads us onto unfamiliar ground, as we set aside the familiar traditions of poetic influence or a "critical heritage" to explore a web of cultural transmission that weaves together previously unexamined moments of citation, appropriation, and redeployment. The unpredictable and unreliable capillaries through which knowledge of Byron and his works was transmitted require us to attend to contingencies of mediation. While there is evidence that Spurgeon read a number of Byron's poems in reliable editions, his understanding of Byron was also—and more importantly— mediated by anthologies, collections of anecdotes, books of quotations, and citations in other texts. This process of mediation was also intermedial: one of Spurgeon's most memorable encounters with Byron was produced not by a book but by a statue, and some of his congregation had their most memorable encounter with Byron while listening to a sermon. Spurgeon mediated Byron to others in his turn, including both those who were already familiar with his works and those who had no firsthand knowledge of them. When a number of anecdotes about Byron and quotations from his works became part of the fund that Spurgeon could draw on when speaking extempore, they became open to appropriation and redeployment. As a result, Byron's texts were broken into fragments, placed in new contexts, spliced with other people's words, misremembered, misattributed, and rendered strange.

Instead of lamenting this process, we might learn to understand it by developing new approaches to reception history. Rather than acquiring a monolithic cultural authority, Romantic authors' writings, their images, and elements of their biographies developed what Charles Martindale calls a distributed "iterability."[52] Whereas the iterations that Martindale examines are mostly in the mainstream of the classical tradition, the religious reception tradition examined in this part of the book reveals the importance of other kinds of iteration. Romantic writers remained in the public eye not because the "sincerity and strength" that Swinburne and Arnold found in Byron's poetry enabled them to endure the vicissitudes of time, but because their writing was continually appropriated and iterated in new ways.[53] Texts continue to speak because they are perpetually being made to speak anew in the web of reception, in ways that address local, specific needs within several distinct traditions. Each iteration allows a text (or the discursive field surrounding a person) from the past to "resonate," in Wai Chee Dimock's terms, with its new context.[54]

The religious reception tradition was one of several discrete but overlapping traditions that allowed Romantic writings to resonate through the web of reception. Like the tradition of illustration, it operated across media, with printed books and spoken homilies supplementing one another in order to reach new audiences across the social spectrum. When Romantic writers entered this reception tradition, their words and their biographies were put to work by preachers eager to spread the gospel in the challenging context of broad secularization. These men and women willingly took up Romantic writings as tools to sustain their mission. As a result, Victorians not only encountered Romantic writers through a variety of books, including the popular illustrated volumes already examined, but also heard about the Romantics when they went to church. And—as we'll see in the next part of the book— when they walked out of the churches and chapels and into the streets, parks, and public buildings of Victorian cities, they found Romantic writers there too, depicted in a variety of statues and memorials, like the one C. H. Spurgeon encountered in Cambridge.

PART IV

Statues

10

Secular Pantheons for the Reformed Nation

BYRON IN CAMBRIDGE

FROM THE agitation that preceded the Reform Bill of 1832 to the repercussions that followed that of 1885, Great Britain was engaged in an especially intense period of reflection on who constituted the nation and what they shared. The old membership badges were not sufficient any more: the slow waning of the landed interest meant that membership of the nation could no longer be equated with ownership of its territory; rapid imperial expansion meant that it could no longer be linked to residence in the metropole; and Reform agitation meant that, in the full political sense, it could no longer be restricted to a governing elite. As entrenched understandings of British society, which had been under pressure at least since the 1790s, began to lose ground, new forms of cultural consensus had to be created. Whether that consensus took the form of an imagined community mediated by print, as Benedict Anderson argues, or a shared opposition to external threat, as Linda Colley suggests, it required a set of common cultural references that was sufficiently cohesive to structure an identity and yet sufficiently vague to unite diverse individuals under a single flag.[1] Only by promoting forms of cultural consensus that could be shared by both parties and all classes could the "Two Nations" that Benjamin Disraeli surveyed in *Sybil* (1845) become one Reformed whole.

Creating a shared identity in the present meant constructing a shared past. The political scientist Consuelo Cruz, who studies the connections between collective memory and national identity, asserts that "*how* we remember shapes *what* we can imagine as possible."[2] This idea was especially potent for those who sought to articulate a conservative approach to Reform, which turned to the past in order to create what Disraeli called in *Sybil* "the remedial future."³ Responding to the Reform agitation, Tennyson looked back as well as forward:

> I trust the leaders of the land
>> May well surmount the coming shock
> By climbing steps their fathers carved
>> Within the living rock.⁴

Tennyson attempts through dexterously mixed metaphors to calm his readers' fears by transforming a shock, which could only be withstood, into a mountain or a cliff, which could be ascended. The point is clear: those who look back correctly can move forward confidently. For many Victorians, Reform was a process of identifying the best in the past in order to revive or sustain it in the future. Thomas Babington Macaulay put it succinctly in his speech to the House of Commons in March 1831 when he sought to persuade conservatives that to embrace Reform was "our best security against a revolution."⁵ He urged his fellow MPs to act "now, while old feelings and the old associations retain a power and a charm which may too soon pass away," in order to "[r]enew the youth of the State."⁶ Macaulay's conservative support for reform, like Tennyson's and Disraeli's, aimed to renovate and sustain forms of collective memory: "Turn where we may," he famously told Parliament, "the voice of great events is proclaiming to us, Reform, that you may preserve."⁷ In a country that seemed worryingly fissiparous, remembering the past was thus central to creating the new forms of cultural consensus on which the Reformed nation would rely.

Collective memory could be anchored in events, traditions, places, or attributes, and crystallized in *lieux de mémoire*.⁸ But the Great Man theory of history, elaborated most fully by Carlyle, underpinned the common assumption that the consensus required was primarily about individuals. A shared set of heroes or a pantheon of great men would provide examples of civic virtue and artistic achievement for emulation. Private pantheons, such as the Temple of British Worthies at Stowe, completed in 1735, constructed lists of the great, but did not necessarily represent public consensus.⁹ From the 1790s on, however, "plans for national pantheonic structures were rife."¹⁰ Pantheons could be discursive, like Hazlitt's *Spirit of the Age* (1825), or sculptural, like those in Westminster Abbey and St. Paul's Cathedral. Or they could be popular, like the waxworks in Madame Tussaud's collection (which the *Edinburgh Review* ironically described as "that British Valhalla") and the busts that decorated the "pantheon" assembly rooms in Oxford Street (1772–1814).¹¹ The BBC's 2002 effort to draw up a list of one hundred "Great Britons" suggests the continuing relevance of efforts to construct a national consensus around notable individuals, but the stakes were higher during the Reform agitations of the nineteenth century. Drawing up lists of the individuals who counted from the past helped produce a consensus about the nation's shared heritage, during a period of intense uncertainty about who would be counted—literally counted at the ballot box—in the present.

Part 4 of this book tells a story about how that consensus emerged, and how Byron and Scott were merged into it. The two were often commemorated together: Madame Tussaud was displaying waxworks of Byron and Scott alongside each other by 1828.[12] But the long process of establishing them securely in the British pantheon also meant engaging in complex acts of selective forgetting. In order to render them suitable for the admiration of wider audiences and later generations, admirers of Byron and Scott had to marginalize some parts of their oeuvres and neutralize some elements of their politics. This was true of both authors, despite their political differences, because the problem for commemorative projects that fostered consensus was not a particular kind of political commitment but political factionalism per se. When they were admitted to the pantheon, Byron and Scott were removed from the hubbub of history and installed in the quieter precincts of heritage.

One way to accomplish this shift from controversy to consensus was to link it to a shift from one medium to another. Remediation distanced the specifics of a person's work or life and transformed him or her (usually him) into an element in the national consciousness, a fixture in the pantheon. Statues were important to this process, because they provided an escape from a contentious and overcrowded discursive field. An art without words could sidestep some of the controversies that erupted in print. The story I tell here extends to other writers too, as well as many nonwriters, but I restrict myself to statues of Byron and Scott because their commemoration shows in detail how Victorians turned back to Romantic authors when trying to imagine new forms of national consensus. Byron and Scott were not only new members of a British pantheon; they were key figures in the process of imagining what a British pantheon for the Reformed nation would be. The projects to commemorate them highlighted cultural and political problems with existing pantheons, and the monuments they received in Cambridge, Edinburgh, and London helped to forge new pantheons around them, drawing existing memorials into new pantheonic alignments.

Although all three statues considered here generated large amounts of commentary both before and after they were erected, they were fundamentally antidiscursive. None bears a detailed inscription. There was no public unveiling of Byron's statue in Cambridge and no speeches were made. When Lord Rosslyn invited Benjamin Disraeli to unveil Byron's statue in London's Hyde Park, he made clear that "[n]o ceremony need be entered upon & no discourse pronounced," and that Disraeli would "only pull a string—such as tied the Pyjamas of the Maid of Athens!"[13] Disraeli was not available, and the statue was unveiled in a private ceremony by members of the committee that had organized its erection, with no members of the public present. The ceremonies at the beginning and completion of the Scott monument in Edinburgh—lavish as they were—could not find space for any readings from his work. Sculpted pantheons' nondiscursive nature allowed them to simulate the inclusive community that Reformers envisaged. Once they had been consigned to marmoreal silence, even politically opposed figures such as Byron and Scott could be conscripted into the construction of a national consensus. Statues paid for by private or public subscription could also appear to be distanced from commerce. None of the memorials I examine here was commissioned or paid for by the state, but they all sought to associate themselves with public individuals and institutions, and were displayed in public or publicly accessible locations. The property of no one but the nation, they could not be bought or sold and, in theory, they could never be removed.

William Godwin's *Essay on Sepulchres* (1809) was an early and prescient example of the rising interest in constructing a national pantheon. Rejecting "sumptuousness of decoration" in funerary monuments, Godwin proposed to erect simple markers over the graves of notable individuals throughout the country.[14] Contemporary commentators found it difficult to reconcile this plan with Godwin's politics: the *Monthly Review* pointedly remarked that the proposal was "more in the style of *antient piety* than of *modern philosophy*." "Modern philosophy" is a code word here for radicalism, but although Godwin's proposal was not avowedly radical, it was nonetheless part of his Reformist agenda.[15] He insisted that honoring the past was not "hostile to that tone of spirit which should aspire to the boldest improvements in future." "The genuine heroes of the times that have been," he asserted, "were the reformers."[16] Commemoration might inspire emulation. Godwin's concluding claim that maps showing the location of the monuments would be more valuable than "the 'Catalogue of Gentlemen's Seats,' which is now appended to the 'Book of Post-Roads through Every Part of Great Britain'" reveals his Reformist agenda.[17] His scheme would help to redraw the imaginative map of Britain; no longer navigating by aristocratic landmarks, the citizens of the Reformed nation would locate themselves in relation to the great individuals of the past, whatever their class or party.

Godwin's pantheon aimed not to transform the national landscape so much as to reform the national consciousness. Drawing on contemporary associationist psychology, he explained that his object was "to mark the place where the great and excellent of the earth repose, and to leave the rest to the mind of the spectator."[18] The resulting pantheon would exist as much in the consciousness of the informed individual as in the physical environment. Godwin didn't hope to incite dissent by celebrating historical radicals but to foster consensus.

He wanted the list of those commemorated to be "made on the most liberal scale," claiming that his project offered "scanty room for party and cabal."[19] The new national pantheon needed to be sufficiently "liberal" to transcend party and class allegiance, and embody a new consensus about the nation's identity.

Westminster Abbey seemed to be the most eligible location for a national pantheon in the early nineteenth century. In *Sybil*, Disraeli described the Abbey "ris[ing] amid the strife of factions" and imagined it as a neutral space, where the hostilities of the adjacent Houses of Parliament were suspended. "[I]n this age of mean passions and petty risks," he wrote, "it is something to step aside from [...] a dull debate [...] to enter the old abbey and listen to an anthem."[20] By seeking to place monuments in the Abbey, supporters of Byron and Scott hoped to connect them to a line of English poets stretching back to Chaucer, who was buried in the Abbey's east aisle in 1400. In fact, however, this understanding of the Abbey as a pantheon was largely an eighteenth-century invention. Richard Jenkyns notes that the idea that "entombment in the Abbey should be for the great alone did not get fully established until near the end of the century."[21] And Matthew Craske has documented the extent to which, throughout the century, commemoration in the Abbey had more to do with private interest than public consensus.[22] Poets' Corner, especially, was the result of eighteenth-century innovations and not the product of a long tradition. Joseph Addison had referred to a "poetical quarter" of the Abbey in 1711, but the term "Poets' Corner" was not in use until the middle of the century, after retrospective monuments had been erected in rapid succession to Dryden (1720), Jonson (c. 1723), Milton (1737), and Shakespeare (1740). As Philip Connell has argued, the Abbey's monuments remained contentious throughout the eighteenth century; it was unclear whether they should be understood as "expression[s] of private grief, personal vanity, public-spirited patronage, or shared cultural tradition." Only by "sublimating the multiple, contested meanings of eighteenth-century commemorative practice" was Westminster Abbey able to establish itself as a national pantheon.[23]

John Murray applied to the Dean of Westminster for permission to bury Byron in the Abbey but was refused.[24] John Cam Hobhouse approached the dean, Samuel Ireland, in 1826 with a formal request to place a monument to Byron in Poets' Corner. He hoped that the statue by Bertel Thorwaldsen he helped to commission would find a place in the Abbey. Dr. Ireland was a friend of William Gifford, who had often read Byron's poems in manuscript and made comments that the poet valued. When Gifford died in 1826, Ireland acted as his executor.[25] But Gifford had come to believe that Byron had prostituted his talents in *Don Juan*, and Ireland shared his view. The Abbey again refused Byron a place. Although it was complete by 1831, Thorwaldsen's statue didn't arrive in England until 1835, when it was stored in the cellars of Custom House.

With nowhere else to go, it would languish there for a decade. Hobhouse and his committee hoped that the Abbey would change its mind after the death of the dean in 1842, but Byron was still not welcome in Poets' Corner. In 1870, Charles William Williams wrote to *The Times*, asking, "Is there no voice to ask why the Poets' Corner lacks the name of him who (save one) dwarfed them all?" and in April 1875, "C.R.L." added his voice, suggesting that Byron's bones should be relocated to the Abbey.[26] In the same year, Richard Edgcumbe approached the dean (at that time Arthur Penrhyn Stanley) about a monument and was rebuffed.[27] Edgcumbe felt that the statue of Byron in Hyde Park by Richard Charles Belt that he helped to commission was "a step in the direction of the Abbey" and he still hoped in 1883 that some of the remaining funds from that statue's subscription could be used to place a memorial tablet in Poets' Corner.[28] That wish would not be granted until 1969—145 years after Byron's death—when what *The Times* described as a "congregation of middle-aged ladies and modern poets" gathered to witness the unveiling of a stone tablet in Byron's memory.[29]

Scott was buried in the ruins of Dryburgh Abbey, according to his own preferences and amid much ceremony. But half a century would pass before he was admitted to the other Abbey. In the 1880s, a private subscription was taken up in Edinburgh for the purpose of commemorating him at Westminster. That subscription raised enough money to commission a medallion of the poet, but in August 1888 the Dean of Westminster (now George Granville Bradley) rejected it as unsuitable for the Abbey.[30] In 1896, a better-connected committee was formed in London. With the Marquess of Lothian (a former secretary for Scotland) in the chair, they met at John Murray's. The dean relented after being petitioned by a number of eminent Scots, many of them in the House of Lords, and the committee resolved to purchase a copy of the bust of Scott by Sir Francis Chantrey at Abbotsford.[31] The Duke of Buccleuch unveiled the bust in Westminster Abbey on 21 May 1897.[32]

Partly as a result of its slowness to admit Byron and Scott, the Abbey began to seem increasingly unfit to serve as a truly national pantheon. (Coleridge was not commemorated there until 1885, nearly fifty years after his death.) Already overcrowded and lacking any systematic arrangement or criteria for admission, the Abbey could not accommodate enough new memorials and was arguably unsuitable for the range of individuals who deserved commemoration. Some Romantic writers had an easier passage into the Abbey: a statue of Wordsworth was installed in 1854, four years after his death. And some controversial installations seemed to promise a more inclusive policy, including memorials to Isaac Newton (1727), David Garrick (1779), and the engineer James Watt (1825, removed 1960).[33] But from early in the nineteenth century, many people expressed misgivings about Westminster Abbey's status as a national pantheon. In 1868, the Dean of Westminster himself lamented, "how extremely unequal and uncertain is the commemoration, or absence of commemoration, of our famous men" and admitted that "the Abbey [was], after all, but an imperfect monument of greatness."[34]

These concerns about Westminster Abbey produced demands for an alternative, inclusive, and secular pantheon. Godwin was prompted to conceive his new pantheonic scheme when he visited the Abbey and was "struck with the capriciousness of the muse of monumental fame."[35] In an 1838 pamphlet, Henry Austen Driver canvassed Byron's qualifications for admission to Westminster Abbey and asked, "Is it wise, at all, to pay worldly honours to worldly eminence in edifices consecrated to religious purposes?"[36] His answer was to call for the construction of a secular edifice for commemorating British achievements. The Bishop of Exeter, speaking in the House of Lords in 1844, agreed with Driver when he wished for "some national place, not a church, in which these monuments might be fitly placed."[37] A representative commentator claimed that "it is fit that we should possess some national edifice" for commemorating great men "without violence to the pious and conscientious scruples of those who are trustees of places of public worship."[38] Although there was a revival of interest in Poets' Corner at the end of the nineteenth century, which led to a disproportionate number of late Victorian writers being interred there, this kind of dissatisfaction with Westminster Abbey's commemorative function was widespread in midcentury, and produced a search for alternative places to display monuments to departed genius.[39]

Several alternatives were suggested. Hobhouse initially told Thorwaldsen that his statue of Byron would be placed in Westminster Abbey, St. Paul's Cathedral, the British Museum, or the National Gallery.[40] The founding of the National Gallery (1824), National Portrait Gallery (1856), Scottish National Gallery (1859), and Scottish National Portrait Gallery (1889) offered prominent places to display images of notable individuals. The National Portrait Gallery in London acquired a portrait of Byron in 1862 and one of Scott in 1867, but the galleries had other functions to serve besides that of a pantheon. St. Paul's Cathedral was discussed as another possibility. When she imagined future tourists visiting the ruins of London in "Eighteen Hundred and Eleven" (1812), Anna Letitia Barbauld pictured them musing in St. Paul's amid a pantheon of individuals who epitomized Britain's faded glory:

With throbbing bosoms shall the wanderers tread
The hallowed mansions of the silent dead,
Shall enter the long isle and vaulted dome
Where Genius and where Valour find a home;

Awe-struck, midst chill sepulchral marbles breathe,
Where all above is still, as all beneath;
Bend at each antique shrine, and frequent turn
To clasp with fond delight some sculptured urn,
The ponderous mass of Johnson's form to greet,
Or breathe the prayer at Howard's sainted feet. (177–86)[41]

In Barbauld's imagined future, Britain's power as a cultural exemplar rises as its geopolitical power falls. That cultural power is manifested in its literature and philosophy, but also in its pantheon of great individuals in St. Paul's. During the Napoleonic wars, St. Paul's began to emerge as a military pantheon but was subject to continuing misgivings about the propriety of celebrating military sacrifices in a house of worship consecrated to the supreme sacrifice of Christ.[42] By the middle of the century, many of the same concerns that dogged Westminster Abbey were also being voiced about St. Paul's.

During the 1830s, the Library of Trinity College, Cambridge emerged as another contender for a quasi-national, secular pantheon. Since the eighteenth century, the library had included plaster busts of thirteen ancient and thirteen modern authors, placed atop the bookshelves designed by the building's architect, Christopher Wren. The ancients represented included Homer, Horace, and Virgil; the moderns included Shakespeare, Spenser, and Milton. In the 1770s, a stained-glass window designed by Giovanni Battista Cipriani was installed at the south end of the library.[43] It anachronistically depicts Isaac Newton being presented to George III, while Francis Bacon looks on. Between 1748 and 1766, the college had also acquired a number of marble busts of famous contemporary alumni, mostly by Louis-François Roubiliac, an eminent French sculptor working in London who had produced several works for Westminster Abbey.[44] Four of the busts were placed in the library and the others were housed elsewhere in the college, where Byron and Hobhouse would have seen them when they were undergraduates. During the 1830s, however, fifteen of these marble busts were gathered together in the library, where they were placed on wooden plinths at the ends of the bookcases.[45] This more than doubled the number of busts in the library and gave it the appearance of a pantheon.

In 1843, a member of Hobhouse's committee approached William Whewell, master of Trinity College, about the possibility of finding a home for Thorwaldsen's statue in Cambridge. Initially, Whewell thought he was being asked to buy the statue, which he said was out of the question. Once he realized it was being offered for free, he warmed to the idea considerably and suggested either the Fitzwilliam Museum (then under construction) or the library of Trinity as possible locations.[46] Finally, in 1844, Hobhouse took decisive action. First, he wrote a furious pamphlet called *Remarks on the Exclusion of Lord Byron's Monument from Westminster Abbey* and circulated it privately.[47] Second, he went to Cambridge—traveling on the new railway— and made arrangements for the statue to be housed in the library of Byron's old college.[48] Thorwaldsen's statue was placed at the far end of the library in 1844, locating Byron in ironic proximity to the monarch he had satirized, and giving the impression that the viewer approached his statue through a guard of honor provided by busts of ancient and modern authors and the college's most distinguished alumni, including Newton and Bacon (fig. 11). When Hobhouse returned to Cambridge in February 1847, he was pleased with the effect:

> I walked to Trinity College Library and saw the Byron statue. It is a beautiful work of art and is in an admirable position. Little did he or I think, when we used to idle about the college—that he would have a statue, and the only statue, in that splendid building.[49]

Hobhouse had secured an "admirable position" for the statue in one of the buildings that was set to assume the role of a secular national pantheon, designed by the closest thing England had to a national architect. Placing Byron's statue in a library that also held such treasures as Milton's shorter

FIGURE 11. Photograph of the library of Trinity College, Cambridge showing the statue of Byron by Bertel Thorwaldsen at the head of rows of busts. Photograph by Ernest Clennett, 1894. The National Archives, ref. COPY1/415 (128).

poems in holograph was a concrete representation of Byron's place in the canon of English poets. And having the only statue in the building made Byron appear at the head of the ranks of luminaries represented in the library busts, turning Newton and Bacon, Shakespeare and Spenser, Homer and Virgil into supporting players in Byron's commemoration.[50] Byron was therefore a key figure in reconfiguring the nineteenth-century British pantheon as a site that could generate new kinds of cultural consensus for an increasingly inclusive nation. As both someone whose commemoration highlighted limitations of the existing pantheon in Westminster Abbey and who featured prominently in an alternative, secular pantheon, Byron was part of the problem *and* part of its solution.

Bertel Thorwaldsen based his statue on his own *ad vivum* bust of Byron, but he elaborated it to make Byron appear suitable for inclusion in the British pantheon. He offered a highly Romantic image of the poet sitting amid ruins, with his foot on a broken column, a pencil in one hand and a copy of *Childe Harold's Pilgrimage* in the other (fig. 12). The statue represented Byron in the act of composition on the spot, drawing inspiration from one of the ruined but beautiful locales that he had traveled through and written about in his first great poem.[51] A *memento mori* was inserted at the bottom of the statue, and the owl of Athena to the rear. On the pedestal, Thorwaldsen carved a winged figure holding a classical Greek tortoise-shell lyre, which he called the "genius of poetry."[52] This statue therefore repeated Byron's own self-representation as a poet who responded powerfully to potent places, but it ignored Byron's objections to being depicted with such trappings of authorship as pens, books, and laurel wreaths.[53] Thorwaldsen showed him as a poet, rather than a man of the world, and specifically as the author of *Childe Harold*, rather than of *Don Juan*, the verse tales, or the political dramas. Rendered in plain white marble, Byron was assimilated in person to the neoclassical aesthetic canons that had influenced his response to sculpture in *Childe Harold* canto 4. Even if they hadn't read Winckelmann, when readers of *Childe Harold* came to view Thorwaldsen's statue they entered an overdetermined loop of repetitions and recognitions. Admiring Byron's image in marble, they could enjoy an aesthetic experience similar to those that Byron had had in Rome while admiring other marble statues. With their responses schooled by *Childe Harold* canto 4, they could step into Byron's shoes while keeping him in front of their eyes. Such a response allowed viewers to identify with Byron, but only in his most sober mood of aesthetic contemplation, and to gaze on his image, but only in admiration and not in desire.

By soft-pedaling the most controversial elements of his oeuvre and the most sensational aspects of his reputation, Thorwaldsen's statue rendered Byron suitable for Trinity's secular pantheon and safe for a wider audience. Here

FIGURE 12. Photograph of the statue of Byron by Bertel
Thorwaldsen in the library of Trinity College, Cambridge.
Reproduced by permission of the Conway Library,
The Courtauld Institute of Art, London.

Byron's statue could be seen not only by Cambridge undergraduates (who
almost doubled in number between 1815 and 1840) but also by a much larger
public of tourists and visitors.[54] As early as 1847, the statue was mentioned in

tourist guides, such as the pocket-sized *Pictorial Guide to Cambridge*, which commented on Trinity's good fortune in securing it:

> Busts on pedestals are arranged on either side of the room; they are all beautifully sculptured, and are by Roubiliac and Scheemakers. But the most prominent object is Thorwaldsen's magnificent statue of Byron, which stands facing the door towards the further end. This splendid piece of sculpture lay for some years in the Vaults of the Custom House, at London, being intended for Westminster Abbey, but the Dean refused his permission for its erection there. Trinity has indeed been a gainer by the Dean's scruples.[55]

When Charles Tennyson Turner, elder brother of the more famous Tennyson, published a double sonnet entitled "On the Statue of Lord Byron, by Thorwaldsen, in Trinity College Library, Cambridge" in 1864, he described how the statue surveyed:

> All forms that throng this learned vestibule;
> Women and men, and boys and girls from school,
> Who gaze with admiration all uncheck'd
> On thy proud lips, and garment's moveless folds,
> So still, so calm, so purely beautiful! (10–14)[56]

Lady Liddell, encountering Byron unexpectedly in Rome, had warned her daughter, "Don't look at him, he is dangerous to look at."[57] But as a result, in part, of statues like Thorwaldsen's, Byron was rendered safe for women and children's admiration, and became wholesome enough to be included in school trips and on tourist itineraries. Robert Sinker, the librarian, recalled showing the statue to "two American ladies" who had come from London for the express purpose of seeing it, and "paid not the least attention to anything else in the library."[58]

Having been denied a place for his Byron memorial in Poets' Corner, Hobhouse had found a new, recently established pantheon that Byron could not simply occupy but dominate.[59] His commemorative project sought to extricate Byron from the embarrassments of celebrity and politics and, through remediation, to immerse him in an uncontentious conception of heritage. That heritage, materialized in a new pantheonic structure, was like a great river of unsullied intellect flowing from ancients to moderns, in which the political differences between a sculpted Byron and a stained-glass George III could be dissolved. Purged of its associations with the flashy superficiality of celebrity culture and the subversive tendencies of democratic politics, a sanitized and aestheticized image of Byron was handed down to modernity with all the cultural capital of marble. And while the poet received a lasting memorial, the nation acquired a new pantheon that supplied the deficiencies of its existing pantheonic structures and sought to bolster a fragile cultural consensus.

11

The Distributed Pantheon

SCOTT IN EDINBURGH

THE DESIRE to identify and commemorate great men as part of constructing a new national consensus began with the search for alternative venues for a pantheon, as I showed in the last chapter, but it did not end there. Neither Trinity College Library nor any of the other contenders was recognized universally as supplying the pantheonic structure Britain seemed to lack. While deprecating Westminster Abbey's claim to be a national pantheon in 1875, *The Standard* asserted: "we object to centralisation in such matters. Let us have many places of pilgrimage, not one only. Let not London devour England's places of sacred interest."[1] This reluctance to accept any building as a suitable pantheon was partly the result of not wanting to follow the French Panthéon too closely. (Richard Edgcumbe, who organized the subscription for the Byron statue discussed in the next chapter, rejected any scheme "to tamper with the dead" as having "a strong Gallic savour.")[2] But it also stemmed from the pantheon's function as a *lieu de mémoire*, an element in the construction of a Reformed national consciousness. If the pantheon is considered not as an end in itself but as the means to achieve this broader and more elusive cultural aim, the fact that no other building successfully replaced Westminster Abbey, despite repeated calls for such a building, becomes explicable.

It was initially essential for such *lieux de mémoire* to be embedded in institutions with established authority for ascribing cultural capital; but for the sociocultural project of the pantheon to be fully successful, commemorative acts had to move beyond the walls of their sponsoring institutions and be reiterated both in civic space, as an expression of public consensus, and in domestic space, as an expression of individual desire. In one respect, Godwin was prescient when he called in 1809 for a commemorative scheme that was not centered in a single structure but distributed across the nation. But his insistence on marking the exact spot where a great man's remains were interred led him to ignore the potential significance of locating monuments in relation to one another, creating new commemorative clusters and new ley lines of affinity extending across the map. When the pantheon ceased to be a structure and became an idea, it demanded not to be built in a single edifice but to be imagined stretching across the nation. Britain didn't *acquire* a secular pantheon in the nineteenth century: it *became* one.

The distributed pantheon spread outward from the twin centers of Edinburgh and London, whose streets, squares, and parks slowly became more and more haunted by the mighty dead as the century went on. Edinburgh's urban space had been undergoing a reconfiguration since James Craig's plans for the New Town were adopted in 1767, inaugurating what Ian Duncan calls "a sixty-year boom of construction and civic improvement, fuelled by the Edinburgh Town Council's combination of visionary enthusiasm and deficit spending."[3] In one of the most notable planned urban developments of the period before Haussmann's renovation of Paris, the New Town's streets and squares rendered Edinburgh an unmistakably modern Georgian city. The modernization of Charlotte Square, to a 1791 design by Robert Adam, the extensive improvements of Leith docks (1806–17), the creation of Waterloo Place (1815–19), and the construction of the Royal Institution on Princes Street, to a design by William Playfair (1822–26), were emblems of the city's self-confidence. As Duncan argues, this rapid development of the city's physical environment was accompanied by a rethinking of Edinburgh's distinctive identity. No longer universally acknowledged as the commercial, political, or intellectual powerhouse it had been at the end of the eighteenth century, the city evolved a new identity centered in part on its natural beauty and its literary heritage. Beginning with George IV's visit in 1822 (largely staged by Scott), the city promoted itself as "a new kind of national capital—not a political or commercial metropolis, but a cultural and aesthetic one."[4] Its central railway station was called Waverley from the middle of the nineteenth century.

The physical renovation of Edinburgh and its imaginative recreation came together in an extraordinary range of plans for new public memorials to distinguished individuals. Similar developments took place in London, as the next chapter shows. What Stephen Behrendt has called an "explosion of public monumental sculpture" at the beginning of the nineteenth century remade the cities' public spaces as quasi-national galleries of civic memorials.[5] As part of the "statuemania" that seized several European capitals in the nineteenth century, many public memorial sculptures were erected in London, including Nelson's Column (1839–43), the Albert Memorial (1872–76), and *Eros* in Piccadilly Circus (1893), which commemorates the Earl of Shaftesbury.[6] In Edinburgh, monuments were erected to Robert Burns in Regent Road (1831) and to Prince Albert in Charlotte Square (1876). But the city's principal monuments were arranged along an axis from Calton Hill through Waterloo Place to Princes Street Gardens. The Nelson

Monument was constructed on Calton Hill between 1807 and 1815 (and modified in 1853), where it was joined in 1822 by the National Monument to commemorate the Scottish contribution to the Napoleonic wars, and in 1831 by the monument to Dugald Stewart. The axis was extended westward by the Scott Monument (1840–46), the equestrian statue of the Duke of Wellington outside Register House in Waterloo Place (1852), and the paired statues of John Wilson and Allan Ramsay in Princes Street Gardens (both 1865). Urban development in both cities made new places available for displaying statues and, according to David Getsy, "used sculptures to beautify or mask new kinds of urban site."[7] Throughout the century, the number of working sculptors in London and Edinburgh increased, as did the number of public bodies wishing to support sculpture, the number of available sites, and the number of candidates for commemoration, as engineers and explorers were memorialized alongside writers, soldiers, and statesmen.[8] At a time when, in Benedict Read's words, "sculpture could be said to have ranked virtually as an industry," both London and Edinburgh developed significant clusters of commemorative sculpture, formed into pantheons that were not enshrined in a single structure but distributed across newly developed geographies of urban space.[9]

Like the statue of Byron in Trinity College's refurbished library, the Scott Monument in Edinburgh was positioned at the center of a recently reconceived pantheon, whose cultural authority it helped to solidify and proclaim. The earliest proposals to commemorate Scott envisaged creating a new pantheon built around him, much like the pantheon constructed around Byron in Cambridge. Just a month after Scott's death, a letter to the *Caledonian Mercury* proposed completing the National Monument—a structure modeled on the Parthenon, which had stood unfinished on Calton Hill since funds ran out for its construction in 1829—and turning it into a Scottish pantheon with Scott at its center:

> Let us suppose, Sir, this noble building completed, the interior consisting of a vast hall, in the centre, or at one end of which, a colossal statue of the poet to be placed, with no inscription marking the edifice as peculiarly dedicated to him, as its great presiding spirit. I should then propose, that along each side there should be pedestals and niches, for the distinguished men of Scotland, from the earliest period of their history down to the most remote futurity. The one wall should contain the busts or statues, or where no resemblance remained, the names, at least, or some characteristic emblem, of the Scottish worthies, previous to Sir Walter's death;—the other side should have similar receptacles prepared for those which are to follow, down to the latest posterity. In this splendid array of the virtues and talents of the nation, the Poet would seem as the great magician who had conjured them up around him.[10]

Like Byron in Trinity College Library, Scott is recruited here not simply as a member of the new pantheon but as its "great presiding spirit," who brings the pantheon into existence by "conjur[ing]" it. Conceived in the year of the first Reform Act, this proposal is self-consciously forward-looking; it gathers the great men of the past but also makes room for the new heroes the Reformed nation will produce. At the head of the pantheon, Scott is also a pivotal historical figure, the fulcrum of Scotland's modernity, with the past on one side and the future on the other. The fact that this proposal was abandoned in favor of the monument to Scott that was built is evidence of a shift in conceptions of the pantheon in the age of Reform, as it moved from being a single structure to being a network of distributed monuments. Whereas Trinity College's pantheon gained its prestige by being in a prestigious building, the Edinburgh pantheon was located at the heart of a culturally prestigious city.

Pierre Nora asserts that "[s]tatues or monuments to the dead [...] owe their meaning to their intrinsic existence; even though their location is far from arbitrary, one could justify relocating them without altering their meaning."[11] But a Geertzian "thick description" of the Scott Monument would be inadequate if it didn't pay attention to its environment.[12] The monument's site was certainly not chosen for its convenience, and the effort expended to place it there reveals how significant the choice was. A special Act of Parliament was required to permit the monument's construction, because Princes Street Gardens was protected from new building works by a previous Act.[13] Sir William Rae—lifelong friend of Scott, MP for Bute, and member of the Privy Council—introduced a Private Member's Bill for the purpose on 15 March 1841, which swiftly passed into law.[14] Several months of work and great expense were then necessary to construct an "underground structure [...] of the most substantial masonry" that would raise the site fifty-two feet to the level of Princes Street and provide an adequate foundation for the monument (fig. 13).[15]

The pains required to secure the site in Princes Street Gardens were worth taking because they placed Scott at the crux of Edinburgh's pantheon-in-progress (fig. 14). Rising above Princes Street, the Scott Monument answered the Nelson Monument and the National Monument, both on Calton Hill to the east. It shared the Nelson Monument's towering, tapering shape and was clearly visible from it, positioning Scott as a literary hero on a par with Britain's military hero. It also had the National Monument in its sights, placing a celebration of Scott's contribution to Britain's literary heritage opposite a celebration of Scotland's contribution to Britain's military supremacy. The Burns Monument, installed in 1831 on Regent Road to the south of Calton Hill, was close to this axis but obliquely situated in relation to it. As time went on, the pantheonic axis that connected these monuments would be consolidated and extended by three other memorials designed by John Steell, who

FIGURE 13. View from the Mound, Edinburgh, across Princes Street Gardens,
facing east, with Scott Monument at midpoint during its construction,
c. 1840, Glasgow University Library Special Collections HA0472.
Photograph by David Octavius Hill and Robert Adamson.
By permission of University of Glasgow Library, Special Collections.

sculpted Scott's statue: Wellington (1852) to the east of Scott, and Wilson and
Ramsay (both 1865) to the west. I've been told that Wellington's statue was
popularly known as "the Iron Duke, in bronze, by Steell." Taken together, these
monuments were the center of an Edinburgh pantheon, a string of memorials
less than a mile apart that celebrated the role of Scottish cultural and military
heroes in ensuring Britain's preeminence.

A potentially controversial addition to this pantheonic axis was the obelisk
erected in Calton Hill Burial Ground to commemorate the "political martyrs"
deported on charges of treason in 1793–94.[16] Its foundation stone was laid in
August 1844, and it was completed in September 1845, making its construction
contemporaneous with that of the Scott Monument. Like the Scott Monument,
promoting its construction involved the coordinated activity of committees in
Edinburgh and London and it was funded by subscriptions collected since the
early 1830s. The leading lights of the project were radicals such as the MP Joseph
Hume (1777–1855) and the publisher William Tait (1793–1864). They hoped
to advance the cause of radical Reform in the 1830s and '40s by celebrating

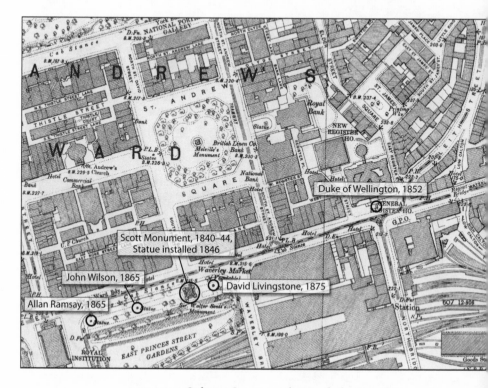

FIGURE 14. Ordnance Survey map showing the location of monuments
Reproduced by permission of the

a radical heritage. But, despite the debate surrounding their proposals, the
resulting monument became more a symptom of the moderate consensus the
new pantheon promoted than a focal point for renewed radicalism. The Town
Council insisted on approving the design by Thomas Hamilton, which was
unobjectionably plain. The monument's location did not allow it to become
a site for political gatherings because of the limited space surrounding it. The
inscriptions avoided acrimony, simply naming the martyrs and quoting statements by two of them, Thomas Muir and William Skirving, at their trials. The
inscription "Erected by the Friends of Parliamentary Reform in England and
Scotland" was sufficiently vague to include both moderates who were satisfied
with the reforms of 1832 and radicals who hoped for further concessions in the

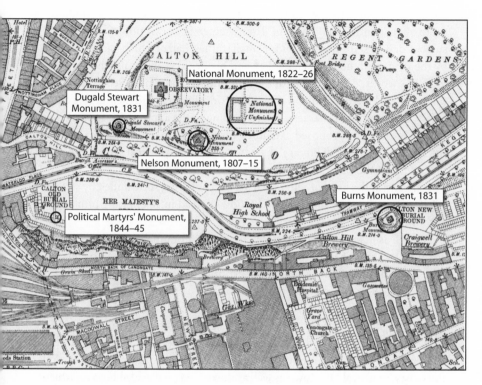

National Monument, 1822–26

Dugald Stewart Monument, 1831

Nelson Monument, 1807–15

Burns Monument, 1831

Political Martyrs' Monument, 1844–45

on Calton Hill and Princes Street, Edinburgh, 1893–94.
National Library of Scotland.

future. Inserted between the monuments on Calton Hill and those in Princes Street Gardens (but set well back from the street that connected them), the obelisk took its place in an Edinburgh pantheon that—considered as a whole—promised to dissolve political differences and promote national consensus.[17]

The Scott Monument contributed to a pantheon in Edinburgh that promoted cultural consensus, then, but it also constituted a micropantheon in its own right. The structure included likenesses of sixteen Scottish writers, positioned around the statue of Scott. The selection was significant. It was weighted toward the previous century, and included James Hogg, Robert Burns, and James Beattie. But it placed those writers within a Scottish literary tradition extending back to the early modern period, represented by likenesses of William Drummond of Hawthornden, King James I, and Queen Mary (both monarchs featured here as Scottish *authors*). That tradition appeared as distinctly Scottish in character, but the inclusion of Lord Byron, Tobias Smollett, and James Thomson was a reminder that it overlapped with a literary tradition more often identified as "English." These sixteen Scottish authors were in turn surrounded by sixty-four niches for small statues, half of which had been filled by the 1870s with fictional characters and historical individuals who featured in Scott's works.[18] This feature of the monument represented Scott's works as themselves a kind of pantheon of great historical figures and memorable characters, and promoted character-based reading as the appropriate approach to them. Godwin had proposed extending his grave-marking scheme to include the imaginary tombs of literary characters, because "poetical scenes affect us in somewhat the same manner as historical."[19] While the Scott Monument placed Scott at the head of a literary national pantheon, surrounded by sixteen supporting players, it also followed Godwin's lead in celebrating him as the author of a pantheonic oeuvre.

As well as being a micropantheon, the Scott Monument was also a microcosm of the city of Edinburgh. Situated on the dividing line between the Old Town and the New Town, it incorporated elements of both. William Watson (1858–1935) grasped the significance of this in his sonnet on the Scott Monument.[20] He noted that it was located "in this highway proud, that arrow-straight / Cleaves at one stroke the new world from the old. / On this side, Commerce, Fashion, Progress, Gold; / On that, the Castle Hill, the Canongate" (3–6). The monument's gothic architectural structure recalled the twisty, medieval Old Town as well as the ruined medieval abbeys on which George Kemp explicitly based its design. The marble statue at the monument's center, in contrast, recalled the neoclassical Georgian style of the New Town. *The Times* complained that "the pedestal does not partake of the character of the building, and gives rather an incongruous effect to the whole."[21] But this missed the point: the monument's combination of seemingly incongruous elements was actually part of its import in the age of Reform. Combining a marble statue in the aristocratic neoclassical style with a canopy in the gothic style that was associated with democracy, it modeled the unity-in-diversity of the Reformed nation. John Ruskin had praised gothic ornament as "revolutionary" because it celebrated the imperfect efforts of individual workmen and proceeded from "a healthy love of change."[22] Ruskin might have been describing the Reform agitation when he characterized the gothic temper as founded on "[s]trength of will, independence of character, resoluteness of purpose, impatience of undue control, and that general tendency to set the individual reason against authority, and the individual deed against destiny."[23]

The Scott Monument thus enshrined in stone the tolerance of difference that the Reformed nation would require. Watson did not approve ("O Scotland, was it well and meetly done?"[11]), but he did recognize that unifying these different elements was a progressive gesture: "For see! he sits with back turned on the Past" (12). Invoking the ancient, lower-class Old Town and the modern, upper-class New Town, the Scott Monument attempted to combine them into a single whole, while facing toward a future in which their inhabitants could coexist as equal members of the Reformed nation.

The significance of this unifying project extended far beyond Edinburgh; as well as being a micropantheon, a fixture in the Edinburgh pantheon, and a focal point for the city, the Scott Monument was also located in a force field that extended across Britain and beyond. From the start, the monument was represented not simply as an undertaking for Edinburgh or Scotland but one for a Reformed and unified British nation. At the ceremony to lay the foundation stone in 1840, a military band played "Rule Britannia" and "God Save the Queen." As part of the ceremony, a glass jar containing coins of the realm showing George IV, William IV, and Victoria was placed in the monument's foundations. And when the structure was completed in October 1844 (two years before the statue was installed), a Union Jack was flown from the top to mark the event.[24] These gestures helped to create the impression that commemorating Scott was not just a Scottish duty but also a British one.

Flying the Union Jack over the Scott Monument seemed appropriate in 1844 because of a sustained campaign over the twelve years since Scott's death to represent him as a national treasure and his monument as an exemplary undertaking of the Reformed nation. Raising funds, gathering subscriptions, and organizing competitions for the design of the monument and its statue involved the coordinated action of committees in Edinburgh, London, and Glasgow. When the funds raised threatened to fall short of what was required, *The Times* reinforced the point that this was the business of the whole nation. The newspaper acclaimed "this truly national work" and admonished its readers to take an interest:

> We cannot conceive of a greater humiliation to any nation than the fact that a monument to such a man should remain unfinished. This claim to respect and distinction should not be confined either to the city or the land of his birth. The only limit we would propose would be that the sum required should be raised by subscription from those only who have derived pleasure and instruction from his works.[25]

The paper's vocabulary tellingly slips here between the "land" that bore Scott and the "nation" that is now duty-bound to commemorate him, suggesting that the "land" of Scott's inspiration is nested within the "nation" that justly claims his works as its own.

For a work to be "truly national" in the era of Reform required it to mobilize different social classes. The project of commemorating Scott did so effectively, from royalty downward, offering a form of cultural consensus that could model and promote a new kind of political consensus. The committees were able to attract the patronage of two monarchs: William IV contributed £300 to the initial subscription and Victoria and Albert answered a subsequent appeal for funds by subscribing £100 and £25 respectively.[26] The initial meetings held "in various parts of the kingdom" to discuss a monument for Scott were "addressed by most distinguished noblemen and gentlemen" and the Acting Committee of fifteen boasted four knighthoods between them. But when funds fell short, an "Auxiliary Committee" consisting of "300 of the chief merchants and other influential townspeople of Edinburgh and Leith" was formed to raise subscriptions. By the time the foundation stone was laid, according to the monument's official history, "all classes [were] vying with each other in expressions of sympathy in the grand national movement" to commemorate Scott.[27] The committees adapted their fundraising to different classes, from the "Waverley Balls" held for the wealthy and fashionable in London (in July 1844) and Edinburgh (in April 1844 and April 1845) to the "house-to-house visitation" undertaken by the Auxiliary Committee among those of more modest means.[28] The Scott Monument was represented as a shared enterprise in which everyone played a part: the monarch, the nobility and gentry, the beau monde, the mercantile middling sort, and finally "all classes." In the years immediately following the first Reform Act, participating in the commemoration of Scott was a way of sharing in a unified but stratified national consciousness, engaging in the collaborative project of recognizing a great man whom everyone admired within a pantheon on which everyone could agree.

Two reassuringly meritocratic competitions—one for the design of the monument's architectural structure and the other for the statue—also brought together social classes, without by any means negating their differences. The unknown, lower-class George Meikle Kemp won the first competition and the well-established John Steell (later Sir John) won the second. Queen Victoria had already sat to Steell for her bust. Kemp, a shepherd's son from Lanarkshire, appears in the monument's official history as an exemplary citizen of the Reformed and newly meritocratic nation. Kemp had largely educated himself, working as a journeyman joiner in England and Continental Europe while honing his skill as an architectural draftsman by studying ruins and cathedrals. He is portrayed as "an humble artist, not far removed from the position of an ordinary workman," who rebuts objections to his design from "enemies and detractors" in order to convince the committee and secure the commission.[29] At the laying of the foundation stone, Sir William Rae praised Kemp for being "unassuming and meritorious" and claimed him as a "native artist."[30] On the foggy night of 6 March 1844, seven months before the builders realized his design, Kemp fell into the Union Canal and drowned. The monument's *History* mourned him as "a native genius cut down in his prime."[31] His "indefatigable industry and self-culture" would earn him a place in Samuel Smiles's *Self-Help* (1859)—itself an alternative, purportedly meritocratic pantheon—where he is praised for being "exceedingly taciturn and habitually modest" and for "living as an ordinary mechanic, whilst executing drawings which would have done credit to the best masters in the art."[32]

In his combination of talent, industry, and humility, Kemp resembled the dominant posthumous image of Scott himself. Scott's obituary in *The Times* had praised his "personal simplicity of character and total absence of literary affectation," and Lockhart's biography expanded this to present a massively detailed story of self-sacrifice following the financial collapse of his publishers, and redemption through his enormous exertions to pay off his creditors at the expense of his health.[33] Noticing the first volume of Lockhart's biography, *The Times* returned to this theme. Scott was perhaps "not the first literary man of his age," but he was at least one who "had certainly the most healthy and wholesome mind among all the tribe."[34] This was not faint praise of Scott but an indication that a wholesome mind was worth more than a literary one. Thus framed, Scott could be accepted as a moral exemplar for the nation as a whole. "Who can tell how many dormant spirits have been roused to arduous and successful exertion by the honourable example of Scott," remarked the lord provost at the ceremony to inaugurate the monument.[35] The lord provost at the time was Adam Black, the publisher who would secure Scott's copyrights in 1851 and join the Edinburgh pantheon himself when his statue was erected in Princes Street Gardens in 1877. In his remarks, Scott appears less as a literary genius and more as a commercial success. Rather than portraying Scott as the "Wizard of the North," several posthumous commentators made him into a paragon of personal application capable of inspiring men such as Kemp to the "arduous and successful exertion" required to succeed in modern capitalist society. Exhibiting the diligence in a worldly calling that Smiles would enjoin in *Self-Help*, and that Max Weber would identify as key to the development of capitalism, Scott is made to model a form of conduct well adapted to the bourgeois industrial society of the nineteenth century.[36]

Equipped with authors who exhibited these virtues and with citizens who were prepared to emulate them, the Reformed nation was ready not only to grow commercially but also to expand imperially. Inaugurating the Scott Monument, the lord provost won "loud cheers" when he said:

> Continents as yet unexplored will be taught by the wisdom of Scott, and enlivened by his wit; and rivers unknown to song will resound with the lays of his minstrelsy; but nowhere will his memory be cherished with fonder attachment and more enduring delight than in the cities and the hamlets of his own beloved Scotland.[37]

Perhaps Black had one eye on the export revenues Scott's copyrights would generate, but the undertones of his rhetoric are imperial as well as commercial. The lord provost here bears out Ian Duncan's claim that Romantic Edinburgh stands at "the threshold of what we are used to reading as a Victorian story of world empire."[38] Adapting the colonial logic of Macaulay's *Minute on Indian Education* (1835), which advocated educating Indians in English about British culture to the exclusion of indigenous languages and cultures, he recruits Scott to a project of supposedly benevolent imperialism. His references to "[c]ontinents as yet unexplored" and "rivers unknown to song" invoke the exploration of Africa's interior along its rivers. Scott is thus yoked with a line of Scottish explorers who would soon join him in the British pantheon: Mungo Park (1771–1806) was commemorated with a statue in Selkirk in 1859, and David Livingstone (1813–1873) was commemorated with a statue just yards from the Scott Monument in Princes Street Gardens in 1875.

FIGURE 15. Photograph of the Scott Monument by William Henry Fox Talbot, from *Sun Pictures in Scotland* (1845). Private collection.

For the Scott Monument to do the cultural work that I am attributing to it, it had to reach an audience beyond those who could visit it in Edinburgh. It did this when it was reproduced in engravings and on silverware, and using the new technologies of photography and chromolithography. The committee produced an engraving of the monument's design, which was given to everyone who subscribed a guinea or more, and when it was complete the monument was engraved for the frontispiece of its official history. It also became a subject for some of the first photographs ever taken. These include one by

William Henry Fox Talbot (1800–1877), inventor of the negative-positive process, who captured the monument for his second photographically illustrated book, *Sun Pictures in Scotland* (1845) (fig. 15), and a number by David Octavius Hill (1802–1870) and Robert Adamson (1821–1848), who photographed the monument at every stage of its construction.

There are many connections between early photography and Romanticism, and Talbot's own interest in Romantic writing was—forgive the pun—well developed. John Wood straightforwardly claims that early photography was "a product of English Romanticism"; Sonia Hofkosh suggests that Talbot's photographs should "be viewed in the context of late Romanticism"; and Andrea Henderson has shown how Talbot's understanding of photography was ambiguously shaped by Romantic aesthetic ideals.[39] Talbot knew at least one Romantic writer well. Thomas Moore was one of Talbot's neighbors at Lacock Abbey and the two became close friends.[40] Talbot photographed Moore in April 1844, when Moore was sixty-five.[41] Employing the new, indexical technology of photography to depict a visibly aging writer signaled both photography's connections with Romanticism and its potential for memorializing its subjects.

Sometime in 1840, Talbot made a photographic facsimile of the manuscript of Byron's "Ode to Napoleon"; Moore may have lent him the document.[42] Talbot probably understood this image partly as a demonstration of photography's ability to reproduce text, but he also conceived it as one image in a projected set that would memorialize Romantic poets. In February 1840, Talbot jotted into his notebook a plan for "The Tribute of Science to Poetry, two views of house, and one copy of manuscript," which Larry Schaaf interprets as "a proposal for a small memorial publication to Lord Byron."[43] Manuscripts feature in several of Talbot's early photographs, perhaps because handwriting and photography both offer traces and guarantees of anterior presence. The photograph—which Talbot repeatedly characterizes as light inscribing itself— testifies that its subject really was there in front of the lens at the moment of exposure. The manuscript—which is the physical trace of the writing body that inscribed it—testifies to the presence of the living hand that held the pen. A photograph of a manuscript, especially in an era when all photographs were developed and printed by hand, therefore offers its viewer a chain of indexical connections back to the manuscript's writer. The viewer holds in her hand a photograph that was printed by the hand of the photographer, who held in his hand the manuscript that was written by the hand of the author.

The twofold assertion of presence offered by a photographed manuscript, however, is shadowed by a twofold reminder of absence. The moment of exposure, when the manuscript was really present, took place elsewhere and in the past, while the living hand that wrote the manuscript is now in the icy silence of the tomb. Talbot's attempt to memorialize Byron by photographing one of his manuscripts, then, was compromised by the media that enabled it. This may explain why, although Talbot continued to think of reproducing text as one of photography's possible applications, he did not complete the projected memorial to Byron and did not include a facsimile of Scott's handwriting in *Sun Pictures in Scotland*. Instead, Talbot—like Hill and Adamson around the same time—connected the new technology of photography with the newly emerging pantheon to produce a more effective "Tribute of Science to Poetry."

The *Pencil of Nature*, Talbot's first book, published in six fascicles from 1844 to 1846, demonstrates various possible uses of photography, from depicting objects to reproducing artworks and documents, to creating original artistic compositions inspired by Dutch genre painting, to recording architectural subjects. *Sun Pictures in Scotland*, which appeared between the fourth and fifth installments of *Pencil*, differs in trying to do only one thing: adapt the genre of the illustrated travel book to the medium of photography. The subscription advertisement claims that "[m]ost of the views represent scenes connected with the life and writings of Sir Walter Scott" and prominently lists the Scott Monument among them.[44] Gillen D'Arcy Wood argues that Talbot fails as an illustrator of Scott because "the uncompromising 'clearness' of Fox Talbot's images [. . .] effectively de-romanticizes the myth of Waverley" and suggests that this explains the relative neglect of *Sun Pictures in Scotland* compared to *The Pencil of Nature*.[45]

FIGURE 16. Photograph of the Scott Monument under construction, by David Octavius Hill and Robert Adamson, 1844, Glasgow University Library Special Collections HA0469. By permission of University of Glasgow Library, Special Collections.

One strand of Talbot's practice that cuts across both books, however, is his interest in documenting new monuments. In May or June 1843, he photographed the Panthéon in Paris, and he included a photograph of Westminster Abbey in *The Pencil of Nature*.[46] That September, he took several photographs of the Martyrs' Monument in Oxford, which had been completed earlier in the year.[47] The following April, he photographed Nelson's Column in London, which was still under construction.[48] That

FIGURE 17. Photograph of the Scott Monument before installation of the statue, by David Octavius Hill and Robert Adamson, May 1845, Glasgow University Library Special Collections HA0751. By permission of University of Glasgow Library, Special Collections.

October, Talbot was in Edinburgh photographing the Scott Monument.[49] The choice of these subjects suggests that, during a key moment in photography's development, Talbot participated in the contemporary concern with memorializing the dead and creating a dispersed, secular pantheon. Documenting the construction of that pantheon was, it seems, one of the roles he envisioned for the new technology of photography. Hill and Adamson, who opened their photographic studio at Rock House on Calton Hill, not far from the site of the Scott Monument, in 1843, shared this interest. Over the next few years, Hill and Adamson photographed most of the monuments in the emerging Edinburgh pantheon and documented the construction of the Scott Monument very thoroughly, photographing it at least twenty times (figs. 16, 17).

Neither Talbot nor Hill and Adamson showed any interest in waiting until the Scott Monument was finished to photograph it. Instead, their photographs show the monument still under construction, before the statue was installed, supported by scaffolding and only partly complete. Hill and Adamson also photographed the statue before it was put in place, and took pictures of some of the masons who worked on the monument. Having photographed the monument under construction, Talbot never returned to record its finished state. Talbot's photograph of Nelson's Column also shows it half finished, with the incomplete top of the column cut off by the photograph's edge and its base surrounded by wooden scaffolding. In these photographs, we see not simply a desire to represent the monuments of the new pantheon but also a desire to document the process of memorializing. Their focus is not the fact of commemoration but the act of commemorating. In using the new technology of photography to record the creation of new monuments, these photographers stressed the modernity of the secular pantheon and allowed its marmoreal figures to circulate widely in mechanical reproductions.

That circulation was extended with the appearance of the picture post-card at the end of the century. The Penny Post, introduced in Britain in 1840, allowed anyone to send a letter anywhere in the country for only a penny, in one of several posts each day. It produced a huge rise in the amount of material circulating through the mail and was accompanied by a variety of innovations in communications technology, including the postage stamp and the pre-paid envelope.[50] Postcards were introduced in 1870.[51] Initially the only cards allowed to be sent through the post were those printed by the Post Office, which included the cost of postage in the purchase price, but from 1872 private firms were also allowed to produce postcards. Picture postcards were intro-duced in 1894, making use of cutting-edge technologies of image reproduction such as chromolithography. (Photographic postcards were not technologically or commercially viable until the twentieth century.) Initially the picture took up only part of the card, leaving space for the address on the other side (fig. 18), but from 1902 regulations changed, allowing pictures to cover the whole front surface of the card, with the back divided in the middle, providing space for the address on one half and a message on the other.

Postcards caught on rapidly and sold in enormous numbers. By some esti-mates, 75 million were sent in 1870, the first year of the postcard's existence in Britain. That figure rose to a staggering 600 million postcards carried through the mail in 1903.[52] The Victorians adopted the postcard so enthusiastically

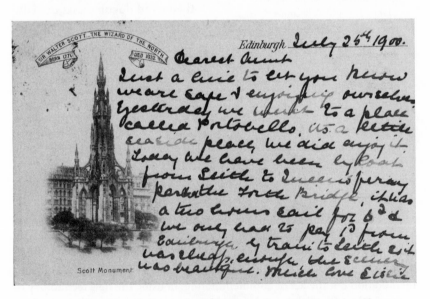

FIGURE 18. Postcard showing the Scott Monument, c. 1900. Reproduced by permission of the University of Edinburgh Centre for Research Collections. Private collection.

because it was cheap, efficient, and modern, but also because it was connected to contemporary developments such as the rise of middle-class tourism, the increasing popularity of sending greetings cards on Valentine's Day or at Christmas, and the greater mobility of the labor force as more people relocated to find work.[53] The firm of Raphael Tuck was one of the earliest and largest producers of picture postcards, with over ten thousand different cards in production by 1903.[54] In 1900, Tuck organized a postcard collecting competition, with £1000 in prizes for those individuals who collected the most cards that had been sent through the post. The competition neatly reveals how postcards were bound up with economies of both circulation and accumulation.

The winner had a collection of over twenty thousand different cards.[55]

Scott Monument, Edinburgh.

50.

FIGURE 19. Cigarette card showing the Scott Monument, Cope Bros., c. 1900. Reproduced by permission of the University of Edinburgh Centre for Research Collections. Private collection.

The Scott Monument was a very popular subject for picture postcards: I have located more than twenty different examples issued by various publishers. Tuck produced at least four different images of the Scott Monument, usually as part of sets of six postcard views of Edinburgh or Midlothian, each of which had a likely print run of several thousand. The Scott Monument also appeared in other kinds of Victorian collectable printed ephemera, such as cigarette cards. The Cope Brothers tobacco company produced a set of fifty Scott-themed cards around 1900, including an image of the monument (fig. 19).[56] The monument was completed twenty-five years before the postcard boom, so unlike photographers, postcard artists did not depict it under construction. Instead, they represented it as the landmark achievement of a thriving modern city that was striding into the future without forgetting the past.

A 1902 image in the Oilette series, a high-end line that Tuck described as "veritable miniature oil paintings," shows the monument at the center of a respectable and commercial city (fig. 20). In the foreground, figures stroll in well-kept public

FIGURE 20. Postcard showing the Scott Monument, Tuck and Co. Oilette series, c. 1902.

gardens filled with potted flowers. The glass skylights of Waverley market, adjacent to the railway station that connects Edinburgh to the rest of the nation, form a line leading the viewer's eye toward the Scott Monument. To the right of the monument, the commercial artery of Princes Street extends into the distance, bustling with new cable-hauled trams (installed in the 1880s), horse-drawn delivery vehicles, and private motorcars, and lit by municipal streetlights. Canvas awnings stretch over the windows of large shops, including Jenner's Department Store (rebuilt in 1895 after a fire) immediately opposite the Scott Monument.[57] Behind the Scott Monument, the Royal Scottish Academy and Edinburgh Castle can be seen. Commerce, history, and the arts come together in an image of a thriving modern city with Scott at its heart.

Postcards such as this one circulated images of the Scott Monument widely and provided another second-order remediation in Scott's reception. They incorporated the monument into formal and informal groups of monuments, because postcards were published in series and because collecting them was encouraged. These collections formed another iteration of the new pantheon, one that was not confined to a single location but circulated through the mail and could be assembled by individual collectors. Postcards promoted the Scott Monument as a tourist attraction, emphasizing the claim made repeatedly by its supporters that it was not intended for the citizens of Edinburgh alone but for people across the nation and beyond. When postcards gained in popularity as a new medium of communication, the media ecology shifted once again. The many postcards that depicted the Scott Monument ensured

that Romantic poets and their memorials would continue to feature prominently in the new media ecology as well as the new urban environment.

Victorian consumers could also carry the Scott Monument in their pockets.
It appeared on a large number of personal objects, such as card cases, snuff
boxes, and vinaigrettes (small boxes containing a sponge soaked in sweet-
smelling oil, for warding off noxious odors).[58] These boxes were often made of
silver and decorated with architectural images, and were known as "castle-top"
boxes. As well as the Scott Monument, images of Abbotsford and Newstead
Abbey were popular, along with Westminster Abbey and St. Paul's Cathedral.
The Birmingham silversmith Nathaniel Mills and sons, who operated from
1803 to 1853, produced many such items in the 1840s and '50s. Bourgeois consumers could afford them, while those with sufficient means could collect
them. Card cases, snuff boxes, and vinaigrettes depicting memorials, writers'
houses, or pantheonic buildings remediated the pantheon and allowed consumers to possess a version of it among their personal effects.

By the second half of the century, then, the movement to create a new pantheon for the Reformed nation had ceased to be a search for a new structure.
Instead, the new pantheon took shape as a loose collection of monuments,
distributed across the nation's rapidly developing cityscapes and remediated
in its shifting and innovative mediascapes. The Scott Monument was a key
fixture of this new distributed pantheon. Its location placed it at the center of
the emerging Edinburgh pantheon, located along the axis between the Old
Town and the New. The campaign to build the monument was framed as an
exemplary undertaking for a nation seeking new forms of cultural consensus. Its construction unified aesthetic styles associated with different social
groups and combined elements designed by individuals from different ends
of the social spectrum. Its fundraising campaign brought different social strata
together in a national project to which every sector of the Reformed nation
could contribute. It reached across the nation when it circulated through
new media such as photography and featured in the postcard boom. And its
supporters positioned Scott as a paragon of professional application and an
ambassador for a modern commercial and imperial power. In these ways, Scott
was recruited to the project of creating a new secular pantheon for Reformed
Britain that took shape not as a grand new building but as a network of monuments distributed across the nation.

12

The Networked Pantheon

BYRON IN LONDON

THE DISTRIBUTED pantheon that emerged in Edinburgh in the 1840s also took shape in London, and Byron was key to its development. As an increasingly dense network of monuments spread across the land, the new pantheon developed a signifying infrastructure of growing complexity. As the pantheon became progressively more distributed, each new monument gained meaning not only in relation to its closest neighbors but also with reference to others across the city, the country, and even the world (witness the copy of the Scott Monument's statue erected in New York's Central Park in 1872). This chapter shows how efforts to memorialize Byron in London embedded his commemoration in the city's evolving imaginative map and twinned his statue with Scott's monument at the other end of the island. Situated on a politically significant site, and bringing existing monuments into newly meaningful constellations, the Byron statue erected in Hyde Park in 1880 served to foster the liberal political consensus about figures from the past that was required by a nation in the process of modernizing its self-image.

Like Edinburgh, nineteenth-century London experienced a reconfiguration of urban space brought about by a variety of factors. The city's population exploded, rising from about one million in 1801 to over seven million by 1911, leaving the metropolis feeling teeming and sprawling.[1] New civil engineering projects were undertaken, such as the Chelsea, Victoria, and Albert embankments (1874), and new landmarks constructed, such as the Crystal Palace (1851, relocated 1854), the rebuilt Houses of Parliament (1840–70), and the Albert Hall (1871). New transport links were required, including new roads and railways, several bridges across the Thames, and the London Underground Railway (from 1863). Gaslight and smog changed the experience of the city streets, while music halls and the new London Zoo (opened to the public in 1847) offered new ways to pass leisure time. These developments were accompanied by an imaginative remapping of the city undertaken by writers and artists such as Thomas De Quincey, Pierce Egan, Gustave Doré and Blanchard Jerrold, Henry Mayhew and, above all, Charles Dickens.

In 1863, William Ewart rose in the House of Commons to propose a scheme whose aim was nothing less than to reimagine London itself as a space ennobled and rendered historically legible as a pantheon of great men.[2] The Society of Arts (later the Royal Society of Arts) undertook the scheme, initially forming a committee in 1864 "to consider and report how the Society may promote the erection of statues or other memorials of persons eminent in Arts, Manufactures, and Commerce, and whether it is desirable that the Society should contribute to the monuments of distinguished individuals."[3] On reflection, the committee recommended leaving statues to others, and the society set up an ambitious scheme to produce "memorial tablets to distinguished persons, to be affixed to houses in which they were born or dwelt."[4] The scheme's earliest supporters were closely associated with the cause of Reform. Ewart was "a Liberal with radical leanings" who advocated widening the reforms of 1832.[5] When his own commemorative plaque was installed in 1963, it described him simply as "Reformer."[6] The scheme's "convenor" at the Society of Arts was George C. T. Bartley, a civil servant and later Member of Parliament who established the National Penny Bank in 1875 to promote thrift among the poor.[7] The first tablet the society installed was on Byron's birthplace on Holles Street, in 1868.[8] This inaugurated what became the well-known "blue plaque scheme," which continues to place markers on buildings once occupied by notable individuals, and is now administered by English Heritage.[9] The society published annual lists of the memorials it had installed; there were thirty-three of them by the end of the century, with many more planned.[10]

The coordination and ambition that the society brought to the scheme was unprecedented, but the conception was Romantic through and through, from the understanding of the city it endorsed, to the experience of the city it promoted, to the individuals it memorialized. In his *Essay on Sepulchres*, Godwin acknowledged that the simple wooden cross he prescribed for marking graves might be impractical in the crowded city. In this case, he asserted, "A horizontal stone on the level of the pavement, or a mural tablet, where the grave is enclosed within a building, is abundantly enough."[11] Samuel Rogers, in the "Genoa" section of his poem *Italy* (1822–28), visited the house of Andrea Doria, the admiral who reestablished the Republic of Genoa in the sixteenth century, and took special note of the memorial plaque on its outside wall:

He left it for a better; and 'tis now
A house of trade, the meanest merchandise
Cumbering its floors. Yet, fallen as it is,
'Tis still the noblest dwelling—even in Genoa!

And hadst thou, Andrea, lived there to the last,
Thou hadst done well; for there is that without,
That in the wall, which monarchs could not give,
Nor thou take with thee, that which says aloud,
It was thy Country's gift to her Deliverer. (9–17)[12]

The custom of marking houses in this way, Rogers added in a note to this passage, was "well worthy of notice"; remarking how "rare are such memorials among *us*," he asserted that they were "evidences of refinement and sensibility in the people."[13] Rogers's note (but not his poem) was quoted in the *Journal of the Society of Arts* when the idea of setting up memorial tablets was being mooted.[14]

The text that shaped the society's understanding of the city most, even if it went unmentioned, was *The Prelude*. Among the wonders he looked forward to seeing in London in the 1805 version, Wordsworth included "Statues, with flowery gardens in vast Squares" (7.134). In 1850, he made clear that he expected these statues to be elements of a well-ordered and maintained pantheon of mostly military heroes: "Statues—man, / And the horse under him—in gilded pomp / Adorning flowery gardens, 'mid vast squares" (7.133–35). When he arrived, however, he found a pantheon not among statues (which are not mentioned again) but among shop signs showing "physiognomies of real men, / Land-warriors, kings, or admirals of the sea, / Boyle, Shakespeare, Newton, or the attractive head / Of some quack-doctor, famous in his day" (7.164–67). These commercial signs were accompanied by a cacophony of written messages, "blazon'd Names [. . .] [on] fronts of houses, like a title page / with letters huge inscribed" (7.158–61). Wordsworth's simile here probably fuses two observations: first, booksellers' practice of pasting up title pages on boards outside their shops to serve as advertisements, and second, tradesmen's practice of using a famous author's name or likeness as a shop sign, especially if the site of the shop was associated with him or her.[15] The piratical publisher William Benbow used Byron's head as his shop sign in the 1820s, and a pub in Fetter Lane bore the sign "Here lived Dryden, the poet" in the 1860s.[16] One source of the complex anxiety that London generated for Wordsworth in *The Prelude*, then, was the realization that the city did not have a stable, prestigious pantheon of great men commemorated in statues, as he had imagined, but a shifting, commercialized, and debased pseudo-pantheon of advertisements and shop signs, in which Boyle, Shakespeare, and Newton were pressed into the service of tradesmen and forced to mingle with quack doctors.

The Society of Arts' plan to mark the houses of eminent men in London aimed to provide the benefits that Rogers praised, while counteracting the disappointment Wordsworth felt. Having noted that some foreign cities displayed signs at the houses of notable individuals which "few would notice [. . .] if to do so required hunting in a 'Murray's Guide,' " Bartley imagined an annotated city, whose buildings would be written over with its own tourist handbook.[17] Unlike Wordsworth's cacophonous experience of the city, in which every building seemed to be shouting at once, he imagined a decorous register of past achievements. *The Times* remarked that "[n]othing could be more fertile in interest than to make our houses their own biographers."[18] The intended readers of the plaques, however, were not primarily tourists but residents of the city, especially the lower classes who were the focus of Ewart and Bartley's philanthropic and political work. "To travellers up and down in omnibuses, &c," Bartley wrote, the plaques would provide "an agreeable and instructive mode of beguiling a somewhat dull and not very rapid progress through the streets."[19]

In order not to be confused with the pseudo-pantheon Wordsworth discovered in London's shop signs, this scheme carefully distanced itself from the taint of commerce. Bartley cautioned that "any attempt which might be made in this advertising age to utilize the memory of a former inhabitant for commercial advantages [. . .] should be as much as possible avoided."[20] For the lower-class man on the omnibus, only recently admitted to full political membership of the nation, the city was imagined by the scheme's supporters as a space of monotony and alienating drudgery, choked with traffic and studded with advertisements. The blue plaque scheme offered an alternative experience of the city, a kind of augmented reality in which its monotony was relieved by instructive diversions, its commercialism was accompanied by civic pride, and its alienating character was overcome by a sense of shared inheritance. Everyday reminders of past greatness could make the modern city navigable, intelligible, and edifying. The plaques offered to construct a pantheon that would not be gathered in one structure but distributed across the whole city. It would be equally accessible to all its inhabitants, and would invite them to imagine themselves as part of the same nation as each other and as the celebrated city-dwellers of the past.[21] Having been established in London, the practice spread rapidly: Shelley's house in Marlowe was reportedly marked with an inscription by the 1880s.[22]

The plaque marking Byron's birthplace was quickly followed by proposals for a London statue of the poet. The process began in 1875, when Richard Edgcumbe visited Byron's grave in Nottinghamshire. As early as 1860, *Harper's* magazine had visited "The Home and Grave of Byron" as part of the growing interest in the "homes and haunts" of authors, and reported its disappointment at his tomb, where "there was very little of that beauty peculiar to English village churches."[23] By 1866 there were reports that the tomb was dilapidated and the visitors' book had been stolen, and in 1875 Edgcumbe "found that

Byron's resting-place was inadequately marked, and indeed almost lost, within the chancel at Hucknall Torkard." He decided to "[follow] the example of Mr Hobhouse" by forming a committee to commemorate him, and initially intended to remedy the situation by placing a new marker on Byron's grave.[24] In his *History of the Byron Memorial* (1883), Edgcumbe claimed that this was simply "a preliminary step" designed "not to startle a somewhat sensitive public" and that he wanted only "a small slab, inscribed with Byron's name."[25] But the circular that he distributed to potential subscribers mentioned "a handsome and costly marble slab (inlaid either with brass or mosaic)," and *The Times* reported that "the memorial is intended to take the form of a costly marble slab, richly inlaid, and with a suitable inscription."[26] This evidence suggests that Edgcumbe's plan to mark Byron's grave was more ambitious than he later admitted.

Edgcumbe also disguised the reasons he abandoned his intention to place a slab in a provincial church, and concentrated instead on erecting a statue in a metropolitan civic space. According to Edgcumbe, when he recruited Benjamin Disraeli to chair the fundraising committee for the memorial, the prime minister "expressed himself by no means satisfied with the modest proposals" and "[w]ith that indomitable 'pluck' for which he was famous" pressed for "a really national memorial."[27] The committee therefore resolved in June 1875 to use any money left over after the slab had been installed to place "a statue, or bust of Byron" in "some public place in London," and to make "a further and more earnest appeal" to the public for that purpose.[28] Not everyone liked the idea of a marble slab in the church where Byron was buried: the architects who had recently restored the building thought the slab would be impractical, and Edward John Trelawny called it "a bauble" (he advocated making a copy of Thorwaldsen's statue in bronze instead).[29] Most importantly, Lady Anne Blunt, Byron's granddaughter, wrote to Disraeli to say that the simple monument placed on Byron's grave still seemed sufficient to his family, and that "it is not for the public which denied a worthier grave to take now, after 50 years, unasking, from his family the guardianship of their dead."[30]

The guardianship of their dead was not wrested from the family's control, but the stewardship of Byron's memory certainly was. At a public meeting held on 16 July 1875 to raise subscriptions, Earl Stanhope opined that "no monument in a remote and small village church could be appropriately described as a national memorial to the Poet."[31] The inscribed slab, which would have required a description of Byron's achievements that was bound to be contentious, was dropped in favor of a statue that would represent Byron without comment, and the idea gradually took hold that Byron was the property of the nation and that his memorial was to be a "really national" undertaking. Writing to *The Standard* in April 1875, Edgcumbe explained he could have raised sufficient funds for a memorial from private donors (as Hobhouse had done for Thorwaldsen's statue), "but the committee are of the opinion that such tribute should be national in every sense of the word, and that it should be in the power of every Englishman to take part in the work of doing honour to the poets of his country."[32] By December, a meeting had been arranged in Manchester "for the purpose of promoting a Local Subscription in aid of the proposed National Memorial of Lord Byron," and Edgcumbe reported to Disraeli that similar meetings were planned in Edinburgh, Aberdeen, Plymouth, Liverpool, and Birmingham, in the hope of "making the memorial in every sense national."[33] Like the Scott Monument discussed in the last chapter, then, the Byron memorial involved coordinating fundraising efforts across different cities and classes. *The Standard* imagined Byron's memorial as a source of national consensus, predicting that "the nation will act in the matter, as becomes it, unanimously."[34]

Creating a national memorial meant appealing to an idea of Englishness. A *Times* editorial in May 1875 looked forward to the day "when England shall at last possess some national monument of Byron."[35] When Disraeli addressed the public meeting, he called Byron "one of the greatest of England's sons" and envisaged the monument as "a national expression of admiration and gratitude."[36] The Earl of Rosslyn picked up the theme when he said that if they failed to commemorate Byron "they, as Englishmen, would be doing an injustice to their own feelings and to their national character," and William Michael Rossetti wrote in *The Academy* that it was "a burning shame to the English people" that Byron had no "public monumental recognition."[37] By the time the committee took out a paid advertisement in *The Times* listing subscriptions received, it seemed natural that it should be headed "The National Byron Memorial."[38]

In his effort to establish Byron's commemoration as a matter of civic pride, Edgcumbe assiduously associated his undertaking with the individuals and institutions of the British establishment. The committee he assembled included literary men (such as Tennyson, Arnold, and Wilkie Collins), associates of Byron (including his son-in-law Lord Lovelace, Trelawny, and Murray), aristocrats, churchmen, and such civic notables as the mayor of Nottingham. The public meeting that opened the subscription took place at Willis's Rooms on St. James's Street, a stone's throw from Byron's publisher. Willis's Rooms had previously been Almack's, one of Regency London's most prestigious social gathering places, and so the venue connected the meeting to Byron's years of fame, as well as to a number of worthy civic and political enterprises that had begun life under Willis's roof.[39] Five years before, Willis's Rooms had held a "Waverley Ball" on the centenary of Scott's birth.[40] The committee held an open competition and exhibited the entries in 1876 in the South Kensington Museum (renamed the Victoria and Albert Museum in 1899). However, the committee judged that none of the entries was up to standard, and they reopened the competition, holding another exhibition the following year at the Royal Albert Hall. Holding exhibitions in these buildings forged additional links between the Byron memorial and the institutions of the British establishment.[41]

Edgcumbe's biggest success in this respect was to involve Benjamin Disraeli, then in his second term as prime minister, who took time out of "a busy and an urgent" life (in his words) to chair the public meeting.[42] Writing to Disraeli's private secretary, Edgcumbe was in no doubt that "The *presence of Mr Disraeli* will undoubtedly put the seal upon our endeavour," stressing that "the absence of Mr Disraeli would ruin our chances of success" and reiterating that "I consider that his name [...] is absolutely necessary to success."[43] In his vote of thanks to the prime minister, Earl Stanhope said "[t]hat he should have withdrawn himself for a brief interval from the anxious affairs of State, and from his arduous and continuous labours in the House of Commons was in itself no slight tribute to the genius of Byron."[44] This simultaneously expressed gratitude for Disraeli's condescending to pay heed to Byron and asserted that the national Byron memorial was on a par with the affairs of state that usually absorbed his attention. Raising a memorial to Byron, Stanhope suggested, *was* an affair of state, worthy of the prime minister's support and that of every Englishman.

Disraeli was a significant asset to the committee because he embodied exactly the kind of transformation they hoped to bring about. The ultimate outsider-turned-insider, Disraeli had risen from social, racial, and religious marginalization to the height of power. In the process, he had been instrumental in reshaping the nation's membership, most notably when, in his first term as prime minister, he steered the Reform Act of 1867 through Parliament. Having idolized and emulated Byron in his youth, Disraeli had shown how a Byronic outsider could become an esteemed Victorian. And if Victorian society had embraced, even tentatively, such a formerly Byronic figure as Disraeli, could it not posthumously embrace Byron himself? Paul Smith has described Disraeli's "task of integrating what he described as his 'continental' and 'revolutionary' mind into his English environment in a way which would enable him to achieve not a mere passive assimilation but the pinnacle of power."[45] The committee's task on Byron's behalf was comparable: to integrate the expatriate, irreligious poet into a place—and an exalted one—in the British pantheon. In the process, they would have to rethink the pantheon in order to allow it to accommodate him. That process was not only analogous to the reimagining of the nation that accompanied political Reform: it was part of it.

Expropriating Byron from his family and entrusting him to the nation also meant extricating him from the care of women and returning him to the

company of men. In her letter to Disraeli, Anne Blunt, Byron's granddaughter, wrote that Byron's grave marker was placed by "his sister, Mrs Leigh, and
his friend, Mr Hobhouse." But in the public meeting, George Sala referred
to it as "the touching memorial which Mrs Leigh had, out of her sisterly
affection, caused to be erected."[46] By eliding Hobhouse's contribution, Sala
represented the memorial as the product of feminized domestic emotions.
This effectively set up an opposition between two mutually exclusive spheres
of commemorative practice, indexed to two gendered spheres of social life.
The existing grave marker was imagined as private, domestic, and provincial.
Placed by one female relative and defended by another, it belonged in a feminized realm of familial cares. That domestic sphere was uncomfortably close
to the scandalous private life "exposed" by Lady Byron in conversations with
Harriet Beecher Stowe. The proposed statue, in contrast, was public, national,
and metropolitan, and therefore it appeared as men's business. Although *The
Times* reported that "many ladies were present" at the public meeting, and a
number subscribed, none of them spoke in support of the statue, which was
now understood as the civic duty of men. Commemorating the poet was no
longer motivated primarily by a feminine affection for Byron, but by a masculine concern for patriotism and justice. (Similarly, the Scott Monument had
been inaugurated with a dinner attended by five hundred men but no women.)

Memorializing Byron in this way inevitably entailed foregrounding aspects
of his life and work that seemed to be worth remembering, while sidelining
aspects that seemed to be best forgotten. We can trace these strategies of
selective forgetting by examining the designs that the committee rejected.
The sketch models that were exhibited have not survived, but a catalog of the
second exhibition was published and the press reported what some of the
entries looked like.[47] *The Times* "express[ed] astonishment at the general weak-
ness and melodramatic extravagance":

> In some he has the air and address of a Greek brigand; or, as a fierce free-
> booter, he stamps his foot on a pile of volumes, which the artist explains
> are his "literary adversaries, the reviewers, while he stands inspired among
> the classic ruins he has so nobly described." In another guise, he is in full
> Court dress, perched on the top of a portico of columns, or, with dishev-
> elled hair, he stands on the top of the Choragic Monument of Lysicrates,
> which the artist suggests might have the intercolumnar spaces filled with
> bas reliefs of his principal characters. In another he stands on a huge ped-
> estal, with bronze figures in the round, really very cleverly modelled if they
> were for chimney ornaments, of an angel branding Cain on the forehead,
> the Prisoner of Chillon, Sardanapalus, and Haidee, at the four faces of the
> pedestal.[48]

The problem with all these designs is that they represent Byron either *with* his characters or *as* his characters.[49] To show him as "a Greek brigand," as "a fierce freebooter," or "with dishevelled hair" would recall the outcast heroes of his tales, introducing an unwelcome reminder of Byron's fascination with the margins of society, when the monument should introduce him to the polite company of the canon. To show him stamping on "his literary adversaries, the reviewers" or to include an image of Cain would rekindle controversies surrounding his works, when the monument should move Byron beyond controversy. To show Haidee would evoke *Don Juan*'s offenses against good taste, when the monument should be tasteful. Indeed, the monument's task was to move beyond any specific engagement with Byron's works at all and toward a vague, generalized appreciation of his merits. Only one of Byron's poems could be safely invoked. Throughout the debate surrounding his monument, Byron's supporters called him "the author of *Childe Harold*," and the only statue in the first exhibition that *The Times* endorsed followed Thorwaldsen in drawing on the landscape of *Childe Harold's Pilgrimage*, by showing Byron "leaning with his right elbow on a broken column."[50] In the second exhibition, of the nine entries that were accompanied by epigraphs, five quoted from *Childe Harold*, including Richard Belt's winning entry.[51] The statues by both Thorwaldsen and Belt are careful to disassociate Byron from most of his poetry by selectively forgetting elements of his oeuvre.

While Belt's design sought to distance itself from questionable aspects of Byron's work, it also sought to associate itself with existing monuments in the national pantheon. The Scott Monument provided the obvious model for a truly national literary monument, and Alfred Austin wrote to *The Times* suggesting that "a memorial rivalling in pomp and beauty that of Scott at Edinburgh" would be suitable for Byron.[52] Belt's statue of Byron closely resembled Steell's of Scott; both figures are seated on a rock, holding books, wearing a somewhat stylized version of contemporary dress, with cloaks (Scott's wrapped around him and Byron's lying beside him), and accompanied by dogs, each of whom sits at his master's right hand and looks up at him (fig. 21). An ornamental canopy for the Byron statue was initially proposed, but the idea was abandoned after a canopy, influenced by that of the Scott Monument but much grander, was erected for the Albert Memorial in 1872 (before Albert's statue was installed in 1875).

The similarities between Byron's and Scott's statues invited those viewers who could parse the allusions to distinguish themselves from those who saw only generic props and costume. More importantly, they positioned Byron and Scott as focal points within a British national identity that, as Linda Colley argues, was still less than a century old. Byron's statue in London evoked Scott's in Edinburgh, positioning him as an English bard comparable to the

FIGURE 21. Statue of Byron by R. C. Belt, Hyde Park, London.
Photo by the author.

Scottish writer who had done so much to forge the identity of Scotland as
both a distinctive ancient nation and a part of the modern British state. (The
rejected design for a Byron memorial based on the Choragic Monument of
Lysicrates would have produced a similar effect by invoking the Burns Monument in Edinburgh, which was based on the same Greek model.) Colley argues
that a British national identity was overlaid on existing allegiances, so that it
was possible to identify as Scottish or English and British simultaneously.[53]

The statues of Byron and Scott materialize that understanding by celebrating two recently deceased writers, in two capital cities, who are at once focuses for English and Scottish sentiments and poles structuring a British pantheon extending from one end of the island to the other and constructing that island as a unified nation at the center of a worldwide empire. The pantheonic network was complicated not only by Byron's Scottish ancestry and upbringing but also by the way in which the literary pantheon was embedded within a more general one. The Albert Memorial and the Byron monument, constructed almost contemporaneously, both drew on elements of the Scott monument in their designs, somewhat blurring the "twinning" effect that Belt may have hoped to achieve.

The need to embed a literary pantheon within a more general one also influenced the statue's final location in London's Hyde Park. As with the Thorwaldsen statue in the library of Trinity College and the Scott Monument in Princes Street Gardens, this monument's location is essential to understanding its meaning. As early as 1858, *The Times*, discussing a statue of Edward Jenner, had insisted on the importance of placing statues in an appropriate relation to each other. While medical men were deserving of statues, "we would not see them placed in ridiculous juxtaposition with men whose careers and merits were entirely different from their own" because "certainly it cannot be desirable to group together inconsistent figures."[54] The committee first wanted to put the Byron statue in Green Park, but the Queen denied permission to do so.[55] Next, they considered a site at the bottom of St. James's Street, while Disraeli suggested a site at the top of the street, on Piccadilly.[56] The local Parish Church Council denied this site on the grounds that it would narrow the roadway.[57] The committee also talked about the Embankment and Holles Street (Byron's birthplace), but rejected these sites as respectively "prosaic" and "inconvenient."[58] The statue was finally erected in Hamilton Gardens, near Hyde Park Corner, in 1880.[59] This location was significant, because it placed Byron in close proximity to the fountain endowed by Marian Mangan Brown, designed by Thomas Thornycroft, and installed in 1875 (fig. 22). This fountain was twenty-four feet high and featured marble statues of Chaucer, Shakespeare, and Milton, as well as bronze figures of the muses of Tragedy, History, and Comedy.[60] The Byron statue was installed less than five hundred feet from the poetry fountain, and each was visible from the other. The same Red Mansfield stone was used for the base of both. Placing Byron close to this recently unveiled monument helped to extend its cluster of poetic giants into modern times.

If Britain was becoming a large-scale, distributed version of the pantheon that was once imagined in Westminster Abbey, it now had two Poets' Corners. One, as I showed in the last chapter, occupied the area around

FIGURE 22. The Poetry Fountain, designed by Thomas Thornycroft, National Archives. Unknown photographer, 1928. The National Archives, ref. Work 20/189.

Princes Street Gardens in Edinburgh; the other occupied the east side of Hyde Park in London. And like the original Poets' Corner, both of these were constructed not by a long tradition of commemorating recently deceased poets but by a fairly rapid sequence of retrospective installations. Baedeker's 1885 guide to London directed Hyde Park's visitors to the "handsome *Fountain* by Thornycroft, adorned with figures of Tragedy, Comedy, Poetry [*sic*], Shakspeare [*sic*], Chaucer, and Milton, and surmounted by a statue of Fame. In Hamilton Gardens, a little further to the S[outh]," the guide continued, "is a statue of *Lord Byron*."[61] Similarly, Baedeker's 1887 guide to Edinburgh situates the Scott Monument in relation to surrounding statues: "To the E[ast] of the Scott Monument is a statue of *Livingstone* (d. 1873), the African traveller; to the W[est] are statues of *Adam Black*, a prominent citizen, and *John Wilson*."[62] In both cases, Baedeker invites the tourist to experience Hyde Park or Princes Street Gardens as a gallery of statues to great men. Byron is only a short walk from Shakespeare, Chaucer, and Milton, and Scott is buttressed by his prominent countrymen.

But Belt's statue had closer, and more problematic, neighbors (fig. 23). It faced the enormous statue of Achilles by Sir Richard Westmacott, erected in 1822 to honor the Duke of Wellington; it was close to Apsley House, the duke's home until his death in 1852, and not far from the massive equestrian statue

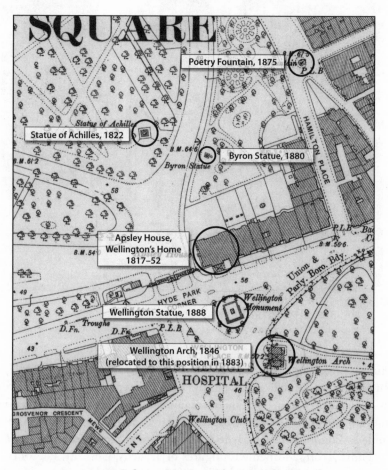

FIGURE 23. Ordnance Survey map showing the location of monuments around Hyde Park Corner, 1894. Reproduced by permission of the National Library of Scotland.

of the duke by Matthew Cotes Wyatt, erected atop a triumphal arch in 1846.[63] Hyde Park Corner was definitely Wellington's turf. Like the ironic proximity of Thorwaldsen's statue to a stained-glass George III in Cambridge, the proximity of Belt's Byron to these tributes to Wellington helped to neutralize Byron's oppositional politics, divert attention from his attacks on Wellington as "the best of cut-throats" in Don Juan (9.4), and soft-pedal his enthusiasm for Wellington's enemy Napoleon. Byron and Wellington both appeared as great Englishmen who deserved statues in London. (Similarly, Wellington's statue in Edinburgh was placed a short walk from Scott's monument.) If the proximity of Byron's statue to Chaucer, Shakespeare, and Milton presented him as a poet of comparable aesthetic merit, its proximity to Wellington promoted cultural consensus by presenting both men as occupying equivalent positions in the national pantheon. The original significance of the statue's location has been blurred by the fact that both Thornycroft's fountain and Wyatt's equestrian statue have subsequently been removed, although the choice of Hyde Park as the site of the Diana, Princess of Wales memorial fountain (opened in 2004), and the memorial to those killed in the London bombings of 7 July 2005 (opened in 2009) suggests its continuing importance as a location for British memorials.

Imagining Hyde Park as a space of memorial consensus meant forgetting that within recent memory it had been a flashpoint of political contention. The Hyde Park riots of July 1866 had been an expression of popular frustration at the failure of the 1866 Reform Bill, which caused the Liberal government to fall.[64] This opened the way for a minority Conservative government, led by Disraeli, to engineer the passage of the Reform Act of 1867, doubling the size of the electorate. When Disraeli, one of the Reformers' most influential political allies, supported the commemoration of Byron, one of the Reformers' most admired poets, in Hyde Park, site of one of the Reformers' most important London demonstrations, it must have reminded Britons how divided the nation had been. The statue's supporters hoped it would also reassure them that such upheavals were a thing of the past. Britons could now accept that both Wellington and Byron should be represented in the national pantheon, despite their political differences, just as Wellington's High Tory followers and Byron's Chartist readers could both be represented in Parliament. That consensus relied on and promoted a strategically vague idea of British greatness, which was celebrated and given shape through the construction of secular pantheons for the Reformed nation.

While the pantheon moved outward from Westminster Abbey, St. Paul's Cathedral, or Trinity College to the parks, streets, and squares of Britain's cities, it also moved inward to the nation's domestic interiors, where it was recreated in miniature. Many of the individuals commemorated in statues, monuments, or plaques were also represented in collectable figurines and busts. A number of collectable figures of Byron and Scott were produced in Staffordshire pottery, Parian (a highly finished kind of porcelain developed in the 1840s, which resembled marble), and spelter (an affordable alternative to bronze) (figs. 24, 25).[65]

FIGURE 24. Parian bust of Byron, produced by Robinson and Leadbeater, c. 1870–85. Reproduced by permission of the Byron Society Collection, Special Collections and Archives, Drew University Library.

FIGURE 25. Parian bust of Scott, unknown producer, c. 1865–80. Reproduced by permission of the Byron Society Collection, Special Collections and Archives, Drew University Library.

They included busts and full-length figures, both of which were sometimes derived from existing statues of the poets (fig. 26). These artifacts were often marketed in pairs or groups for display on mantelpieces or in domestic interiors. Byron was often paired with the "Maid of Athens," and Scott with Robert Burns, and both appeared alongside nonliterary figures such as Wellington and Nelson.[66] Byron and Scott were also routinely paired with each other, and Robert Copeland's catalog of Parian figures listed several different sized busts of Scott "to match Byron."[67] When T. S. Eliot wrote, "I have always seen, or imagined that I saw, in busts of [Byron and Scott], a certain resemblance in the shape of the head," he was recalling this convention of pairing authors' busts.[68]

Displaying Byron and Scott as a pair of poets, including them in a private collection of busts or figurines, or reading their names in a potter's catalog were ways of reiterating the construction of distributed, secular pantheons in London and Edinburgh. Busts of Wordsworth, Shelley, Goethe, and Thomas Moore—as well as of older poets like Shakespeare and Dante and modern poets like Tennyson and Browning—were also produced.[69] Female poets, however, tend to be underrepresented.

FIGURE 26. Porcelain statuette
of Byron based on Thorwaldsen
statue, Copenhagen: Kongelige
Porcelainsfabrik, c. 1835.
Reproduced by permission of the Byron
Society Collection, Special Collections
and Archives, Drew University Library.

The miniature pantheons constituted by potters' catalogs and materialized in private collections, well-appointed private libraries, and tastefully decorated drawing rooms offered what Rohan McWilliam calls "a form of consensus building" producing "kinds of cultural integration."[70] Displayed in the rooms of the house where guests were received, these artifacts occupied liminal sites between public and private that offered a space in which to construct and exhibit one's identity, even if what to display and where was also sometimes a source of disagreement among the members of the household. The subjectivity displayed on the mantelpiece was relationally derived: family portraits indicated connections to the family, a picture of the Queen or a souvenir of the Great Exhibition signaled membership of the nation, and an author's bust or a reproductive print referred to the shared experience of literature or art. The objects on the mantelpiece reflected back the identities of their owners, much as the mirrors often placed above the mantelpiece reflected back their image.

A key rhetorical aim of the sculpted pantheon had been to move its inhabitants beyond the realm of commerce, just as the plaques put up in London had to distinguish themselves from advertisements. But when the pantheon was reiterated in the domestic interior (or, as we saw in the last chapter, in postcards and silverware), it was also reconciled to commerce. Purchasing a figurine of a canonical individual was a way for citizens to indicate, through consumption, that they concurred in the national consensus: a way to bring one's own desire into conformity with the national self-image and to turn one's private, domestic space into a miniaturized version of public, civic, or institutional space. The sense of belonging to a public that could be obtained by contributing to a subscription fund for a public statue (and seeing one's name in a socially stratified subscription list) was here transformed into a reason for purchasing a commodity, literally buying into the consensus. Images of Byron and Scott had been placed at either end of Victorian Britain; by also placing them at either end of Victorian mantelpieces, individuals could proclaim their membership of a nation with a shared pantheon of heroes. These were the kind of belongings that signified belonging.

Efforts to raise memorials to Scott and Byron brought to light problems with the eighteenth-century conception of a national pantheon, and helped to shape a new version of the pantheon, with its own monumental sites and forms, which contributed to a new understanding of the national identity. As I've presented it in this part of the book, the new pantheon was characterized by six key attributes. First, it was liberal. It could include figures with opposed political outlooks, such as Byron and Scott, and even place them in close proximity—for example, when Byron appeared close to Wellington or George III, and Scott appeared close to the political martyrs of 1794. Second, it was secular. It was not located in a house of worship, and so it could include people of different denominations, as well as those like Byron whose conduct and beliefs seemed questionable. Third, it was distributed across the country. Initially conceived as a single structure and connected to the buildings of the British establishment, by the end of the century it was an imaginative construct reiterated in the municipal spaces of city streets and parks, in the institutional spaces of Trinity College or St. Paul's, in the popular, commercial spaces of waxwork galleries, in the domestic spaces of houses decorated with figurines or busts, and among individuals' personal possessions. Fourth, it was networked. Individual monuments took on significance in relation to other monuments locally, nationally, and even internationally. They became nodes in a pantheonic network that recalibrated the nation's imaginative geography. Fifth, it was nondiscursive. Rather than offering readings of Byron or Scott, their monuments offered ways *not* to read them. For all the commentary that surrounded them in pamphlets and newspapers, the statues and figurines were fundamentally antitextual. They provided nondiscursive ways of encountering their subjects, which avoided the requirement to enter a debate whose language risked becoming contentious. And finally, it was iterable across media. Statues of Byron and Scott were reproduced in photographs, postcards, and engravings as well as in Parian, spelter, pottery, and silverware. The drive to memorialize them unfolded alongside the process of canonization found in editions of their works, but it was also folded into them—for example, when an engraving of Poets' Corner appeared as the frontispiece to an anthology produced under the direction of the Society for the Promotion of Christian Knowledge in 1833, when Thorwaldsen's statue was engraved for the frontispiece of Matthew Arnold's selected edition of Byron's poems in 1881, or when a photograph of the Scott Monument was used to illustrate an edition of Lockhart's memoir in 1901.[71]

The new kind of secular pantheon gained its cultural significance by aiming to banish contention and celebrate individuals whose merits were a matter of common consensus. The silence of a sculpted pantheon simulated the cultural consensus that it claimed to represent, and by doing so helped to bring it about. It imagined a nation that could include Tories, Whigs, and radicals, Anglicans, dissenters, and deists. It served an electorate who passed statues of their heroes on the way to work, rather than visiting them in special shrines. It offered citizens ways to buy into the pantheon, by owning representations of its heroes and their monuments. Functioning as a *lieu de mémoire* unconfined by a particular location or medium, the pantheon gave material existence, in the present, to the past shared by the newly enfranchised subjects of a Reformed nation that not only had to legislate itself into existence but also had to imagine itself into being.

PART V

Anthologies

13

Scattered Odes in Shattered Books

QUANTIFYING VICTORIAN ANTHOLOGIES

ONE WARM evening in the 1890s, a young man and a young woman sat down together in the shade of the trees at the bottom of a garden in an English village and read poems to one another. Shaping their relationship through the shared experience of literature, they were reenacting a scene of reading repeatedly depicted in poetry, from Dante's *Inferno* to Hunt's *The Story of Rimini*. We don't know if their reading had the erotic charge of Paolo and Francesca's, or even if they knew about their ill-fated poetic predecessors. Neither Willie, an apprentice carpenter, nor his friend Laura, a post office worker, had more than the most basic formal education, and they owned no more than a handful of books between them. But Willie did own an anthology of poetry, so that was what they read. There were probably many scenes of reading similar to this, across the country and across the century, that left no historical trace. This one survives because it was recorded in Flora Thompson's slightly fictionalized memoir of village life, *Candleford Green* (1943), part of her trilogy *Lark Rise to Candleford* (1945). Laura is Thompson's alter ego:

> Willie was fond of reading too, and did not object to poetry. Somehow he had got possession of an old shattered copy of an anthology called *A Thousand and One Gems*, [...] and after office hours Laura and he would sit among the nut-trees at the bottom of the garden and take turns at reading aloud from it.
>
> Those were the days for Laura when almost everything in literature was new to her and every fresh discovery was like one of Keats's own *Magic casements opening on the foam*. Between the shabby old covers of that one book were the "Ode to a Nightingale", Shelley's "Skylark", Wordsworth's "Ode to Duty", and other gems which could move to a heart-shaking rapture.[1]

Anthologies, as this passage indicates, were very widely read, even—perhaps especially—among those who had access to very few books. Anthologies were

assigned in classrooms, given as school prizes, used for elocution manuals, pen-
manship practice, and preparation for public examinations. They structured
the leisure of many nineteenth-century readers looking for pleasure or self-
improvement, and embedded literary works in the educational institutions
that produced a new class of civic and imperial administrator. As the new time
of modernity took hold, leisure emerged as a distinct kind of time that was
defined as not being work, but that had to leave you refreshed to return to
work. Anthologies became the delivery system for literary leisure in capitalist
modernity, injecting bite-sized chunks of culture into the intervals of a life
of labor. Francis Turner Palgrave imagined his *Golden Treasury* being picked
up in "the scanty hours that most men spare for self-improvement."[2] But in
Thompson's description, the book's superior contents are at odds with its
inferior form, which is "old," "shabby," and "shattered." Anthologies were often
thought of as books for amateurs and tyros, who skipped and dipped and were
disproportionately female, as opposed to serious readers, by implication male,
who immersed themselves in collected editions. They often targeted lower-
class audiences, offering what Palgrave called "a storehouse of delight to Labour
and to Poverty."[3] Offering the choicest poetry in the cheapest formats, anthologies circulated the most refined thoughts to the most unrefined readers.

Thompson's description also hints at how anthologies affected the reception of their contents. Obviously the anthologist's choices determined what
the anthology's readers read. But the anthology's paratexts also shaped how
the poems it contained were read. In this passage, the word "gems," which the
anthology uses in its title, quietly becomes Thompson's own in the following
paragraph. Her description of the poems that were held in "that one book"
endorses the anthology's self-depiction as a casket of jewels overflowing with
treasure, a magic box containing multitudes, a window onto an undreamt-of
world. In reading the anthology, Laura is learning not only how to enjoy literature but also how to deploy it. Describing her anthology reading, she elevates
her diction into a lyrical mode ("a heart-shaking rapture") and freely quotes
Keats's "Ode to a Nightingale" to make her point. Thompson's description of
Laura's rapturous awakening to the power of poetry is modeled on Keats's
description of his own rapture in "On First Looking into Chapman's Homer,"
which also appeared in Willie's anthology.[4] Both Keats in "Chapman's Homer"
and Laura here (through Keats) present themselves standing on the edge of
literature's unexplored ocean, with an exhilarated sense of potential. But both
of them also foreground the channel through which literature is mediated to
them: Chapman's translation, Willie's "shattered" anthology.

The anthology Willie owned was *A Thousand and One Gems of English
Poetry*, edited by Charles Mackay, which first appeared in 1867 and went
through twenty-three editions by the end of the century.[5] It aimed, in

Mackay's words, "to present one great panoramic view of the masterpieces of English poetry [. . .] in a form and at a price which would recommend it to the taste of the rich, without placing it beyond the means of the poor."[6] Its depiction of poems as gems—small, attractive, and timelessly valuable— was a common trope among nineteenth-century literary anthologies.[7] I have counted over thirty with the word "gems" in the title. It suggests the premium placed on short forms in the anthologies, and their dedication to lyrics above all. This raises a problem for the anthologies' handling of Romantic poetry, since many of the most famous Romantic poems are long, narrative, or even epic. How would a collection of poetic "gems" find room for such Romantic poems as *The Prelude*? What about *The Excursion, The White Doe of Rylstone, The Ancient Mariner, Thalaba the Destroyer, The Curse of Kehama, The Lay of the Last Minstrel, Marmion, Queen Mab, Alastor, Prometheus Unbound, Childe Harold's Pilgrimage, The Corsair, Don Juan, The Eve of St. Agnes, Lamia, The Forest Sanctuary, The Siege of Valencia, The Improvisatrice,* or *The Story of Rimini?* The problem here was not thematic but pragmatic. Even if the subjects and ideas of Romantic poetry continued to appeal to Victorian readers, there was a mismatch between the formats in which that poetry originally appeared— usually as individual poetry volumes—and the formats in which poetry from earlier periods mostly circulated to wide audiences in the later nine- teenth century—in various kinds of anthologies. To handle this mismatch, nineteenth-century anthologies functioned like "magic casements opening on the foam": they offered a portal to the oceanic breadth of Romantic poetry, while also framing and limiting the reader's view of it.

In this final section of the book, I argue that poems by Byron, Hemans, and Shelley were made to conform to the format of the anthology, and that their oeuvres and their reputations were reshaped for Victorian readers as a result. To make this argument, I employ some quantitative data about Victorian antholo- gies. In this chapter, I explain how I gathered those data and discuss the advan- tages and limitations of this approach. In the following chapters, I identify the most commonly anthologized short poems by Byron, Hemans, and Shelley, show how anthologies abridged or excerpted their long poems, and explore how these choices changed over time. Overall, I suggest that by selecting and reprinting in these ways, anthologies reshaped Victorian readers' experience of Romantic poetry, naturalized Romantic poems in the Victorian anthology, suppressed material that might offend Victorian sensibilities, elided or neu- tralized political content, and fostered ways of encountering and responding to Romantic poetry that ramified in the new media ecology more generally.

Anthologies had this impact because they were (and are) privileged sites of reading, capable of producing interpretive effects felt far beyond their pages. Their authority was compounded by the educational settings in which they were often assigned as set texts and reinforced when people like Willie and Laura used them for recitation or shared reading.[8] Partly as a result of their connections with education, recitation, and shared reading, many anthologies circulated more widely than single-author volumes.[9] The fact that readers typically encountered anthologies early and in educational settings gave these books a disproportionate power to shape canons, construct publics, and form reading habits that extended to other books. Anthologies defined canons of literature with embedded gendered assumptions, as Margaret Ezell has documented.[10] They constructed literary fame, as Anne Ferry argues, rather than reflecting it, and fostered the authority of individuals, rather than dissipating it.[11] They brought into being the reading publics they ostensibly served, as Leah Price and Barbara Benedict both suggest.[12] They played a formative role in the emergence of English literature as an academic discipline, as Laura Mandell claims.[13] In all these ways, anthologies fostered readerly assumptions that carried over to other books, producing what Stefanie Lethbridge calls "anthological reading habits": approaches to literature learned from the anthologies that treated long poems and novels as though they were anthologies of shorter passages that could be dipped into at will.[14] To examine the anthologies' mediation of Romantic poetry, then, is not only to reveal strategies internal to the anthology but also to identify approaches to Romantic poetry that resonated throughout nineteenth-century culture.

As I suggest at the end of chapter 15, the anthology's power as a mediator was as ambiguous as it was extensive. Anthologies could promote certain kinds of response to Romantic poetry and discourage other kinds, but they could not enforce their preferences. Not every purchaser of an anthology read every poem it contained, few readers encountered poetry exclusively through the medium of anthologies, and no one reader looked at all the anthologies I have surveyed. When I refer to "readers of anthologies," then, I am not conjuring up imaginary individuals who read anthologies from cover to cover and read nothing else. Instead, I intend to invoke the power of anthologies to shape how their readers read, including how they read books apart from anthologies. This power, I conclude, was at once pervasive and unstable. While the processes of selecting, abridging, excerpting, framing, and mediating employed in the anthologies had significant impact on the experiences of many readers, the anthologies could not always produce the effects their compilers desired.

Romantic poetry occupies a special place in the history of anthologies as a publishing form, as well as a special place in the Victorian anthology's pages. The few literary historians who have attended to the anthology make the Romantic period a hinge in the anthology's history. Broadly speaking, the period witnessed a shift from eighteenth-century miscellanies, which acted as focal points for communities of readers who were also contributors, to nineteenth-century anthologies, which were commercial products reprinting previously published texts, constructed by publishers to target consumers. Some Romantic writers were directly or tangentially involved in these developments. Walter Scott collected and edited *Minstrelsy of the Scottish Border* (1802–3). Byron contributed nine poems to John Cam Hobhouse's miscellany of original and translated poetry (1809).[15] Anna Barbauld edited *The Female Speaker*, an 1811 anthology for girls. Southey edited the short-lived *Annual Anthology* (1799) and collaborated with Coleridge on *Omniana* (1812), a collection of miscellaneous notes and essayistic fragments.[16] Leigh Hunt, William Hazlitt, and Charles Lamb all edited anthologies. Once this generic shift from miscellanies to anthologies played out, the new genre of the modern anthology diversified into multiple overlapping subgenres aimed at a variety of audiences. In the process, anthologies emerged as a powerful tool for classifying, glossing, repackaging, redacting, and understanding the writing of the past.

Anthologies constitute a distinct reception tradition. They are far from unanimous in their approach to Romantic poetry—remember Alasdair MacIntyre's already-quoted assertion that traditions "embody continuities of conflict."[17] But because later compilers often consulted earlier anthologies when making their selections, they sustained a self-referential tradition with a surprising level of consensus. This tradition, like the tradition of sermons discussed in part 3, had its own favorite bits of Romantic poetry, and it recalled those bits to serve its own agenda. When Stephen Gill claims that anthologies "were offshoots of the work of construction already taking place and they ministered to received notions" about Wordsworth's poetry, he suggests that anthologies reflected a reception history unfolding somewhere else, rather than producing one of their own.[18] By contrast, I contend that anthologies are an important and distinctive site of reception, with a sometimes conflicted relationship to other reception traditions. In particular, the anthology tradition sits awkwardly alongside the tradition of academic literary criticism. As Leah Price notes, "extracts underwrite the discipline of literary criticism as we know it," but "the anthologies which provide a vehicle for literary history have rarely become its object."[19] The two traditions took on their modern form at roughly the same time in the early nineteenth century and became intertwined without merging together. Anthologies remain central to the university teaching of literature, but while we rely on them for undergraduate teaching, we expect our graduate students to graduate from anthologies to scholarly editions of an author's collected works. This divided attitude toward anthologies reflects an underlying division in the professional identity of literary scholars as, on one hand, guardians and curators of our written heritage and, on the other, producers of new knowledge about it. These factors make anthologies a particularly fraught example of the multiple intersecting traditions that make up the web of reception.

This chapter and the following two base their arguments on a larger corpus of anthologies than any previously examined, and investigate this corpus in more detail than any existing study. Although anthologies have received some scholarly attention at least since Richard Altick's pathbreaking book *The English Common Reader* (1957), the number of anthologies discussed is often small.[20] In William St. Clair's *The Reading Nation in the Romantic Period*, the appendix "Romantic Poets in Victorian Times" lists only five anthologies.[21] Ian Michael's *The Teaching of English* (1987) offers the most comprehensive quantitative study of anthologies to date, focusing on a sample of 114 classroom anthologies from the nineteenth century. However, Michael restricts his analysis to counting which poets appeared in the anthologies, arguing that "any analysis of the anthologies must be confined to their superficial aspects"; while he offers some basic statistical comparisons, he is reluctant to "press [his] figures very far."[22] Michael's approach can tell us which poets featured most commonly in nineteenth-century anthologies, then, but it cannot tell us anything about which poems were included, or which sections of long poems, or how the anthologies shaped the reception of those poems.

Using the British Library catalog as a starting point, I identified a corpus of 210 literary anthologies published in Britain between 1822 (when Shelley died) and the end of the century.[23] The subgenres of anthologies, textbooks, readers, and books of quotations were not as clearly defined in the nineteenth century as they are now. Many anthologies did not include the word "anthology" in the title and some books that modern readers would not recognize as anthologies, such as collections of very short quotations, did. I identified a set of keywords often used in anthology titles, such as "Library," "Cabinet," "Museum," "Treasury," "Garland," "Bouquet," "Casket," and others, and combined these in catalog searches with the keywords "verse," "poet," "poem," "literature," and their cognates. This produced a "long list" of books. I excluded periodical or annual publications, song-books, hymnals, and books of only local interest (such as collections of poems about a particular place). This produced the corpus of 210 anthologies. It includes several different kinds of anthologies, produced in different formats, aimed at different readers and intended for different kinds of use. There are duodecimos and quartos; single- and multivolume works; books aimed at children and adults, men and women; books for recitation, study, self-culture, and pleasure. There were certainly other literary anthologies published in Britain in this seventy-eight-year period, but these books provide a substantial sample.

Having identified the corpus, I examined each of the 210 books, with the help of student assistants, and recorded information about the frontmatter and arrangement of contents, as well as each poem, or extract from a poem, by Lord Byron, Felicia Hemans, or Percy Shelley that appeared in them. Choosing these individuals allows me to trace the figures cut in the anthologies by poets with different reception histories. Byron was enormously popular in his lifetime, but the reputation of at least some of his poems fell with at least some parts of the reading public after his death. Shelley was not read by a wide audience in his lifetime, and his volumes sold in small numbers, but his reputation slowly grew posthumously. Hemans, while never achieving Byron's sales, was sufficiently popular in her lifetime to support herself from her writing and continued to have a strong following among Victorian readers. Examining how these three poets appeared in the anthologies, then, allows comparisons between different trajectories of reception. It also allows us to compare male and female authors, and to limit the primary focus to posthumous reception.

Every time a poem by Byron, Hemans, or Shelley was reprinted in one of the anthologies in the corpus, we recorded whether the poem was complete, and if not, noted the first and last line included. We noted whether the poem's original title was used, or recorded any editorial title given to it. We transcribed any headnote, footnotes, or editorial commentary. We also gathered information on the poem or extract that immediately preceded and followed the one in question. The resulting database is a powerful research tool. It contains details of 210 anthologies, containing 1,055 poems or extracts from Byron, 554 from Hemans, and 402 from Shelley. These data can be queried in sophisticated ways, allowing us to see not just which poets were most commonly anthologized but also which of their poems were most popular, and which sections of long poems were anthologized. It allows us to explore how these selections changed over time, or between anthologies of different lengths, anthologies published in different places, or anthologies that arranged their contents in different ways. It sets the poems, or extracts from poems, in context, showing how the anthologies presented them among other poems, and framed them with headnotes, footnotes, or glosses. The argument I make here does not by any means exhaust the data gathered, but indicates, I hope, how this approach permits an account of the nineteenth-century literary anthology that is at once robust and granular: grounded in a wider range of evidence than existing studies and able to incorporate more relevant detail.[24] This methodology is also transferable; it could be applied to other authors in Britain in this period, or, if a new corpus were identified, in other places and periods.

As it stands, this approach has some limitations. Most seriously, my results take no account of sales figures. Anthologies that fell stillborn from the press are given the same weight as bestsellers. Information on print runs and sales figures for nineteenth-century publications is difficult to obtain. While Richard Altick, William St. Clair, James Raven, and other historians of print culture have compiled some information about print runs for novels and poetry volumes, our knowledge of anthologies' print runs remains very limited.[25] The account books of a few publishers, such as John Murray and Longmans, are well preserved, but most are lost.[26] As a result, it is infeasible to gather data on the print runs or sales figures of all anthologies in the sample. This makes it impossible to "weight" my analysis to account for the relative popularity of different anthologies. Second, the quantitative data gathered from the anthologies need to be triangulated with close readings of both the anthologies' editorial matter and the responses of individual readers, where available, in order to produce a thick description of the cultural work that the anthologies performed. Finally, although the studies of Byron, Hemans, and Shelley presented here yield similar results, suggesting that they offer insights into the anthologies' overall approach to Romantic poetry, it remains difficult to generalize these findings with certainty to other Romantic poets, or poets from earlier periods. More confident generalizations will require further research.

Even with these limitations, though, this method has some advantages. I have chosen it in part because it offers an alternative approach to issues of exemplarity that beset more traditional approaches based on case studies. Historians and literary critics have found the case study to be a powerful tool for linking the small number of texts that can be illuminated in detail to the dark mass of the archive. But as James Chandler impressively shows, this approach raises a variety of methodological concerns.[27] I don't intend to enter into an epistemological debate about exemplarity here, nor to engage with the long history of case-based argument in the tradition of casuistry. Instead, I want simply to note that the quantitative methodology I employ in this part of the book responds to concerns about how one particular thing can be treated as an example, or case, of something more general.

Concerns about exemplarity press on historicist critics who seek to connect texts to a grid of social, historical, and political contexts, which can be recovered from their archival traces. For New Critics explicating the central texts of a stable canon, close reading was an end in itself and the archive's submerged mass was not a pressing concern. The poems on which they focused their attention were "exemplary" only in the sense of being claimed as aesthetically superior. But historicist critics—working with a radically expanded and destabilized canon, and treating texts as embedded in discursive contexts—connect individual texts to the literary, cultural, and historical concerns manifested in broader swathes of archival materials. Their texts and anecdotes are "exemplary" in the sense that they contain in miniature larger cultural formations and structures of power. From an early stage, therefore, New Historicist critics faced questions about the evidentiary value of their examples. Alan Liu, for example, charged in 1989 that "A New Historicist paradigm holds up to view a historical context on one side, a literary text on the other, and, in between, a connection of pure nothing."[28] In a 2005 interview, Stephen Greenblatt described moments of inspiration when "I feel I could run up and down these shelves [. . .] and open books at random and things would jump out at me."[29] New Historicism has sometimes been accused of picking its cases "at random," rather than finding examples that are truly representative of the historical matrix they are supposed to illuminate.

While these questions trouble historicist critics in general, they also concern critics of Romanticism in particular. As Chandler argues, the procedure of making a claim about a large field of knowledge on the basis of minute analysis of particular cases has antecedents in Romantic-period historiography. Romantic authors were self-consciously concerned with whether the characters and situations they represented exemplified the spirit of the age they inhabited. Moreover, they were among the first writers to think in these terms, as the concept of historical situatedness itself became increasingly normalized. Choosing certain texts or authors to serve as examples of Romantic writing, then, or trying to uncover the relationship between Romantic poetry and "history," pitches the critic into a set of debates that already exercised the Romantics.

And if questions of exemplarity concerned Romantic writers, they also exercised the compilers of Victorian anthologies. Their selective procedures inevitably raised questions. Did the poets they included reflect their age? Were the short poems they reprinted good examples of their authors' work? Could the excerpts they made from long poems be taken as representative of those poems as a whole? Or had the extracts been selected precisely because they *differed* from the rest of the long poem, the author's work, or the literature of their age? These concerns were sometimes reflected in anthologies' titles, which presented their contents as "specimens"—or in one case "quiddities"—of literature.[30] What Leah Price calls the anthologies' "synecdochal esthetic" guaranteed that questions about exemplarity would always be present beneath the appeals to consensus they made in their paratexts.[31]

In this part of the book, I examine a number of examples of Romantic poems in Victorian anthologies in detail. But I situate those examples with quantitative evidence drawn from a broad survey of the surviving material. In some respects, adding quantitative data to the evidentiary mix raises the issue of exemplarity to a higher level rather than resolving it. Readers who wondered if the case studies undertaken in other parts of this book were representative of larger archival trends might now ask whether the corpus of anthologies studied here is representative of the total population of nineteenth-century literary anthologies. My claim here is not that numerical evidence is inherently superior or sufficient in itself, but that a broad statistical survey of anthologies can be combined with more familiar kinds of evidence to create a fuller picture of Romantic reception history. Developing a variant on the "distant reading" advocated by Franco Moretti, this approach nonetheless involves careful examination of the volumes in the corpus, attention to textual variants, and close reading of the anthologies' paratexts.[32] It is therefore a contribution to what scholars like Martin Mueller have now begun to call "scalable reading."[33]

Byron, Hemans, and Shelley all commonly appeared in anthologies, although Shelley was not as popular as the other two. Of the 210 books surveyed, Byron's poetry appeared in 134 (64%), Hemans's in 119 (57%), and Shelley's in 81 (39%). This lends support to Ian Michael's claim—based on his "weighted" figures— that Byron is one of the three most popular authors in the nineteenth-century anthology (after Shakespeare and Wordsworth), and Paula Feldman's assertion that, partly because of her inclusion in anthologies, Hemans was "even more widely read in the Victorian era than in the Romantic."[34] Byron's poetry also saturated the anthologies more than Hemans's or Shelley's: a quarter of the books that included some poetry by Byron included ten or more poems, as opposed to 15 percent of books for Hemans and 17 percent for Shelley. Nineteenth-century readers opening anthologies of poetry, then, usually encountered poetry by Byron and Hemans, and often poetry by Shelley as well.

In the next two chapters, I show how the nineteenth-century anthologies offered their readers versions of Byron, Hemans, and Shelley that were distinctive. The anthologies' versions were unlike those offered by the poets' first publications, their posthumously published collected works, their modern scholarly editions, or today's classroom anthologies. The poets of the anthologies were not the poets that we know—not because nineteenth-century anthologies did not include the writers we have come to view as canonical, but because they constructed their own versions of those writers. In some cases the poems they preferred remain central to our understanding of Romanticism; in others they are now often overlooked. "Casabianca" retained its currency into the twentieth century, largely thanks to anthologies, and became a central poem in the academic recovery of Hemans. "The Destruction of Sennacherib," by contrast, lost the currency the nineteenth-century anthology gave it; although it is included in some modern selected editions of Byron's poetry, it is not included in any modern classroom anthology of Romanticism.[35] The anthologies, then, offer their own, still underexamined tradition of reception history, which is distinct from better-known traditions yet intersects with them and shapes them in unacknowledged ways. Flora Thompson's Laura found in Willie's anthology a "magic casement" that opened onto the ocean of literature, but framed and shaped her view of it. I use a quantitative survey of a corpus of anthologies, alongside close readings of some examples, as a similar casement—though not a magic one—that can reveal this history while providing a distinctive new perspective on it.

14

Romantic Short Poems in Victorian Anthologies

WHEN THEY opened their "shattered" anthology, Laura and Willie tended to find short or abridged poems: the longest poem Laura mentions by name is 105 lines long. Victorian anthologies favored lyrics and lyrical passages from longer poems. Anthologists reprinted short poems by Byron, Hemans, and Shelley that neither the poets nor their first critics thought of as highlights of their collected works. When they promoted these previously marginal poems to a central place in their remediation of Romantic poetry, they gave them wider currency than they would otherwise have had. They also framed them with editorial notes that reflected gendered assumptions about the supposed femininity of short poems. Faced with longer poems of several hundred lines, anthologies abridged them—sometimes drastically and usually silently—in order to make them fit into the format of the anthologies and the interpretations of Byron, Hemans, and Shelley that they sponsored. The anthologies' extensive circulation gave their selections and interpretations wide cultural reach.

The passage by Byron the anthologies reprinted most often was the address to the ocean from the conclusion to *Childe Harold's Pilgrimage*. Close behind it in the ranked table (table 1) is "The Destruction of Sennacherib" from *Hebrew Melodies*. "The Destruction of Sennacherib" ("The Assyrian came down like a wolf on the fold") was one of the most popular poems by Byron in the anthologies. This six-quatrain poem appeared thirty-five times in the anthologies surveyed, and was always published in its entirety. This makes it the second most quoted piece of Byron's poetry overall and the poem most often quoted in full. "Sennacherib" is included more than twice as often as the next most popular independent lyric, "On This Day I Complete My Thirty-Sixth Year," and almost three times as often as "She Walks in Beauty," which is now far better known. "Lord Byron's work in poetry may best be described as 'splendid,'" commented one editor in a footnote to "Sennacherib," "[b]ut its splendour is often lurid or gloomy, for the poet's life was reckless and profligate,

TABLE 1. The Most Popular Poems, or Sections of Poems, by Byron in a Corpus of Victorian Anthologies

Poem, or Extract from a Long Poem, by Byron	Number of Anthologies to Include It
Closing address to the ocean from *Childe Harold*, beginning at 4.177, "Oh that the Desert were my dwelling place"	40
"The Destruction of Sennacherib"	35
Waterloo stanzas from *Childe Harold*, beginning at 3.17, "Stop!—For thy tread is on an Empire's dust!"	34
"The Isles of Greece" from *Don Juan* 3	23
Description of Lake Leman from *Childe Harold*, beginning at 3.85, "Clear, placid Leman!"	16
Description of a dying gladiator from *Childe Harold*, beginning at 4.138, "The seal is set.—Now welcome, thou dread power," or at 4.140, "I see before me the Gladiator lie"	16
Childe Harold's "Good Night" from *Childe Harold* 1	15
Lines from *Childe Harold* beginning at 2.23, " 'Tis night, when Meditation bids us feel"	15
"On This Day I Complete My Thirty-Sixth Year"	14
Lines from the shipwreck scene from *Don Juan* 2 (often with elisions)	13
"Fare Thee Well"	12
"She Walks in Beauty"	12
"When We Two Parted"	12
"It is the Hour" (lines printed as a separate poem in *Hebrew Melodies* and subsequently incorporated in *Parisina* 1–14)	12
"Farewell! If Ever Fondest Prayer"	11
"Stanzas for Music," "There's not a joy the world can give"	10
Description of a thunderstorm from *Childe Harold*, beginning at 3.92, "The sky is changed!—and such a change!"	10
"The Castled Crag of Drachenfels," from *Childe Harold* 3	9
Lines beginning "Know ye the Land" from *The Bride of Abydos*, I.1–19 (a free translation of Mignon's Song from Goethe's *Wilhelm Meister's Apprenticeship*)	8
"Bright be the Place of thy Soul"	8

Note: Identifying sections of long poems in the anthologies cannot be as simple as identifying their opening and closing lines. In this table, therefore, excerpts that are recognizably from the same passage in a long poem are counted together, even if they don't start and end on exactly the same lines. The anthologies' handling of long poems is discussed in more detail in chapter 15.

and his wealth of imagination and language was sometimes perverted to evil uses."[1] Given this view of Byron's life and work, "Sennacherib" had obvious attractions: with its biblical subject and impersonal voice, it must have seemed to anthologists like a jewel salvaged from the rubble of Byron's moral ruin, displaying all of his splendor and none of his profligacy, a memory of better days before the perversion of *Don Juan* set in, and an indication of what Byron could have achieved if his "wealth of imagination" had been better invested.

The table as a whole shows how popular Byron's lyrics were in the anthologies (with nine of the top twenty spots), as well as lyrics embedded in longer poems such as "The Isles of Greece" from *Don Juan* (the fourth most popular lines, appearing 23 times) and "Childe Harold's Good Night" (seventh most popular, appearing 15 times). Byron's verse tales also featured: *The Giaour* was excerpted 39 times in all, *The Siege of Corinth* 23 times, and *The Corsair* 21 times. However, there was no consensus among the anthologies about which sections of these poems should be included. Lyrics and lyrical passages from longer poems were therefore the most popular selections from Byron's poetry in the anthologies. The anthologies drastically underrepresented the narrative poems he published at the height of his celebrity, and almost completely ignored his dramas and his overtly political verse. His canonical reputation now rests to a large extent on his two long poems, *Childe Harold* and *Don Juan*. *Childe Harold's Pilgrimage*, with an aggregated total of 247 excerpts in seventy-four anthologies, was a far more popular choice for anthologists than *Don Juan*, with 119 excerpts in fifty-five anthologies. But—as I show in the next chapter—most anthologies included only short extracts from these poems, and most of the lines from each poem never appeared in any anthology.

"Casabianca" was Felicia Hemans's most commonly anthologized poem. It appeared 28 times in the anthologies surveyed, followed by "The Homes of England," "The Better Land," "The Graves of a Household," and "The Voice of Spring," which all appeared 18 or more times (table 2). Hemans's most commonly anthologized poems were all short. Her fifteen most popular poems in the anthologies all have fewer than one hundred lines, and twelve, including nine of the top ten, have fewer than sixty lines. At seventy-eight lines, "The Voice of Spring" is the longest poem in the top ten, but, as I discuss in detail below, most of the anthologies that included it cut it down. Even "The Homes of England" was too long for some anthologies: over a third of the books to include it (nine out of twenty-six) cut the poem from forty lines to thirty-two. Hemans's long poems were almost completely excluded from the anthologies (table 3). Short extracts from *Modern Greece* (1817), *The Sceptic* (1820), and *The Forest Sanctuary* (1825) appeared in only three or four books each, lines from *The Restoration of the Works of Art to Italy* (1816) appeared in only two, and her poetic drama *Vespers of Palermo* (1823) did not appear in any volume surveyed. *The Siege of Valencia* (1823) was Hemans's most popular long poem in the anthologies, but it appeared much less often than her short poems: twelve volumes included extracts from it, reprinting just under 10 percent of the poem (a total of 235 out of 2,528 lines).

TABLE 2. The Most Popular Poems, or Sections of Poems, by Hemans in a Corpus of Victorian Anthologies

Poem by Hemans	Number of Anthologies to Include It
"Casabianca"	28
"The Homes of England"	26
"The Better Land"	24
"The Graves of a Household"	18
"The Voice of Spring"	18
"The Treasures of the Deep"	15
"Bernardo del Carpio"	13
"The Hour of Prayer"	11
"The Trumpet"	11
"The Palm-Tree"	9
"The Landing of the Pilgrim Fathers in New England"	9
"The Adopted Child"	8
"Gertrude, or Fidelity till Death"	8
"Ivan the Czar"	8
"Coeur de Lion at the Bier of His Father"	8
"The Hour of Death"	7
"The Sunbeam"	7
"Ah! Cease—those fruitless tears" (translation from Camoens)	6
"Christ Stilling the Tempest"	6
"The Boon of Memory"	5

TABLE 3. The Number of Extracts from Long Poems by Hemans in a Corpus of Victorian Anthologies

Poem by Hemans	Number of Anthologies to Include It
The Siege of Valencia	12
The Forest Sanctuary	4
Modern Greece	3
The Sceptic	3
The Restoration of the Works of Art to Italy	2
Sebastian of Portugal	0
Vespers of Palermo	0

"To a Skylark" was Shelley's most anthologized poem (appearing 36 times), followed by "The Cloud" (27 times), "The Indian Girl's Serenade" (17 times), and "To Night" (15 times) (table 4). Sylva Norman reflected the anthologies' preferences when she called her 1954 study of Shelley's reception *Flight of the Skylark*.[2] The ten most anthologized poems by Shelley were all short lyrics almost always reprinted in their entirety. "To a Skylark" was the longest at 105

TABLE 4. The Most Popular Poems, or Sections of Poems, by Shelley in a Corpus of Victorian Anthologies

Poem, or Extract from a Long Poem, by Shelley	Number of Anthologies to Include It
"To a Skylark"	36
"The Cloud"	27
"I arise from dreams of thee" (known as "The Indian Girl's Serenade")	17
"To Night"	15
"The Sensitive Plant" (complete or abridged)	13
"Stanzas written in Dejection—December 1818, Near Naples"	13
"Ode to the West Wind"	13
"Love's Philosophy"	11
"Song" ("Rarely, rarely comest thou")	10
"To ———" ("One word is too often profaned")	9
"To ———" ("Music, when soft voices die")	9
Description of evening scene from *Queen Mab*, beginning at 4.1, "How beautiful this night! The balmiest sigh"	8
"When the lamp is shattered"	7
"Autumn, A Dirge"	7
Beatrice's description of the place for Count Cenci's ambush, from *The Cenci*, beginning at III.i.242	5
Lines from *Epipsychidion* beginning at 53, "Sweet Lamp! my moth-like Muse has burnt its wings"	5
Lines from *Alastor* beginning at 420, "The noonday sun / Now shone upon the forest"	5
Lines from *Queen Mab* beginning at 1.1, "How wonderful is Death"	4
"On a Faded Violet"	4
"A Dream of the Unknown"	4

lines. While Shelley's long poems did feature in the anthologies, there was little or no consensus about which passages to excerpt. Nine anthologies included some lines from *Prometheus Unbound*, for example, but in only one case did more than one book choose the same lines.[3] Some of the poems by Shelley that are now staples in critical discussions were almost never reprinted in the anthologies surveyed. "Ozymandias" appeared only three times, "Hymn to Intellectual Beauty," "Mont Blanc," and "The Mask of Anarchy" only once each, and "Julian and Maddalo" and "England in 1819" not at all.

The most anthologized poems by Hemans and Shelley originally appeared in a very small number of their published volumes. Hemans published nineteen volumes of poetry in a career that spanned twenty-seven years, but fourteen of her fifteen most anthologized poems came from just three of those volumes, published in a three-year period. Seven came from *Records of Woman: With Other Poems* (1828), five came from *The Forest Sanctuary: With Other Poems* (2nd ed., 1829), and two came from *Songs of the Affections, with Other Poems* (1830).[4] These were the volumes that, according to Susan Wolfson, "clinched" Hemans's fame, when, as Paula Feldman writes, her "poetic career was at its height."[5] Percy Shelley published fourteen books in twelve years, and Mary Shelley edited his *Posthumous Poems* for publication two years after his death.[6] His most anthologized poems came overwhelmingly from only one lifetime volume and *Posthumous Poems*. Of the fourteen most anthologized poems or extracts by Shelley, nine were originally published in *Posthumous Poems* (1824) and four in *Prometheus Unbound and Other Poems* (1820).

The anthologies' favored poems had typically been relegated to sections of "miscellaneous poems" at the back of these books, like afterthoughts. Hemans and Shelley tended to prefer a similar arrangement for their mature published volumes (Byron does not follow this pattern so consistently). Their books were anchored by a long poem, which gave the volume its title. This was followed by a selection of shorter poems. Among the top fifteen poems or extracts by Hemans reprinted in the anthologies, all five from *The Forest Sanctuary* volume came from the sections entitled "Lays of Many Lands" (one poem) or "Miscellaneous Pieces" (four poems), not from the title poem. One of the poems from the volume *Records of Woman* came from the title sequence, while six came from among the "Miscellaneous Pieces" included in the book. One of the two from *Songs of the Affections* came from the title sequence, and the other came from the "Miscellaneous Pieces." Only two of the fifteen most anthologized poems by Hemans came from sequences and none were extracts from long poems. Likewise, only two of Shelley's fifteen most anthologized pieces were extracted from long poems: descriptive passages from *Queen Mab* and *The Cenci*, discussed in the next chapter. The rest all came from the "Miscellaneous Poems" that occupied the last fifty pages of *Prometheus Unbound [. . .] with*

Other Poems, or the ninety-page section of "Miscellaneous Poems" that formed the largest subdivision of *Posthumous Poems*. The majority of Hemans's and Shelley's most anthologized poems were labeled "miscellaneous" when they first appeared in book form.

Neither Hemans nor Shelley thought of these "miscellaneous" poems as their most important works. As Susan Wolfson notes, Hemans repeatedly used the heading "Miscellaneous Pieces" at the back of her volumes for poems previously published in periodicals, not forming sequences, which "increased the income of her labour and widened its circulation."[7] Periodical publication ensured a steady cash flow, while allowing Hemans to profit from her poems a second time when they appeared in volumes; both the amount and regularity of payments for her writing were especially important after her husband left her in 1818 with no other means to support their five sons.[8] "It has ever been one of my regrets," Hemans reflected late in life, "that the constant necessity of providing sums of money to meet the exigencies of the boys' education, has obliged me to waste my mind in what I consider mere desultory effusions."[9] Hemans's miscellaneity was a response to circumstances, rather than an aesthetic principle. For Shelley, too, miscellaneous lyrics seemed incidental to his sense of his own vocation and achievement.[10] He withheld many of his shorter poems from publication in his lifetime and, like Hemans, he never published a mature volume of poetry that did not begin with a long poem that gave the book its title.[11] Mary Shelley collected her husband's magazine poetry in *Posthumous Poems*, along with "[m]any of the Miscellaneous Poems, written on the spur of the occasion, and never retouched, [...] found among his manuscript books" on the grounds that "every line and word he wrote is instinct with peculiar beauty."[12] "I do not know whether the critics will reprehend the insertion of some of the most imperfect among these," she wrote in her preface.[13] The anthologies promoted to the center of Hemans's and Shelley's oeuvres poems that the poets considered peripheral and in some cases chose not to publish.

If Hemans and Shelley didn't especially value these poems, neither did their reviewers. "Casabianca" appeared in the *Monthly Magazine* in August 1826 and was then reprinted with the "Miscellaneous Pieces" at the back of the second edition of *The Forest Sanctuary* (1829). Its publication was therefore very modest and unlikely to attract attention; neither periodical poetry nor subsequent editions of poetry volumes were commonly reviewed, and the poem went unnoticed in the press. "To a Skylark" was the last poem in *Prometheus Unbound [...] with Other Poems* (1820). In his long *Blackwood's* review of the volume, John Gibson Lockhart mentioned the poem in passing ("There is an 'Ode to the West Wind,' another 'To a Sky-Lark,' and several smaller pieces"), but it was not otherwise discussed in reviews, with the exception of the *Dublin Magazine*, which quoted it in full as "convey[ing] some general idea of [Shelley's] style."[14] Although it was not labeled as a "miscellaneous" poem, Byron's first reviewers similarly neglected "Sennacherib." When it was published in *Hebrew Melodies* (1815), only two of the book's fifteen reviews quoted the poem.[15] Like "Casabianca" and "To a Skylark," it initially occupied a rather minor place in its author's collected works and the reviews.

Why, then, did the anthologies reprint these poems so often? One reason was that they were suitable for recitation. "Sennacherib" and "Casabianca" are both of manageable length, with regular tetrameter lines, pronounced stresses (anapests in "Sennacherib," iambs in "Casabianca"), and heroic subject matter. Both incorporated strong elements of balladry in their narrative content and quatrain form, making them especially suitable for speaking aloud, or for hearing. As such, they became central texts in the tradition of "percussive Romanticism" identified by Andrew Elfenbein.[16] Percussive rhythm was not necessarily an inherent feature of these poems, however. As Catherine Robson points out in her excellent study of recitation, the metrical variation of "Casabianca" has been beaten out of it by repeated sing-song recitations. " 'Casabianca' *became* an ultraregular poem, and thus a byword for unthinking jog-trot metre, through [...] constrained and unthinking recitation," she writes. " 'Casabianca' has come to be remembered as a poem with uniform metre because of the particular circumstances of its assimilation into a culture."[17] The recitation tradition didn't just identify some poems as suitable for recitation; the processes of repeatedly selecting certain poems, assigning them for classroom memorization, and reprinting them in anthologies aimed at recitation also *made* some poems appear more suitable for recitation. Many readers looking for poems to recite found them in anthologies, and many anthologies were specifically designed to provide material for recitation, in a symbiosis that ensured the popularity of "Sennacherib" and "Casabianca" throughout the second half of the nineteenth century.[18]

"Casabianca," "To a Skylark," and "Sennacherib" all appeared far more often in the anthologies as the century went on (fig. 27). Their popularity snowballed as later anthologies copied earlier ones. "Casabianca" appeared only twice in the 1830s (or in 6.8% of the anthologies surveyed), but it appeared eight times in the 1860s (21%), and nine in the 1880s (32.1%). "To a Skylark" appeared only once in each of the first three decades surveyed, but it rose hugely in popularity from the middle of the century, appearing in eight books in the 1850s (29.6%), ten in the 1860s (26.3%), and nine in the 1880s (32.1 %).[19] "Sennacherib" appeared only three times in the 1830s (10.3%), but it appeared in ten of the thirty-eight anthologies examined from the 1860s (26.3%). These poems became more widely known through the century as more anthologies included them.

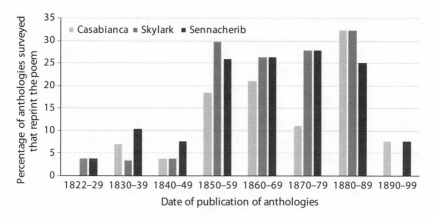

FIGURE 27. Reprints of three Romantic lyrics in a corpus of Victorian anthologies,
by decade.

This gave them a currency beyond the anthologies that they wouldn't
otherwise have enjoyed. The number of parodies that appeared points to their
popularity. As Isaac Disraeli noted, "unless the prototype is familiar to us, a
parody is nothing."[20] In his collection of parodies, published in six volumes from
1884 to 1889, Walter Hamilton gathered fourteen parodies of "The Destruction of Sennacherib" ("Great Gladstone came down his new Bill to unfold,"
for example), making that poem a more common subject than "The Isles of
Greece" from *Don Juan* (which was parodied eleven times) or anything from
Childe Harold (which was parodied twelve times in all). Hamilton includes
one parody of "Sennacherib" from 1828, but all the others that are dated come
from the 1840s and after, when the anthologies had started to give the poem
greater currency.[21] Hamilton collected seven parodies of "Casabianca"—more
than any Hemans poem except "The Homes of England." (Perhaps one of them
was the parody of her own work that Hemans apparently "relish[ed], without
reserve."[22]) All but two are undated and those two date from 1875 and 1884.[23]
"To a Skylark," "The Cloud," and "The Sensitive Plant" are the only poems by
Shelley of which Hamilton found parodies: one of "Skylark" from 1885 called
"To a Bicycle" ("Hail to thee, blithe roadster!"); three of "The Cloud" from
1847, 1880, and 1885; and one undated travesty of "The Sensitive Plant."[24] While
the late dates of these parodies may reflect the ephemeral nature of parodies
generally, which led Hamilton to collect more parodies from the more recent
past, they may also suggest that these poems became more familiar to readers—
and therefore more readily available to parodists—as the century went on.

The way the anthologies framed and circulated these poems reflected and
reinforced gendered assumptions about poetry. In Hemans's case, it supported
the perception that women were incapable of sustaining long poems, because

they were unsuited for either the lofty conceptions or the extended intellectual application required. Women "rarely succeed in long works," wrote Francis Jeffrey in his review of *The Forest Sanctuary*, "their natural training rendering them equally averse to long doubt and long labour."[25] John Neal, writing in *Blackwood's Magazine*, characterized Hemans as an essentially feminine poet and therefore most herself when writing in short forms. "Her *poetry*, however—that which I call *her* poetry—the tender, profound, and spiritual part of it—is only to be met with in her smaller pieces," he claimed, emphasizing the identification of women and short poems through the pointed use of italics.[26] Her friend and biographer Henry Chorley chose his words carefully when he wrote that "one or two" of Hemans's lyrics were "certain to survive so long as the short poem shall be popular in England."[27]

Anthologies reinforced this perception of Hemans as a writer of short, feminized lyrics through their editorial framing of her poetry. One editor wrote:

> She has too rarely concentrated her energies on a single topic, and has, consequently, produced no great poem worthy of her talents; but many of her scattered odes are among the noblest and most affecting lyrics of our language. They resemble in their effect some of those wondrous snatches of music that, when heard, imprint themselves on the memory at once and for ever.[28]

Another anthologist described these miscellaneous poems tartly as "an immense number of fugitive pieces of various merit [. . .] admired rather, it may be presumed, for a certain elegance and taste than for originality or profoundness of thought."[29] William Davenport Adams, in *The Student's Treasury of English Song* (1873), concurred both in associating Hemans with the lyric and in patronizing her with muted praise:

> Her genius was rather lyrical than dramatic, and is seen to better advantage in short lays and ballads than in her sustained efforts. [. . .] Her longer works are now little read, though containing many graceful and tender passages; but some of her briefer songs will always occupy a place in our English anthologies.[30]

Hemans in fact produced long poems throughout her career, and identified the long poem as the height of her aspiration. "My wish ever was to concentrate all my mental energy in the production of some more noble and complete work," she wrote to a friend three months before her death.[31] But the anthologies showed comparatively little interest in the long poems and sequences that Hemans herself thought of as her greatest achievement. Instead, Victorian anthologies preferred the miscellaneous poems and "scattered odes" that she described as "written as if in the breathing-times of storms and billows."[32] The perception of miscellaneous writing as feminine meshed with the perception that anthologies were suited to women readers. Feminized writing circulated readily in a feminized publication venue.

The same gendered set of assumptions operated on Shelley's posthumous reputation. If short poems were the natural home of female poets, and Shelley was most at home when writing short poems, then he was feminized by a kind of dubious syllogism. Adams praised Shelley for feminine-coded qualities, while denying him masculine ones. Shelley "possessed imagination, fancy, an exquisite sense of melody, a high and spiritual feeling;" he wrote, "but he lacked judgement, unity, and depth of thought, and the power of realising his abstract conceptions."[33] Lacking intellectual stamina, Shelley was constitutionally unfitted to write a successful long poem, just as Jeffrey had argued that women poets were. He could be praised only for his short lyrics. "Let it be owned, however," Adams continued, "that Shelley was great as a lyrist [sic]."[34]

For readers of the volumes Shelley and Hemans published in their lifetimes, or the collected editions that began to appear after their deaths, both poets appeared as writers of long dramatic, narrative, or discursive poems, or (in Hemans's case) poetic sequences. These long poems and sequences anchored their published volumes and gave them their titles, and they dominated their collected works. For readers of the anthologies, however, Shelley and Hemans were not primarily writers of long poems or sequences. Instead, they were writers of short lyrics, most of which had appeared among sections of "Miscellaneous Pieces" in their published volumes. In some cases, these poems initially appeared in the contingent context of a periodical, surrounded by other poetry and prose that their authors could not control. From there, they traveled to the new context of a volume, where they appeared under the rubric of miscellaneity. That label implied that their new context was more accidental than meaningful, and that each poem made sense on its own rather than in relation to the collection as a whole. Having traveled into new poetic and bibliographical contexts once made it easier for them to do so again, migrating to a new home in the anthology. There they were situated within a gendered editorial discourse and the supposed femininity of miscellaneous writing was reinforced by the supposed femininity of anthology reading.

Anthologies routinely abridged poems, and rarely mentioned this fact.[35] Cutting lines from longer poems served both practical and ideological purposes: it made the poems fit into the anthology's pages, but it also made them fit into the anthologist's preconceptions.[36] Since anthologists often referred to each other's books, there was considerable consensus about which sections of these poems should be cut. Hemans's poem "The Homes of England" was abridged in nine out of twenty-six anthologies that included it. Eight of the nine anthologies that abridged the poem cut exactly the same lines: the third stanza, beginning "The blessed homes of England." This rejigged the poem's vision of English society from a four-part to a three-part structure. The complete poem offers a vision of English society as a quasi-feudal organic whole, held together from "hut" to "hall" (34) by domestic affection and shared religion. In the abridged version, this becomes a society with three distinct strata, set out in three stanzas about "stately Homes," "merry Homes," and "cottage Homes," which conformed more closely to the emerging nineteenth-century understanding of a society divided into upper, middle, and working classes. The poem's model of a stable and stratified society—stable *because* it was stratified—was thus updated, ironically, to reflect social change.

"The Voice of Spring" was abridged drastically in eleven of the eighteen anthologies that reprinted it. Once again, the compilers agreed on which lines to cut. The poem is a thirteen-stanza evocation of spring spoken by a personification of the season. *Blackwood's* called it "a lump of pure gold."[37] It begins with Spring celebrating its long-awaited arrival:

> I come, I come! ye have call'd me long,
> I come o'er the mountains with light and song!
> Ye may trace my step o'er the wakening earth,
> By the winds which tell of the violet's birth,
> By the primrose-stars in the shadowy grass,
> By the green leaves, opening as I pass. (1–6)[38]

It continues in this vein for five stanzas, cataloguing Spring's effect on the natural world and its northward progress through the hemisphere. Then Spring invokes its addressees in the imperative—"Come forth, O ye children of gladness, come!" (31)—and it becomes clear that this is not a melody sung gratuitously out of pure joy (like the "night-bird's lay" in line 21), but a message for these children in particular:

> Ye of the rose lip and dew-bright eye,
> And the bounding footstep, to meet me fly!
> With the lyre, and the wreath, and the joyous lay,
> Come forth to the sunshine, I may not stay. (33–36)

Here the children are associated with spring, implicitly compared to its roses and dews, and their lyrical song joins the spring chorus. The springtime of the year addresses those in the springtime of life. But this connection between youth and spring also introduces the poem's first darker shades, as Spring insists, "I may not stay." Hemans explained in a letter:

> The "Voice of Spring" expresses some peculiar feelings of my own [...]
> I cannot but feel every year, with "the return of the violet," how much the

shadows of my mind have deepened since its last appearance, and to me the spring, with all its joy and beauty, is generally a time of thoughtfulness rather than mirth.[39]

The poem pivots sharply from mirth to thoughtfulness in line 43, as Spring exclaims: "But ye!—ye are changed since ye met me last!" The following five stanzas make clear that, over the winter, several children have died. "Ye have look'd on death since ye met me last!" (60), Spring discerns, "They are gone from amongst you, the young and fair / Ye have lost the gleam of their shining hair!" (67–68). The children's "wreath" in line 35, which at first seemed to be a wreath of spring flowers, now seems to hark back to the funeral wreath in line 10, and to foreshadow their own deaths. What starts out as a pastoral celebration of spring's annual return, then, suddenly becomes one of Hemans's many poems about dead children. Life's spring never returns in this world, and to mature is to experience the death of loved ones. This is not a pastoral elegy, but a poem in which pastoral succumbs to elegy. The poem offers some religious consolation ("But I know of a land where there falls no blight, / I shall find them there, with their eyes of light!" [69–70]), but it is muted and ineffectual. Spring tells the children, "Ye are mark'd by care, ye are mine no more" (76) and forsakes them, ending the poem "farewell" (78).

Most of the anthologies that included this poem cut its gloomy second half completely. Of the eighteen that reprinted the poem, only seven published all seventy-eight lines. Of the other eleven, eight printed as far as line 42, stopping just before death's entry into the poem, one printed as far as line 36, and two only printed as far as line 30, eliding the children from the poem completely and leaving only Spring's joyous celebration of its arrival. By abridging the poem like this, the anthologies turned it into a straightforward pastoral. They eliminated Hemans's layered presentation of spring as both a literal season that returns annually and a metaphor for youth that never returns. They truncated the poem's movement from joyous song to sober elegy, and restricted it to its upbeat early stanzas. This made it more acceptable for a wider range of readers, including children, as well as more manageable for recitation, and therefore more suitable for inclusion in many anthologies.[40]

The problem here, however, was not the discussion of death per se. The most-reprinted poems by Hemans are marked by her characteristic concern with death. Her "death-haunted consciousness" dwells in these poems on the deaths of family members: sons die in "Casabianca," "The Graves of a Household," and "Ivan the Czar" (and a son's death is foretold in "The Trumpet"); a daughter dies in "Graves of a Household"; fathers die in "Bernardo del Carpio" and "Coeur de Lion at the Bier of His Father"; a mother dies in "The Adopted Child" and a husband in "Gertrude, or Fidelity till Death."[41] There are general evocations of death in "The Better Land" ("beyond the clouds, and beyond the tomb" [27]), "The Treasures of the Deep" ("Restore the dead, thou sea!" [36]), and "The Hour of Prayer" ("Mourner, haunted by the tone / Of a voice from this world gone" [11–12] and "Woman, o'er the lowly slain / Weeping on his burial plain" [19–20]). In many of these poems, as Paula Feldman remarks, "love [. . .] seems to require death or the threat of death for its most intense expression."[42] The only poems among Hemans's fifteen most anthologized that are untouched by death are "The Homes of England," "The Palm-Tree," and "The Landing of the Pilgrim Fathers."

Rather, the problem with "The Voice of Spring" was that the consolation it offered in the face of death was too muted. In Hemans, death is rarely in vain and mourners are seldom unconsoled. Henry Chorley acknowledged that Hemans's poems were "often deeply melancholy, and dwel[t], it may be, a little too exclusively upon the farewells and regrets of life," but he maintained that they were "never morbid in their tone—never convey[ed] a word or thought of questionable morality."[43] If these poems appealed to readers accustomed to the Victorian cult of mourning, they also reassured those readers that bereavement could be borne if understood in the context of nationhood, empire, family, and faith. The Book of Gems told its readers that, although Hemans's poetry was "often sad," it "never exhibits a 'discontented or repining spirit;' and [. . .] it manifests no unwillingness to bear meekly, patiently and trustingly, the thousand ills that flesh is heir to."[44] On this view, "The Voice of Spring" offered insufficient consolation in the face of death. Hemans was not writing like herself. Anthologists therefore abridged the poem to create a pastoral lyric that would fit into their books both physically and ideologically.

Shelley's "The Sensitive Plant" was similarly abridged, and for similar reasons. The poem has three parts plus a short conclusion. Part First (114 lines) describes the sensitive plant, or *mimosa pudica*, and the garden in which it is found in spring. Part Second (60 lines) introduces an unnamed Lady who tends the garden, but ends with the sudden revelation that she died "ere the first leaf looked brown" (2.60). Part Third (117 lines) catalogs the garden's decay as winter arrives and it becomes overrun by weeds, frozen, and finally desolate. The Conclusion (24 lines), however, invites us to hope that the decay of beauty and life are only apparent, not real, and that their continuation is only obscured by the limits of human perception. Like Hemans's "Voice of Spring," then, "The Sensitive Plant" pivots between spring and winter, between growth and decay, between beauty and death, before turning to a brief, muted expression of consolation. Shelley devotes equal poetic energy to the garden's initial beauty and its subsequent ugliness. Several readings of the poem are possible: it may obliquely reflect Shelley's political concerns after the Cato Street Conspiracy, it may express his existential uncertainty as he sought for evidence of underlying meaning in the natural world, it may show the influence of his study of Plato, or it may be understood as a literary exercise in natural description.

Of the thirteen anthologies to include the poem, only five quoted it in full. The other eight all focused on the poem's first part, with its luxurious description of a lush garden in spring. One anthology quoted the whole of the first part, while the other seven that abridged the poem quoted a section of the first part beginning between line 1 and line 13 and ending between line 40 and line 65. This passage of the poem is a descriptive catalog of the flowers that surround the sensitive plant in the garden. ("[H]e knew every plant by its name," Mary Shelley noted in her preface to *Posthumous Poems.*)[45] Two of these seven anthologies also included a forty-four-line section from the third part (lines 5–49), which describes autumn coming to the garden, but stopped short of the description of it being overrun by weeds and parasites. None of the anthologies that abridged this poem included any lines from the second part or the conclusion.

The Lady and her death were thus elided from the poem entirely, like the deaths of the children in "The Voice of Spring." In most cases the balance between the first and third parts of the poem was ignored completely, while in some cases the "morbid extravagance" of the third part (in Timothy Webb's words) was greatly reduced.[46] Most of the anthologies to include this poem shrunk it to a sunny passage of natural description. This sustained the view found in Mary Shelley's preface, and endorsed by some of the religious commentators discussed in chapter 8, that Shelley was a poet especially gifted in natural description, or even one mainly concerned with it. "The Voice of Spring" and "The Sensitive Plant" therefore offer two examples of how the anthologies abridged longer poems, reducing their length and complexity. In both cases many anthologies truncated the poems, limited the abridged version to springtime visions of joy and delight, and omitted any mention of death and decay. In doing so, they sustained the reputations of Hemans as a poet of pious optimism and Shelley as a poet of luxurious natural description. The abridged versions conformed both to the format of the anthology and to the anthologists' understanding of Hemans and Shelley in ways that the original poems did not.

Like other cultural products that mediated or remediated Romantic writing to Victorian audiences, nineteenth-century literary anthologies faced the challenge of accommodating Romanticism to new readerly expectations, new social contexts, and new media of cultural transmission. Anthologists tended to privilege short poems that fit the anthology form best, and to intervene to make longer poems conform to it. Short poems—such as Byron's "The Destruction of Sennacherib," Hemans's "Casabianca," and Shelley's "To a

Skylark"—thus gained in prominence within their authors' oeuvres. These poems came from a narrow selection of the poets' published volumes, and were not necessarily thought of as their best or most representative work, either by the poets themselves or by their first critics. They were often originally published in sections of "miscellaneous" poems at the back of volumes and therefore were especially suited to the miscellaneous format of the anthology. As a result of their popularity in the anthologies, they became more widely known, were common choices for recitation and parody, and were loved by readers who might not otherwise have encountered them, such as Flora Thompson's Laura, who was moved "to a heart-shaking rapture" by "To a Skylark." Longer poems—such as Hemans's "The Voice of Spring" and Shelley's "The Sensitive Plant"—were drastically abridged. This made them fit into the format of the anthology, but also excised content that seemed objectionable or uncharacteristic of their authors. Book-length Romantic poems provided anthologists with even more of a challenge; the next chapter shows how the Victorian anthologies handled them.

15

Romantic Long Poems
in Victorian Anthologies

VICTORIAN ANTHOLOGISTS developed several strategies for handling book-length Romantic poems that they could not reprint in full. Rather than deciding which lines to leave out—as we saw them doing with poems of several hundred lines in the last chapter—with book-length poems, the anthologists had to decide which lines to put in. They were not abridging but excerpting. In this chapter, I examine the passages anthologies excerpted, showing how they disembedded lyrics that were embedded in long poems, extracted descriptive passages, and even constructed new poems by stitching together discontinuous lines. Through these procedures, I suggest, they decontextualized the gobbets they excerpted, minimized the political content of the poems they came from, neutralized objectionable material, and bleached out complexity. But in the process, the anthologies also guaranteed the wide circulation of these excerpts, making them available to readers who might not otherwise have encountered them, prompting some readers to seek out the long poems from which they had been ripped, and facilitating new approaches to them. The anthologies' effects as mediators in the web of reception, like those of other artifacts and practices examined in this study, were therefore powerful but not monolithic. I conclude this chapter—and the book—by theorizing their ambiguous effects.

Anthologies often began by disembedding the lyrics that had been embedded in long poems. John Wesley Hales introduced his very popular anthology *Longer English Poems* (1872) with a discussion of Walter Scott's poem "Rosabelle," without once mentioning that these lines were originally part of *The Lay of the Last Minstrel* (1805), where they appeared as one of several lyrics sung by different poets taking part in a competition.[1] Francis Jeffrey had already excerpted "Rosabelle" in his review of the *Lay* in the *Edinburgh Review*, where he called it "one specimen of the songs which Mr. Scott has introduced into the mouths of the minstrels," but in Hales's anthology the lines were treated as a fully independent poem, floating free of their poetic context.[2] Anthologists similarly disembedded lyrics from Byron's *Childe Harold's Pilgrimage*. "Childe Harold's Good Night" was reprinted fifteen times and "The Castled Crag of Drachenfels" nine times. Two anthologies presented "The Castled Crag" as addressed to Byron's sister, an assumption for which the poem provides no support.[3] Anthologists disembedded four songs from Hemans's *The Siege of Valencia*: the opening ballad sung by Ximena (reprinted twice), Theresa's song "Why is the Spanish maiden's grave / So far from her own bright land?" (reprinted once), the nuns' chant beginning "A sword is on the land" (reprinted twice), and the eight-line funeral hymn beginning "Calm on the bosom of thy God" (reprinted once). In their long poems, Scott, Byron, and Hemans marked off these lyrics with introductory gestures (such as "Thus to the elements he poured his last 'Good Night'" [*CH* 1.13]), a change of meter or stanza form, stanza numbers that are not continuous with the rest of the poem, subheadings, stage directions, or changes in page layout. These kinds of embedded lyrics were a common feature of Romantic long poems and some novels and were often reprinted in Victorian anthologies.

Their authors would not have been surprised to find these lyrics detached from the poems in which they had embedded them. Hemans anticipated the anthologies when she detached the funeral hymn "Calm on the bosom of thy God" from *The Siege of Valencia*, added a stanza, and republished it as "A Dirge" in the "Lays of Many Lands" section of *The Forest Sanctuary*.[4] In *The Siege of Valencia*, Hemans reflected on this capacity of poems to travel into new contexts. The embedded lyrics in *Siege* are typically treated not as extempore effusions by the characters but as songs they already know. Theresa, Ximena's maid, introduces her song with the words "Rest here, ere you go forth, and I will sing / The melody you love" (V.40–41). She indicates that her song is already well known to her and her mistress. Theresa's song, "Why is the Spanish maiden's grave / So far from her own bright land?" shares many characteristics with Hemans's most popular short poems. It tells the story of a woman's death in a faraway land, as a result of her devotion to her husband and her faith. After hearing the song, Ximena remarks:

> Those notes were wont to make my heart beat quick,
> As at a voice of victory; but to-day
> The spirit of the song is changed, and seems
> All mournful. (V.86–89)

The song produces different effects in different circumstances; Ximena acknowledges that the song's current context is only one of its possible contexts. *The Siege of Valencia*, then, is self-conscious about how its songs can be detached from the contexts in which they are presented. Even familiar lines,

Ximena suggested, gained new dimensions of meaning from this redeployment, because "The spirit of the song [was] changed" by the circumstances in which it was encountered. When "Why is the Spanish maiden's grave" was reprinted in the anthology *Lyrical Gems* (1825) under the generic editorial title "Ballad," with no reference to the play in which it first appeared, the editor was extending an understanding of the poem already implicit in Hemans's verse drama.[5]

In other cases, embedded lyrics were not presented as detachable from their first publication contexts. But this did not stop the anthologies from detaching and reprinting them. "The Isles of Greece" was reprinted twenty-three times in the volumes surveyed, making it the fourth most popular piece of Byron's poetry and by far the most often-quoted section of *Don Juan*. The anthologies handled "The Isles of Greece" as though it were a freestanding lyric, abstracted from its poetic context and detached from its specified speaker. Framing it with headnotes and footnotes that sketched Byron's biography made it seem like Byron was speaking the lines in his own voice. In fact, Byron spends seventy lines in *Don Juan* canto 3 cementing the poem into its context, introducing the poem's speaker —"a sad trimmer" (3.82)—and locating the poem as the utterance of a particular man, at a specified time in his life, occupying a particular social situation, in a stated location, for a particular audience and with a specific set of (mixed) motives. Jerome McGann has argued that the poem's speaker blends elements of Robert Southey and Byron himself, creating a complex, layered, mobile, and self-conscious poetic utterance.[6] In the anthologies, however, Byron's careful specification of the poem's speaking voice and the occasion of its delivery were sheared off. The editor of *Lyrical Gems* called "The Isles of Greece" "one of the first lyrical compositions of modern times," but the idea that this was an independent lyric reflecting Byron's sentiments was largely the product of how the anthologies handled it.[7]

Disembedding lyrics that had been embedded in long poems provided a paradigm for the anthologies' approach to Romantic long poems more generally. Anthologies extracted sections from long poems and treated them as though they were independent short poems. Examples from Byron include the description of the dying gladiator and the address to the ocean from *Childe Harold* canto 4; the description of a thunderstorm from *Childe Harold* canto 3; and the lines beginning " 'Tis sweet" from *Don Juan* canto 1. Speeches from plays could also be disembedded in this fashion and treated as though they were independent monologues; this happened to Manfred's soliloquy on the Jungfrau on nine occasions in the anthologies surveyed.

When passages that suited their purposes did not exist, editors intervened to create them. Five speeches by the priest Hernandez in Hemans's *The Siege of Valencia* were stitched together into one long monologue in *Lyrical Gems* (1825).[8] In it, Hernandez tells Elmina how his son deserted Spain's armies to fight for the

Moors and how Hernandez later met his son in battle and slew him in ignorance of his identity. In the anthology version, Elmina's interjections were elided, as were all remarks Hernandez addressed to her directly, including a whole speech of twenty lines. In each elision, the first half of one line was stitched to the second half of another, with the intervening lines silently omitted. In some cases the text was altered to fill up the meter. The editor called the resulting poem "The Monk's Tale," although Hernandez is not a monk. This synthetic poem is a monologue of 89 lines carved out of 122 lines in the source, a compressed oriental tale in blank verse and a ready-made piece for speech-day declamations.[9] Having been created in one anthology, it was then reprinted in another with identical elisions and variants.[10]

In some cases, anthologies extracted lines that had been composed independently and then seamlessly integrated within longer poems: for example, the lines beginning "It is the Hour," which Byron originally published with *Hebrew Melodies* but later incorporated in *Parisina* (1–14). When Byron made these lines part of the longer poem, he did not mark them with changes of meter, stanza numbering, or page layout, but incorporated them seamlessly. Whereas Byron chose to minimize their independence, the anthologies gave them new life as an independent lyric, typically making no reference to the longer poem from which they came. Of the twelve anthologies to quote the lines beginning "It is the Hour," only two identified the source: one in the title ("From *Parisina*") and the other in a footnote. The other ten made no reference to *Parisina*, or *Hebrew Melodies*, but gave the lines an editorial title such as "Twilight," "Eastern Twilight," "Twilight in Italy," or "The Hour of Love."

In most cases, however, the anthologies extracted lines that were not marked rhythmically or typographically as distinct sections of the poems in which they first appeared, did not circulate independently in manuscript, and were not printed separately in any authorized publication. While some early readers had presumably singled out these sections as highlights of the long poems in which they appeared, there is no evidence that they thought of them as easily detachable from those poems. In excerpting these sections, then, anthologists were effectively creating short poems that did not exist before. When several anthologies followed each other in excerpting the same passage from a long poem and treating it as though it were an independent poem, they collectively reshaped an author's oeuvre, and the canon of English literature as a whole. Anthologies treated long poems as collections of short set pieces, nuggets for extraction, and marginalized poetry that could not be made to conform to their preferred modes of presentation and reading.

The anthologies thus promoted an "anthological" approach to long poems, which encouraged readers to view them as collections of short highlights connected by more prosaic or undistinguished linking passages. In this, they followed and extended a Romantic line of thought about how a long poem should be constructed. Coleridge asserted that "a poem of any length neither can be, nor ought to be, all poetry."[11] Keats imagined a long poem as "a little Region to wander in where [the reader] may pick and choose" his or her favorite bits.[12] Shelley claimed that long poems consisted of "inspired moments" connected "by the intertexture of conventional expressions."[13] Edgar Allan Poe gave this view a terse, ironic formulation, declaring, "[w]hat we term a long poem is, in fact, merely a succession of brief ones."[14] Reflecting on the attribution of *Two Noble Kinsmen*, Coleridge wrote in the margin of the play that he was almost certain it was by Shakespeare, except that some of the writing was "unrelieved by any lyrical interbreathings."[15] Coleridge takes the mark of genius to be not simply the ability to write sublime lyrics but the ability to embed lyrical passages within longer poems, where, like the breathing of his infant son in "Frost at Midnight," they "Fill up the interspersed vacancies / And momentary pauses of the thought" (51–52). Monique Morgan has shown how nineteenth-century long poems, including *The Prelude* and *Don Juan*, suspend moments of lyricism in their narrative form.[16] Literary anthologies gave an independent existence to such lyrical breathing spaces, reprinting them alongside short poems "written as if in the breathing-times of storms and billows" (as Hemans put it) for readers like Laura and Willie, pausing for breath in busy lives.

This approach to long poems was displayed in the editors' handling of *Childe Harold's Pilgrimage*, which was consistently popular in the anthologies surveyed. Anthologists who could include only a small number of poems by Byron usually chose something from *Childe Harold*. Eighty-one books in the corpus quoted at least one Byron poem but fewer than five; of these, thirty-six included something from *Childe Harold* (and one chose all five of its extracts from that poem).[17] This suggests that *Childe Harold* was one of the "essential" poems by Byron for anthologists. Two-thirds of the poem's lines—67 percent—were quoted at least once in the anthologies surveyed.[18] The most popular sections of the poem were lyrical passages that combined descriptions of sublime natural phenomena with heightened emotional states: the address to the ocean from canto 4 (which appeared 40 times in the anthologies surveyed); the thunderstorm from canto 3 (10 times); the description of Lake Leman (16 times); and the evening reflection from canto 2 beginning, " 'Tis night, when Meditation bids us feel / We once have loved, though Love is at an end" (15 times).

Roughly one-third of *Childe Harold* was never quoted in any anthology surveyed.[19] Some of these unquoted lines were apparently censored. Not a single book reprinted Byron's attack on British foreign policy at the Convention of Cintra from canto 1 (a section of 144 lines, from 315 to 458). His description of Albania from canto 2 was never reprinted, perhaps because of its persistent homoerotic undertones (458 lines, from 235 to 692). And anthologists also judged part of Byron's reflection on his own fall from grace in canto 4 to be unsuitable for their readers (140 lines, from 41 to 180). These preferences and exclusions suggest that, like the statues of Byron discussed in part 4, the anthologies helped to confirm the centrality of *Childe Harold's Pilgrimage* to Byron's oeuvre, but that in the process they reshaped how new generations of readers would encounter the poem. Readers of the anthologies would be less likely, on the whole, to consider *Childe Harold* as a poem of political, sexual, or social dissent, and more likely to read it as a disjointed series of lyrical or descriptive set-pieces prompted by natural sights. This approach, in turn, was reinforced by tourist guidebooks that quoted the poem and landscape illustrations produced to accompany it.

When the anthologies reprinted parts of *Childe Harold* that dealt with the current events of Byron's day, such as the stanzas on the Battle of Waterloo from canto 3, they minimized their political dimensions. Thirty-four of the anthologies surveyed quote some of the Waterloo passage, making it the second most popular section of the poem (after the address to the ocean) and one of the top three bits of Byron overall. After its abrupt beginning, "Stop!—for thy tread is on an Empire's dust!" (3.17), this section of the poem modulates through several phases: it starts with four broadly political stanzas (3.17–20) which oppose the Congress of Vienna's restoration of pre-Revolutionary monarchies ("What! shall reviving Thraldom again be / The patched-up idol of enlightened days?" [3.19]); it then moves on to the ball held by the Duchess of Richmond and the "mounting in hot haste" as officers rushed from the ball to the battle (3.21–28); it continues by singling out Frederick Howard among the fallen (3.29–31); this leads Byron to reflect on mourning ("the heart will break, yet brokenly live on" [3.32]) and memory ("And this is much, and all which will not pass away" [3.35]); and the whole thirty-stanza section concludes with ten stanzas (3.36–45) sympathetically invoking Napoleon as "the greatest, nor the worst of men" (3.36). Throughout, the section is scrupulously balanced between the glamour and valor of the soldiers and the sorrow of those who mourn the fallen, between the individual such as Howard and the collective of which he forms a part, and between description of the battle and reflection on its political significance.

The anthologies had no time for this balance and modulation—or rather no space. Most anthologies—21 out of the 34 that quoted from the Waterloo stanzas—restricted themselves to eight stanzas or fewer describing the Duchess of Richmond's ball and its sequel: 15 of the 34 began at "There was a sound of revelry by night" (3.21) and ended at "Rider and horse,—friend, foe,—in one red burial blent!" (3.28), while a further 6 quoted a shorter extract from the same eight stanzas. For 21 out of the 34 anthologies that quoted some of the Waterloo stanzas, then, Byron's treatment of the battle included no political polemic about "reviving Thraldom," no meditation on mourning, and no mention of Napoleon at all. Nine anthologies did include the four political stanzas that open the Waterloo section, but only one included the stanzas on Napoleon.

Anthologies thus effectively remade some of the Waterloo stanzas into a new poem. It was remarkably similar in some ways to "The Destruction of Sennacherib," which appeared alongside the Waterloo stanzas in four anthologies. Both poems focus on the splendor of the combatants ("his cohorts all gleaming in red and in gold," "Battle's magnificently stern array"). Both end on a rhetorical exclamation ("melted as snow in the sight of the Lord!" "in one red burial blent!"). Neither engages in any discussion of the reasons for the battle or its wider consequences. To notice the similarities is to see the cultural work of the anthologies in progress, as they turn stanzas from Romantic long poems into independent lyrics better suited to the anthology format.

The first three or four stanzas of Hemans's *The Forest Sanctuary* were also turned into a stand-alone poem in three anthologies. These lines begin a two-part, fifteen-hundred-line poem, but they were almost the only part of that poem to be anthologized. Excerpting them turned them into a short poem of twenty-seven or thirty-six lines. Its speaker is an exiled man, who describes being haunted by those he's left behind. But the excerpt stops just before any specifying details about him are revealed. We hear nothing about his Spanish nationality (revealed in stanza 5), his persecution ("torture and the chain," also mentioned in stanza 5), the religious freedom he seeks in America (revealed in stanza 7), or the fact that his son is with him (revealed in stanza 8). The original poem employs a layered set of historical and geographical parallels, in which the Spanish Inquisition's persecution of "heretics" in the sixteenth century raises issues surrounding contemporary resistance to Spain's reactionary regime and the rights of Catholics in Britain in the 1820s. Extracting the first three or four stanzas elides these concerns and turns the lines into a generic lyric that is similar to Hemans's most anthologized miscellaneous pieces. Like "The Palm Tree," it is concerned with fond memories of a faraway country. Like "The Graves of a Household," it mentions the graves of loved ones in distant places. Like "Treasures of the Deep," it recalls those buried at sea. Slicing the opening stanzas of *The Forest Sanctuary* out of the poem in which they first appeared created another miscellaneous lyric of the kind the anthologies preferred.

Anthologists performed similar surgery on three of Shelley's longer poems: *Queen Mab*, *Alastor*, and *The Cenci*. In each case, the lines most often anthologized from these poems were passages of natural description. With its youthful radicalism and outspoken attacks on religion, monarchy, and contemporary society, *Queen Mab* was especially difficult for anthologists to handle. Its publishers had been successfully prosecuted in the past, so editors and publishers had to be cautious about excerpting it in anthologies.[20] Nonetheless, extracts from it appeared in twelve books. The most commonly anthologized passage from *Queen Mab* was the opening of canto 4, which was reprinted eight times. The *Literary Gazette*, in its otherwise very hostile review from 1821, singled this passage out as "the noblest piece of poetry the author ever imagined."[21] It begins with this description of night:

> How beautiful this night! The balmiest sigh,
> Which vernal zephyrs breathe in evening's ear,
> Were discord to the speaking quietude
> That wraps this moveless scene. Heaven's ebon vault,
> Studded with stars unutterably bright,
> Through which the moon's unclouded grandeur rolls,
> Seems like a canopy which love had spread
> To curtain her sleeping world. (4.1–8)

The passage goes on to describe the snowy hills surrounding the speaker, and the castle visible in the distance, "Whose banner hangeth o'er the time-worn tower / So idly, that rapt fancy deemeth it / A metaphor of peace" (4.13–15). These lines provide the only hint of discord in the scene, in their faint sugges- tion that only "rapt fancy" would see the flag as a metaphor of peace, while a more clear-eyed and disenchanted observer would see it as a sign of strife. The speaker then reflects that this scene is one:

> Where musing solitude might love to lift
> Her soul above this sphere of earthliness;
> Where silence undisturbed might watch alone,
> So cold, so bright, so still. (4.16–19)

Five anthologies stopped there, while another three extended the extract to line 70. *Queen Mab* employs fantastical, romantic passages to introduce the religious and political polemic that appears both in the poem's central cantos and in the prose notes on free love, Necessity, atheism, Christian dogma, and vegetarianism. The *Literary Gazette* found this passage acceptable, even "noble," because it bore no trace of Shelley's opinions on these topics. By extracting calm moments such as this description of the night, anthologies inoculated themselves against *Queen Mab*'s radical content, protected them- selves against prosecution, and reiterated their focus on Shelley's lyrical and descriptive poetry.

Alastor featured in ten of the anthologies surveyed. One quoted almost the whole poem, apart from 132 lines describing the Poet's physical decline (492–624). The other nine books all excerpted the poem, quoting seven distinct passages, six of which were included in only one or two books. One passage, however, was quoted in five books: a description from the middle of the poem of a well in a shady forest. Four books quoted this whole section (420–68), while one quoted only the last fifteen lines (454–68). In a dense, slow-moving passage of lush description, Shelley enumerates the trees in the wood—the oak, beech, cedar, ash and acacia—the flowers that grow around them, "[s]tarred with ten thousand blossoms" (440), the intertwining leaves in the canopy, which "make net-work of the dark blue light of day" (446), and the mossy forest floor "[f]ra-grant with perfumed herbs" (450). He then turns to the well, whose liquid surface reflects the forest canopy, the stars twinkling through the branches, the birds asleep in the trees, and the insects of the wood (459–68).

The passage is pervaded by anthropomorphic tropes of beauty and love, as though the flora and fauna of the forest were a loving family or community. It is "Nature's dearest haunt" (429), where the oak "expanding its immense and knotty arms, Embraces the light beech" (433) and the creepers twine around the trees "as gamesome infants' eyes, / With gentle meanings, and most inno-cent wiles, / Fold their beams round the hearts of those that love" (441–43). The overlapping tree branches are "wedded boughs" (444) and the creepers "unit[e] their close union" (445). Even the insects are "gorgeous" (466). Time seems suspended here. The forest's dense canopy creates a perpetual "twilight" (427), making "the dark blue light of day" seem like night and "the night's noontide clearness" seem like day (446–47). Stillness reigns both day and night: the surface of the water in the well is never disturbed by anyone using it. It reflects a sleeping bird by night and a motionless insect by day, but nothing that moves (465–67). Immediately after this passage, the Poet reenters the poem on his quest, but the anthologies were not concerned with him. Their interest in *Alastor*, like their interest in "The Sensitive Plant" and *Queen Mab*, was in its passages of natural description, especially those that took place in a suspended lyrical present, free from narrative, tension, and decay. In this, they followed some of the poem's first reviews. The *Eclectic Review* called *Alastor* a "heartless fiction" that failed "in accomplishing the legitimate purposes of poetry" but the reviewer conceded that "[i]t cannot be denied that very con-siderable talent for descriptive poetry is displayed in several parts."[22] As we saw in chapter 8, Shelley's religious readers shared this preference for his descrip-tive poetry, because it seemed comparatively untainted by troublesome ideas.

The most anthologized passage from *The Cenci* was also a natural descrip-tion. Seven anthologies included lines from the play, with some including more than one extract. Five of these anthologies included the same description of a rocky landscape from Act 3 (III.i.242–65). Beatrice speaks these lines, describ-ing to Lucretia and Orsino the spot where Count Cenci can be ambushed and killed. Like the passage from *Alastor*, this passage describes a wooded land-scape, with "Cedars, and yews, and pines," and a place of shadows. "At noonday here / 'Tis twilight, and at sunset blackest night" (264–65). But this landscape is sinister, with a "mighty rock" (247) that hangs over a gulf "with terror and with toil" (249), "Even as a wretched soul hour after hour, / Clings to the mass of life" (252–53). In his preface to *The Cenci*, Shelley singled this passage out as the only one in the play that could be described as "mere poetry":

> I have avoided with great care in writing this play the introduction of what is commonly called mere poetry, and I imagine there will scarcely be found a detached simile or a single isolated description, unless Beatrice's description of the chasm appointed for her father's murder should be judged to be of that nature.[23]

Passages of "isolated description" were something Shelley sought to avoid in *The Cenci*, but they were exactly what the anthologies valued most in his poetry. In *Queen Mab, Alastor,* and *The Cenci*, the only passages excerpted in several anthologies were passages of natural description, extracted from their narrative or dramatic contexts. By reprinting these passages, the anthologies acknowledged Shelley's achievement as an author of long poems—even though they reprinted his short lyrics much more often—while insulating their readers against the political radicalism of *Queen Mab*, the "heartless" poetic quest-narrative of *Alastor*, and the horror and moral complexity of *The Cenci*.

Whether they excerpted the Waterloo stanzas from *Childe Harold* canto 3, or the "Monk's Tale" from *The Siege of Valencia*, reprinted only the opening stanzas of *The Forest Sanctuary*, or extracted passages of natural description from *Queen Mab, Alastor,* or *The Cenci*, the anthologists weren't seeking a manageable part that faithfully represented the whole. Leah Price writes that "each anthology-piece functions (at least in theory) as a representative synecdoche for the longer text from which it is excerpted."[24] But all these examples suggest that the approach of nineteenth-century anthologists to Romantic long poems was not fundamentally synecdochal. In extracting these lines from the long poems in which they first appeared, the anthologists sought not a synecdochal excerpt from the longer poem but a stand-alone substitute for it.

Perhaps no Romantic long poem was harder for Victorian anthologies to handle than *Don Juan*. The poem's offenses against propriety and discretion, its political outspokenness, and its supposedly immoral subject matter all caused problems for the anthologies. Its digressive, contingent unfolding made it difficult to isolate passages of description or lyrical reflection that were free from undesirable elements. Byron's masterpiece resisted extracting at multiple levels, and anthologists had to work hard to contain it within their operating procedures. Some sections of *Don Juan* appeared regularly in the anthologies, most notably the embedded lyric "The Isles of Greece" from canto 3. But over three-quarters of the poem—twelve and a half thousand out of its sixteen thousand lines—was never quoted in any anthology.[25]

The excerpts that did appear were skewed severely toward the earlier cantos of the poem, plus some parts of the English cantos (fig. 28). Three-quarters of all quotations from *Don Juan* in the anthologies came from the first four cantos. For those nineteenth-century readers who only experienced *Don Juan* through anthologies—and there must have been many who were disinclined to read the poem as a whole because of its length and its reputation for immorality—Juan's adventures in the slave market, the Sultan's harem, the siege of Ismail, and the court (and bed) of Catherine the Great might as well have never been written. The preference for the earlier cantos reflects in part a Victorian aversion to the harder satirical edge and dissenting politics that Byron brought to the poem's later cantos.[26] For most Victorian readers of the anthologies, *Don Juan* ends somewhere in the third canto.

The anthologies' interest in the poem appears to increase slightly in the English cantos: seven books quote lines from canto 15. In fact, however, all seven books reproduce the same four lines from the canto (one of them also reprints another short extract):

> There's music in the sighing of a reed;
> There's music in the gushing of a rill;
> There's music in all things, if men had ears;
> Their earth is but an echo of the spheres. (15.5)

None of these anthologies identify the lines as coming from *Don Juan*, preferring either to leave them without a title or to supply an editorial title such as "Music" or "Music Everywhere." As I noted in chapter 9, C. H. Spurgeon was one reader who found these lines in an anthology, but apparently did not associate them with the poem in which they first appeared.

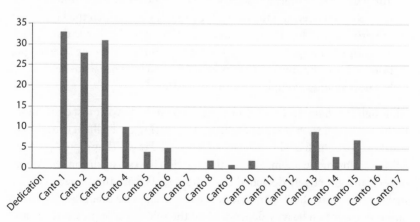

FIGURE 28. Number of excerpts from Byron's *Don Juan* printed
in a corpus of Victorian anthologies, by canto.

As well as being highly selective in their treatment of *Don Juan*, the anthologies tended to present the poem in very short gobbets of text. Roughly half the extracts from the poem in the volumes surveyed consisted of two stanzas or less. *Don Juan* also appeared in books of quotations and bon mots. *Quips and Quiddities* (1881), for example, included nineteen extracts from *Don Juan*, some as short as one line and none longer than eight.[27] It did not include any extracts from *Childe Harold*. The usual way for a Victorian reader of anthologies to encounter *Don Juan*, then, was in disjointed fragments with little sense of the poem's narrative or its recurrent concerns. The result was often to make short passages from *Don Juan* read like separate lyrics. One anthology printed three extracts from *Don Juan*, all less than six stanzas long and appearing in the first four cantos, under the editorial titles "First Love," "The Lovers," and "A Dream."[28] It did not identify any of the lines as coming from *Don Juan*. On either side of these extracts, the anthology reprinted several of Byron's lyrics under their original titles, giving the impression that the passages from *Don Juan* were short lyrics in their own right.

This approach provided the anthologies with a strategy for neutralizing the supposedly immoral content of *Don Juan* without censoring it altogether, similar to their handling of *Queen Mab*. The poem's first reviewers pioneered this approach: *Blackwood's* was "willing to quote a few of the passages which can be read without a blush" on the understanding that "the comparative rarity of such passages will, in all probability, operate to the complete exclusion of the work itself, from the libraries of the greater part of our readers."[29] An 1873 anthology echoed this judgment when it justified its inclusion of two short passages from *Don Juan* ("The Isles of Greece" and a description of Haidee):

> The work was roundly abused for its immorality, but all acknowledged its marvellous power, and the brilliant gems of poetry which thickly studded the production throughout—they were the stars which gave their light to good and bad impartially. [...] Notwithstanding, it is only selected portions, such as the above, that may be safely read by those whose judgement has not obtained complete control of passion.[30]

Although *Don Juan* was, overall, one of the poems by Byron most often quoted in the anthologies, they tended to treat it as a string of "brilliant gems"—that word again—which could be detached, recut, and reset. They reproduced only a tiny fraction of the poem, divided that fraction into small, disjointed gobbets of text, and effectively detached those fragments from their poetic context, making them into short, stand-alone poems. In all these examples, we can see anthologists, often heavily dependent on the selections of previous anthologists, scanning the long works of Romantic authors in search of passages that could be removed from their poetic contexts, shorn of specific narrative and political references, detached from their individualized speakers, and made

into independent lyrics, treating "universal" themes, and spoken in the deper-
sonalized lyric voice of "pure" (or "mere") poetry.

Through these maneuvers, nineteenth-century anthologies occluded most
of the lines in most of the long poems that we now think of as among the central texts of Romanticism. The lines from these long poems that *were* included
could be disembedded lyrics, passages of natural description, detachable bon
mots, poetic highlights such as Byron's stanzas on Waterloo, or even synthetic
poems created by stitching together lines of poetry across silent elisions.
Whatever their provenance, in the anthologies these lines were stripped of
their poetic context, encouraging readers to approach them as though they
were short poems of the kind the anthologies preferred. This anthological
reading protocol could be carried over to the long poems as a whole, or even to
an author's collected works; both could be treated as strings of brilliant gems
to be experienced discreetly. The extracts in anthologies were not offered as
synecdoches for the long poem as a whole but as substitutes for it.

A "pessimistic" understanding of this history would dwell on how the
anthologies censored or misrepresented Romantic poetry. This understanding
assumes that the relevant interpretive context for poetry is either its author's
oeuvre as a whole or the context of its creation and first publication; when
the anthologies remove poems from these contexts, their artistic power and
richness seems to be diminished. On this account, anthologies reduced the
formal variety of Romantic poetry, marginalizing forms of writing that did
not share the anthologies' focus on lyric brevity, and contributing to the
"lyricization" of literature in the nineteenth century. They flattened out the
complexities of Romantic poetry's speaking voices by obscuring their individ-
ualizing features. In doing so, they made Romantic poetry seem more earnest
and less ironic—as though "The Isles of Greece" were written in Byron's own
voice, and Hemans unproblematically endorsed every word of "Casabianca."
And at the same time, they made it seem as though Romantic poets could
only speak in their own voices, however individualized, while Victorian poets
experimented with the new form of the dramatic monologue. The anthologies
removed poems and excerpts from the context of the poetry that surrounded
them, the context of their first publication, and the social, economic, political,
and historical contexts of their production. The poems in Willie's anthology
were as shattered as the "old shattered" book itself.

Shattered, but not dead. A more "optimistic" reading of the anthologies' cultural work would argue that shattering Romantic long poems was actually key
to ensuring their continued vitality. Roland Barthes, in S/Z, describes his practice of breaking the text up "in the manner of a minor earthquake" into "blocks
of signification" or *lexias*, in order to facilitate analysis.[31] He calls the result
"le texte étoilé".[32] Richard Miller translates *étoilé* as "starred" ("On étoilera donc
le texte": "We shall therefore star the text"), but it could also be translated

as "shattered" ("We shall therefore *shatter* the text").[33] A shattered car wind-screen, for example, can be called *étoilé*. For Barthes, this process of shattering is initiated by the commentator; it is "arbitrary in the extreme" and produces a "broken" text (*texte brisé*), which, "separated from any ideology of totality," cannot be reassembled.[34] It is therefore part of his project of empowering read-ers: the text is shattered to make active reading possible. Barthes's *texte étoilé* might point the way to a more "optimistic" understanding of the anthologies' cultural work. Breaking long poems into short sections made those sections available for reading by people who might otherwise have overlooked them. It must have directed some anthology readers to approach long poems or vol-umes of collected works wholesale. And it encouraged readers who had already read the long poems to consider parts of them in more detail, and perhaps to make use of them in new ways, as we saw C. H. Spurgeon drawing on antholo-gies and books of quotations for citations from Byron, even though he had read Byron's collected works. While Barthes's method of shattering the text is a tool in the hands of the empowered reader, the anthologist uses a similar procedure to "administer" long poems for readers. Nonetheless, anthologists could not control the readings they made possible. The anthologies, then, propagated new kinds of encounter with Romantic poems, some of which, at least, must have been the resistant readings that Michel de Certeau calls "poaching."[35]

To ask which of these accounts of the cultural work of anthologies in the web of reception is "correct" seems to me less important than to recognize how deeply implicated each is in the other. The anthologies censored poems in the process of circulating them, but also, ironically, circulated poems in the process of censoring them. Even poems as ideologically problematic for Vic-torian audiences as *Queen Mab* and *Don Juan* featured in the pages of anthol-ogies, albeit in drastically reduced form and sometimes hedged around with defensive commentary. The anthology made Romantic poems conform to Victorian media of cultural transmission, and in the process elided elements of those poems that seemed alien or threatening to Victorian sensibilities. But as they did so, the volumes examined here acted as capillaries of cultural trans-mission, circulating Romantic poetry to new generations of readers. While the anthologies' paratexts attempted to shape the responses of those readers, they could not finally control them. And so these 210 books, containing thousands of poems and extracts, produced tens of thousands of moments of reading—some of them culturally dissident, most of them historically fugitive—in schools, evening classes, and universities, reading societies and public librar-ies, at kitchen tables and in attic bedrooms, and in an English village, at the bottom of a garden, in the shade of the trees, one warm evening in the 1890s.

Coda

Ozymandias at the Olympics; or, She Walks in Brixton

What is the point of remembering a past that can't be made into a present?

—SØREN KIERKEGAARD[1]

THE CLOSING ceremony of the London Olympics, 12 August 2012. The new Olympic Stadium, built at a cost of £486 million in the once working-class neighborhood of Stratford, was lit up by spotlights and smiles. Huge screens relayed close-ups of the pageantry to the ten thousand athletes and eighty thousand spectators in the arena, while an estimated 750 million people around the world watched on television.[2] Its organizers described it as "a celebration of all that's good about London, British people, our music and our culture."[3] Wordsworth, Byron, Shelley, and Keats were all there.

The ceremony's first section, called "Rush Hour," featured a scaled-down London cityscape, including the London Eye, the Houses of Parliament, and Battersea Power Station, all apparently wrapped up in newspapers. Newspaper-wrapped taxis drove through newspaper-covered streets, while people dressed in newspaper clothes made their way to work. Emeli Sandé sang part of her hit song "Read All about It." Closer inspection revealed that the newspapers' text was made up of quotations from classic British literature, including lines from Shelley's "Ozymandias" (fig. 29) and Byron's "She Walks in Beauty" (fig. 30). Turning poetry into newsprint suggested that the canon of literature was still as topical as the day's headlines. The newsprint-covered taxis seem to have taken their cue from an advertising campaign for the London *Evening Standard*, which brought together two familiar London sights by covering the city's iconic black taxis in images of the newspaper sold on its streets. The newspaper-clad buildings shared the ambition of the blue plaque scheme, discussed in chapter 12, to construct an annotated city made intelligible to its population in part through

FIGURE 29. Taxi at the closing ceremony of the London Olympic
Games 2012, showing lines from Shelley's "Ozymandias."
Courtesy of the International Olympic Committee.

FIGURE 30. Taxi at the closing ceremony of the London Olympic
Games 2012, showing lines from Byron's "She Walks in Beauty."
Courtesy of the International Olympic Committee.

its connections with past writers. The Olympics closing ceremony offered a vision of London as a palimpsest of poetry, sedimented with generations of words, as though the bricks themselves were books.

London taxi drivers are renowned for their ability to navigate through the city's streets, but no one could navigate this city of words, this undifferentiated mass of discourse. The size of the stadium meant that the spectators could read the words only when they appeared on the giant screens, while television viewers could decipher only a few lines before the pageant moved on or the camera shot changed. Fractured gobbets of text, folded, wrapped, and mobile, turned the words from lexical signifiers into visual background, rendering them effectively illegible. Those who already knew what they were looking for could pick out and identify familiar quotations as the camera cut from one shot to another. But for most viewers, most of the time, the scene was a disordered expanse of signs with more noise than signal. It was as though someone had torn all the pages out of a million dictionaries of quotations, shuffled them, and used them to wallpaper the whole city.

Rather than a legible anthology of literary works, then, the scene offered a spectacle of heritage. Byron and Shelley, along with many other writers, were positioned as supporting players in a pageant of British life. English literature was here presented as one component of a national identity imagined not as a set of propositions to which one could give assent, so much as an affective state into which one could be absorbed. Literature was presented as part of our surroundings, concrete poetry literally merged into London's built environment, and we were invited not to read it or engage with it critically but to inhabit it. Literature wrapped itself around a cityscape in which the eye moved unblinkingly from monuments of culture such as the Royal Albert Hall to icons of unrestrained capitalism such as the "Gherkin" skyscraper (30 St. Mary Axe), in the heart of London's financial district.

If we could stop to read "Ozymandias," as a bit of it went by on the back of a taxi, the poem would disrupt the smooth operation of this celebratory pageant. A sonnet about the fate of hubristic grand projects and the relationship of art, money, and power, it might prompt uncomfortable questions for the politicians who invested public money in the Games and the artists they commissioned to design the closing ceremony. Shelley contrasts Ozymandias's vain boast "look on my works, ye mighty, and despair" with the ravages of time that have reduced his kingdom to dust (11). The work of art commissioned to celebrate Ozymandias outlives the achievements of its subject and provides an ironic commentary on them. But Shelley does not simply assert the claims of art against those of power; instead, he probes their complicity. The tyrant and the sculptor may both be guilty of hubris: the tyrant's works have crumbled and, although the sculptor's work lasts longer, it is broken, "shattered," and "half sunk" and will soon share the same fate (4). The sculptor achieves technical mastery (he has "well those passions read" [6]), but his work exists only because the tyrant commissioned it and, presumably, was satisfied with the result. Art does not simply serve power, however: Shelley's ambiguous choice of the word "mocked" to describe the sculptor's representation of Ozymandias—meaning "imitated" but also feasibly "ridiculed"—allows the possibility that the sculptor encoded dissent in his work and resisted the tyrant's bombastic self-image even as he was commissioned to shape it (8).

Shelley's poem could prompt us to ask whether the London Olympic Games faced similar tensions, collusions, and trade-offs. But the way in which the poem was used in the ceremony made it unlikely that it would serve as a springboard for critique. Like many examples discussed in this book, the Olympic closing ceremony provided a remediation of Romantic poetry that was based on reading selectively, uncritically, or not at all. It appropriated Romantic writing for a new, contemporary purpose, boosting the national mood and constructing an inclusive version of national identity in which key tensions could be overlooked because dissenting voices were co-opted into a chorus of assent. It would not take long before the euphoria of that Olympic summer wore off, and the underlying discontent became apparent.

"She Walks in Beauty" also appeared on a taxi at the Olympic closing ceremony, but if you walked out of the stadium and into London's streets you could find it there too. The graffiti artist Arofish stenciled the poem's first line on walls around the city, next to a picture of a woman (fig. 31). Byron was something of a graffiti artist himself. He reportedly carved his name into a tree in the grounds of Newstead Abbey, a wooden panel at Harrow School, a pillar at Sounion, a wall at Château de Châtelard near Clarens, and another pillar at the Castle of Chillon.[4] Arofish is a London-based stencil artist, often compared to Bristol-based Banksy and the Parisian artist Blek le Rat. He has also made graffiti in Palestine and Iraq.[5] Arofish's stenciled graffito "She Walks in Beauty" is one of several images he has repeated many times with variations. It both implies a reading of Byron's poem and redeploys the poem in a new context. We can understand the graffito better once we understand the poem; but we might also understand the poem better once we understand the graffito.

The poem describes a woman whose beauty results from the perfect balance of dark and light. Byron structures his description around a series of poised oppositions between "dark and bright" (3), or "shade" and "ray" (7): dark hair, a pale face, dark eyes. This balance is reflected prosodically: key lines of the poem hinge on a medial caesura, whose position is almost unvaried. There are five midline commas in the poem: the first is positioned after the fifth of eight syllables in the line (1), while the other four all appear at the exact

FIGURE 31. Photograph of graffito by Arofish, London.

midpoint, after the fourth syllable (7, 13, 14, 15).[6] Arofish also works through a series of oppositions between "dark and bright," composing his picture from black masses and unsprayed space. (In some versions of the picture, he appears to have painted the wall white before spraying the stencil to emphasize the contrast.) Stenciling allows for no shading or cross-hatching, and this image is partly a display of skill that shows, like some of Aubrey Beardsley's prints, what can be achieved with solid black alone. The figure's legs and her left arm appear without being outlined, as the viewer's brain fills in the form of the limbs from the parts of them that appear in shadow.

Both Byron and Arofish impose restrictions on themselves and then strategically deviate from them in order to produce effects. "She Walks in Beauty" restricts itself to words of one or two syllables, with two exceptions: "eloquent" (14) and "innocent" (18). These three-syllable words both occur at the end of lines in the final stanza (including the last line of the poem). The restricted ababab rhyme scheme is perfectly maintained until the final stanza, when Byron deviates minimally in the half rhyme of "brow" with "glow" and "below," and the rhyme "eloquent"/ "spent"/ "innocent," which—by encouraging the reader fully to sound the final syllable of "eloquent"—emphasizes the extra syllable in that word. The poem is minimally punctuated, which increases the effect of the exclamation mark after "innocent." The emphasis placed on "eloquent" and "innocent" supports the claim that the woman's beauty is the sign of her moral goodness. The natural balance of dark and light in "her aspect and her eyes" becomes the outward and visible sign of inward virtue (4). Her appearance is "eloquent" (14) of "days in goodness spent" (16) partly because she doesn't seem to be straining after effect. She inhabits beauty ("walks *in* beauty") rather than possessing it or aspiring to it. Her beauty bespeaks "A mind at peace" because her looks, like her thoughts, hold potentially discordant elements in equilibrium (17). Arofish also employs small departures from self-imposed restrictions to disproportionate effect. He adds two touches of red in a composition otherwise restricted to black: the red ribbon he places in his figure's hair and the red lettering (which is black in some iterations of the piece). The red ribbon adds the "tints that glow" (15) without succumbing to "gaudy" display (6). This minimalism turns a practical limitation of the medium—the need to work fast, often under the gaze of surveillance cameras, before the police arrive—into an artistic strength.

Byron wrote "She Walks in Beauty" after seeing Anne Wilmot, the wife of his cousin, at a party hosted by Lady Sitwell in June 1814.[7] Thomas Moore was the first to report that Mrs. Wilmot was dressed in mourning, with spangles on her black dress.[8] The dress doesn't appear in the poem, although it may have prompted the image of "cloudless climes and starry skies," which also clearly references Byron's recent travels.[9] Like Byron's lyric, Anne Wilmot's dress made the most of small departures from conventional restraint. Her mourning dress acknowledged her grief in the conventional way, but its daring spangles were ironic points of light signaling that her grief was borne with grace, even with flair. Arofish's stenciled lady displays the same confidence in the power of judicious adornment. She may be in a bad part of town and she may be cleaned off the wall tomorrow. She may be at risk—one version of the image is painted on a police sign appealing for witnesses to a robbery. But the red ribbon in her hair, like the spangles on Anne Wilmot's dress, is a sign of grace under pressure, a gesture of elegance in the face of adversity.

Arofish's stenciled lady could be the gypsy muse of this book. *What the Victorians Made of Romanticism* has traced a variety of material artifacts and cultural practices that mediated Romantic writing to Victorian audiences and shaped the reputations of Romantic authors. It shows how the Romantics became naturalized in the Victorian media ecology and how they were recruited to address new cultural concerns. As this coda suggests, that process of remediation is not over but continues in the present as our media ecology shifts once again. At the edge of the web of reception, the stenciled lady continues to weave her threads. Each material artifact and every cultural practice examined here simultaneously implied a reading of the author or the work it engaged with, and appropriated them to address some contemporary issue. Recovering and examining this reception history reveals how Romantic writing was and is continually redeployed in social, political, historical, medial, and cultural contexts far from those of its composition and first publication.

Tracing the web of reception across several media foregrounds the intermedial nature of reception history and the cultural work of remediation. Victorians encountered Romantic authors and their works not only by reading but also in statues, illustrations, photographs, sermons, and cigarette cards. Crossing the boundaries between media entailed metamorphoses in reception history, especially when the media themselves were new. The artifacts and practices studied here were organized by their producers and consumers into several traditions and regimes of value, which sustained conflicts and moments of cross-pollination. People in different traditions put Romantic writing to different uses. Romantic authors and their works did not offer the same pleasures and satisfactions to all Victorians; instead they were renovated and revitalized in unpredictable ways.

Focusing exclusively on the context in which Romantic authors wrote and published, and trying to read like their first readers, makes it hard to see the intermedial web of reception history this book has adumbrated. Suturing texts so firmly to their earliest historical context makes it difficult to understand how they function in later contexts. Isolating our objects of study in the past can also make it harder for us to advocate for their study in the present, at a time when such advocacy is everywhere demanded. By following Romantic writing out of its context of production and into contexts of reception beyond the lifetimes of its authors, I hope to understand not how it transcended its first context but how it was repeatedly made meaningful in other contexts. Tracing that unfinished history of exploitation, remediation and curation might suggest how the web of reception is still being woven in the present moment of media change. Rather than bricking up our texts in the contexts of the past, we might learn new ways to mobilize them as resources of consolation and critique in our own dispiriting times.

NOTES

Introduction: Don Juan in the Pub

1. Claes Oldenburg, "I Am for an Art" (1961), in Claes Oldenburg and Emmett Williams, eds., *Store Days: Documents from the Store (1961) and Ray Gun Theater (1962)* (New York: Something Else Press, 1967), 39–42 (39).

2. For Disraeli's northern tour, see Robert Blake, *Disraeli* (London: Eyre and Spottiswoode, 1966), 181–82. Martin Fido notes that Disraeli probably read a description of an entertainment room in Stockport called "The Temple of the Muses" in William Dodd's *The Factory System Illustrated in a Series of Letters to Lord Ashley* (1842). See Martin Fido, " 'From His Own Observation': Sources of Working Class Passages in Disraeli's *Sybil*," *Modern Language Review* 72 (1977): 272–73. Sheila M. Smith identifies two other Manchester entertainment rooms that might have provided a source for Disraeli's description. See Benjamin Disraeli, *Sybil: or The Two Nations*, ed. Sheila M. Smith (Oxford: Oxford University Press, 1981), 437.

3. In addition to the sources mentioned in the previous note, Disraeli may been referring obliquely to the bookseller James Lackington's shop in Finsbury Square, also known as "The Temple of the Muses." By refusing to extend credit to his customers, Lackington was able to offer books at lower prices than his competitors. See Richard G. Landon, "Small Profits Do Great Things: James Lackington and Eighteenth-Century Bookselling," *Studies in Eighteenth-Century Culture* 7 (1976): 387–99.

4. Benjamin Disraeli, *Sybil: or, The Two Nations* (1845), in *The Bradenham Edition of the Novels and Tales of Benjamin Disraeli*, vol. 9 (London: Peter Davies, 1927), 106.

5. Ibid., 111.

6. On adaptations of *The Lady of the Lake*, see Philip Cox, *Reading Adaptations: Novels and Verse Narratives on the Stage, 1790–1840* (Manchester: Manchester University Press, 2000), 44–76. On adaptations of Scott's novels, see Henry A. White, *Sir Walter Scott's Novels on the Stage* (New Haven, CT: Yale University Press, 1927), and H. Philip Bolton, *Scott Dramatized* (London: Mansell, 1992). On adaptations of *Mazeppa* and the actress Adah Isaacs Menken, who made her name in the role, see Antony D. Hippisley Coxe, "Equestrian Drama and the Circus," in *Performance and Politics in Popular Drama: Aspects of Popular Entertainment in Theatre, Film and Television*, ed. David Bradby, Louis James, and Bernard Sharratt (Cambridge: Cambridge University Press, 1980), 109–18, and Renée M. Sentilles, *Performing Menken: Adah Isaacs Menken and the Birth of American Celebrity* (Cambridge: Cambridge University Press, 2003), 91–114. On Romanticism and hippodrama, see Michael Gamer, "A Matter of Turf: Romanticism, Hippodrama, and Satire," *Nineteenth-Century Contexts* 28, no. 4 (2006): 305–34.

7. Disraeli, *Sybil* (*Bradenham* ed.), 490.

Chapter 1. Romantic Writers in the Victorian Media Ecology

1. [John Gibson Lockhart], review of "Prometheus Unbound," *Blackwood's Edinburgh Magazine* 7, no. 42 (September 1820): 679–87 (687). Samuel Taylor Coleridge, *Marginalia,* ed. H. J. Jackson and George Whalley, 6 vols. (Princeton, NJ: Princeton University Press, 1980–2001), 4 (1998): 76. Coleridge did, however, think Scott would be remembered as a novelist.

2. John Todd, *The Student's Manual* (Northampton: J. H. Butler, 1835), 150.

3. Review of John Gibson Lockhart, "Memoirs of the Life of Sir Walter Scott," *Quarterly Review* (January 1868): 1–54 (1). Thomas Carlyle, "Signs of the Times" (1829), in *The Works of Thomas Carlyle: Centenary Edition,* ed. H. D. Traill, vol. 27, *Critical and Miscellaneous Essays II* (New York: AMS Press, 1974), 56–82 (78).

4. Orestes Brownson, cited in James Barcus, ed., *Shelley: The Critical Heritage* (London: Routledge and Kegan Paul, 1975), 380. Review of "The Poetical Works of Mrs. Felicia Hemans," *The Graphic* (19 July 1873): 16. *The Anti-Slavery Reporter* (1 October 1886): 27. Stopford A. Brooke, *The Development of Theology as Illustrated in English Poetry from 1780 to 1830* (London: Philip Green, 1893), 36.

5. *Selections from the Poems of William Wordsworth, Chiefly for the Use of Schools and Young Persons,* ed. Joseph Hine (London: Edward Moxon, 1831); *Readings for the Young, from the Works of Sir Walter Scott,* 2 vols. (Edinburgh: Robert Cadell, 1848).

6. Walter Bagehot, "Wordsworth, Tennyson, and Browning: or Pure, Ornate, and Grotesque Art in English Poetry" (1864), in *The Collected Works of Walter Bagehot,* ed. Norman St. John-Stevas, 15 vols. (Cambridge, MA: Harvard University Press, 1965–86), 2 (1965): 318–67 (321).

7. T. S. Eliot, introduction to *The Use of Poetry and the Use of Criticism* (London: Faber and Faber, 1964), 13–36 (33). T. S. Eliot, "Shelley and Keats" (1933), in *The Use of Poetry and the Use of Criticism,* 87–102 (89). T. S. Eliot, "Byron" (1937), in *On Poetry and Poets* (London: Faber and Faber, 1957), 193–206 (196).

8. Tom Mole, *Byron's Romantic Celebrity: Industrial Culture and the Hermeneutic of Intimacy* (Basingstoke: Palgrave, 2007); Tom Mole, ed., *Romanticism and Celebrity Culture, 1750–1850* (Cambridge: Cambridge University Press, 2009).

9. On Robinson's funeral, see Paula Byrne, *Perdita: The Life of Mary Robinson* (London: Harper Collins, 2004), 417. Robinson's fading celebrity partly reflected her own ambivalence about her fame. See Tom Mole, "Mary Robinson's Conflicted Celebrity," in *Romanticism and Celebrity Culture,* 186–206.

10. William Hazlitt, "On Reading New Books," in *The Selected Writings of William Hazlitt,* ed. Duncan Wu, 9 vols. (London: Pickering and Chatto, 1998), 9:141–51 (141, 147).

11. Benjamin Disraeli to Lord Rosslyn, 5 July 1876, Scottish Record Office GD 164/1832/9.

12. Review of Lockhart, "Memoirs of the Life of Sir Walter Scott," *Quarterly Review* (January 1868): 1.

13. Carlyle, "Signs of the Times," 56.

14. Francis Turner Palgrave, "On Readers in 1760 and 1860," *Macmillan's Magazine* 1 (1859– 60): 489.

15. Walter Benjamin, "Theses on the Philosophy of History," in *Illuminations,* ed. Hannah Arendt, trans. Harry Zohn (London: Fontana, 1992), 245–55 (247).

16. Reinhart Koselleck, "Concepts of Historical Time and Social History," trans. Adelheis Baker, in *The Practice of Conceptual History: Timing History, Spacing Concepts*, trans. Todd Samuel Presner et al. (Stanford, CA: Stanford University Press, 2002), 115–30 (118–19).

17. Bernard Williams, *Truth and Truthfulness: An Essay in Genealogy* (Princeton, NJ: Princeton University Press, 2002), 149–71.

18. François Hartog, *Regimes of Historicity: Presentism and Experiences of Time*, trans. Saskia Brown (New York: Columbia University Press, 2015), 41–63.

19. Charles Taylor, *A Secular Age* (Cambridge, MA: Harvard University Press, 2007), 54–61.

20. Reinhart Koselleck, "The Eighteenth Century as the Beginning of Modernity," trans. Todd Samuel Presner, in *The Practice of Conceptual History*, 154–69 (162).

21. Peter Fritzsche, *Stranded in the Present: Modern Time and the Melancholy of History* (Cambridge, MA: Harvard University Press, 2004), 47–48, 202.

22. Hayden White, paraphrasing Koselleck, writes, "only in its modern phase—sometime between 1750 and 1850—did European society begin to think and act as if it existed in history, as if its 'historicity' was a feature, if not the defining feature of its identity." Hayden White, foreword to *The Practice of Conceptual History*, x.

23. In the entry for "modernity," *OED* records that sense 1a "The quality or condition of being modern; modernness of character or style" was supplemented by a specific sense 1b "An intellectual tendency or social perspective characterized by departure from or repudiation of traditional ideas, doctrines, and cultural values" around 1900. James's handling of "modernity" as a buzzword requiring inverted commas suggests that this development began earlier.

24. Reinhart Koselleck, "Time and History," trans. Kerstin Behnke, in *The Practice of Conceptual History*, 100–114 (102–4). See also White, foreword to *The Practice of Conceptual History*, xii.

25. Fritzsche, *Stranded in the Present*, 204; see also 10, 53.

26. James Chandler, *England in 1819: The Politics of Literary Culture and the Case of Romantic Historicism* (Chicago: University of Chicago Press, 1998), 78. It is in the Romantic period, Chandler claims, that "the normative status of the period becomes a central and self-conscious aspect of historical reflection" (91).

27. Koselleck, "The Eighteenth Century as the Beginning of Modernity," 164–65. Fritzsche quotes the neat formulation by Hans Blumenberg: "Modernity (*Neuzeit*) was the first and only age that understood itself as an epoch and, in so doing, simultaneously created the other epochs" (52). See also Fritzsche, *Stranded in the Present*, 203.

28. Obituary for Sir Henry Taylor, *The Standard* (London) (30 March 1886): 5. *Gale NewsVault*. Web. Accessed 13 June 2011.

29. Fritzsche, *Stranded in the Present*, 130.

30. Examples include Hilary Fraser, *The Victorians and Renaissance Italy* (Oxford: Blackwell, 1992); Timothy Lang, *The Victorians and the Stuart Heritage: Interpretations of a Discordant Past* (Cambridge: Cambridge University Press, 1995); and B. W. Young, *The Victorian Eighteenth Century* (Oxford: Oxford University Press, 2007).

31. Pierre Nora, "Between Memory and History: *Les Lieux de Mémoire*," trans. Marc Roudebush, *Representations* 26 (1989): 7.

32. Ibid., 8.

33. Raphael Samuel, *Theatres of Memory: Past and Present in Contemporary Culture* (London: Verso, 1994), x.

34. "In Memory of Mrs Hemans," *Aberdeen Weekly Journal* (25 January 1899): 12.

35. Nora, "Between Memory and History," 7.

36. Ibid., 12.

37. Samuel, *Theatres of Memory*, x.

38. Clifford Siskin and William Warner, eds., *This Is Enlightenment* (Chicago: University of Chicago Press, 2010), 5.

39. Bruno Latour, *Reassembling the Social: An Introduction to Actor-Network Theory* (Oxford: Oxford University Press, 2005), 39.

40. McKenzie Wark aphorizes: "The role assigned to media within the rhetoric of a not-yet-dead modernity is always to be the very sign of the new." McKenzie Wark, *Telesthesia: Communication, Culture and Class* (Cambridge: Polity, 2012), 12.

41. Lisa Gitelman, *Always Already New: Media, History, and the Data of Culture* (Cambridge, MA: MIT Press, 2006), 5.

42. Janine Barchas, *Graphic Design, Print Culture, and the Eighteenth-Century Novel* (Cambridge: Cambridge University Press, 2003).

43. Christina Lupton, *Knowing Books: The Consciousness of Mediation in Eighteenth-Century Britain* (Philadelphia: University of Pennsylvania Press, 2012).

44. Celeste Langan and Maureen N. McLane, "The Medium of Romantic Poetry," in *The Cambridge Companion to British Romantic Poetry*, ed. James Chandler and Maureen N. McLane (Cambridge: Cambridge University Press, 2008), 242.

45. Kittler, for example, describes gramophones, films, and typewriters as "the first technological media," but does not explain why moveable type and the printing press do not count as "technologies." Friedrich A. Kittler, *Gramophone, Film, Typewriter* (Stanford, CA: Stanford University Press, 1999), xl.

46. For an account of some of these changes and an analysis of their effect on poetry publication, see Lee Erickson, *The Economy of Literary Form: English Literature and the Industrialization of Publishing, 1800–1850* (Baltimore: Johns Hopkins University Press, 1996), 19–48.

47. Joseph A. Dane, "'Ca. 1800': What's in a Date?" in *Blind Impressions: Methods and Mythologies in Book History* (Philadelphia: University of Pennsylvania Press, 2013), 37–57.

48. James Moran, *The Printing Press: History and Development from the Fifteenth Century to Modern Times* (Berkeley: University of California Press, 1973), 101–72; Michael Twyman, *The British Library Guide to Printing: History and Techniques* (London: British Library, 1998), 38–46 and 69–75.

49. Stereotyping involves making a mold from type that has been set up for printing, and then casting that mold in metal and printing from the metal plate instead of directly from the type. After several experiments in the eighteenth century, the stereotype process using papier-mâché molds originated in France around 1830 and was in general use from the middle of the century. See "Stereotype," in Geoffrey Ashall Glaister, *Glossary of the Book* (London: George Allen and Unwin, 1960), 387–91.

50. Richard L. Hills, *Papermaking in Britain, 1488–1988: A Short History* (London: Athlone Press, 1988), 119–55.

51. See Raymond Lister, *Prints and Printmaking: A Dictionary and Handbook of the Art in Nineteenth-Century Britain* (London: Methuen, 1984); David Bindman, "Prints," in *An Oxford Companion to the Romantic Age: British Culture 1776–1832*, gen. ed. Iain McCalman (Oxford: Oxford University Press, 1999), 207–13.

52. Basil Hunnisett notes that "The first type of book to benefit from steel engraving was the newly created annual" (121). Basil Hunnisett, *Engraved on Steel: The History of Picture Production Using Steel Plates* (Aldershot: Ashgate, 1998), esp. 110–43. See also Lister, *Prints and Printmaking*, 54–66.

53. See Lister, *Prints and Printmaking*, 28–42.

54. Michael Twyman, *Breaking the Mould: The First Hundred Years of Lithography* (London: British Library, 2001). See also Lister, *Prints and Printmaking*, 14–27, and Twyman, *British Library Guide to Printing*, 47–50.

55. Wolfgang Schivelbusch, *The Railway Journey: Trains and Travel in the Nineteenth Century*, trans. Anselm Hollo (Oxford: Blackwell, 1980); p. 36 provides comparative maps showing the huge development of the railway network between 1840 and 1850.

56. Neil Postman, *Technopoly: The Surrender of Culture to Technology* (New York: Vintage, 1993), 18. Ecology is not in fact Postman's preferred metaphor for the relations among media: he prefers to think of media as at war with one another.

57. Paul Duguid, "Material Matters: The Past and Futurology of the Book," in *The Future of the Book*, ed. Geoffrey Nunberg (Berkeley: University of California Press, 1996), 65.

58. Gitelman, *Always Already New*, 6.

59. Langan and McLane, "The Medium of Romantic Poetry," 257.

60. John Guillory, "Genesis of the Media Concept," *Critical Inquiry* 36 (2010): 321; see also John Guillory, "Enlightening Mediation," in *This Is Enlightenment*, ed. Siskin and Warner, 37–63. Also useful here are Raymond Williams, "Media" and "Mediation," in *Keywords: A Vocabulary of Culture and Society*, rev. and expanded ed. (London: Fontana, 1983), 203–7. Guillory usefully explicates Williams's view of media in "Genesis of the Media Concept," 355–57.

61. Bolter and Grusin examine how "new" media construct their own cultural value and significance by "remediating" existing media, and observe a dual logic of "hypermediacy"—a fascination with mediation itself—and "immediacy"—an attempt to do away with mediation altogether. J. David Bolter and Richard Grusin, *Remediation: Understanding New Media* (Boston: MIT Press, 2000).

62. Walter Benjamin, "The Medium through Which Works of Art Continue to Influence Later Ages," trans. Rodney Livingstone, in *Selected Writings*, ed. Marcus Bullock et al., 4 vols. (Cambridge, MA: Belknap, 2002), 1:235.

63. Ann Rigny makes a similar point about the two aspects of Scott's reception that she calls "mobility" and "monumentality." Ann Rigny, *The Afterlives of Walter Scott: Memory on the Move* (Oxford: Oxford University Press, 2012), 13.

Chapter 2. Reception Traditions and Punctual Historicism

1. Frank Kermode, *The Classic: Literary Images of Permanence and Change* (Cambridge, MA: Harvard University Press, 1975), 16, 117.

2. Jerome McGann puts it neatly: "We need to do more than explain what our texts are saying [. . .]; we need to understand *what they are doing in saying what they say*." Jerome J. McGann, *Social Values and Poetic Acts: The Historical Judgment of Literary Work* (Cambridge, MA: Harvard University Press, 1988), viii. Italics in original.

3. Leah Marcus, *Puzzling Shakespeare: Local Reading and Its Discontents* (Berkeley: University of California Press, 1988), 1. I differ from Marcus here because where she opposes the local to the "general," I oppose the tendency to localize in one historical moment with the possibility of repeated localization in different historical moments.

4. Jerome J. McGann, *The Beauty of Inflections: Literary Investigations in Historical Method and Theory* (Oxford: Clarendon Press, 1988), 343.

5. Marjorie Levinson, "Insight and Oversight: Reading 'Tintern Abbey,'" in *Wordsworth's Great Period Poems* (Cambridge: Cambridge University Press, 1986), 14–57; Nicholas Roe, *John Keats and the Culture of Dissent* (Oxford: Clarendon Press, 1997), 253–67; McGann, *Beauty of Inflections*, 49–62; Alan Liu, "Wordsworth and Subversion, 1793–1804: Trying Cultural Criticism," *Yale Journal of Criticism* 2, no. 2 (1989): 55–100, repr. as "Trying Cultural Criticism: Wordsworth and Subversion," in Alan Liu, *Local Transcendence: Essays on Postmodern Historicism and the Database* (Chicago: University of Chicago Press, 2008), 71–108; Marilyn Butler, *Jane Austen and the War of Ideas* (Oxford: Clarendon Press, 1975). I leave aside the other key tenet of historicism—that the important context is primarily sociopolitical rather than literary. This idea has been challenged by neoformalist approaches, which tend to stress the importance of literary contexts.

6. Stephen Greenblatt, *Shakespearean Negotiations: The Circulation of Social Energy in the Renaissance* (Berkeley: University of California Press, 1988), 7; Jerome J. McGann, *Byron and Romanticism*, ed. James Soderholm (Cambridge: Cambridge University Press, 2002), 3.

7. Thomas Pfau, *Romantic Moods: Paranoia, Trauma, and Melancholy, 1790–1840* (Baltimore: Johns Hopkins University Press, 2005), 340.

8. http://www.cornellpress.cornell.edu/collections/?collection_id=133, retrieved 1 November 2013; http://www.euppublishing.com/series/EEWN, retrieved 1 November 2013.

9. The doctrine of final intention is descended from R. B. McKerrow, *Prolegomena for the Oxford Shakespeare: A Study in Editorial Method* (Oxford: Clarendon Press, 1939); W. W. Greg, "The Rationale of Copy-Text," *Studies in Bibliography* 3 (1950): 19–36, repr. in *Collected Papers*, ed. J. C. Maxwell (Oxford: Clarendon Press, 1966), 374–91; and Fredson Bowers, "Textual Criticism," in *The Aims and Methods of Scholarship in Modern Languages and Literatures*, ed. James Thorpe (New York: Modern Language Association of America, 1963), 23–42. It has been clarified by G. Thomas Tanselle, "The Editorial Problem of Final Authorial Intention," *Studies in Bibliography* 29 (1976): 167–211, repr. in *Textual Criticism and Scholarly Editing* (Charlottesville: University Press of Virginia, 1990), 27–71.

10. Stephen Parrish, "The Whig Interpretation of Literature," *TEXT* 4 (1988): 343–50. James Thorpe was among the first to challenge this doctrine in his *Principles of Textual Criticism* (San Marino, CA: Huntington Library, 1972), esp. 37–47.

11. Jerome J. McGann, *A Critique of Modern Textual Criticism* (Chicago: University of Chicago Press, 1983).

12. Jack Stillinger, "Textual Primitivism and the Editing of Wordsworth," *Studies in Romanticism* 28 (1989): 3–28. See also Jack Stillinger, "A Practical Theory of Versions," in

Coleridge and Textual Instability: The Multiple Versions of the Major Poems (Oxford: Oxford University Press, 1994), 118–40.

13. Roe, *John Keats and the Culture of Dissent*, 257; Marilyn Butler, "Against Tradition: The Case for a Particularized Historical Method," in *Historical Studies and Literary Criticism*, ed. Jerome J. McGann (Madison: University of Wisconsin Press, 1985), 31.

14. Jerome J. McGann, introduction to the *New Oxford Book of Romantic Period Verse*, ed. Jerome J. McGann (Oxford: Oxford University Press, 1993), xxv. McGann controversially prints only those poems that were "printed and distributed at the time" (xxiv), follows their earliest published texts, and arranges them in chronological order of first appearance. *The Complete Poetry of Percy Bysshe Shelley*, ed. Donald H. Reiman and Neil Fraistat, 2 vols. (Baltimore: Johns Hopkins University Press, 2000–2004), 1:xxix.

15. Rita Felski, *Uses of Literature* (Oxford: Blackwell, 2008), 120.

16. Andrew Bennett, *Romantic Poets and the Culture of Posterity* (Cambridge: Cambridge University Press, 1999).

17. George H. Ford, *Keats and the Victorians: A Study of His Influence and Rise to Fame, 1821–1895* (New Haven, CT: Yale University Press, 1945); James Najarian, *Victorian Keats: Manliness, Sexuality, and Desire* (New York: Palgrave, 2003); Stephen Gill, *Wordsworth and the Victorians* (Oxford: Clarendon Press, 1998); Andrew Elfenbein, *Byron and the Victorians* (Cambridge: Cambridge University Press, 1995).

18. The Critical Heritage series, published by Routledge, and the Reception of British and Irish Authors in Europe series, published by Bloomsbury, exemplify this approach. See also Annika Bautz, *The Reception of Jane Austen and Walter Scott: A Comparative Longitudinal Study* (London: Continuum, 2007).

19. Alison Milbank, *Dante and the Victorians* (Manchester: Manchester University Press, 1998); Adrian Poole, *Shakespeare and the Victorians* (London: Arden Shakespeare, 2004); Erik Gray, *Milton and the Victorians* (Ithaca, NY: Cornell University Press, 2009).

20. On collected editions, see Michael Gamer, *Romanticism, Self-Canonization, and the Business of Poetry* (Cambridge: Cambridge University Press, 2017), and Andrew Piper, *Dreaming in Books: The Making of the Bibliographic Imagination in the Romantic Age* (Chicago: University of Chicago Press, 2009). On volumes of "remains," see Samantha Matthews, *Poetical Remains: Poets' Graves, Bodies, and Books in the Nineteenth Century* (Oxford: Oxford University Press, 2004); on reprinting, see William St. Clair, *The Reading Nation in the Romantic Period* (Cambridge: Cambridge University Press, 2004); Meredith L. McGill, *American Literature and the Culture of Reprinting, 1834–1853* (Philadelphia: University of Pennsylvania Press, 2002). On editors' interventions in the nineteenth century, Michael O'Neill, "'Trying to Make It as Good as I Can': Mary Shelley's Editing of Shelley's Poetry and Prose," in *Mary Shelley in Her Times*, ed. Betty T. Bennett and Stuart Curran (Baltimore: Johns Hopkins University Press, 2000), 185–97; and Kathryn Sutherland, *Jane Austen's Textual Lives: From Aeschylus to Bollywood* (Oxford: Oxford University Press, 2007), 1–54. See also Joel Faflak and Julia M. Wright, eds., *Nervous Reactions: Victorian Recollections of Romanticism* (Albany: SUNY Press, 2004).

21. Nicola J. Watson, *The Literary Tourist: Readers and Places in Romantic and Victorian Britain* (Basingstoke: Palgrave, 2006); Catherine Robson, *Heart Beats: Everyday Life and the Memorized Poem* (Princeton, NJ: Princeton University Press, 2012); Leah Price, *How to Do Things with Books in Victorian Britain* (Princeton, NJ: Princeton University Press, 2012).

22. Gill, *Wordsworth and the Victorians*, 81–113; Sutherland, *Jane Austen's Textual Lives*, 338–58; John Wiltshire, *Recreating Jane Austen* (Cambridge: Cambridge University Press, 2001); Sarah Wootton, *Consuming Keats: Nineteenth-Century Representations in Art and Literature* (Basingstoke: Palgrave, 2006); Atara Stein, *The Byronic Hero in Film, Fiction and Television* (Carbondale: Southern Illinois University Press, 2004). Wootton's study remains largely within a high-art tradition, while Stein's relies on pointing out similarities between nineteenth-century literary culture and twentieth-century film and television, but offers no account of the process of cultural transmission. Mike Goode, "Blakespotting," *PMLA* 121, no. 3 (2006): 769–86, argues that Blake's proverbs survive and circulate precisely because their form allows them to be appropriated and reused in unfamiliar contexts. The proverb form, he suggests, produces "a kind of centrifugal force [. . .] a pressure his poetry exerts on readers to break off chunks of poems, to circulate its texts out of their contexts, to stop reading its lines and start repeating them instead" (774). Goode's essay, however, places reception history in the service of an argument about authorial agency, claiming that if Blake couldn't foresee *how* his proverbs would be appropriated, he nonetheless intended that they *would* be.

23. Charles Martindale argues, with respect to Latin poetry, that "our current interpretations of ancient texts, whether or not we are aware of it, are, in complex ways, constructed by the chain of receptions through which their continued readability has been effected." Charles Martindale, *Redeeming the Text: Latin Poetry and the Hermeneutics of Reception* (Cambridge: Cambridge University Press, 1993), 7.

24. The history of English as an academic discipline is complex, but the key institutional developments occurred in this period, and included the following. A Regius Chair of Rhetoric and Belles Lettres was established at the University of Edinburgh in 1762; University College, London had a chair of English Language and Literature from 1828; a Regius Chair in English Literature was established at the University of Glasgow in 1861; Oxford University had a Merton Professor of English Literature from 1885; the King Edward VII Chair in English Literature at Cambridge University was first filled in 1912. Harvard University had an English Department from 1876 and the Modern Language Association (MLA) was founded in 1883. For more information, see Terry Eagleton, *Literary Theory: An Introduction* (Oxford: Blackwell, 1983), 15–46; Chris Baldick, *The Social Mission of English Criticism: 1848–1932* (Oxford: Clarendon Press, 1983); Franklin E. Court, "The Social and Historical Significance of the First English Literature Professorship in England," *PMLA* 103, no. 5 (1988): 796–807.

25. These titles and others are noted by Giovanni Cianci and Jason Harding, introduction to *T. S. Eliot and the Concept of Tradition* (Cambridge: Cambridge University Press, 2009), 2.

26. T. S. Eliot, "Tradition and the Individual Talent," in *The Norton Anthology of Theory and Criticism*, ed. Vincent B. Leitch et al. (New York: W. W. Norton, 2001), 1093.

27. Ibid.

28. Ibid.

29. Raymond Williams, *Keywords: A Vocabulary of Culture and Society*, rev. and expanded ed. (London: Fontana, 1983), 13.

30. Ibid., 318–19.

31. Cf. also Raymond Williams, "Culture Is Ordinary" (1958), in *Resources of Hope* (London: Verso, 1989), 3–18. Here Williams refuses simply to equate the "high art" tradition with the bourgeois class that sponsors it, writing, "As for the arts and learning, they are in a real sense a national inheritance, which is, or should be, available to everyone" (8).

32. T. S. Eliot, "The Waste Land," in *The Poems of T. S. Eliot*, ed. Christopher Ricks and Jim McCue, 2 vols. (London: Faber and Faber, 2015), 1:415.

33. Robert Crawford, *Young Eliot: From St Louis to "The Waste Land"* (London: Jonathan Cape, 2015), 170, 174–75; Peter Ackroyd, *T. S. Eliot* (London: Penguin, 1993), 37, 47.

34. I leave aside here, as irrelevant for present purposes, the subsequent evolution of Eliot's understanding of tradition, both in poems such as *Four Quartets* and in prose works such as "What Is a Classic?" (1944).

35. T. S. Eliot, *After Strange Gods: A Primer of Modern Heresy* (London: Faber and Faber, 1933), 41.

36. "What I am," MacIntyre writes, "is in key part what I inherit [. . .] I find myself part of a history and that is generally to say, whether I like it or not, whether I recognise it or not, one of the bearers of a tradition." Alasdair MacIntyre, *After Virtue: A Study in Moral Theory*, 2nd ed. (London: Duckworth, 1984), 221.

37. MacIntyre's thinking about tradition has shifted through his career. Initially proposed as a category of moral inquiry in *After Virtue* (1981, 1984, 2007), it subsequently shifted emphasis to become a constitutive feature of subjectivity and rationality in *Whose Justice? Which Rationality?* (1988). See Jean Porter, "Tradition in the Recent Work of Alasdair MacIntyre," in *Alasdair MacIntyre*, ed. Mark C. Murphy (Cambridge: Cambridge University Press, 2003), 38–69.

38. MacIntyre, *After Virtue*, 222.

39. Ibid.

40. "So when an institution—a university, say, or a farm, or a hospital—is the bearer of a tradition of practice or practices, its common life will be partly, but in a centrally important way, constituted by a continuous argument as to what a university is and ought to be or what good farming is or what good medicine is." Ibid.

41. Alasdair MacIntyre, *Whose Justice? Which Rationality?* (Notre Dame, IN: University of Notre Dame Press, 1988), 349–69.

42. Felski, *Uses of Literature*, 20.

43. I draw here on Barbara Herrnstein Smith, *Contingencies of Value: Alternative Perspectives for Critical Theory* (Cambridge, MA: Harvard University Press, 1988); John Frow, *Cultural Studies and Cultural Value* (Oxford: Clarendon Press, 1995); and Richard Rorty's seminal work *Contingency, Irony, and Solidarity* (Cambridge: Cambridge University Press, 1989).

44. MacIntyre, *Whose Justice?* 370–88 (esp. 374–75) and 394–95. MacIntyre's point is not affected by the fact that his analogy may not be factually accurate, as simultaneous bilingualism is now thought to be very common worldwide.

45. For a gloss on this aspect of MacIntyre's thought, see Jack Russell Weinstein, *On MacIntyre* (Toronto: Wadsworth/Thomson, 2003), 69–71, and Thomas D. D'Andrea, *Tradition, Rationality, and Virtue: The Thought of Alasdair MacIntyre* (Aldershot: Ashgate, 2006), 327–40.

46. MacIntyre analyzes and critiques the Enlightenment's claim to break free from tradition in *After Virtue*, 51–61, and in *Three Rival Versions of Moral Enquiry: Encyclopaedia, Genealogy, Tradition* (Notre Dame, IN: University of Notre Dame Press, 1990), esp. 170–95. Confusingly, he appears to present tradition as one version of moral inquiry here, whereas in *Whose Justice? Which Rationality?* he describes tradition as the ground of possibility for any moral inquiry. Michael Fuller explains that "All knowledge and rationality are indeed involved in some tradition or other, but the problem is that neither Encyclopaedia nor Genealogy understand this properly. As a result of not understanding this, both are incoherent in their different ways." Michael Fuller, *Making Sense of MacIntyre* (Aldershot: Ashgate, 1998), 127.

47. MacIntyre, *Whose Justice?* 395. For a gloss on this passage, see Weinstein, *On MacIntyre*, 71.

48. Charles Martindale, "Introduction: Thinking Through Reception," in *Classics and the Uses of Reception*, ed. Charles Martindale and Richard F. Thomas (Oxford: Blackwell, 2006), 3–4.

Chapter 3. Minding the Generation Gap

1. Matthew Arnold, "Stanzas in Memory of the Author of 'Obermann'" (1849), 69–70, in *The Poems of Matthew Arnold*, ed. Kenneth Allott (London: Longman, 1965), 129–38 (133). Marshall Berman, *All That Is Solid Melts into Air: The Experience of Modernity* (New York: Simon and Schuster, 1982), 15.

2. Arnold, "Stanzas in Memory of the Author of 'Obermann,'" 77–79.

3. Byron, *Manfred* (1817), I.i.14–21, in *The Complete Poetical Works*, ed. Jerome J. McGann, 7 vols. (Oxford: Clarendon Press, 1980–93), 4 (1986): 53; Manfred is himself, of course, closely following Marlowe's *Doctor Faustus* at this point. Arnold, "Stanzas from the Grand Chartreuse" (1855), 127–28, in *Poems*, ed. Allott, 285–94 (291).

4. Henry James, in the *English Illustrated Magazine* (January 1884), cited in *Matthew Arnold: The Critical Heritage*, vol. 2, *The Poetry*, ed. Carl Dawson (London: Routledge/Taylor and Francis, 2005), 282. Arnold, "Rugby Chapel" (1867), in *Poems*, ed. Allott, 444–52; Arnold, "Stanzas from the Grand Chartreuse," 85–86.

5. John Stuart Mill, "The Spirit of the Age," *The Examiner* (January–May 1831), in *Collected Works of John Stuart Mill*, gen. ed. John M. Robson, vol. 22, *Newspaper Writings*, ed. Ann P. Robson and John M. Robson (Toronto: University of Toronto Press, 1986), 230.

6. *A Selection from the Works of Lord Byron*, ed. Algernon Charles Swinburne (London: Edward Moxon, 1866), v.

7. Ibid.

8. Arnold, "Memorial Verses" (1850), in *Poems*, ed. Allott, 225–29.

9. *A Selection from the Works of Lord Byron*, ed. Swinburne, v; Arnold, "Wordsworth" (1879), in *The Complete Prose Works of Matthew Arnold*, ed. R. H. Super, 11 vols. (Ann Arbor: University of Michigan Press, 1960–77), vol. 9, *English Literature and Irish Politics* (1973), 36–55 (37).

10. Jerome J. McGann, "Who's Carving Up the Nineteenth Century?" *PMLA* 116, no. 5 (2001): 1415–21; Charles J. Rzepka, "The Feel of Not to Feel It," *PMLA* 116, no. 5 (2001): 1422–31; Susan J. Wolfson, "Our Puny Boundaries: Why the Craving for Carving Up the Nineteenth Century?" *PMLA* 116, no. 5 (2001): 1432–41.

11. Frank Kermode, *Romantic Image* (London: Routledge, 1957; repr. 2002), 16, 18.

12. Ibid., 19.

13. Arnold, "Empedocles on Etna," in *Poems*, ed. Allott, 147–94.

14. Kermode, *Romantic Image*, 19.

15. Arnold, *Poems*, ed. Allott, 591.

16. Ibid., 591, 592.

17. Benjamin Disraeli, *Venetia* (1837), in *The Bradenham Edition of the Novels and Tales of Benjamin Disraeli*, vol. 7 (London: Peter Davies, 1927), v. Dedication to Lord Lyndhurst.

18. For details of the attitudes toward her father that permeated Ada Byron's upbringing, see Malcolm Elwin, *Lord Byron's Family: Annabella, Ada and Augusta 1816–1824* (London: John Murray, 1975).

19. Richard Cronin calculates that Carducis dies "at least a few months" before Byron, his principal historical model, was born. Richard Cronin, *Romantic Victorians: English Literature, 1824–1840* (Basingstoke: Palgrave, 2002), 40.

20. Eve Kosofsky Sedgwick takes the concept of "triangulation" from René Girard and others, and uses it to analyze male homosocial desire: Eve Kosofsky Sedgwick, *Between Men: English Literature and Male Homosocial Desire* (New York: Columbia University Press, 1985), 21–27.

21. Andrew Elfenbein, for example, reads *Venetia* and Bulwer Lytton's *Pelham* as examples of novels that allowed their authors to adopt an attention-seeking pose of homoerotic Byronic flamboyance before rejecting that pose and entering political life. Andrew Elfenbein, *Byron and the Victorians* (Cambridge: Cambridge University Press, 1995), 217–29. Michael Flavin reads *Venetia* as a transitional work, coming between the self-dramatizing autobiographical novels of Disraeli's youth and the political consciousness of his mature writing. Michael Flavin, *Benjamin Disraeli: The Novel as Political Discourse* (Brighton: Sussex Academic Press, 2005), 59–64. Emily Allen and Dino F. Felluga read *Venetia* as Disraeli's attempt to place the exotic, cosmopolitan energies of Romanticism into the service of a domestic, Tory political agenda. Emily Allen and Dino F. Felluga, "Feeling Cosmopolitan: The Novel Politician after Byron," *European Romantic Review* 20, no. 5 (2009): 651–59.

22. Ann R. Hawkins, "Evoking Byron from Manuscript to Print: Benjamin Disraeli's *Venetia*," *Papers of the Bibliographical Society of America* 98, no. 4 (2004): 449–76 (475).

23. Elfenbein notes that "the attachment of Herbert and Carducis underscores the extent to which they are both outdated as literary and political figures, despite their age difference" (*Byron and the Victorians*, 227).

24. "To the Queen" ("Revered, beloved—O you that hold"), in *The Poems of Tennyson*, ed. Christopher Ricks, 2nd ed., 3 vols. (Berkeley: University of California Press, 1987), 2:462–64.

25. Stephen Gill, *William Wordsworth: A Life* (Oxford: Oxford University Press, 1990), 373.

26. Arthur Henry Hallam to William Gladstone, 14 September 1829, in *The Letters of Arthur Henry Hallam*, ed. Jack Kolb (Columbus: Ohio State University Press, 1981), 319.

27. Hallam Tennyson, *Alfred Lord Tennyson: A Memoir by his Son*, 2 vols. (London: Macmillan, 1897), 1:123.

28. John D. Jump, ed., *Tennyson: The Critical Heritage* (London: Routledge and Kegan Paul, 1967), 245–46.

29. Hallam Tennyson, ed., *Tennyson and his Friends* (London: Macmillan, 1911), 297.

30. Ibid., 296.

31. Ibid., 382.

32. *The Complete Notebooks of Henry James*, ed. Leon Edel and Lyall H. Powers (New York: Oxford University Press, 1987), 33.

33. Henry James, *The Aspern Papers* (London: J. M. Dent, 1994), 15.

34. Ibid., 82.

35. Ibid., 83.

36. Ibid., 8.

37. Ibid.

38. Ibid., 7.

39. Ibid., 8.

40. For a study of the concept in a French context, see Pierre Nora, "Generation," in *Realms of Memory: The Construction of the French Past*, ed. Pierre Nora, trans. Arthur Goldhammer, 3 vols. (New York: Columbia University Press, 1998), 1:499–531.

41. Walter Scott, *Rob Roy* (1817; rev. ed. 1829), ed. Ian Duncan, Oxford World's Classics (Oxford: Oxford University Press, 1998), 217, 277, 294.

42. John Keats, "Ode to a Nightingale" (1820), 62, in *The Poems of John Keats*, ed. Jack Stillinger (London: Heinemann, 1978), 369–72 (371).

43. Raymond Williams, "Generation," in *Keywords: A Vocabulary of Culture and Society*, rev. and expanded ed. (London: Fontana, 1983), 140–41. Williams points to a shift in the implications of the word that is registered by *The Oxford English Dictionary* but not precisely located historically. *OED* records that "generation" can mean simply a particular sort of person (sense 4), without any connotation of succession, but that it can also mean "[a]ll of the people born and living at about the same time, regarded collectively" (sense 5). *OED* notes that "in later use" the word frequently carries the "implication of shared cultural and social attitudes" (sense 5a).

44. Walter Scott, *Waverley* (1814), ed. Claire Lamont, Oxford World's Classics (Oxford: Oxford University Press, 1986), 5, 341.

45. Karl Mannheim, "The Problem of Generations" (1927), in *Essays on the Sociology of Knowledge* (London: Routledge and Kegan Paul, 1952), 276–320 (303). See also Bryan S. Turner and June Edwards, *Generations, Culture and Society* (Buckingham: Open University Press, 2002).

46. Franco Moretti, *Graphs, Maps, Trees: Abstract Models for Literary History* (London: Verso, 2005), 21 and 22n.

47. Both Arnold and Swinburne, however, tend to conflate the previous two generations, speaking of Wordsworth and Byron as part of the same cohort and not following the twentieth-century academic protocol of dividing Romanticism into "first" and "second" generations.

48. Gertrude Stein reportedly coined this phrase, and Ernest Hemingway used it as the epigraph of *The Sun Also Rises* (1926).

49. T. S. Eliot, "The Romantic Generation If It Existed," *Athenaeum* (18 July 1919): 616–17. Eliot's remark about disliking the word "generation" is quoted in F. O. Matthiessen, *The Achievement of T. S. Eliot* (London: Oxford University Press, 1935), 106 (apparently from Matthiessen's conversations with Eliot).

50. "Byron's Contemporaries," *The Times* (20 October 1874): 2.

51. Obituary for Sir Henry Taylor, *The Standard* (London) (30 March 1886): 5.

52. William Graham, *Last Links with Byron, Shelley, and Keats* (London: Leonard Smithers, 1898). As William Michael Rossetti noted, several details of these interviews are erroneous and unreliable: *Some Reminiscences of William Michael Rossetti*, 2 vols. (New York: Charles Scribner's Sons, 1906), 2:354–55.

53. All *OED*. These neologisms are discussed by Robert Douglas-Fairhurst, who notes that "'neo-Catholic' is 'the first such 'neo-' neologism cited by the *OED*." Robert Douglas-Fairhurst, *Victorian Afterlives: The Shaping of Influence in Nineteenth-Century Literature* (Oxford: Oxford University Press, 2002), 75.

54. *The Poetical Works of Robert Browning*, vol. 5, *Men and Women*, ed. Ian Jack and Robert Inglesfield (Oxford: Clarendon Press, 1995), 256.

Chapter 4. Illustration as Renovation

1. William Wordsworth, "Illustrated Books and Newspapers" (1846), in *Last Poems, 1821–1850,* ed. Jared Curtis, The Cornell Wordsworth (Ithaca, NY: Cornell University Press, 1999), 405–6.

2. Wordsworth, "Prefatory Sonnet" ("Nuns Fret Not at Their Convent's Narrow Room") (1807), 11, in *Poems, in Two Volumes, and Other Poems, 1800–1807,* ed. Jared Curtis, The Cornell Wordsworth (Ithaca, NY: Cornell University Press, 1983), 133.

3. William Galperin, *The Return of the Visible in British Romanticism* (Baltimore: Johns Hopkins University Press, 1993), 19.

4. Walter Scott to George Ellis, 21 August 1804, in *The Letters of Sir Walter Scott,* ed. H.J.C. Grierson, 12 vols. (London: Constable, 1932–37), 1:227. On illustrations to Scott's works, see Catherine Gordon, "The Illustration of Sir Walter Scott: Nineteenth-Century Enthusiasm and Adaptation," *Journal of the Warburg and Courtauld Institutes* 34 (1971): 297–317; Richard D. Altick, *Paintings from Books: Art and Literature in Britain, 1760–1900* (Columbus: Ohio State University Press, 1985), 163–64, 424–36, and passim.

5. Gillen D'Arcy Wood, *The Shock of the Real: Romanticism and Visual Culture, 1760–1860* (Basingstoke: Palgrave, 2001), 1–16.

6. W.J.T. Mitchell, *Iconology: Image, Text, Ideology* (Chicago: University of Chicago Press, 1986), 25.

7. On Wordsworth's portraits, see Frances Blanshard, *Portraits of Wordsworth* (London: George Allen and Unwin, 1959). On his engagement with landscape artists, see Timothy Fulford, "Virtual Topography: Poets, Painters, Publishers and the Reproduction of the Landscape in the Early Nineteenth Century," *Romanticism and Victorianism on the Net* 57–58 (2010). On the visual appearance of his later editions, see Peter Simonsen, *Wordsworth and the Word-Preserving Arts: Typographic Inscription, Ekphrasis and Posterity in the Later Work* (Basingstoke: Palgrave, 2007).

8. Peter Manning, "Wordsworth's 'Illustrated Books and Newspapers' and Media of the City," in *Romanticism and the City,* ed. Larry Peer (New York: Palgrave Macmillan, 2011), 223–40.

9. See the "Illustrating Scott" database compiled by Peter Garside and Ruth McAdams: http://illustratingscott.lib.ed.ac.uk, and Richard J. Hill, *Picturing Scotland through the Waverley Novels: Walter Scott and the Origins of the Victorian Illustrated Novel* (Farnham: Ashgate, 2010).

10. Raymond Lister notes that "if it had not been for the illustration of books it is unlikely that reproductive printmaking techniques would have developed so quickly or so plentifully as they did." Raymond Lister, *Prints and Printmaking: A Dictionary and Handbook of the Art in Nineteenth-Century Britain* (London: Methuen, 1984), 1.

11. On the Boydell Shakespeare Gallery, see Winifred H. Friedman, *Boydell's Shakespeare Gallery* (New York: Garland, 1976); Frederick Burwick and Walter Pape, eds., *The Boydell Shakespeare Gallery* (Bottrop: Peter Pomp, 1996); and Christopher Rovee, *Imagining the Gallery: The Social Body of British Romanticism* (Stanford, CA: Stanford University Press, 2006), 75–104. On Fuseli's Milton Gallery, see Luisa Calè, *Fuseli's Milton Gallery: Turning Readers into Spectators* (Oxford: Clarendon Press, 2006).

12. John Dryden, *The Works of John Dryden: Now First Collected in Eighteen Volumes Illustrated with Notes, Historical, Critical, and Explanatory, and a Life of the Author, by Walter Scott, esq.* (London: William Miller, 1808).

13. Robert Cadell, "Notice to the *Waverley Novels*" (Edinburgh: Robert Cadell, 1844), n.p., cited by Wood, in *The Shock of the Real*, 250; "Illustrated Works," *London Review* 22 (January 1859): 475; "Tennyson Illustrated by Doré," *The Times* (29 December 1868): 10.

14. "Illustrated Books," *Journal of the Society of Arts* (22 January 1864): 159. Richard Maxwell notes that an "unprecedented range of extraordinary illustrated books" in the nineteenth century "absorbed a huge amount of artistic activity into mass-market publishing": Richard Maxwell, *The Illustrated Victorian Book* (Charlottesville: University of Virginia Press, 2002), xxi, xxiii. See also Paul Goldman, *Victorian Illustration: The Pre-Raphaelites, the Idyllic School and the High Victorians* (Burlington, VT: Lund Humphries, 2004), and John Buchanan-Brown, *Early Victorian Illustrated Books: Britain, France and Germany, 1820–1860* (London: British Library; New Castle, DE: Oak Knoll Press, 2005).

15. "The Reader," review of William Michael Rossetti, *Lives of Famous Poets, The Graphic* (21 March 1885): 23; "Christmas Books," *Daily News* (7 November 1863): 2.

16. Samuel Taylor Coleridge, *The Rime of the Ancient Mariner*, illus. Gustave Doré (London: Doré Gallery and Hamilton, Adams and Co., 1876); *The Illustrated Byron, with upwards of two hundred engravings from original drawings* (London: Henry Vizetelly, 1854–55).

17. "Illustrated Selections of Poetry," *Illustrated London News* (29 December 1866): 11.

18. "New Illustrated Books," *Morning Post* (8 December 1860): 2. This passage specifically concerns books produced for Christmas, but it also applies more generally.

19. "The Illustration Nuisance," *Pall Mall Gazette* (28 December 1866): 12.

20. Review of Christopher Wordsworth, *Greece: Pictorial, Descriptive and Historical, Morning Chronicle* (12 January 1853): 7.

21. David Blewett, *The Illustration of "Robinson Crusoe," 1719–1920* (Gerrards Cross: Colin Smythe, 1995), 15.

22. Walter Scott to Mrs. Hughes, 9 or 10 October 1828, in *Letters*, 11 (1936): 7.

23. William St. Clair, *The Reading Nation in the Romantic Period* (Cambridge: Cambridge University Press, 2004), 32–40.

24. Carol M. Armstrong, *Scenes in a Library: Reading the Photograph in the Book, 1843–1875* (Cambridge, MA: MIT Press, 1998), 3.

25. William Henry Fox Talbot, *The Pencil of Nature (Facsimile Edition)* (Chicago: KWS, 2011), xxxi.

26. Jerome J. McGann, *The Textual Condition* (Princeton, NJ: Princeton University Press, 1991), 77.

27. This edition is discussed in Stephen Gill, *Wordsworth and the Victorians* (Oxford: Clarendon Press, 1998), 93–98.

28. G. Thomas Tanselle, *Literature and Artifacts* (Charlottesville: Bibliographical Society of the University of Virginia, 1998).

29. J. Hillis Miller, *Illustration* (London: Reaktion, 1992), 9.

30. For a counterargument, which aims to recover images of the sister arts working in concert from the beginning of the ekphrastic tradition, see Andrew S. Becker, "Contest or Concert? A Speculative Essay on Ecphrasis and Rivalry between the Arts," *Classical and Modern Literature: A Quarterly* 23, no. 1 (2003): 1–14.

31. Morris Eaves, "The Sister Arts in British Romanticism," in *The Cambridge Companion to British Romanticism*, ed. Stuart Curran (Cambridge: Cambridge University Press, 1993), 236;

Julia Thomas, *Pictorial Victorians: The Inscription of Values in Word and Image* (Athens: Ohio University Press, 2004), 8.

32. James A. W. Heffernan, *Museum of Words: The Poetics of Ekphrasis from Homer to Ashbery* (Chicago: University of Chicago Press, 1993), 6.

33. "Our Address," *Illustrated London News* (14 May 1842): 1.

Chapter 5. Renovating Romantic Poetry: Retrofitted Illustrations

1. *Lord Byron's Don Juan: with Life and Original Notes by A. Cunningham Esq. and Many Illustrations on Steel* (London: Charles Daly, 1852). Charles Daly was a publisher in London by 1832 and issued a pirated edition of *Childe Harold's Pilgrimage* (London: C. Daly, 1839) in sextodecimo. He went bankrupt in 1841 but was back in business by 1850, when he published a duodecimo edition of *Don Juan* and *Lord Byron's Poetical Works, with Life and Notes by Allan Cunningham, Esq. Select Family Edition* (London: Charles Daly, [1850?]). This book omitted *Don Juan* and *Childe Harold* entirely. Its editor, Allan Cunningham, was an assistant to the sculptor Sir Francis Chantrey, an acquaintance of James Hogg and Walter Scott, a minor poet and a regular contributor to periodicals. He died in 1842, and it is unclear whether his editorial work on Byron was complete at his death or finished by one of his sons. (He had five sons, one of whom edited the *Life* of David Wilkie that Cunningham left unfinished at his death.) Apparently Cunningham had undertaken to annotate *Don Juan* as well, since Daly followed the "Family" Byron with the 1852 edition of *Don Juan* discussed here. For details of Daly, see the British Book Trade Index [http://www.bbti.bham.ac.uk, accessed 21 November 2007]. For details of Cunningham, see Leslie Stephen, "Cunningham, Allan (1784–1842)," rev. Hamish Whyte, *Oxford Dictionary of National Biography* (Oxford: Oxford University Press, 2004) [http://www.oxforddnb.com/view/article/6918, accessed 16 January 2008].

2. *Lord Byron's Don Juan*, Don Juan on Haidee's island: image illustrating *DJ* 4.37, facing p. 126; Don Juan in the slave market: image illustrating *DJ* 5.26, facing p. 148.

3. John Harvey, *Men in Black* (London: Reaktion, 1995), 23. Harvey asserts that "up to a certain date in the early nineteenth century, men's evening wear changed freely and could be in many colours," but from "the later 1810s, the smart began to wear black in the evenings, and evening wear has stayed black ever since" (28). For details of costume dating, see Blanche Payne, *The History of Costume* (New York: Harper Collins, 1992), 474–76; and R. Turner Wilcox, *The Mode in Costumes* (New York: Charles Scribner, 1958), 257–58. I am grateful to Catherine Bradley for information on costume history.

4. Iris Brooke and James Laver note that "although ball dresses were very low, and neck and shoulders bare, there was a surprising absence of neck jewellery, a simple brooch in front of the corsage being considered sufficient." Iris Brooke and James Laver, *English Costume from the Fourteenth through the Nineteenth Century* (New York: Macmillan, 1987), 384.

5. Nancy Bradfield, *Historical Costumes of England: From the Eleventh to the Twentieth Century* (London: G. G. Harrap, 1938), 132, 136.

6. Wilcox, *The Mode in Costumes*, 294, 296.

7. Stephen Cheeke has shown how, despite some radically modern attitudes, aspects of *Don Juan* seemed old-fashioned even on its first publication as a result of Byron's detachment from contemporary English politics and his nostalgia for the political scene of the previous

decade (when he had already been nostalgic for the decade before). "This frequently produces an anachronistic effect in the poem, as if Byron has slipped out of time somewhere around 1814, so that even when the poem *appears* to be speaking in an immediate English context about current English affairs, to its original readership it may have seemed marginally out of sync." Stephen Cheeke, *Byron and Place: History, Translation, Nostalgia* (Basingstoke: Palgrave, 2003), 181.

8. *Our English Lakes, Mountains and Waterfalls, as Seen by William Wordsworth, photographically illustrated* [by Thomas Ogle] (London: A. W. Bennett, 1864; 2nd ed. 1866). This book provoked a dispute between the publisher and Wordsworth's heirs over copyright, which led to changes between the first two editions. The images examined here are from the second edition. See Stephen Gill, *Wordsworth and the Victorians* (Oxford: Clarendon Press, 1998), 87–89.

9. The principal reference source on stereo photography remains William C. Darrah, *The World of Stereographs* (Gettysburg, PA: Darrah, 1977).

10. "I made [Jeffrey] admire the song of Lord Clifford's minstrel, which I like exceedingly myself." Walter Scott to Robert Southey, November 1807, in *The Letters of Sir Walter Scott*, ed. H.J.C. Grierson, 12 vols. (London: Constable, 1932–37), 1:390. Cited in Robert Woof, ed., *Wordsworth: The Critical Heritage*, vol. 1, *1793–1820* (London: Routledge, 2001), 235.

11. Susan Sontag, *On Photography* (London: Penguin, 1977), 15.

12. "Some Account of the Art of Photogenic Drawing," *Edinburgh Review* 76 (1843): 309.

13. Bruce Graver, "Wordsworth, Scott, and the Stereographic Picturesque," *Literature Compass* 6, no. 4 (2009): 896–926.

14. Roland Barthes, *Camera Lucida: Reflections on Photography*, trans. Richard Howard (New York: Hill and Wang, 1981).

15. William Wordsworth, note to "Song, at the Feast of Brougham Castle," in *Poems, in Two Volumes, and Other Poems, 1800–1807*, ed. Jared Curtis, The Cornell Wordsworth (Ithaca, NY: Cornell University Press, 1983), 425. Introduction to *Our English Lakes, Mountains and Waterfalls*, vi.

16. Helen Groth, *Victorian Photography and Literary Nostalgia* (Oxford: Oxford University Press, 2003).

17. Henry Chorley, *Memorials of Mrs Hemans: with Illustrations of her Literary Character from her Private Correspondence*, 2 vols. (London: Saunders and Otley, 1836), 1:16.

18. Ibid., 1:80.

19. *The Works of Mrs Hemans, with a Memoir by her Sister*, 7 vols. (Edinburgh: William Blackwood, 1839), 1:14.

20. Susan J. Wolfson, introduction to *Felicia Hemans: Selected Poems, Letters, Reception Materials*, ed. Susan J. Wolfson (Princeton, NJ: Princeton University Press, 2000), xiii–xxix; Paula R. Feldman, "The Poet and the Profits: Felicia Hemans and the Literary Marketplace," *Keats-Shelley Journal* 46 (1997): 148–76.

21. *The Works of Mrs Hemans*, 1:208.

22. Chorley, *Memorials of Mrs Hemans*, 1:16; *The Works of Mrs Hemans*, 1:4–5.

23. [John Wilson], "Small Talk," *Blackwood's Edinburgh Magazine* 5, no. 30 (September 1819): 686.

24. Tricia A. Lootens, *Lost Saints: Silence, Gender, and Victorian Literary Canonization* (Charlottesville: University of Virginia Press, 1996), esp. 1–15.

25. Felicia Hemans, *Poems of Felicia Hemans* (Edinburgh: William Blackwood, 1865).

26. Eric Hobsbawm, "Introduction: Inventing Traditions," in *The Invention of Tradition*, ed. Eric Hobsbawm and Terence Ranger (Cambridge: Cambridge University Press, 1983), 2.

27. Prys Morgan, "From a Death to a View: The Hunt for the Welsh Past in the Romantic Period," in *The Invention of Tradition*, ed. Hobsbawm and Ranger, 43–99.

28. Michael Freeman, "Lady Llanover and the Welsh Costume Prints," *National Library of Wales Journal* 34, no. 2 (2007): 235–51; Christine Stevens, "Welsh Peasant Dress: Workwear or National Costume?" *Textile History* 33 (2002): 63–78; Morgan, "From a Death to a View," 79–81.

29. It is difficult to fix a precise date for the installation of the first steps at the stone. Pocklington owned the land by 1798 and recorded the stone's measurements in a notebook dated 15 May 1799 (now in the Public Record Office in Carlisle). Robert Southey visited the stone in 1807 and listed Pocklington's alterations in his fictional *Letters from England*: "a little mock hermitage, [. . .] a new druidical stone, [. . .] an ugly house for an old woman to live in who is to show the rock [. . .] a hole underneath through which the curious may gratify themselves by shaking hands with the old woman." Robert Southey, Letter XLIII, in *Letters from England: by Don Manuel Alvarez Espriella. Translated from the Spanish*, ed. Jack Simmons (London: Cresset, 1951), 243. Despite the comprehensiveness of his list, Southey does not mention a set of stairs. It seems likely that the stairs were installed after 1807, although a temporary ladder may have been in regular use before this date. I am grateful to Alan Smith for providing information about the stone's history and to Jeff Cowton and Harvey Wilkinson for discussions of its significance.

30. J. B. Pyne, *Lake Scenery in England*, drawn on stone by T. Picken (London: Day and Son, 1859). By composing his image like this, Pyne met the criteria of excellence outlined in his publisher's preface, which conformed to the discourse of the picturesque when it claimed that "without sacrificing truth to those graces of art by which it is sometimes impaired and disguised," Pyne had "treated his subjects in a style which cannot fail to render them acceptable as PICTURES" (ii).

31. William Wordsworth, *Guide to the Lakes*, ed. Ernest de Selincourt with a preface by Stephen Gill (London: Frances Lincoln, 2004), 35.

32. Wordsworth, *Guide to the Lakes*, 79.

33. "Christmas Books," review of *Our English Lakes, Mountains, and Waterfalls, as seen by William Wordsworth*, *Daily News* (7 November 1863): 2.

34. Although she does not discuss the images that I examine here, Helen Groth makes a similar argument when she represents books such as Ogle's as "an effort to modernise Wordsworth's vision" (*Victorian Photography*, 60).

35. Edward Finden and William Finden, *Findens' Illustrations of the Life and Works of Lord Byron*, with notes by William Brockedon, 3 vols. (London: John Murray and Charles Tilt, 1833–34). For a longer discussion of the Findens' illustrations, see Tom Mole, "Impresarios of Byron's Afterlife," *Nineteenth-Century Contexts* 29, no. 1 (2007): 17–34.

36. David Blayney Brown, *Turner and Byron* (London: Tate Gallery, 1992), 99.

37. One hundred and twenty engravings issued as parts, thirty-five additions from the duodecimo life and works edition, and six appearing as frontispieces and title-page vignettes to the three volumes.

38. *Findens' Illustrations*, vol. 1, unnumbered p.

39. Blayney Brown, *Turner and Byron*, 43–51.

40. Thomas Moore, *Letters and Journals of Lord Byron with Notices of His Life*, 2 vols. (London: John Murray, 1830–31), 2:178. See also *Byron's Letters and Journals*, ed. Leslie A. Marchand, 13 vols. (London: John Murray, 1973–94), 6 (1976): 48.

41. Cited in Andrew Rutherford, ed., *Byron: The Critical Heritage* (London: Routledge, 1970), 423.

42. This passage was illustrated with an image of the Rialto in *Thirty Illustrations of Childe Harold* (London: Art Union, 1855), unnumbered p.

43. *Findens' Illustrations*, vol. 3, unnumbered p.

44. For more information on the rise of middle-class European tourism in the Victorian period, see Judith Flanders, *Consuming Passions: Leisure and Pleasure in Victorian Britain* (London: Harper Press, 2006), 206–51.

Chapter 6. Turning the Page: Illustrated Frontmatter

1. Kate Flint, *The Victorians and the Visual Imagination* (Cambridge: Cambridge University Press, 2000), esp. 197–235.

2. Jonathan Crary, *Techniques of the Observer: On Vision and Modernity in the Nineteenth Century* (Cambridge, MA: MIT Press, 1990), argues that the fascination with optical illusions helped to situate perception within the physiology of the individual, producing modern subjects who were both agents of their own perception and open to new forms of control and standardization of vision. Isobel Armstrong, *Victorian Glassworlds: Glass Culture and the Imagination 1830–1880* (Oxford: Oxford University Press, 2008), 253–361, examines the uses of glass lenses, slides, and transparencies in Victorian optical toys.

3. Crary, *Techniques of the Observer*, 98.

4. For an account of this frontispiece, see Derek Pearsall, "The *Troilus* Frontispiece and Chaucer's Audience," *Yearbook of English Studies* 7 (1977): 68–74. Whether the reading figure is actually intended as a likeness of Chaucer remains debatable, but the figure does resemble other portraits of Chaucer. See Pearsall, 69, n. 3. The manuscript is MS 61 in the Parker Library at Corpus Christi College. A printed facsimile is available: Geoffrey Chaucer, *Troilus and Criseyde: A Facsimile of Corpus Christi, Cambridge Library MS 61*, introductions by M. B. Parkes and Elizabeth Salter (Cambridge: D. S. Brewer, 1978). A digital version is available via www.parkerweb.stanford.edu, accessed 8 August 2013.

5. See David Scott Kastan, *Shakespeare and the Book* (Cambridge: Cambridge University Press, 2001), 50–78; and Leah Marcus, *Puzzling Shakespeare: Local Reading and Its Discontents* (Berkeley: University of California Press, 1988), 2–25.

6. Gérard Genette, *Paratexts: Thresholds of Interpretation*, trans. Jane E. Lewin (Cambridge: Cambridge University Press, 1997).

7. Janine Barchas, *Graphic Design, Print Culture, and the Eighteenth-Century Novel* (Cambridge: Cambridge University Press, 2003), 22.

8. William St. Clair, *The Reading Nation in the Romantic Period* (Cambridge: Cambridge University Press, 2004), 331.

9. Roger Chartier, *The Order of Books: Readers, Authors and Libraries in Europe between the Fourteenth and the Eighteenth Centuries*, trans. Lydia G. Cochrane (Cambridge: Polity, 1994), 52.

10. Gerald Egan, "Radical Moral Authority and Desire: The Image of the Male Romantic Poet in Frontispiece Portraits of Byron and Shelley," *The Eighteenth Century: Theory and Interpretation* 50, no. 2–3 (2009): 185–205; Peter Simonsen, *Wordsworth and the Word-Preserving Arts: Typographic Inscription, Ekphrasis and Posterity in the Later Work* (Basingstoke: Palgrave, 2007), 175.

11. Andrew Piper, *Dreaming in Books: The Making of the Bibliographic Imagination in the Romantic Age* (Chicago: University of Chicago Press, 2009), 59.

12. Barchas, *Graphic Design*, 21.

13. Ben Jonson, *The Complete Poems*, ed. George Parfitt (London: Penguin, 1996), 263.

14. Jacques Derrida, *Of Grammatology*, trans. Gayatri Chakravorty Spivak (Baltimore: Johns Hopkins University Press, 1998), 144.

15. Henry Chorley, *Memorials of Mrs Hemans: with Illustrations of her Literary Character from her Private Correspondence*, 2 vols. (London: Saunders and Otley, 1836), 2:58.

16. This bust existed in two states, a plaster version and a marble version, with minor differences. Both are now held in the National Portrait Gallery in London. See Richard Walker, *Regency Portraits*, 2 vols. (London: National Portrait Gallery, 1985), 1:245.

17. Chorley, *Memorials of Mrs Hemans*, 2:59.

18. *The Works of Mrs Hemans, with a Memoir by her Sister*, 7 vols. (Edinburgh: William Blackwood, 1839), 2:130, quoted in Walker, *Regency Portraits*, 1: 245.

19. Ford Madox Brown completed six illustrations for the Byron volume, which appeared in 1870, and his son Oliver contributed another two. Brown simultaneously or subsequently worked up five of his illustrations into paintings: *Byron's Dream* (1874), oil on canvas, Manchester City Art Galleries; another version (1889), watercolor on paper, Whitworth Art Gallery, University of Manchester. The *Corsair's Return* (1870–71), watercolor on paper, Delaware Art Museum. *The Dream of Sardanapalus* (1871–72), watercolor on paper, Delaware Art Museum; other versions remain untraced. *Jacopo Foscari*, or *Jacopo Foscari in Prison* (1869–70), watercolor, Craven Collection. *Don Juan Found by Haidée* (1870–73, retouched until 1876), oil on canvas, Birmingham Museums and Art Gallery; another oil version is in the Musée d'Orsay, Paris; a watercolor version, 1869–70, is in the National Gallery of Victoria, Melbourne. See Ford Madox Hueffer (Ford Madox Ford), *Ford Madox Brown: A Record of his Life and Work* (London: Longmans, Green, 1896), and Kenneth Bendiner, *The Art of Ford Madox Brown* (University Park: Pennsylvania State University Press, 1998).

20. William Michael Rossetti to Algernon Charles Swinburne, 18 March [1869], in *Selected Letters of William Michael Rossetti*, ed. Roger W. Peattie (University Park: Pennsylvania State University Press, 1986), 210. Edward Moxon himself had died in 1858; his widow Emma ran the firm after his death, with help from administrators, until 1864, when she appointed J. Bertrand Payne, who had worked under Moxon, as a manager. Payne sold his share of the firm in April 1869 and Emma Moxon was bought out in 1871 by Ward, Lock, and Tyler, who continued to publish books under the Moxon imprint until 1877. Hans Ostrom, "Moxon, Edward (bap. 1801, d. 1858)," *Oxford Dictionary of National Biography* (Oxford: Oxford University Press, 2004) [http://www.oxforddnb.com/view/article/19463, accessed 17 January 2008]; Harold G. Merriam, *Edward Moxon, Publisher of Poets* (New York: Columbia University Press, 1939), 194.

21. William Michael Rossetti, ed., *Rossetti Papers, 1862–1870: A Compilation* (New York: Charles Scribner's Sons, 1903), 381.

22. William Michael Rossetti to Dante Gabriel Rossetti, 12 September 1869, in *Selected Letters*, 228.

23. *The Poetical Works of Lord Byron*, ed. William Michael Rossetti, illus. Ford Madox Brown (London: E. Moxon, Son and Co., 1870), xv.

24. Ibid., xx.

25. The tissue guard is present in most, but not all, copies of the first edition of this book that I have examined. It seems likely that books in this series were issued with tissue guards, some of which have become detached.

26. *A Selection from the Works of Lord Byron*, ed. Algernon Charles Swinburne (London: Edward Moxon, 1866).

27. To be accurate, the quotation should read: "The grass upon my grave will grow as long, / And sigh to midnight winds, but not to song." Lord Byron, *The Complete Poetical Works*, ed. Jerome J. McGann, 7 vols. (Oxford: Clarendon Press, 1980–93), 5 (1986): 235.

28. *Byron's Dream*, illus. Mrs. Lees (London: Dickinson and Co., 1849).

29. William Michael Rossetti, preface to *The Poetical Works of Lord Byron*, xi.

30. William Michael Rossetti to Algernon Charles Swinburne, 11 August 1870, in *Selected Letters*, 261. Swinburne's 1866 *Selection from the Works of Lord Byron* had taken advantage of the expiry, in that year, of copyright on the final poems published during Byron's lifetime.

31. Rossetti, preface to *The Poetical Works of Lord Byron*, xii.

32. *The Poetical Works of William Wordsworth*, ed. William Michael Rossetti, illus. Henry Dell (London: E. Moxon, Son and Co., [1870]).

33. William Michael Rossetti, prefatory notice to *The Poetical Works of William Wordsworth*, ed. William Michael Rossetti, illus. Edwin Edwards (London: Edward Moxon, Son and Co., 1871), xxi.

34. The point had been made even more clearly by the frontispiece to the 1845 Moxon edition of Wordsworth's poems, which is an engraving by William Finden of Francis Chantrey's 1820 bust of the poet, produced with his approval. *The Poems of William Wordsworth* (London: Edward Moxon, 1845). For a discussion of this frontispiece and its construction of Wordsworth's late poetic identity, see Simonsen, *Wordsworth and the Word-Preserving Arts*, 159–84. This image was reused for the Wordsworth volume in Moxon's series of Miniature Poets (1865), edited by Francis Turner Palgrave. *A Selection from the Works of William Wordsworth*, ed. Francis Turner Palgrave, Moxon's Miniature Poets (London: Edward Moxon and Co., 1865).

35. Rossetti, prefatory notice to *The Poetical Works of William Wordsworth*, xxii.

36. Matthew Arnold, preface to *Poems of Wordsworth*, chosen and edited by Matthew Arnold (London: Macmillan and Co., 1879), xii.

37. William Wordsworth, *The Prelude* (1850), 1.303, in *The Fourteen-Book Prelude*, ed. W.J.B. Owen, The Cornell Wordsworth (Ithaca, NY: Cornell University Press, 1985).

38. Nicola J. Watson, *The Literary Tourist: Readers and Places in Romantic and Victorian Britain* (Basingstoke: Palgrave, 2006), 56–89.

39. William Wordsworth, "Tintern Abbey" (1798), 89, in *Lyrical Ballads, and Other Poems, 1797–1800*, ed. James Butler and Karen Green, The Cornell Wordsworth (Ithaca, NY: Cornell University Press, 1992), 116–20.

Chapter 7. A Religious Reception Tradition

1. *Byron's Letters and Journals*, ed. Leslie A. Marchand, 13 vols. (London: John Murray, 1973–94), 9 (1979): 76.

2. James Kennedy, *Conversations on Religion, with Lord Byron and others, held in Cephalonia, a short time previous to His Lordship's Death* (London: John Murray, 1830), 54.

3. John Sheppard, *Thoughts Chiefly Designed as a Preparative or Persuasive to Private Devotion* (London: G. and B. Whittaker, 1824), 244–45.

4. This was partly due to the work of the Church Building Commission, which operated from 1818 to 1856 and allocated public funds to support building churches. It also, however, reflects significant numbers of churches largely built through voluntary contributions. Joseph S. Meisel, *Public Speech and the Culture of Public Life in the Age of Gladstone* (New York: Columbia University Press, 2001), 109–12.

5. Meisel cites figures for several denominations. Ibid., 108.

6. Callum G. Brown, *The Death of Christian Britain: Understanding Secularisation, 1800–2000*, 2nd ed. (London: Routledge, 2009), 162–63.

7. Brown concludes that "Every major study based on social composition analysis of churchgoers or members shows for every part of Britain from the late eighteenth to the late twentieth centuries, for every denomination, that the working classes were in the majority" (ibid., 155).

8. The census figures are reported and discussed in Meisel, *Public Speech*, 107, and Brown, *The Death of Christian Britain*, 161–62. The figures for Scotland, as Brown points out, are less reliable owing to a higher number of nonreturns from enumerators. Brown also comments that the figures from 1851 are likely to have been historically very high.

9. Simon Eliot, *Some Patterns and Trends in British Publishing, 1800–1919*, Occasional Papers of the Bibliographical Society 8 (London: Bibliographical Society, 1994), esp. 44–58.

10. Leslie Howsam, *Cheap Bibles: Nineteenth-Century Publishing and the British and Foreign Bible Society* (Cambridge: Cambridge University Press, 2002); Leah Price examines bookish it-narratives in *How to Do Things with Books in Victorian Britain* (Princeton, NJ: Princeton University Press, 2012), 107–37.

11. Meisel, *Public Speech*, 113.

12. In discussing Christian commentators as a distinct tradition, I don't want to overlook the fact that many of the writers in the critical heritage would also have identified as Christians. Nor, I hope, do I downplay differences within the religious reception tradition between Christians of different denominations.

13. "Lines Written a Few Miles above Tintern Abbey," 97. Stephen Gill, *Wordsworth and the Victorians* (Oxford: Clarendon Press, 1998), 44.

14. Cited by Gill, ibid., 53.

15. Cited by Gill, ibid., 61.

16. Thomas Dick, *The Philosophy of a Future State* (New York: R. Schoyer, 1831). The appendix is on pp. 273–75. In the body of the tract, Dick refers to Byron on p. 267.

17. David Bristow Baker, *A Treatise on the Nature and Causes of Doubt, in Religious Questions* (London: Longman, Rees, Orme, Brown and Green, 1831). The passage from Byron's letter is quoted on p. xii; the appendix is p. 104.

18. John Morison, *Portraiture of Modern Scepticism; or, A Caveat Against Infidelity* (London: Frederick Westley and A. H. Davis, 1832), 45. Rev. W. Cunningham reached for the identical quotation when he addressed the Edinburgh Young Men's Society in 1842. Rev. Andrew Thomson, Rev. W. Cunningham, Rev. Alexander Fraser, and Rev. D.T.K. Drummond, *Four Lectures to Young Men* (Edinburgh: William Innes, 1842), 62.

19. The letter was also reprinted in several American religious magazines. See "Observations on the Character, Opinions, and Writings of the Late Lord Byron," *Christian Observer* (Boston) 25, no. 2 (1 February 1825): 79; "A Prayer for Lord Byron: To the Right Hon. Lord Byron, at Pisa" and "Byron: The Answer," *Zion's Herald* (Boston) 3, no. 17 (27 April 1825): 2; E. R., "Lord Byron's Answer," *Christian Spectator* (New Haven, CT) 7, no. 9 (September 1825): 450–52; and "Lord Byron's Religious Opinions," *New-England Magazine* (Boston) 1 (August 1831): 112.

20. "Lord Byron," *Bury and Norwich Post* (5 September 1832): 4.

21. [Matthew Iley], *The Life, Writings, Opinions and Times of [. . .] Lord Byron* (London: the author, 1825), 356, 361–66. Iley devoted a chapter to refuting the charges brought against Byron since his death by other writers, including the claim made by Sir Egerton Brydges, in his *Letters on the Character and Poetical Genius of Lord Byron* (1824), that Byron's "attacks on our religious faith are too positive, and too revolting, to be palliated." Iley responded that "no man ever professed, or entertained, a more unequivocal respect for the established religion of his country than Byron did" and, to support this assertion, he reprinted the exchange of letters between Sheppard and Byron in its entirety. Moore did not comment on Byron's letter, but Mrs. Sheppard's prayer prompted him to reprove those who attacked Byron posthumously for lacking Christian charity. Thomas Moore, *Letters and Journals of Lord Byron with Notices of His Life*, 2 vols. (London: John Murray, 1830–31), 2:561–62. The American author of *A Review of the Character and Writings of Lord Byron* (London: Sherwood, Gilbert and Piper, 1826) also retailed the story and reprinted Byron's letter, claiming that it was "more creditable to him in a moral point of view, than any other composition of his which has been published" (144). (The author of this anonymous work is identified in the catalog of the New York Public Library as either Willard Phillips [1784–1873] or Norton Andrews [1786–1853].)

22. John Nichol, *Byron* (London: Macmillan, 1880), 157. *The Works of Lord Byron*, ed. E. H. Coleridge and Rowland E. Prothero, 13 vols. (London: John Murray, 1898–1904), vol. 5, *Letters* (1901), 488–91.

23. Alasdair MacIntyre, *Whose Justice? Which Rationality?* (Notre Dame, IN: University of Notre Dame Press, 1988), 7–8.

24. William R. McKelvy, *The English Cult of Literature: Devoted Readers, 1774–1880* (Charlottesville: University of Virginia Press, 2007), 12.

25. Richard D. Altick, "The Sociology of Authorship: The Social Origins, Education, and Occupations of 1,100 British Writers, 1800–1935," in *Writers, Readers, and Occasions* (Columbus: Ohio State University Press, 1989), 106.

26. McKelvy, *The English Cult of Literature*, 35.

27. Rev. K. Arvine, ed., *The Book of Entertaining and Instructive Anecdote, Moral and Religious* (London: T. Nelson and Sons, 1852), 95; *Anecdotes: The Holy Scriptures* (London: Religious Tract Society, n.d.), 168–69; Charles Carroll Bombaugh, ed., *Gleanings from the Harvest-Fields of Literature, Science and Art* (Baltimore: T. Newton Kurtz, 1860), 79; Rev. James Lee, ed., *Bible Illustrations*, 6 vols. (London: published by subscription, 1867), 6:271; Donald Macleod, *New Cyclopaedia of Illustrative Anecdote, Religious and Moral* (London: E. Stock, 1872), 133.

28. Baker, *Treatise*, 104.

29. Charles Taylor, *A Secular Age* (Cambridge, MA: Harvard University Press, 2007). I draw here especially on pp. 1–22.

30. Ibid., 374.

31. John Stuart Mill, *Autobiography*, in *Collected Works of John Stuart Mill*, gen. ed. John M. Robson, vol. 1, *Autobiography and Literary Essays*, ed. John M. Robson and Jack Stillinger (Toronto: University of Toronto Press, 1981), 47.

32. Matthew Arnold, "Dover Beach," 25, 21, in *The Poems of Matthew Arnold*, ed. Kenneth Allott (London: Longman, 1965), 242.

33. Mill, *Autobiography*, 45.

34. Meisel, *Public Speech*, 109.

35. Boyd Hilton, *A Mad, Bad and Dangerous People? England 1783–1846*, The New Oxford History of England (Oxford: Clarendon Press, 2006), 183.

36. On the "myth of the unholy city," see Brown, *The Death of Christian Britain*, 18–29.

37. Ibid., 37–40.

38. Deidre Shauna Lynch, *Loving Literature: A Cultural History* (Chicago: University of Chicago Press, 2015), 167.

39. M. H. Abrams, *Natural Supernaturalism: Tradition and Revolution in Romantic Literature* (New York: W. W. Norton, 1973); Mark Canuel, *Religion, Toleration, and British Writing, 1790–1830* (Cambridge: Cambridge University Press, 2005); Daniel E. White, *Early Romanticism and Religious Dissent* (Cambridge: Cambridge University Press, 2010).

Chapter 8. Converting Shelley

1. *The Courier* (5 August 1822): 3. Cited in Richard Holmes, *Shelley: The Pursuit* (London: Flamingo, 1995), 730.

2. Stopford A. Brooke, "Inaugural Address to the Shelley Society" (1886), in *Studies in Poetry* (London: Duckworth, 1907), 115–43 (126).

3. Karsten Klejs Engelberg, *The Making of the Shelley Myth: An Annotated Bibliography of Criticism of Percy Bysshe Shelley, 1822–1860* (London: Mansell, 1988), 3.

4. Stopford A. Brooke, *The Development of Theology as Illustrated in English Poetry from 1780 to 1830* (London: Philip Green, 1893), 47.

5. Leigh Hunt, "Canting Slander," *The Examiner* 778 (22 December 1822): 806.

6. The estimate of Wade's religious views is taken from Richard Garnett, "Thomas Wade (1805–1875)," *Dictionary of National Biography* (London: Smith Elder, 1885–1900), 58:419.

7. Thomas Wade, "Shelley," in *Mundis et Cordis* (London: John Miller, 1835), 120.

8. Kristin G. Doern, "Balfour, Clara Lucas (1808–1878)," *Oxford Dictionary of National Biography* (Oxford: Oxford University Press, 2004) [http://www.oxforddnb.com/view/article/1183, accessed 22 December 2015].

9. William McGonagall, "An Address to the Rev. George Gilfillan" (1877), in *Collected Poems*, ed. Chris Hunt (Edinburgh: Birlinn, 2006), 294.

10. *George Gilfillan: Letters and Journals, with Memoir*, ed. Robert A. Watson and Elizabeth S. Watson (London: Hodder and Stoughton, 1892), iv.

11. George G. Armstrong, *Richard Acland Armstrong: A Memoir, with Selected Sermons* (London: Philip Green, 1906), 57, 81.

12. Ibid., 71.

13. Letter from an unnamed college friend, quoted by George Armstrong, ibid., 36–37.

14. Fred L. Standley, *Stopford Brooke* (New York: Twayne, 1972), 13.

15. Stopford A. Brooke, *Theology in the English Poets: Cowper, Coleridge, Wordsworth and Burns*, 10th ed. (London: Kegan Paul, 1907), vi.

16. Standley, *Stopford Brooke*, 73–74.

17. Brooke, *Development of Theology*, 5. Brooke gave the inaugural lecture in 1892. Armstrong lectured in 1897: G. Armstrong, *Richard Acland Armstrong: A Memoir*, 91.

18. Angela Dunstan, "The Shelley Society, Literary Lectures, and the Global Circulation of English Literature and Scholarly Practice," *Modern Language Quarterly* 75, no. 2 (2014): 279–96.

19. Standley, *Stopford Brooke*, 36.

20. Lawrence Pearsall Jacks, *Life and Letters of Stopford Brooke*, 2 vols. (London: John Murray, 1917), 1:304–5.

21. Clara Lucas Balfour, *Sketches of English Literature, from the Fourteenth to the Present Century* (London: Longman, Brown, Green, and Longmans, 1852), 347; George Gilfillan, *A Gallery of Literary Portraits* (Edinburgh: William Tait, 1845), 73.

22. Balfour, *Sketches*, 348.

23. Ibid.

24. Gilfillan, *Gallery*, 73.

25. Coleridge to John E. Reade, December 1830, in *The Collected Letters of Samuel Taylor Coleridge*, ed. E. L. Griggs, 6 vols. (Oxford: Clarendon Press, 1956–71), 6:849.

26. Balfour, *Sketches*, 361.

27. Richard Armstrong, *Faith and Doubt in the Century's Poets* (London: James Clarke, 1898), 4, 9; Balfour, *Sketches*, 347; Gilfillan, *Gallery*, 89.

28. Balfour, *Sketches*, 361.

29. Gilfillan, *Gallery*, 83.

30. George Gilfillan, *A Third Gallery of Portraits* (Edinburgh: James Hogg, 1854), 498.

31. Stopford A. Brooke, preface to *Poems from Shelley*, ed. Stopford A. Brooke (London: Macmillan, 1880), xi.

32. Gilfillan, *Gallery*, 88.

33. Gilfillan, *Gallery*, unnumbered advertisement leaf.

34. George Gilfillan, *The History of a Man* (London: Arthur Hall, Virtue and Co., 1856), 150, 303.

35. Balfour, *Sketches*, 350.

36. Armstrong, *Faith and Doubt in the Century's Poets*, 4.

37. Gilfillan, *Gallery*, 76.

38. Ibid., 75.

39. James E. Barcus, ed., *Shelley: The Critical Heritage* (London: Routledge and Kegan Paul, 1975), 370 (Ossoli), 418 (Hawthorne).

40. Gilfillan, *Gallery*, 76.

41. Shelley to John and Maria Gisborne, 19 July 1821, in *The Letters of Percy Bysshe Shelley*, ed. Frederick L. Jones, 2 vols. (Oxford: Clarendon Press, 1964), 2:310.

42. Stopford A. Brooke, *English Literature* (London: Macmillan, 1876), 161.

43. Gilfillan, *History of a Man*, 104; Balfour, *Sketches*, 352; Brooke, "Epipsychidion," in *Studies in Poetry*, 176–201 (193). James Thomson's 1860 essay on Shelley supported this view of Shelley's poetry as music first and thought only a distant second. Shelley's poetry was so full of "sweet and rich [. . .] tones" and "perfect cadences," Thomson wrote, that the "meaning of the words" was "lost and dissolved in the overwhelming rapture of the impression." James Thomson, "Shelley," in *The Speedy Extinction of Evil and Misery: Selected Prose of James Thomson (B.V.)*, ed. William David Schaefer (Berkeley: University of California Press, 1967), 199–207 (201).

44. Brooke, *English Literature*, 163.

45. Brooke, "The Lyrics of Shelley," in *Studies in Poetry*, 144–75.

46. Gilfillan, *Gallery*, 92.

47. Ibid., 77.

48. Balfour, *Sketches*, 352.

49. Brooke, *English Literature*, 163.

50. Brooke, *Theology in the English Poets*, 2.

51. Ibid., 3.

52. Brooke, "Inaugural Address," 135.

53. Brooke, *Development of Theology*, 18.

54. Ibid., 44.

55. Stopford A. Brooke, *The New Aspect of Christian Theology* (London: Macmillan, 1873), 13.

56. This view gained support from early biographies of Shelley, which suggested that he had been mentally deranged in some episodes of his life, to the point of hallucinating (Engelberg, *Making of the Shelley Myth*, 44).

57. Gilfillan, *Gallery*, 75; *History of a Man*, 149.

58. Gilfillan, *Third Gallery*, 498.

59. Balfour, *Sketches*, 347.

60. Gilfillan, *History of a Man*, 66.

61. The story of the Gerasene demoniac is told in Matthew 8.28–34, Mark 5.1–20, and Luke 8.26–39. Gilfillan alludes to it in *Gallery*, 73, and *Third Gallery*, 499.

62. Gilfillan, *Gallery*, 73.

63. Gilfillan, *Third Gallery*, 500. Italics in original.

64. Balfour, *Sketches*, 352.

65. Thomson, "Shelley," 204.

66. Apollodorus [George Gilfillan], review of editions of Shelley and Keats, *The Critic: London Literary Journal* (1852), cited in Engelberg, *Making of the Shelley Myth*, 347.

67. Brooke, *Theology in the English Poets*, 3.

68. Thomson, "Shelley," 203.

69. Armstrong, *Faith and Doubt in the Century's Poets*, 9.

70. Stopford A. Brooke, *Religion in Literature and Religion in Life* (London: Philip Green, 1900), 11.

71. Brooke, *Religion in Literature*, 9; Balfour, *Sketches*, 361.

72. Thomson, "Shelley," 204; Brooke, "Inaugural Address," 127; Balfour, *Sketches*, 349.

73. Gilfillan, *History of a Man*, 66.

74. Armstrong, *Faith and Doubt in the Century's Poets*, 6.

75. Cited in Stephen Hebron and Elizabeth C. Denlinger, *Shelley's Ghost: Reshaping the Image of a Literary Family* (Oxford: Bodleian Library, 2010), 170.

76. Gilfillan, *Gallery*, 73.

77. Armstrong, *Faith and Doubt in the Century's Poets*, 9. Isaiah 6.6–7.

78. Brooke, *Religion in Literature*, 9. Ezekiel 37.9.

79. Harold Bloom, *Shelley's Mythmaking* (New Haven, CT: Yale University Press, 1959).

80. Brooke, "The Lyrics of Shelley," 159.

81. Brooke, *Religion in Literature*, 9.

82. P. G. Wodehouse, *Piccadilly Jim* (London: Arrow, 2008), 9.

83. Brooke, *Development of Theology*, 19.

84. Brooke, *Religion in Literature*, 5.

85. Brooke, *Theology in the English Poets*, 1.

86. Brooke, preface to *Poems from Shelley*, xxvii.

87. Brooke, *Development of Theology*, 19.

88. Brooke, "Inaugural Address," 126.

89. Brooke, preface to *Poems from Shelley*, xxvi.

90. Brooke, *Development of Theology*, 47.

91. Brooke, *New Aspect*, 6, 12.

92. Jacks, *Life and Letters of Stopford Brooke*, 1:87; *George Gilfillan*, ed. Watson and Watson, 90; G. Armstrong, *Richard Acland Armstrong: A Memoir*, 64.

93. Brooke, *Development of Theology*, 18–19.

94. Ibid., 10.

95. Brooke, *Theology in the English Poets*, vi–vii.

96. Brooke, *Development of Theology*, 50–51.

97. Jacks, *Life and Letters of Stopford Brooke*, 1:310. Jacks suggests that the strain this placed on his commitment to the Thirty-Nine Articles was a key factor in his departure from the Church of England.

98. Cited in Standley, *Stopford Brooke*, 101.

Chapter 9. Spurgeon, Byron, and the Contingencies of Mediation

An earlier version of this chapter was published as "Spurgeon, Byron, and the Contingencies of Mediation," *Romanticism and Victorianism on the Net* 58 (2010; pub. 2012).

1. C. H. Spurgeon, *The Autobiography of Charles H. Spurgeon, Compiled from his Diary, Letters, and Records by his Wife and his Private Secretary*, 3 vols. (Chicago: F. H. Revell, 1898–1900), 1:297–98.

2. Byron, *Manfred*, I.ii.40–41, in *The Complete Poetical Works*, ed. Jerome J. McGann, 7 vols. (Oxford: Clarendon Press, 1980–93), 4 (1986): 63.

3. Spurgeon, *Autobiography*, 1:242. The voice echoes Jeremiah 45.5.

4. The best modern biography of Spurgeon is Patricia Stallings Kruppa, *Charles Haddon Spurgeon: A Preacher's Progress* (New York: Garland, 1982). Apologetic treatments of his life include Ernest W. Bacon, *Spurgeon: Heir of the Puritans* (London: George Allen and Unwin, 1967), and Lewis A. Drummond, *Spurgeon: Prince of Preachers* (Grand Rapids, MI: Kregel Publications, 1992). See also Rosemary Chadwick, "Spurgeon, Charles Haddon (1834–1892),

in *Oxford Dictionary of National Biography* (Oxford: Oxford University Press, 2004) [http://www.oxforddnb.com/view/article/26187, accessed 8 March 2007], and Joseph S. Meisel, *Public Speech and the Culture of Public Life in the Age of Gladstone* (New York: Columbia University Press, 2001), 127–36. Kruppa says Spurgeon preached to "nearly twenty-seven thousand" people in Crystal Palace in 1857 (68); Chadwick says it was twenty-four thousand; Meisel gives the figure from the turnstiles as 23,654 (129).

5. Matthew Arnold, *Culture and Anarchy and Other Writings*, ed. Stefan Collini (Cambridge: Cambridge University Press, 1993), 147, 155–59, 199.

6. Cited in Kruppa, *Charles Haddon Spurgeon*, 96.

7. Cited in Russell Herman Conwell, *The Life of Charles Haddon Spurgeon, the World's Great Preacher* (Philadelphia: Edgewood Publishing Co., 1892), 479.

8. Cited in Kruppa, *Charles Haddon Spurgeon*, 101.

9. C. H. Spurgeon, *The Letters of Charles Haddon Spurgeon*, ed. Charles Spurgeon (London: Marshall Bros., 1923), 57.

10. Kruppa, *Charles Haddon Spurgeon*, 102–5.

11. "Sermons of the Rev. C. H. Spurgeon," *North American Review* 86, no. 178 (1858): 275.

12. Bacon, *Spurgeon*, 47.

13. Spurgeon, *Autobiography*, 3:63.

14. C. H. Spurgeon, *Sermons in Candles* (London: Passmore and Alabaster, 1890). Spurgeon had previously expressed his conviction that useful illustrations could be drawn from current events in *The Bible and the Newspaper* (London: Passmore and Alabaster, 1878).

15. Cited in Robert H. Ellison, *The Victorian Pulpit: Spoken and Written Sermons in Nineteenth-Century Britain* (London: Associated University Presses, 1998), 73.

16. Drummond, *Spurgeon*, 412; Kruppa, *Charles Haddon Spurgeon*, 22.

17. Cited by Kruppa, in *Charles Haddon Spurgeon*, 368.

18. Cited by Kruppa, ibid., 367.

19. For further details on Spurgeon's reading, see Bacon, *Spurgeon*, 108–9, and Kruppa, *Charles Haddon Spurgeon*, 209, 366–68.

20. Cited by Kruppa, in *Charles Haddon Spurgeon*, 217.

21. For the hymns, see Kruppa, *Charles Haddon Spurgeon*, 25; for the quotation from Spurgeon's brother, see Drummond, *Spurgeon*, 96.

22. Cited in Lewis Ormond Brastow, *Representative Modern Preachers* (New York: Hodder and Stoughton, 1910), 391.

23. Walter Benjamin, "What Is Epic Theatre?" in *Illuminations*, ed. Hannah Arendt, trans. Harry Zohn (London: Fontana, 1992), 144–51 (148).

24. C. H. Spurgeon, *The Metropolitan Tabernacle Pulpit*, 63 vols. (London: Passmore and Alabaster, 1855–1917), 16 (1870): 584. Hereafter cited parenthetically as *MTP*. The first six volumes of Spurgeon's sermons were published while he was pastor of the New Park Street Chapel and were entitled *The New Park Street Pulpit* (1855–60). The title *Metropolitan Tabernacle Pulpit* was adopted from volume seven onward (1861). For ease of reference, I have used the abbreviation *MTP* to refer to all volumes in this series. After his death in 1892, Spurgeon's associates continued to issue new volumes of the *Metropolitan Tabernacle Pulpit*, containing transcribed but (usually) unpublished sermons, for another twenty-five years.

25. C. H. Spurgeon, *The Treasury of David*, 7 vols. (London: Passmore and Alabaster, 1882), 5:220–21, quoting George Bowen, *Daily Meditations* (London: Presbyterian Board of Publication, 1865), 89.

26. I gratefully acknowledge the assistance I have received from the staff of the seminary, especially its librarian, Craig Kubic, and from the librarian of the Spurgeon College in London, Judy Powles.

27. *The Works of Lord Byron*, 2nd ed., 5 vols. (Leipzig: Bernhard Tauchnitz, 1866). These volumes were part of Tauchnitz's reprint series of British authors, inaugurated in 1841. After the international copyright act of 1844, Tauchnitz paid small fees to British publishers or authors, as did Galignani in France, and so was not technically a pirate. See William St. Clair, *The Reading Nation in the Romantic Period* (Cambridge: Cambridge University Press, 2004), 523; and Simon Nowell-Smith, *International Copyright Law and the Publisher in the Reign of Queen Victoria* (Oxford: Clarendon Press, 1968), 41–63. Only the second of this edition's five volumes remains in the Spurgeon collection at Midwestern Baptist Theological Seminary. It seems very likely that Spurgeon originally owned all five volumes, and I have made this assumption in what follows.

28. Lord Byron, *Childe Harold's Pilgrimage: Canto the Fourth* (London: John Murray, 1818). The first nonce volume contains *Childe Harold* canto 3 (1st ed.), *The Prisoner of Chillon and Other Poems* (1st ed.), *The Giaour* (9th ed.), *The Corsair* (3rd ed.), *The Bride of Abydos* (5th ed.), and the spurious volume *Lord Byron's Farewell to England: with Three Other Poems*. The second nonce volume contains *Hebrew Melodies* (1st Murray ed.), *Ode to Napoleon Buonaparte* (8th ed.), *The Siege of Corinth and Parisina* (2nd ed.), *The Lament of Tasso* (2nd ed.), and *Manfred* (1st ed.).

29. D. Carey, ed., *Beauties of the Modern Poets in Selections from the Works of Byron, Moore, Scott &c.* (London: Wightman and Cramp, 1826). *Beautiful Poetry: A Selection of the Choicest of the Present and the Past*, 7 vols. (London: J. Crockford, 1853–59). Spurgeon's library contains volumes 1–5.

30. *Truths Illustrated by Great Authors*, 4th ed. (London: William White, 1855).

31. Austin Dobson, *The Civil Service Handbook of English Literature* (London: Lockwood, 1874). This is an introductory literary history consisting of capsule biographies; the biography of Byron appears on 174–77. George Gilfillan, *Galleries of Literary Portraits*, 2 vols. (London: R. Groombridge, 1856–57). The biography of Byron appears at 1:64–74, where we are told, "vain it is to struggle against those austere and awful laws by which moments of sin expand into centuries of punishment. Yet this was Byron's own life-long struggle, and one which, like men who fight their battles o'er again in sleep, he renewed again and again in every dream of his imagination" (71).

32. H. J. Jackson, *Romantic Readers: The Evidence of Marginalia* (New Haven, CT: Yale University Press, 2005).

33. The similarity of the marks suggests that the annotated Byron volumes in Spurgeon's collection were all annotated by the same person, and although it cannot be proved that this was Spurgeon himself, this seems overwhelmingly likely.

34. Spurgeon, *The Treasury of David*, 4:190 (quoting Edwin Paxton Hood, *Dark Sayings on a Harp: and Other Sermons on Some of the Dark Questions of Human Life* [London: Jackson, Walford, and Hodder, 1865], 26); *Treasury of David*, 7:43; *MTP* 1889, 35:332; *MTP* 1891, 37:64; *MTP* 1893, 39:302.

35. These lines appear in later editions of *Truths Illustrated by Great Authors* but not in the fourth edition, which Spurgeon owned.

36. C. H. Spurgeon, *Words of Wisdom for Daily Life* (London: Passmore and Alabaster, 1892), 126; Spurgeon, *Autobiography*, 1:298.

37. [John Agg,] *Lord Byron's Farewell to England: with Three Other Poems* (London: J. Johnston, 1816).

38. *Byron's Letters and Journals*, ed. Leslie A. Marchand, 13 vols. (London: John Murray, 1973–94), 5 (1976): 84, 138; for further comments of the incident, see 5:143, 150, 151, and 159. Samuel Chew reminded readers of *Notes and Queries* in 1919 that these poems had long been disattributed (Samuel Chew, "The Byron Apocrypha," *Notes and Queries* 92 [1919]: 113–15), and Howard Mumford Jones identified the author as John Agg (Howard Mumford Jones, "The Author of Two Byron Apocrypha," *Modern Language Notes* 41, no. 2 [1926]: 129–31).

39. *Truths Illustrated from Great Authors*, 354.

40. *MTP* 1867, 13:532; *MTP* 1869, 15:139; Spurgeon, *The Treasury of David*, 2:423.

41. Byron's paraphrase of the 137th Psalm is praised as "perhaps the best" in Spurgeon's commentary to that psalm in *The Treasury of David*, 7:193. "The Destruction of Sennacherib" is quoted in the same book, 3:405.

42. Carey, *Beauties of the Modern Poets*, 26.

43. *Truths Illustrated from Great Authors*, 448.

44. Cited in C. H. Spurgeon, *The Saint and His Saviour: The Progress of the Soul in the Knowledge of Jesus* (Nashville: Graves, Marks and Co., 1857), 165.

45. *Truths Illustrated from Great Authors*, 381; *Beautiful Poetry*, 5 (1858): 191.

46. Leslie A. Marchand, *Byron: A Biography*, 3 vols. (London: John Murray, 1957), 2:647.

47. *MTP* 1902, 48:72, quoting William Cowper, *The Task*, 5.733–34. See *The Poems of William Cowper*, ed. John D. Baird and Charles Ryskamp, vol. 2, *1782–1785* (Oxford: Clarendon Press, 1980), 109–303.

48. George Eliot to Sara Sophia Hennell, 18 November 1870, in *The George Eliot Letters*, ed. Gordon S. Haight, 9 vols. (New Haven, CT: Yale University Press, 1954–78), 5 (1955): 121; and George Eliot to Sara Sophia Hennell, 5 September 1858, in *Letters*, 2 (1954): 478.

49. After remarking that "Spurgeon was a preacher to whom one sent the servants," Ruskin's biographer Tim Hilton writes: "Between Ruskin and Spurgeon there developed an unlikely, warm friendship. They had next to nothing in common apart from their knowledge of the Bible and a love of its exegesis. Ruskin simply ignored all aspects of Spurgeon's views that would annoy him. The Baptist's fiery hatred of Carlyle he overlooked. He was not drawn by Spurgeon's insistence that all churches should be Greek rather than Gothic. Instead [. . .] they would spar over their intimacy with Scripture and their utterly different natures, Ruskin provocative, Spurgeon laughing at him, each capping the other" (Tim Hilton, *John Ruskin: The Early Years* [New Haven, CT: Yale University Press, 1985], 260–61). Hilton notes that the friendship was fading by 1860 but suggests that "something of Spurgeon's bluntness and expository manner enters *Unto This Last*" (Tim Hilton, *John Ruskin: The Later Years* [New Haven, CT: Yale University Press, 2000], 12).

50. Marjorie Garber, *Quotation Marks* (London: Routledge, 2003), 2.

51. Jacques Derrida, "Signature Event Context," *Glyph* 1 (1977): 172–97 (185).

52. Charles Martindale argues for a reception hermeneutics in which "a classic becomes a text whose 'iterability' is a function of its capacity, which includes the authority vested in

its reception, for continued reappropriations by readers." Charles Martindale, *Redeeming the Text: Latin Poetry and the Hermeneutics of Reception* (Cambridge: Cambridge University Press, 1993), 28.

53. Algernon Charles Swinburne, "Byron," in *The Complete Works of Algernon Charles Swinburne*, ed. Sir Edmund Gosse and Thomas James Wise, 20 vols. (New York: Russell and Russell, 1925; repr. 1968), 15:121.

54. Wai Chee Dimock, "A Theory of Resonance," *PMLA* 112, no. 5 (1997): 1060–71.

Chapter 10. Secular Pantheons for the Reformed Nation: Byron in Cambridge

1. Benedict Anderson, *Imagined Communities: Reflections on the Origin and Spread of Nationalism* (London: Verso, 1983); Linda Colley, *Britons: Forging the Nation, 1707–1837* (London: Vintage, 1996).

2. Consuelo Cruz, "Identity and Persuasion: How Nations Remember Their Pasts and Make Their Futures," *World Politics* 52 (2000): 311.

3. Benjamin Disraeli, *Sybil: or, The Two Nations* (1845), in *The Bradenham Edition of the Novels and Tales of Benjamin Disraeli*, vol. 9 (London: Peter Davies, 1927), 491.

4. Alfred Lord Tennyson, "I loving Freedom for herself," 13–16, in *The Poems of Tennyson*, ed. Christopher Ricks, 2nd ed., 3 vols. (Berkeley: University of California Press, 1987), 2:43–46 (44).

5. Thomas Babington Macaulay, "Speech on Parliamentary Reform," delivered 2 March 1831, in *Selected Writings*, ed. John Clive and Thomas Pinney (Chicago: University of Chicago Press, 1972), 168.

6. Ibid., 180.

7. Ibid.

8. Pierre Nora, "Between Memory and History: *Les Lieux de Mémoire*," trans. Marc Roudebush, *Representations* 26 (1989): 7–24.

9. See John Martin Robinson, *Temples of Delight: Stowe Landscape Gardens* (London: National Trust, 1994).

10. Alison Yarrington, "Popular and Imaginary Pantheons in Early Nineteenth-Century England," in *Pantheons: Transformations of a Monumental Idea*, ed. Richard Wrigley and Matthew Craske (Aldershot: Ashgate, 2004), 107.

11. "Mr Disraeli: His Character and Career," *Edinburgh Review* 97 (1853): 421.

12. Kate Berridge, *Madame Tussaud: A Life in Wax* (New York: William Morrow, 2006), 240.

13. Lord Rosslyn to Benjamin Disraeli, Earl of Beaconsfield, 7 May 1880, Disraeli Archive, Queen's University, HA/IV/N/153 and HA/IV/N/152. I am grateful to Michel Pharand and Ellen Hawman of the Disraeli Archive at Queen's University in Kingston, Ontario, for their assistance.

14. William Godwin, *Essay on Sepulchres*, in *Political and Philosophical Writings of William Godwin*, ed. Mark Philp, vol. 6, *Essays* (London: Pickering and Chatto, 1993), 18.

15. *Monthly Review* 61 (1810): 111, cited in Godwin, *Essay on Sepulchres*, 3.

16. Ibid., 6.

17. Ibid., 30.

18. Ibid., 18. On the connection between Godwin's *Essay on Sepulchres* and associationist psychology, see Mark Salber Phillips, *Society and Sentiment: Genres of Historical Writing in Britain, 1740–1820* (Princeton, NJ: Princeton University Press, 2000), 324–27.

19. Godwin, *Essay on Sepulchres*, 27. For an examination of comparable issues surrounding how public memorials should respond to shifting political climates, principally in the American South, see Sanford Levinson, *Written in Stone: Public Monuments in Changing Societies* (Durham, NC: Duke University Press, 1998).

20. Disraeli, *Sybil*, 267, 268.

21. Richard Jenkyns, *Westminster Abbey* (Cambridge, MA: Harvard University Press, 2004), 86.

22. Matthew Craske, "Westminster Abbey 1720–70: A Public Pantheon Built Upon Private Interest," in *Pantheons: Transformations of a Monumental Idea*, ed. Richard Wrigley and Matthew Craske (Aldershot: Ashgate, 2004), 57–79.

23. Philip Connell, "Death and the Author: Westminster Abbey and the Meanings of the Literary Monument," *Eighteenth-Century Studies* 38, no. 4 (2005): 559, 563, 578.

24. Leslie Marchand, *Byron: A Biography*, 3 vols. (London: John Murray, 1957), 3:1256.

25. Samuel Smiles, *A Publisher and His Friends: Memoir and Correspondence of the Late John Murray, with an Account of the Origin and Progress of the House, 1768–1843*, 2 vols. (London: John Murray, 1891), 2:44.

26. Charles William Williams, "Byron's Grave," *The Times* (25 April 1870): 11; C.R.L., "The Grave of Lord Byron," *The Times* (23 April 1875): 11.

27. Richard Edgcumbe, *History of the Byron Memorial* (London: Effingham Wilson, 1883), 10.

28. Ibid., 12.

29. Byron Rogers, "Byron the Rover Returns to the Abbey," *The Times* (9 May 1969): 12.

30. H. B., "Memorial to Sir Walter Scott in Westminster Abbey," *The Times* (20 April 1889): 4.

31. "Sir Walter Scott Memorial," *The Times* (3 July 1896): 8.

32. "Scott Memorial in Westminster Abbey," *The Times* (22 May 1897): 16.

33. Details of Westminster Abbey's memorials are available at http://www.westminster-abbey.org/our-history/people, accessed 28 October 2011.

34. Arthur Penrhyn Stanley, *Historical Memorials of Westminster Abbey* (London: John Murray, 1868), 330, cited in Nicola J. Watson, *The Literary Tourist: Readers and Places in Romantic and Victorian Britain* (Basingstoke: Palgrave, 2006), 29.

35. Godwin, *Essay on Sepulchres*, 12.

36. Henry Austen Driver, *Byron and "The Abbey"* (London: Longman, Orme, Brown, Green and Longmans, 1838), 26.

37. *Journals of the House of Lords*, 14 June 1844, vol. 75, 3rd series (London: Hansard, 1844), 886–91 (891).

38. "Lord Byron's Statue," *Berrow's Worcester Journal* (30 August 1838): 4.

39. For further discussion of Westminster Abbey and the politics of literary commemoration, see Samantha Matthews, *Poetical Remains: Poets' Graves, Bodies, and Books in the Nineteenth Century* (Oxford: Oxford University Press, 2004), esp. 222–55.

40. Hobhouse's letter is reproduced in Robert Sinker, *The Library of Trinity College, Cambridge* (Cambridge: Deighton, Bell and Co., 1891), 127.

41. Anna Letitia Barbauld, *Selected Poetry and Prose*, ed. William McCarthy and Elizabeth Kraft (Peterborough, ON: Broadview, 2002), 160–73 (167–68).

42. Holger Hoock, "The British Military Pantheon in St Paul's Cathedral: The State, Cultural Patriotism, and the Politics of National Monuments, c.1790–1820," in *Pantheons: Transformations of a Monumental Idea*, ed. Richard Wrigley and Matthew Craske (Aldershot: Ashgate, 2004), 81–105; Alison Yarrington, *The Commemoration of the Hero, 1800–1864: Monuments to the British Victors of the Napoleonic Wars* (New York: Garland, 1988), 61–78.

43. David McKitterick, ed., *The Making of the Wren Library, Trinity College, Cambridge* (Cambridge: Cambridge University Press, 1995), 25.

44. For Roubiliac's work in Trinity College, see Malcolm Baker, "The Portrait Sculpture," in McKitterick, *Making of the Wren Library*, 110–37 (116–19); for his work in Westminster Abbey, see Jenkyns, *Westminster Abbey*, 87–92.

45. Baker, "Portrait Sculpture," 129.

46. Sinker, *Library of Trinity College*, 129–31.

47. [John Cam Hobhouse], *Remarks on the Exclusion of Lord Byron's Monument from Westminster Abbey* (London: the author, 1844).

48. See Doris Langley Moore, *The Late Lord Byron* (London: John Murray, 1961), 207–13, 502–8; and E.W.B., "The Statue of Byron in the Library of Trinity College Cambridge," *Notes and Queries*, 6th series, 4 (1881): 421–23.

49. Cited in Moore, *The Late Lord Byron*, 507.

50. Trinity College's pantheon was extended from the library to the chapel later in the century, when Roubiliac's standing statue of Newton (1755) was joined by seated statues of Francis Bacon by Henry Weekes (1845), the mathematician Isaac Barrow by Matthew Noble (1853), Thomas Macaulay (1868), and the master of the college, William Whewell (1872), both by Thomas Woolner.

51. Stephen Cheeke argues for the importance of writing on the spot for *Childe Harold's Pilgrimage*. "In short," he writes, "*Childe Harold's Pilgrimage* is authored by Byron *in place*—and so rather than being a poem about the growth of a poet's mind, or even about a fantastic journey—it seems first and foremost to be a poem written through the experience of place." Stephen Cheeke, *Byron and Place: History, Translation, Nostalgia* (Basingstoke: Palgrave, 2003), 42.

52. Annette Peach, "Portraits of Byron," *The Walpole Society* 62 (2000): 85.

53. Byron had written to Thomas Phillips in 1814, while the artist was working on his portrait, "I don't care what becomes of the arms so that *pens* [&] *books* are *not* upon ye. Canvas," and when Hobhouse suggested in 1817 that the original Thorwaldsen bust should show Byron crowned with laurels, Byron objected: "I won't have my head garnished like a Xmas pie with Holly—or a Cod's head and Fennel—or whatever the damned weed is they strew around it." *Byron's Letters and Journals*, ed. Leslie A. Marchand, 13 vols. (London: John Murray, 1973–94), 3 (1974): 113; 5 (1976): 243.

54. Student numbers from McKitterick, *Making of the Wren Library*, 138.

55. *The Pictorial Guide to Cambridge: Containing Descriptions of its Colleges, Halls [...] Illustrated with [...] Engravings on Wood* (Cambridge: T. King, 1847), 13.

56. Charles Tennyson Turner, *Sonnets* (London: Macmillan, 1864), 34.

57. Cited in Marchand, *Byron*, 2:692.

58. Sinker, *Library of Trinity College*, 125.

59. By 1865, Byron had even eclipsed George III. *The Excursionist's Guide to Cambridge* criticized the Cipriani window and noted that "[a]s the tints reflected by this miserable window

were cast upon the exquisite statue of Lord Byron, by Thorwaldsen, it has for some years been covered with a curtain." *The Excursionist's Guide to Cambridge* (Cambridge: E. Johnson, [1865?]), 46.

Chapter 11. The Distributed Pantheon: Scott in Edinburgh

1. *The Standard* (London) (26 April 1875): 4.

2. Richard Edgcumbe, *History of the Byron Memorial* (London: Effingham Wilson, 1883), 14. For differences between French and English commemorative practices, as well as a thoughtful account of Nora's *Lieux de Mémoire*, see Stefan Collini, "French Contrasts: From the *Panthéon* to Poets' Corner," in his *English Pasts: Essays in History and Culture* (Oxford: Oxford University Press, 1999), 38–66. On the French Panthéon, see Mona Ozouf, "The *Panthéon*: The École Normale of the Dead," in *Realms of Memory: The Construction of the French Past*, ed. Pierre Nora, trans. Arthur Goldhammer, 3 vols. (New York: Columbia University Press, 1998), 3:325–46. Also relevant is Michael D. Garval, *"A Dream of Stone": Fame, Vision, and Monumentality in Nineteenth-Century French Literary Culture* (Newark: University of Delaware Press, 2004).

3. Ian Duncan, *Scott's Shadow: The Novel in Romantic Edinburgh* (Princeton, NJ: Princeton University Press, 2007), 9.

4. Ibid.

5. Stephen C. Behrendt, "The Visual Arts and Music," in *Romanticism: An Oxford Guide*, ed. Nicholas Roe (Oxford: Oxford University Press, 2005), 72.

6. For a comparative account of Parisian statuemania, see Sergiusz Michalski, *Public Monuments: Art in Political Bondage, 1870–1997* (London: Reaktion, 1998), 13–55. The history of the Albert Memorial is examined in detail in Chris Brooks, ed., *The Albert Memorial. The Prince Consort National Memorial: Its History, Contexts, and Conservation* (New Haven, CT: Yale University Press, 2000); Stephen Bayley, *The Albert Memorial: The Monument in Its Social and Architectural Context* (London: Scolar Press, 1981); and G. Alex Bremner, "The 'Great Obelisk' and Other Schemes: The Origins and Limits of Nationalist Sentiment in the Making of the Albert Memorial," *Nineteenth-Century Contexts* 31, no. 3 (2009): 225–49. Alfred Gilbert's *Eros (Memorial to Antony Ashley Cooper, 7th Earl of Shaftesbury)* is discussed in David J. Getsy, *Body Doubles: Sculpture in Britain, 1877–1905* (New Haven, CT: Yale University Press, 2004), 87–117 passim. Useful reference works on London's statuary include Philip Ward-Jackson, *Public Sculpture of the City of London* (Liverpool: Liverpool University Press, 2003), and Margaret Baker, *Discovering London Statues and Monuments*, 5th ed. (Princes Riseborough, Bucks: Shire Publications, 2002).

7. Getsy, *Body Doubles*, 4.

8. On the heroic depiction of engineers in nineteenth-century Britain, see Christine MacLeod, *Heroes of Invention: Technology, Liberalism and British Identity, 1750–1914* (Cambridge: Cambridge University Press, 2007).

9. Benedict Read, *Victorian Sculpture* (New Haven, CT: Yale University Press, 1982), 67.

10. R. M., "Monument for Sir Walter Scott," *Caledonian Mercury* (Edinburgh) (29 October 1832): 3.

11. Pierre Nora, "Between Memory and History: Les Lieux de Mémoire," trans. Marc Roudebush, *Representations* 26 (1989): 22.

12. Clifford Geertz, *The Interpretation of Cultures* (New York: Basic Books, 1973), 3–32.

13. Nor Loch, which had been created in 1450 by damming streams in what is now Princes Street Gardens, was drained in 1760. In 1818, the Crown, which owned the land, agreed a long-term, low-rent lease to the proprietors of Princes Street to make the area open to the public. This lease transferred to the City of Edinburgh in 1876.

14. The Bill (4 & 5 Vict. CAP XV) received the Royal Assent on 18 May 1841.

15. *History of the Scott Monument, Edinburgh* (Edinburgh: Printed for the Magistrates and Town Council, 1881), 89.

16. The five men transported, in a blatant political abuse of judicial power, were Thomas Muir, Joseph Gerrald, Thomas Fyshe Palmer, William Skirving, and Maurice Margarot. Scott did not comment on the affair, but his sympathies seem likely to have been with the prosecutors. He attended subsequent treason trials in 1794, which, he wrote, "displayd to the public the most atrocious & deliberate plan of villany which has occurrd perhaps in the annals of G. Britain" (*The Letters of Sir Walter Scott*, ed. H.J.C. Grierson, 12 vols. [London: Constable, 1932–37], 1:34).

17. For an account of this monument's erection (which differs from my conclusions here), see Alex Tyrrell with Michael T. Davis, "Bearding the Tories: The Commemoration of the Scottish Political Martyrs of 1793–94," in *Contested Sites: Commemoration, Memorial and Popular Politics in Nineteenth-Century Britain*, ed. Paul A. Pickering and Alex Tyrrell (Aldershot: Ashgate, 2004), 25–56.

18. *History of the Scott Monument*, 96.

19. William Godwin, *Essay on Sepulchres*, in *Political and Philosophical Writings of William Godwin*, ed. Mark Philp, vol. 6, *Essays* (London: Pickering and Chatto, 1993), 24.

20. William Watson, "The Scott Monument, Princes Street, Edinburgh," in *The Collected Poems of William Watson* (London: George G. Harrap, 1936), 46.

21. *The Times* (2 April 1842): 5.

22. John Ruskin, "The Nature of Gothic," in *The Stones of Venice*, ed. Jan Morris (Boston: Little, Brown, 1981), 120, 122.

23. Ibid., 131.

24. *History of the Scott Monument*, 68, 73, 76.

25. *The Times* (11 May 1844): 7.

26. For William IV's contribution, see *History of the Scott Monument*, 62; for Victoria and Albert's, see *The Times* (9 February 1842): 6.

27. *History of the Scott Monument*, 61, 74, 66.

28. On Waverley Balls, see ibid., 77–78. On house-to-house visitation, ibid., 74.

29. Ibid., 64, 65.

30. Ibid., 72.

31. Ibid., 76.

32. Samuel Smiles, *Self-Help: With Illustrations of Character and Conduct* (London: John Murray, 1859), 221–22.

33. *The Times* (25 September 1832): 2.

34. *The Times* (18 March 1837): 5.

35. *History of the Scott Monument*, 83.

36. Max Weber, *The Protestant Ethic and the Spirit of Capitalism* (1930), trans. Talcott Parsons (London: Routledge, 2001).

37. *History of the Scott Monument*, 83.

38. Duncan, *Scott's Shadow*, 20.

39. John Wood, *The Scenic Daguerreotype: Romanticism and Early Photography* (Iowa City: University of Iowa Press, 1995), 14 (Wood is referring to the daguerreotype rather than to Talbot's calotype process); Sonia Hofkosh, "Early Photography's Late Romanticism," *European Romantic Review* 22, no. 3 (2011): 296; Andrea K. Henderson, "William Henry Fox Talbot: The Photograph as Memorial for Romanticism," *BRANCH: Britain, Representation and Nineteenth-Century History*, ed. Dino Franco Felluga, extension of *Romanticism and Victorianism on the Net*, accessed 30 May 2016.

40. Moore lived at Sloperton Cottage, near Bromham, Wiltshire, from 1816 until his death in 1852. Ronan Kelly, *Bard of Erin: The Life of Thomas Moore* (London: Penguin, 2008), 301.

41. Hoover H. Jordan identified a previously unknown portrait calotype of Moore in the Science Museum in London. Hoover H. Jordan, "A Photograph of Thomas Moore," *Keats-Shelley Journal* 28 (1979): 24–25.

42. This photogenic drawing, made by contact printing from the original manuscript, was produced sometime before April 1840. There are four very similar negatives showing this manuscript, which are listed in Larry J. Schaaf, *Records of the Dawn of Photography: Talbot's Notebooks P & Q* (Cambridge: Cambridge University Press, 1996), 169, n. 141. For an account of this photograph, see Andrew Burkett, "Photographing Byron's Hand," *European Romantic Review* 26, no. 2 (2015): 129–48.

43. Schaaf, *Records*, 169; see also xxiv. Either this publication was never produced or no copies have survived.

44. The subscription advertisement is reproduced in Graham Smith, "William Henry Fox Talbot's Calotype Views of Loch Katrine," *Bulletin of the University of Michigan Museums of Art and Archaeology* 7 (1984–85): 49–77, reprinted in an abridged form in *William Henry Fox Talbot: Selected Texts and Bibliography*, ed. Mike Weaver (Boston: G. K. Hall, 1993), 117–24 (118).

45. Gillen D'Arcy Wood, *The Shock of the Real: Romanticism and Visual Culture, 1760–1860* (Basingstoke: Palgrave, 2001), 190.

46. The photograph of the Panthéon is reproduced in Michael Gray, Arthur Ollman, and Carol McCusker, *First Photographs: William Henry Fox Talbot and the Birth of Photography* (New York: Powerhouse Books, in association with the Museum of Photographic Arts, San Diego, 2002).

47. Larry J. Schaaf, *William Henry Fox Talbot's The Pencil of Nature, Anniversary Facsimile: Introductory Volume* (New York: Hans P. Kraus, Jr., 1989), 61–62.

48. *William Henry Fox Talbot: Photographs from the J. Paul Getty Museum* (Los Angeles: J. Paul Getty Museum, 2002); see 82–83 for the photograph, and 118–20 for a discussion of it by Geoffrey Batchen, David Featherstone, James Fee, Nancy Keeler, Weston Naef, Larry J. Schaaf, and Michael Ware.

49. In May that year, Talbot's assistant William Henneman photographed a bust of Catherine Walter, daughter of the *Times*'s proprietor, for the frontispiece to her father's privately printed pamphlet commemorating her death. [John Walter], *Record of the Death-Bed of C.M.W.* (London: Gilbert and Rivington, [1844]). At one time this publication was thought to have preceded *Pencil* and thus to be the first photographically illustrated book. The claim was made by Vernon Snow, "The First Illustrated Book," *Times Literary Supplement* 23 (December 1965): 1204, and repeated by Beaumont Newhall, in *The Pencil of Nature* (New York: Da Capo Press, 1969), vi–vii, but refuted by archival documents quoted by Schaaf, *Anniversary Facsimile*, 85, n. 8.

50. Catherine J. Golden, *Posting It: The Victorian Revolution in Letter Writing* (Gainesville: University Press of Florida, 2010).

51. Richard Carline, *Pictures in the Post: The Story of the Picture Postcard and Its Place in the History of Popular Art* (London: Gordon Fraser, 1971); Tonie Holt and Valmai Holt, *Picture Postcards of the Golden Age: A Collector's Guide* (London: Granada, 1971); Arthur W. Coysh, *The Dictionary of Picture Postcards in Britain, 1894–1939* (Woodbridge, Suffolk: Antique Collectors' Club, 1984).

52. Holt and Holt, *Picture Postcards*, 28, and Asa Briggs, *Victorian Things* (Chicago: University of Chicago Press, 1988), 362, both give the 1870 figure as 70 million; Golden, *Posting It*, 275 n. 6, as 75 million. For the 1903 figure, see Carline, *Pictures*, 53. For additional estimates, see Frank Staff, *The Picture Postcard and Its Origins* (London: Lutterworth Press, 1966), 90–91.

53. On the rising popularity of Valentine's and Christmas cards, see Judith Flanders, *Consuming Passions: Leisure and Pleasure in Victorian Britain* (London: Harper, 2006), 483–87.

54. For more information, see the database of Tuck postcards maintained at www.tuckdb.org.

55. Briggs, *Victorian Things*, 361–68.

56. A. V. Seaton, "Cope's and the Promotion of Tobacco in Victorian England," *European Journal of Marketing* 20, no. 9 (1986): 5–26.

57. Fiona Sinclair, *Scotstyle: 150 Years of Scottish Architecture* (Edinburgh: Royal Incorporation of Architects in Scotland, 1984), 60.

58. For a selection, see Judith Miller, *Miller's Antiques Handbook and Price Guide, 2012–13* (London: Mitchell Beazley, 2011), 369–71.

Chapter 12. The Networked Pantheon: Byron in London

Part of this chapter previously appeared in "Romantic Memorials in the Victorian City: The Inauguration of the 'Blue Plaque' Scheme, 1868," *BRANCH: Britain, Representation and Nineteenth-Century History*, ed. Dino Franco Felluga (c. 3000 words, pub. 2012), Web.

1. The 1801 census recorded London's population as 1,114,644; the 1911 census recorded it as 7,251,358. See Karl Gustav Grytzell, *County of London: Population Changes 1801–1901* (Lund, Sweden: Royal University of Lund, 1969), 120.

2. *Hansard Parliamentary Debates*, 17 July 1863 ("Residences of Deceased Celebrities").

3. *Journal of the Society of Arts* (22 April 1864): 364.

4. Letter from Epsilon, *Journal of the Society of Arts* (15 April 1864): 362.

5. S. M. Farrell, "Ewart, William (1798–1869)," *Oxford Dictionary of National Biography* (Oxford: Oxford University Press, 2004) [http://www.oxforddnb.com/view/article/9011, accessed 3 September 2009].

6. Emily Cole, ed., *Lived in London: Blue Plaques and the Stories behind Them* (London and New Haven, CT: Yale University Press, 2009), 10.

7. W. B. Owen, "Bartley, Sir George Christopher Trout (1842–1910)," rev. Anita McConnell, *Oxford Dictionary of National Biography* (Oxford: Oxford University Press, 2004) [http://www.oxforddnb.com/view/article/30629, accessed 17 August 2009].

8. Byron's birthplace was demolished in 1889, and the site became part of John Lewis Department Store, which erected a new memorial to Byron, in the form of a bronze relief bust, in 1900 (*Journal of the Society of Arts* [29 June 1900]: 620).

9. The Corporation of London agreed to cooperate in the scheme in 1879; the scheme was taken over by London County Council in 1901 (when the standard blue design was adopted) and then by its successor the Greater London Council in 1965, before passing to English Heritage in 1986. See Cole, *Lived in London*, 1–33.

10. For a list, see *Journal of the Society of Arts* (5 October 1900): 827.

11. William Godwin, *Essay on Sepulchres*, in *Political and Philosophical Writings of William Godwin*, ed. Mark Philp, vol. 6, *Essays* (London: Pickering and Chatto, 1993), 25.

12. Samuel Rogers, *Italy: A Poem* (London: Edward Moxon, 1840), 44.

13. Ibid., 54.

14. "Memorials of Eminent Men," *Journal of the Society of Arts* (11 May 1866): 703.

15. On booksellers' advertisements, see James Raven, *The Business of Books: Booksellers and the English Book Trade, 1450–1850* (New Haven, CT: Yale University Press, 2007), 170.

16. On Dryden's pub sign, see "Memorial Tablets," *Journal of the Society of Arts* (20 June 1866): 688.

17. "Memorials of Eminent Men." On the publishing success of Murray's tourist guidebooks, see Humphrey Carpenter, *The Seven Lives of John Murray: The Story of a Publishing Dynasty* (London: John Murray, 2008), 165–76.

18. *The Times* (4 September 1873): 5.

19. *Journal of the Society of Arts* (11 May 1866): 437.

20. Ibid.

21. Compare Ian McEwan's novel *Saturday*, where the central character thinks complacently of London as the "grand achievement of the living and all the dead who've ever lived here." Ian McEwan, *Saturday* (London: Jonathan Cape, 2005), 77.

22. William Graham, *Last Links with Byron, Shelley, and Keats* (London: Leonard Smithers, 1898), 17.

23. "The Home and Grave of Byron," *Harper's New Monthly Magazine* 21 (1860): 610. Nicola Watson connects the dissatisfaction with Westminster Abbey as a pantheon to the rise of interest in visiting authors' graves, or other places associated with them (Nicola J. Watson, *The Literary Tourist: Readers and Places in Romantic and Victorian Britain* [Basingstoke: Palgrave, 2006], 23–32).

24. On the stolen visitors' book: "Lord Byron's Tomb," *The Times* (6 October 1866): 9. Edgcumbe quotations: Richard Edgcumbe, *History of the Byron Memorial* (London: Effingham Wilson, 1883), 9.

25. Edgcumbe, *History*, 9.

26. Printed circular to be distributed by members of the Byron Memorial Committee, sent to Benjamin Disraeli by Richard Edgcumbe, 3 June 1875, Disraeli Archive, Queen's University, HA/IV/N/108; "Byron's Grave," *The Times* (22 April 1875): 7.

27. Edgcumbe, *History*, 9.

28. Edgcumbe to Disraeli, 30 June 1875, Disraeli Archive, Queen's University, HA/IV/N/111.

29. Evans and Jolley, architects, to Benjamin Disraeli, 12 June 1875, Disraeli Archive, Queen's University HA/IV/N/109: "We do not like the idea of placing a richly sculptured slab in the floor over the Byron Vault—experience shews that such slabs are soon chipped and otherwise injured if they are left uncovered and that if covered up they are rapidly destroyed by damp." They suggested a stained-glass window instead. E. J. Trelawny, MS letter to Richard Edgcumbe, 14 April 1875, private collection. Trelawny had also written to Edgcumbe about the same subject on 5 April 1875 (MS letter, private collection).

30. Lady Blunt's letter to Disraeli was printed in *The Times* (10 July 1875): 10. This put the committee in a difficult position, since they had already asked the Greek government to donate the marble, which it had agreed to do; this marble eventually formed the base of the statue. Richard Edgcumbe to Algernon Turnor, Disraeli's private secretary, 9 July 1875, Disraeli Archive, Queen's University, HA/IV/N/117.

31. "The Byron Memorial," *The Times* (17 July 1875): 9.

32. Richard Edgcumbe, "The Byron Memorial," (letter), *The Standard* (London) (20 April 1875): 3.

33. Printed circular dated 6 December 1875, advertising a meeting in Manchester on 13 December 1875 to raise subscriptions for the Byron Memorial, Disraeli Archive, Queen's University, HA/IV/N/123; Edgcumbe to Disraeli, 11 December 1875, Disraeli Archive, Queen's University, HA/IV/N/124.

34. *The Standard* (London) (26 April 1875): 4.

35. "The Proposed Byron Memorial," *The Times* (20 May 1875): 5.

36. "The Byron Memorial," *The Times* (17 July 1875): 9.

37. Ibid.; William Michael Rossetti, *The Academy* (24 April 1875): 423, cited in *Selected Letters of William Michael Rossetti*, ed. Roger W. Peattie (University Park: Pennsylvania State University Press, 1986), 355n.

38. "The National Byron Memorial," *The Times* (21 January 1876): 8. This advertisement also contains a partial list of the committee.

39. For Almack's, see Venetia Murray, *High Society in the Regency Period: 1788–1830* (London: Penguin, 1999), 48–57; Edwin Beresford Chancellor, "The Annals of Almack's," in his *Memorials of St. James's Street* (London: Grant Richards, 1922), 195–280; and Cheryl A. Wilson, *Literature and Dance in Nineteenth-Century Britain: Jane Austen to the New Woman* (Cambridge: Cambridge University Press, 2009), 40–68.

40. The ball is mentioned in *The Times* (8 July 1871): 11, in a report about two footmen arrested for being drunk and disorderly while waiting for their employers, who were attending it.

41. The archives of the Victoria and Albert Museum contain records of correspondence between Richard Edgcumbe and others and the museum regarding the exhibition of designs for a Byron monument held in 1876. The museum also lent display cases for the models displayed at the Royal Albert Hall the following year. I am grateful to Elizabeth James and James Sutton of the Victoria and Albert Museum for their assistance with these archival materials.

42. "The Byron Memorial," *The Times* (17 July 1875): 9.

43. Richard Edgcumbe to Algernon Turnor, 11 July 1875, Disraeli Archive, Queen's University, HA/IV/N/118.

44. "The Byron Memorial," *The Times* (17 July 1875): 9.

45. Paul Smith, *Disraeli: A Brief Life* (Cambridge: Cambridge University Press, 1996), 6.

46. Anne Blunt, "Byron's Tomb," *The Times* (10 July 1875): 10; "The Byron Memorial," *The Times* (17 July 1875): 9.

47. [Richard Edgcumbe], *Byron Memorial Loan Collection Catalogue*, 2nd ed. (London: William Clowes and Sons, 1877).

48. "The Byron Monument," *The Times* (9 November 1876): 6.

49. The debate surrounding the designs was parodied in *Punch*. See "Shall Byron Have a Statue?" *Punch* (18 November 1876): 212.

50. References to "the author of *Childe Harold*" include the printed circular distributed by members of the Byron Memorial Committee in June 1875, Disraeli Archive, Queen's University, HA/IV/N/108C; R. L.'s letter to *The Times* (23 April 1875): 11; Lord Lovelace's speech at the public meeting (*The Times* [17 July 1875]: 9); Alfred Austin's letter to *The Times* (19 July 1875): 10; and Edgcumbe, *History*, 9. The marble tablet placed on Byron's grave by Augusta also refers to him as "The author of 'Childe Harold's Pilgrimage'" without mentioning any of his other poems.

51. [Edgcumbe], *Catalogue*, 9–12.

52. Alfred Austin, "The Byron Memorial," *The Times* (19 July 1875): 10.

53. Linda Colley, *Britons: Forging the Nation, 1707–1837* (London: Vintage, 1996), 108–54.

54. Editorial, *The Times* (3 May 1858): 8.

55. Sir Henry Ponsonby, private secretary to Queen Victoria, to Algernon Turnor, private secretary to Benjamin Disraeli, 14 November 1876, Disraeli Archive, Queen's University, HA/IV/N/133, reports that the Queen has refused the site in Green Park.

56. Benjamin Disraeli to Lord Rosslyn, 24 September 1878, Scottish Record Office GD164/1832/12 (transcript in Disraeli Archive, Queen's University): "The island, at the top of St James' Street, shd. do well for the statue of our greatest poet since Shakespear [*sic*]."

57. Rosslyn to Benjamin Disraeli (now Lord Beaconsfield), 7 April 1879, Disraeli Archive, Queen's University, HA/IV/N/148, reports the decision and encloses a letter from the vestry clerk of St. George's Church in Hanover Square. See also "Shall Lord Byron Have a Statue?" in *Punch* (3 May 1879): 193.

58. Edgcumbe, *History*, 12.

59. Correspondence and memoranda relating to the statue's installation, cleaning, and maintenance until 1904 is preserved in the Ministry of Works papers at the National Archives, Kew, in file Work 20/47.

60. The monument fell into disrepair, and was removed and destroyed around 1948. Correspondence and memoranda relating to its installation, upkeep, and eventual removal is in the Ministry of Works papers at the National Archives, Kew, in files Work 20/43, Work 20/189, and Work 20/249.

61. Karl Baedeker, *London and its Environs*, 5th ed. (Leipzig: Baedeker; London: Dulau and Co., 1885), 247.

62. Karl Baedeker, *Great Britain* (Leipzig: Baedeker; London: Dulau and Co., 1887), 472.

63. Wyatt's statue was removed to Aldershot in 1887, the orientation of the arch was changed, and a figure representing Victory was placed on the top in place of the statue. At the same time (1884–88), a smaller equestrian statue of Wellington by Sir Edgar Boehm was placed opposite Apsley House. Memoranda and correspondence relating to these alterations are preserved in the Ministry of Works papers at the National Archives, Kew, in file Work 20/49.

64. There were also demonstrations in Hyde Park about Sunday Trading in 1855. See M.J.D. Roberts, *Making English Morals: Voluntary Association and Moral Reform in England, 1787–1866* (Cambridge: Cambridge University Press, 2004), 183–88; and Brian Harrison, "The Sunday Trade Riots of 1855," *Historical Journal* 8, no. 2 (1965): 219–45.

65. For the Staffordshire figures of Byron, see P. D. Gordon Pugh, *Staffordshire Portrait Figures*, new and rev. ed. (Woodbridge, Suffolk: Antique Collectors' Club, 1987), figs. 17–21, 27, 28, pp. 492–95; for Scott, see figs. 54, 57, pp. 493, 500–501. For an extremely thorough

attempt to use a Staffordshire figurine as a window onto aspects of Victorian culture, see F. S. Schwarzbach, "Twelve Ways of Looking at a Staffordshire Figurine: An Essay in Cultural Studies," *Victorians Institute Journal* 29 (2001): 6–60. The three major producers of Parian—Minton, Copeland, and Robinson and Leadbeater—all issued figures or busts of Byron and Scott in the nineteenth century. For Byron figures in Parian, see Paul Atterbury et al., *The Parian Phenomenon: A Survey of Victorian Parian Porcelain Statuary and Busts* (Shepton Beauchamp: Richard Dennis, 1989), 93, 135, 186, 228, 230–31; for Scott, see 96, 126, 186, 198, 202, 233, 246. For further information on Parian ware, see Antoinette Faÿ-Hallé and Barbara Mundt, *Nineteenth-Century European Porcelain* (London: Trefoil Books, 1983), 165–67.

66. Wellington was a popular subject for these kinds of artifacts. See Belinda Beaton, "Materializing the Duke," *Journal of Victorian Culture* 10, no. 1 (2005): 100–107.

67. Robert Copeland, *Parian: Copeland's Statuary Porcelain* (Woodbridge, Suffolk: Antique Collectors' Club, 2007), 225. See also Atterbury et al., *Parian Phenomenon*, 186, where a pair of busts of Byron and Scott is shown.

68. T. S. Eliot, "Byron" (1937), in *On Poetry and Poets* (London: Faber and Faber, 1957), 193–206 (194).

69. Keys and Montford made a bust of Wordsworth (Copeland, *Parian*, fig. 827, p. 245); Robinson and Leadbeater made one of Thomas Moore (fig. 752a, p. 230) and one of Shelley (fig. 757, p. 231).

70. Rohan McWilliam, "The Theatricality of the Staffordshire Figure," *Journal of Victorian Culture* 10, no. 1 (2005): 111.

71. *Readings in Poetry: A Selection from the Best English Poets, from Spenser to the Present Times; and Specimens of Several American Poets of Deserved Reputation* (London: John W. Parker, 1833); Lord Byron, *Poetry of Byron*, ed. Matthew Arnold (London: Macmillan, 1881); John Gibson Lockhart, *Memoirs of the Life of Sir Walter Scott, Bart.*, 10 vols. (Toronto: George N. Morang, 1901), vol. 10, facing p. 186.

Chapter 13. Scattered Odes in Shattered Books: Quantifying Victorian Anthologies

1. Flora Thompson, *Lark Rise to Candleford* (London: Penguin, 2008), 466. Italics in original.

2. Francis Turner Palgrave, *The Golden Treasury of the Best Songs and Lyrical Poems in the English Language: Selected and Arranged with Notes by Francis Turner Palgrave*, ed. Christopher Ricks (London: Penguin, 1991), 7.

3. Ibid., 3.

4. Charles Mackay, ed., *A Thousand and One Gems of English Poetry*, illus. J. E. Millais, John Gilbert, and Birket Foster (London: George Routledge and Sons, 1867), 474–75.

5. It is possible that editions were deliberately misnumbered to exaggerate the book's popularity, or that some "new editions" were in fact old editions with new title pages. On these practices, see William St. Clair, *The Reading Nation in the Romantic Period* (Cambridge: Cambridge University Press, 2004), 180–81, although St. Clair suggests that misnumbering of editions declined by midcentury.

6. Mackay, *A Thousand and One Gems*, iii.

NOTES TO CHAPTER 13   273

7. Mackay expanded on the conceit in his preface: "All the 'Gems' in the volume are not of equal brilliancy. The diamonds, rubies, emeralds, and pearls of literature are few;—but there are other 'gems' than these, of inferior value but still gemlike;—agate, cornelian, amethyst, turquoise, onyx, and scores of others known to the lapidary and jeweler, and prized by them and by the public to whose appreciation they are offered" (ibid., iv).

8. Ian Michael has examined how anthologies reflect changing approaches to education. Ian Michael, *The Teaching of English: From the Sixteenth Century to 1870* (Cambridge: Cambridge University Press, 1987), 169–268.

9. David Latané and Christopher Ricks have both examined the most popular of all Victorian anthologies: *Palgrave's Golden Treasury*. David E. Latané, *Palgrave's Golden Treasury and Victorian Anthologies* (Morganton: West Virginia University Press, 1999); Christopher Ricks, "The Making of *The Golden Treasury*," in Palgrave, *The Golden Treasury*, ed. Ricks, 437–50.

10. On anthologies' role in canon formation, see Barbara Korte, *Flowers for the Picking: Anthologies of Poetry in (British) Literary and Cultural Studies* (Amsterdam: Rodopi, 2000). Margaret Ezell examines the role of anthologies in pushing women writers to the margins of the canon in the nineteenth century; Margaret Ezell, *Writing Women's Literary History* (Baltimore: Johns Hopkins University Press, 1993).

11. Anne Ferry, *Tradition and the Individual Poem: An Inquiry into Anthologies* (Stanford, CA: Stanford University Press, 2001).

12. Leah Price, *The Anthology and the Rise of the Novel: From Richardson to George Eliot* (Cambridge: Cambridge University Press, 2000); Barbara Benedict, *The Making of the Modern Reader* (Princeton, NJ: Princeton University Press, 1996).

13. Laura Mandell, "Putting Contents on the Table: The Disciplinary Anthology and the Field of Literary History," *Poetess Archive Journal* 1, no. 1 (2007).

14. Lethbridge writes, "It seems that the 'anthological' reading habit extended to all kinds of literature, including some novels, and was not restricted to non-narrative poetry or anthologies. Neither was it restricted to the eighteenth century." Stefanie Lethbridge, "Anthological Reading Habits in the Eighteenth Century: The Case of Thomson's *Seasons*," in *Anthologies of British Poetry: Critical Perspectives from Literary and Cultural Studies*, ed. Barbara Korte, Ralf Schneider, and Stefanie Lethbridge (Amsterdam: Rodopi, 2000), 102.

15. John Cam Hobhouse, *Imitations and Translations from the Ancient and Modern Classics, Together with Original Poems Never Before Published* (London: Longman, 1809).

16. [Samuel Taylor Coleridge and Robert Southey], *Omniana*, 2 vols. (London: Longman, Hurst, Rees, Orme and Brown, 1812).

17. Alasdair MacIntyre, *After Virtue: A Study in Moral Theory*, 2nd ed. (London: Duckworth, 1984), 222.

18. Stephen Gill, *Wordsworth and the Victorians* (Oxford: Clarendon Press, 1998), 103.

19. Price, *The Anthology and the Rise of the Novel*, 2, 3.

20. Richard D. Altick, *The English Common Reader: A Social History of the Mass Reading Public, 1800–1900* (Chicago: University of Chicago Press, 1957), esp. 126–27, on "extracts" and Bowdlerization, and 159–60 and 176–77, on school anthologies.

21. St. Clair, *Reading Nation*, 715–23 (722). The rest of this useful appendix concentrates on reprint series of collected or selected works.

22. Michael, *The Teaching of English*, 198.

23. As a copyright deposit library, the British Library provides an almost complete archive of publications in the British Isles in this period. Its catalog is not absolutely comprehensive, but in the absence of a specialized bibliography of literary anthologies it offers the best single source of information available. This kind of methodology is only possible with the assistance of a team of students, whose membership has shifted over the years that this project has developed. I am grateful to Kaiwen Zhang and Samuel Schmidt for database development and support; to Mark Algee-Hewitt for consulting on database design; to Tara Murphy, who helped identify the corpus, and Amy Fox, who helped develop methods for interrogating the data; and to Brenna Baggs, Danielle Barkley, Susan Civale, Melissa Dickson, Matthew Ingleby, Christine Lai, Tara MacDonald, and Lauren Welsh, who helped gather data and offered their insights into the project.

24. A discussion of my methodology appeared in Jeffrey J. Williams, "The Statistical Turn in Literary Studies," in *How to Be an Intellectual: Essays on Criticism, Culture and the University* (New York: Fordham University Press, 2014), 61–64.

25. Writing about the period 1557–1700, D. F. McKenzie cites lack of information about "the number printed of each edition" as one of the three "crippling deficiencies in our knowledge" of book history. D. F. McKenzie, "Printing and Publishing 1557–1700: Constraints on the London Book Trades," in *The Cambridge History of the Book in Britain*, vol. 4, *1557–1695*, ed. John Barnard and D. F. McKenzie with the assistance of Maureen Bell (Cambridge: Cambridge University Press, 2002), 556. St. Clair confirms that "Although, for Great Britain, we have excellent descriptive bibliographies and library catalogues of the titles of English-language books known to have been printed since the fifteenth century, we lack information on costs, prices, print runs, and sales" (*Reading Nation*, 9). Some information on edition sizes and print runs drawn from both published and archival sources is provided by St. Clair, 456, 462–75.

26. The Murray Archive, now at the National Library of Scotland, has been extensively mined by, for example: William Zachs, *The First John Murray and the Late Eighteenth-Century London Book Trade* (Oxford: Published for the British Academy by Oxford University Press, 1998); Samuel Smiles, *A Publisher and His Friends: Memoir and Correspondence of the Late John Murray, with an Account of the Origin and Progress of the House, 1768–1843*, 2 vols. (London: John Murray, 1891); Humphrey Carpenter, *The Seven Lives of John Murray: The Story of a Publishing Dynasty* (London: John Murray, 2008); and Mary O'Connell, *Byron and John Murray: A Poet and His Publisher* (Liverpool: Liverpool University Press, 2014). The Longman Archive at the University of Reading includes copyright ledgers recording the print runs of books published by Longmans. This archive formed the mainstay of Asa Briggs, *A History of Longmans and Their Books, 1724–1990: Longevity in Publishing* (London: British Library; New Castle, DE: Oak Knoll Press, 2008); see in particular "Appendix 1: A Note on Sources" for more details (543–46).

27. James Chandler, *England in 1819: The Politics of Literary Culture and the Case of Romantic Historicism* (Chicago: University of Chicago Press, 1998).

28. Alan Liu, "The Power of Formalism: The New Historicism," *ELH* 56 (1989): 721–71, repr. in Alan Liu, *Local Transcendence: Essays on Postmodern Historicism and the Database* (Chicago: University of Chicago Press, 2008), 28–68 (56).

29. Lucasta Miller, "The Human Factor," interview with Stephen Greenblatt, *The Guardian* (26 February 2005), http://www.theguardian.com/books/2005/feb/26/biography (retrieved 17 February 2015). To be fair, Greenblatt went on to comment, "I don't want to exaggerate it, because it almost sounds like I'm a lunatic."

30. George Ellis, *Specimens of the Early English Poets* (London: Longman, 1790), is the most influential anthology to use this terminology. Ellis expanded his one-volume first edition into three volumes in 1801. The term "specimens" was also used by Robert Southey in his *Specimens of the Later English Poets, with Preliminary Notices* (London: Longman, 1807), George Burnett in *Specimens of English Prose-Writers, from the Earliest Times to the Close of the Seventeenth Century* (London: Longman, 1807), and Charles Lamb in *Specimens of English Dramatic Poets, Who Lived about the Time of Shakspeare* (London: Longman, 1808). See also William H. Davenport Adams, ed., *Quips and Quiddities* (London: Chatto and Windus, 1881).

31. Price, *The Anthology and the Rise of the Novel*, 7.

32. Franco Moretti, *Distant Reading* (London: Verso, 2013); Franco Moretti, *Graphs, Maps, Trees: Abstract Models for Literary History* (London: Verso, 2005).

33. Martin Mueller writes: "[s]calable reading [. . .] does not promise the transcendence of reading—close or otherwise—by bigger or better things. Rather it draws attention to the fact that texts in digital form enable new and powerful ways of shuttling between 'text' and 'context.'" One important difference between his work and mine, however, is that his uses full text datasets, whereas mine uses bibliographic data. See https://scalablereading.northwestern.edu/scalable-reading/ (accessed 23 July 2013).

34. Michael, *The Teaching of English*, 236; Paula R. Feldman, introduction to Felicia Hemans, *Records of Woman: With Other Poems*, ed. Paula R. Feldman (Lexington: University Press of Kentucky, 1999), xii.

35. "The Destruction of Sennacherib" does appear in *Lord Byron: Selected Poems*, ed. Susan Wolfson and Peter Manning (London: Penguin, 1996), and *Byron's Poetry and Prose*, ed. Alice Levine (New York: W. W. Norton, 2010), but not in *Lord Byron: The Major Works*, ed. Jerome J. McGann, Oxford World's Classics (Oxford: Oxford University Press, 2000). It does not appear in any of the following anthologies: *The Broadview Anthology of British Literature: The Age of Romanticism*, ed. Joseph Black et al. (Peterborough, ON: Broadview, 2006), *Romantic Poetry: An Annotated Anthology*, ed. Michael O'Neill and Charles Mahoney (Oxford: Blackwell, 2008), *The Longman Anthology of British Literature: The Romantics and Their Contemporaries*, 4th ed., ed. Susan J. Wolfson and Peter Manning (New York: Longman, 2010), *The Norton Anthology of English Literature: The Romantic Period*, 8th ed., ed. Jack Stillinger and Deidre Lynch (New York: W. W. Norton, 2006), *Romanticism: An Anthology*, 3rd ed., ed. Duncan Wu (Oxford: Blackwell, 2006).

Chapter 14. Romantic Short Poems in Victorian Anthologies

1. *Choice Poems and Lyrics for Study and Delight*, ed. J. T. Ashby (London: Relfe Bros., [1879]), 8.

2. Sylva Norman, *Flight of the Skylark: The Development of Shelley's Reputation* (London: Max Reinhardt; Norman: University of Oklahoma Press, 1954).

3. The lines beginning "Life of life! thy lips enkindle" from *Prometheus Unbound* II.v.48–71 were quoted in three anthologies surveyed, including *Palgrave's Golden Treasury*.

4. I refer here to the volume publication of these poems; some were published in newspapers or periodicals before they appeared in volumes. Of the five poems from *The Forest Sanctuary*, two had appeared in the first edition of 1825 but were reprinted in the second edition of 1829, where the other three referred to appeared for the first time.

5. Susan J. Wolfson, introduction to *Felicia Hemans: Selected Poems, Letters, Reception Materials*, ed. Susan J. Wolfson (Princeton, NJ: Princeton University Press, 2000), xxiii. Paula R. Feldman, introduction to Felicia Hemans, *Records of Woman: With Other Poems*, ed. Paula R. Feldman (Lexington: University Press of Kentucky, 1999), xviii.

6. Percy Shelley published fourteen books in his lifetime, counting *Laon and Cythna* and *The Revolt of Islam* as one book, since they contain two versions of the same poem, albeit with many important variants.

7. *Felicia Hemans*, ed. Wolfson, 324.

8. In 1827, Hemans arranged with William Blackwood to be paid 24 guineas a sheet for poetry in *Blackwood's Edinburgh Magazine*, and to draw on him "for the value of the contributions, at my own convenience" (Hemans to William Blackwood, 13 June 1827, in *Felicia Hemans*, ed. Wolfson, 494). Her rate increased to 2 guineas a page (32 guineas a sheet) in 1831 (*Felicia Hemans*, ed. Wolfson, 515). For further information on Hemans's financial dealings with publishers, see Paula Feldman's important article "The Poet and the Profits: Felicia Hemans and the Literary Marketplace," *Keats-Shelley Journal* 46 (1997): 148–76.

9. Cited in Henry Chorley, *Memorials of Mrs Hemans: with Illustrations of her Literary Character from her Private Correspondence*, 2 vols. (London: Saunders and Otley, 1836), 2:257.

10. Timothy Webb writes that, for Shelley, "it was possible, desirable and cathartic even, to compose verses which were personal and which relieved one's feelings, but the essential aim of poetry was grander and higher." Timothy Webb, *Shelley: A Voice Not Understood* (Manchester: Manchester University Press, 1977), 85.

11. Shelley did publish two pseudonymous juvenile volumes of shorter poems in 1810: *Original Poetry by Victor and Cazire* and *Posthumous Fragments of Margaret Nicholson*.

12. Mary Shelley, preface to *Posthumous Poems of Percy Bysshe Shelley*, ed. Mary Shelley (London: John and Henry L. Hunt, 1824), viii.

13. Ibid.

14. Reviews of Percy Bysshe Shelley, *Prometheus Unbound [. . .] and Other Poems*, in *Blackwood's Edinburgh Magazine* 7, no. 42 (September 1820): 679–87 (685); and *Dublin Magazine* 2 (November 1820): 393–99 (396–99).

15. Reviews of *Hebrew Melodies* are reprinted in *The Romantics Reviewed*, ed. Donald Reiman, 9 vols. (London: Garland, 1972).

16. Andrew Elfenbein, *Romanticism and the Rise of English* (Stanford, CA: Stanford University Press, 2009), 141.

17. Catherine Robson, *Heart Beats: Everyday Life and the Memorized Poem* (Princeton, NJ: Princeton University Press, 2012), 116, 117.

18. Shelley's "To a Skylark" does not seem to have been such a popular choice for recitation. It belonged to what Elfenbein calls "patterned Romanticism," in which sonic harmonies were more important than metrical stresses. These "patterned" poems were thought of as less suitable for recitation during much of the nineteenth century, but they gained in popularity at the beginning of the twentieth century, with the rise of a new style of recitation, backed by professional training, promoted through competitions, and popularized in gramophone recordings. Elfenbein, *Romanticism and the Rise of English*, 193–205.

19. The rise in the popularity of "To a Skylark" is corroborated by Karsten Engelberg's statistics. He found that, of the items catalogued in his bibliography, only one from the 1820s

cited "To a Skylark," compared to six from the 1830s, nine from the 1840s, and twenty from the 1850s. Karsten Klejs Engelberg, *The Making of the Shelley Myth: An Annotated Bibliography of Criticism of Percy Bysshe Shelley, 1822–1860* (London: Mansell, 1988), 100.

20. Isaac Disraeli, *Curiosities of Literature* (London: Moxon, 1843), 340.

21. Walter Hamilton, ed., *Parodies of the Works of English and American Authors*, 6 vols. (London: Reeves and Turner, 1884–89), 3 (1886): 201–9, 279.

22. Her biographer Henry Chorley reports how Hemans enjoyed a parody of one of her own poems, but does not say which one. Chorley, *Memorials of Mrs Hemans*, 1:243.

23. Hamilton, *Parodies*, 3:133–35.

24. Ibid., 5 (1888): 233–36.

25. [Francis Jeffrey], review of *The Forest Sanctuary, with Other Poems*, *Edinburgh Review* 50 (1829): 32.

26. X.Y.Z. [John Neal?], "American Writers," *Blackwood's Edinburgh Magazine* 17, no. 97 (February 1825): 195. Neal is here writing anonymously, but quoting himself discussing his own work and its relation to Hemans's, in a fashion that exemplifies *Blackwood's* typically ludic approach to authorial identity and critical integrity.

27. Chorley, *Memorials of Mrs Hemans*, 1:114. Although Chorley praised Hemans's short poems, he didn't value her sonnets very highly: "Mrs Hemans never having wholly attained the power of compression which is a requisite essential to compositions of this difficult but exquisite class" (2:217).

28. *Readings in Poetry: A Selection from the Best English Poets, from Spenser to the Present Times; and Specimens of Several American Poets of Deserved Reputation* (London: John W. Parker, 1833), 312.

29. Howard Williams, ed., *Anthologia Anglica: A New Selection from the English Poets from Spenser to Shelley* (London: n.p., 1873), 362.

30. William H. Davenport Adams, ed., *The Student's Treasury of English Song: Containing Choice Selections from the Principal Poets of the Present Century* (London: T. Nelson and Sons, 1873), 173.

31. Cited in Chorley, *Memorials of Mrs Hemans*, 2:257.

32. Ibid., 2:258.

33. Adams, *The Student's Treasury*, 389.

34. Ibid., 390.

35. Some of the most popular anthology poems, however, were published in their entirety. Byron's "The Destruction of Sennacherib" was printed in full in all 35 anthologies that included it. Hemans's "The Graves of a Household" also always appeared complete, and "Casabianca" remained uncut 26 out of 28 times. Shelley's "To a Skylark" was reprinted in its entirety 33 out of 36 times, and "The Cloud" 25 out of 27 times.

36. I use the term "longer poems" here to refer to poems of up to three hundred lines, which were sometimes reprinted in their entirety but were often abridged. I use the term "long poems" for book-length poems that were never reprinted in full in anthologies.

37. X.Y.Z. [John Neal?], "American Writers," 195.

38. Felicia Hemans, *Selected Poems, Prose and Letters*, ed. Gary Kelly (Peterborough, ON: Broadview, 2002), 215–18.

39. Cited in Chorley, *Memorials of Mrs Hemans*, 1:94.

40. "The Voice of Spring" was set to music a number of times, and the settings followed the anthologies in drastically abridging it. I have examined seven nineteenth-century settings, six of which cut Hemans's lines on the dead children.

41. The phrase "death-haunted consciousness" is Susan Wolfson's; introduction to *Felicia Hemans*, xvi.

42. Feldman, introduction to *Records of Woman*, xxii.

43. Chorley, *Memorials of Mrs Hemans*, 1:43.

44. S. C. Hall, ed., *The Book of Gems: The Modern Poets and Artists of Great Britain* (London: Whittaker and Co., 1842), 134. This volume did not, in fact, include "The Voice of Spring."

45. Mary Shelley, preface to *Posthumous Poems*, iv.

46. Webb, *Shelley*, 237.

Chapter 15. Romantic Long Poems in Victorian Anthologies

An earlier version of this chapter was published as "Romantic Long Poems in Victorian Anthologies," in *British Romanticism: Criticism and Debates*, ed. Mark Canuel (London: Routledge, 2014), 625–34.

1. J. W. Hales, ed., *Longer English Poems, with Notes, Philological and Explanatory, and an Introduction on the Teaching of English* (London: Macmillan, 1872), xvii–xxxvii. For further discussion of this book and its use in British, American, and colonial educational contexts, see Andrew Elfenbein, *Romanticism and the Rise of English* (Stanford, CA: Stanford University Press, 2009), 186–92.

2. [Francis Jeffrey], review of *The Lay of the Last Minstrel: A Poem*, *Edinburgh Review* 6 (1805): 1–20 (16).

3. *Poets of England and America; Being Selections from the Best Authors of Both Countries* (London: Whittaker and Co., 1853), 263–64; Thomas Shorter, ed., *A Book of English Poetry; for the School, the Fireside, and the Country Ramble* (London: T. J. Allman, 1861), 202.

4. She also cancelled at least two embedded lyrics in the manuscript of *Siege* and wrote new lyrics to replace them. The manuscript songs are reprinted in *Felicia Hemans: Selected Poems, Letters, Reception Materials*, ed. Susan J. Wolfson (Princeton, NJ: Princeton University Press, 2000), 254–55.

5. *Lyrical Gems: A Selection of Moral, Sentimental, and Descriptive Poetry, from the Works of the Most Popular Modern Writers* (Glasgow: Richard Griffin, 1825), 253–54.

6. Jerome J. McGann, "Mobility and the Poetics of Historical Ventriloquism," in *Byron and Romanticism*, ed. James Soderholm (Cambridge: Cambridge University Press, 2002), 36–52.

7. *Lyrical Gems*, 461.

8. Ibid., 84–87.

9. *The Siege of Valencia*, II.274–83, 311–28, 333–44, 353–74, 377–96.

10. "The Monk's Tale" was reprinted from *Lyrical Gems*, without any significant variants, in *The Diadem; or, Poetical Scraps: Comprising a Selection of Lyric, Moral, Sentimental and Humorous Poetry, from the Most Admired Authors* (Leith: Commercial List Office, 1830), 186–88.

11. Samuel Taylor Coleridge, *Biographia Literaria: or, Biographical Sketches of My Literary Life and Opinions*, ed. James Engell and W. Jackson Bate, 2 vols. (Princeton, NJ: Princeton University Press, 1983), 2:15.

12. John Keats to Benjamin Bailey, 8 October 1817, in *Letters of John Keats*, ed. Robert Gittings (Oxford: Oxford University Press, 1970), 27.

13. Percy Bysshe Shelley, "A Defence of Poetry," in *Shelley's Poetry and Prose*, ed. Donald H. Reiman and Sharon B. Powers (New York: W. W. Norton, 1977), 504.

14. Edgar Allan Poe, "The Philosophy of Composition" (1846), in *Selections from the Critical Writings of Edgar Allan Poe*, ed. F. C. Prescott (New York: Gordian Press, 1981), 153.

15. "On the other hand, the *Harshness* of many of these passages and a harshness unrelieved by any lyrical interbreathings, and still more that want of profundity in the thoughts, keep me fluctuating." Samuel Taylor Coleridge, *Marginalia*, ed. H. J. Jackson and George Whalley, 6 vols. (Princeton, NJ: Princeton University Press, 1980–2001), 1:407.

16. Monique R. Morgan, *Narrative Means, Lyric Ends: Temporality in the Nineteenth-Century British Long Poem* (Columbus: Ohio State University Press, 2009).

17. The book to include only quotations from *Childe Harold* was Joseph Edwards Carpenter, ed., *The Public School Speaker and Reader: A Selection of Prose and Verse, from Modern and Standard Authors* (London: Frederick Warne, 1869). They are "Lake Leman by Night" (205–7), "Childe Harold's Farewell" (223–24), "The Field of Waterloo" (416–18), "The Dying Gladiator" (454–55), and "The Ocean" (472–74).

18. This means 3,119 lines out of a total of 4,655.

19. A total of 1,450 lines, including the openings of cantos 1 and 4, are never reprinted in the anthologies surveyed.

20. Details of the prosecutions are supplied in the commentary to *The Complete Poetry of Percy Bysshe Shelley*, vol. 2, ed. Donald H. Reiman and Neil Fraistat (Baltimore: Johns Hopkins University Press, 2004). William Clark (sometimes spelled Clarke) published an unauthorized edition of *Queen Mab* in 1821. He was prosecuted by the Society for the Suppression of Vice and sentenced to four months in Cold Bath Fields Prison in November 1822 (509). Mary Shelley, having made cuts in *Queen Mab* for her 1839 edition of her husband's works to avoid prosecution, restored the complete text in the 1840 edition. Its publisher, Edward Moxon, was convicted of blasphemous libel but received no penalty (518).

21. Review of *Queen Mab*, *Literary Gazette and Journal of Belles Lettres* 226 (May 1821): 305–8, repr. in James E. Barcus, ed., *Shelley: The Critical Heritage* (London: Routledge and Kegan Paul, 1975), 77.

22. Review of *Alastor*, *Eclectic Review* (October 1816): 391–93, repr. in Barcus, ed., *Shelley*, 97–99 (99).

23. Percy Bysshe Shelley, preface to *The Cenci*, in *The Poems of Shelley*, vol. 2, *1817–1819*, ed. Kelvin Everest and Geoffrey Matthews (London: Routledge, 2014), 733.

24. Leah Price, *The Anthology and the Rise of the Novel: From Richardson to George Eliot* (Cambridge: Cambridge University Press, 2000), 68.

25. I calculate that out of a total of 16,068 lines in the poem (including the dedication but not unincorporated stanzas), 12,533 do not appear in any anthology surveyed.

26. The publication history of *Don Juan* may have influenced the anthologies' choices: John Murray published cantos 1–5, while John Hunt published from canto 6 onward. But the anthologies' interest drops off before canto 6, with only ten extracts from canto 4, and only four from canto 5. This suggests that the anthologies are responding to the content of these cantos rather than their publication history.

27. William H. Davenport Adams, ed., *Quips and Quiddities* (London: Chatto and Windus, 1881).

28. James Blackwood, ed., *Selections from the Poets: Popular Poems from the Most Eminent Authors, Illustrated with Fine Steel Engravings* (London: n.p., [1850?]). The sections reprinted from *Don Juan* are 1.123–27 ("First Love," pp. 296–97), 4.11–16 ("The Lovers," pp. 298–99), and 4.31–34 ("A Dream," p. 300).

29. [John Gibson Lockhart?], "Remarks on *Don Juan*," *Blackwood's Edinburgh Magazine* 5, no. 29 (August 1819): 512–18, repr. in *Blackwood's Magazine, 1817–25: Selections from Maga's Infancy*, 6 vols., gen. ed. Nicholas Mason, vol. 5, *Selected Criticism, 1817–19*, ed. Tom Mole (London: Pickering and Chatto, 2006), 315–22 (319).

30. Charles Gibbon, ed., *The Casquet of Literature: Being a Selection in Poetry and Prose from the Works of the Most Admired Authors* (London; Glasgow: n.p., 1873), 173.

31. Roland Barthes, *S/Z*, trans. Richard Miller (New York: Hill and Wang, 1974), 13.

32. Roland Barthes, *S/Z* (Paris: Editions du Seuil, 1970), 18.

33. Barthes, *S/Z*, trans. Miller, 13.

34. Ibid., 13, 14, 15.

35. Michel de Certeau, "Reading as Poaching," in *The Practice of Everyday Life*, trans. Steven Rendall (Berkeley: University of California Press, 1984), 165–76.

Coda. Ozymandias at the Olympics; or, She Walks in Brixton

1. Søren Kierkegaard, *Fear and Trembling*, trans. Alastair Hannay (London: Penguin, 2005), 31.

2. Statistics from "London 2012 Olympics Close with Spectacular Ceremony," http://www.bbc.co.uk/news/uk-19236754, and "2012 Summer Olympics Closing Ceremony," http://en.wikipedia.org/wiki/2012_Summer_Olympics_closing_ceremony, both accessed 9 December 2013.

3. *London 2012 Olympic Closing Ceremony Media Guide*, 8; available online at http://www.scribd.com/doc/103018572/London-2012-Olympic-Closing-Ceremony-Guide, accessed 9 December 2013.

4. Leslie Marchand, *Byron: A Biography*, 3 vols. (London: John Murray, 1957), 1:97 (Harrow), 1:264 (Sounion), 2:480 (Newstead), 2:631n (Chillon, p. 67 of notes section); David Ellis, *Byron in Geneva: That Summer of 1816* (Liverpool: Liverpool University Press, 2011), 126 (Château de Châtelard).

5. I follow a number of online discussions of Arofish's work in using the male pronoun to refer to the artist. For an interview, see http://www.justseeds.org/blog/2005/01/interview_with_arofish.html, accessed 15 December 2013.

6. Discussions of Byron's punctuation are complicated by the fact that his manuscripts (like his letters) are often carelessly or eccentrically punctuated, and that he several times deferred to the suggestions of amanuenses or editors when punctuating his poems. Here I follow the punctuation in Lord Byron, *The Complete Poetical Works*, ed. Jerome J. McGann, 7 vols. (Oxford: Clarendon Press, 1980–93), 3 (1981): 288–89.

7. Lord Byron, *Byron's Letters and Journals*, ed. Leslie A. Marchand, 13 vols. (London: John Murray, 1973–94), 4 (1975): 124 and n; *Complete Poetical Works*, 3:467.

8. Moore recorded the detail in *The Works of Lord Byron, With his Letters and Journals and his Life*, 17 vols. (London: John Murray, 1832), 10:75.

9. Who Anne Wilmot was mourning in June 1814 is unknown. She had probably been in mourning recently, however, as her daughter had died in 1811. See Eric Richards, "Horton, Sir Robert John Wilmot, third baronet (1784–1841)," *Oxford Dictionary of National Biography* (Oxford: Oxford University Press, 2004); online ed., January 2008 [http://www.oxforddnb .com/view/article/13827, accessed 16 Dec 2013].

BIBLIOGRAPHY

I have consulted unpublished documents in several private collections and in the archive of the Victorian and Albert Museum; the Disraeli Archive at Queen's University, Kingston, Ontario; the Scottish Record Office; and the National Archives, Kew. Where appropriate, these are cited in the endnotes.

Abrams, M. H. *Natural Supernaturalism: Tradition and Revolution in Romantic Literature*. New York: W. W. Norton, 1973.

Ackroyd, Peter. *T. S. Eliot*. London: Penguin, 1993.

Adams, William H. Davenport, ed. *The Student's Treasury of English Song: Containing Choice Selections from the Principal Poets of the Present Century*. London: T. Nelson and Sons, 1873.

———, ed. *Quips and Quiddities*. London: Chatto and Windus, 1881.

[Agg, John]. *Lord Byron's Farewell to England: with Three Other Poems*. London: J. Johnston, 1816.

Allen, Emily, and Dino F. Felluga. "Feeling Cosmopolitan: The Novel Politician After Byron." *European Romantic Review* 20, no. 5 (2009): 651–59.

Altick, Richard D. *The English Common Reader: A Social History of the Mass Reading Public, 1800–1900*. Chicago: University of Chicago Press, 1957.

———. *Paintings from Books: Art and Literature in Britain, 1760–1900*. Columbus: Ohio State University Press, 1985.

———. "The Sociology of Authorship: The Social Origins, Education, and Occupations of 1,100 British Writers, 1800–1935." In *Writers, Readers, and Occasions*, 95–109. Columbus: Ohio State University Press, 1989.

Anecdotes: The Holy Scriptures. London: The Religious Tract Society, n.d.

Armstrong, Carol M. *Scenes in a Library: Reading the Photograph in the Book, 1843–1875*. Cambridge, MA: MIT Press, 1998.

Armstrong, George G. *Richard Acland Armstrong: A Memoir, with Selected Sermons*. London: Philip Green, 1906.

Armstrong, Isobel. *Victorian Glassworlds: Glass Culture and the Imagination 1830–1880*. Oxford: Oxford University Press, 2008.

Armstrong, Richard. *Faith and Doubt in the Century's Poets*. London: James Clarke, 1898.

Anderson, Benedict. *Imagined Communities: Reflections on the Origin and Spread of Nationalism*. London: Verso, 1983.

Arnold, Matthew. *The Complete Prose Works of Matthew Arnold*. Edited by R. H. Super. 11 vols. Ann Arbor: University of Michigan Press, 1960–77.

———. *Culture and Anarchy and Other Writings*. Edited by Stefan Collini. Cambridge: Cambridge University Press, 1993.

Arnold, Matthew. *The Poems of Matthew Arnold*. Edited by Kenneth Allott. London: Longman, 1965.

Arvine, Reverend K., ed. *The Book of Entertaining and Instructive Anecdote, Moral and Religious*. London: T. Nelson and Sons, 1852.

Ashby, J. T., ed. *Choice Poems and Lyrics for Study and Delight*. London: Relfe Bros., [1879].

Atterbury, Paul, et al. *The Parian Phenomenon: A Survey of Victorian Parian Porcelain Statuary and Busts*. Shepton Beauchamp: Richard Dennis, 1989.

Austin, Alfred. "The Byron Memorial." *The Times*. 19 July 1875: 10.

Bacon, Ernest W. *Spurgeon: Heir of the Puritans*. London: George Allen and Unwin, 1967.

Baedeker, Karl. *Great Britain*. Leipzig: Baedeker; London: Dulau and Co., 1887.

———. *London and its Environs*. 5th ed. Leipzig: Baedeker; London: Dulau and Co., 1885.

Bagehot, Walter. *The Collected Works of Walter Bagehot*. Edited by Norman St. John-Stevas. 15 vols. Cambridge, MA: Harvard University Press, 1965–86.

Baker, David Bristow. *A Treatise on the Nature and Causes of Doubt, in Religious Questions*. London: Longman, Rees, Orme, Brown and Green, 1831.

Baker, Margaret. *Discovering London Statues and Monuments*. 5th ed. Princes Riseborough, Bucks: Shire Publications, 2002.

Baldick, Chris. *The Social Mission of English Criticism: 1848–1932*. Oxford: Clarendon Press, 1983.

Balfour, Clara Lucas. *Sketches of English Literature, from the Fourteenth to the Present Century*. London: Longman, Brown, Green, and Longmans, 1852.

Barbauld, Anna Letitia. *Selected Poetry and Prose*. Edited by William McCarthy and Elizabeth Kraft. Peterborough, ON: Broadview, 2002.

Barchas, Janine. *Graphic Design, Print Culture, and the Eighteenth-Century Novel*. Cambridge: Cambridge University Press, 2003.

Barcus, James, ed. *Shelley: The Critical Heritage*. London: Routledge and Kegan Paul, 1975.

Barthes, Roland. *Camera Lucida: Reflections on Photography*. Translated by Richard Howard. New York: Hill and Wang, 1981.

———. *S/Z*. Paris: Editions du Seuil, 1970.

———. *S/Z*. Translated by Richard Miller. New York: Hill and Wang, 1974.

Bautz, Annika. *The Reception of Jane Austen and Walter Scott: A Comparative Longitudinal Study*. London: Continuum, 2007.

Bayley, Stephen. *The Albert Memorial: The Monument in Its Social and Architectural Context*. London: Scolar Press, 1981.

Beaton, Belinda. "Materializing the Duke." *Journal of Victorian Culture* 10, no. 1 (2005): 100–107.

Beautiful Poetry: A Selection of the Choicest of the Present and the Past. 7 vols. London: J. Crockford, 1853–59.

Becker, Andrew S. "Contest or Concert? A Speculative Essay on Ecphrasis and Rivalry between the Arts." *Classical and Modern Literature: A Quarterly* 23, no. 1 (2003): 1–14.

Behrendt, Stephen C. "The Visual Arts and Music." In *Romanticism: An Oxford Guide*, edited by Nicholas Roe, 62–76. Oxford: Oxford University Press, 2005.

Bendiner, Kenneth. *The Art of Ford Madox Brown*. University Park: Pennsylvania State University Press, 1998.

Benedict, Barbara. *The Making of the Modern Reader*. Princeton, NJ: Princeton University Press, 1996.

Benjamin, Walter. *Illuminations*. Edited with an introduction by Hannah Arendt. Translated by Harry Zohn. London: Fontana, 1992.

————. "The Medium through Which Works of Art Continue to Influence Later Ages." Translated by Rodney Livingstone. In *Selected Writings*, edited by Marcus Bullock et al., 4 vols., 1:235. Cambridge, MA: Belknap, 2002.

Bennett, Andrew. *Romantic Poets and the Culture of Posterity*. Cambridge: Cambridge University Press, 1999.

Berman, Marshall. *All That Is Solid Melts into Air: The Experience of Modernity*. New York: Simon and Schuster, 1982.

Berridge, Kate. *Madame Tussaud: A Life in Wax*. New York: William Morrow, 2006.

Bindman, David. "Prints." In *An Oxford Companion to the Romantic Age: British Culture 1776–1832*, edited by Iain McCalman, 207–13. Oxford: Oxford University Press, 1999.

Black, Joseph, et al., eds. *The Broadview Anthology of British Literature: The Age of Romanticism*. Peterborough, ON: Broadview, 2006.

Blackwood, James, ed. *Selections from the Poets: Popular Poems from the Most Eminent Authors, Illustrated with Fine Steel Engravings*. London, [1850?].

Blake, Robert. *Disraeli*. London: Eyre and Spottiswoode, 1966.

Blanshard, Frances. *Portraits of Wordsworth*. London: George Allen and Unwin, 1959.

Blayney Brown, David. *Turner and Byron*. London: Tate Gallery, 1992.

Blewett, David. *The Illustration of "Robinson Crusoe," 1719–1920*. Gerrards Cross: Colin Smythe, 1995.

Bloom, Harold. *Shelley's Mythmaking*. New Haven, CT: Yale University Press, 1959.

Blunt, Anne. "Byron's Tomb." *The Times*. 10 July 1875: 10.

Bolter, J. David, and Richard Grusin. *Remediation: Understanding New Media*. Boston: MIT Press, 2000.

Bolton, H. Philip. *Scott Dramatized*. London: Mansell, 1992.

Bombaugh, Charles Carroll, ed. *Gleanings from the Harvest-Fields of Literature, Science and Art*. Baltimore: T. Newton Kurtz, 1860.

Bowen, George. *Daily Meditations*. London: Presbyterian Board of Publication, 1865.

Bowers, Fredson. "Textual Criticism." In *The Aims and Methods of Scholarship in Modern Languages and Literatures*, edited by James Thorpe, 23–42. New York: Modern Language Association of America, 1963.

Bradby, David, Louis James, and Bernard Sharratt, eds. *Performance and Politics in Popular Drama: Aspects of Popular Entertainment in Theatre, Film and Television*. Cambridge: Cambridge University Press, 1980.

Bradfield, Nancy. *Historical Costumes of England: From the Eleventh to the Twentieth Century*. London: G. G. Harrap, 1938.

Brastow, Lewis Orsmond. *Representative Modern Preachers*. New York: Hodder and Stoughton, 1910.

Bremner, G. Alex. "The 'Great Obelisk' and Other Schemes: The Origins and Limits of Nationalist Sentiment in the Making of the Albert Memorial." *Nineteenth-Century Contexts* 31, no. 3 (2009): 225–49.

Briggs, Asa. *A History of Longmans and Their Books, 1724–1990: Longevity in Publishing*. London: British Library; New Castle, DE: Oak Knoll Press, 2008.

————. *Victorian Things*. Chicago: University of Chicago Press, 1988.

Brooke, Iris, and James Laver. *English Costume from the Fourteenth through the Nineteenth Century*. New York: Macmillan, 1987.

Brooke, Stopford A. *The Development of Theology as Illustrated in English Poetry from 1780 to 1830*. London: Philip Green, 1893.

———. *English Literature*. London: Macmillan, 1876.

———. *The New Aspect of Christian Theology*. London: Macmillan, 1873.

———. *Religion in Literature and Religion in Life*. London: Philip Green, 1900.

———. *Studies in Poetry*. London: Duckworth, 1907.

———. *Theology in the English Poets: Cowper, Coleridge, Wordsworth and Burns*. 10th ed. London: Kegan Paul, 1907.

Brooks, Chris, ed. *The Albert Memorial. The Prince Consort National Memorial: Its History, Contexts, and Conservation*. New Haven: Yale University Press, 2000.

Brown, Callum G. *The Death of Christian Britain: Understanding Secularisation, 1800–2000*. 2nd ed. London: Routledge, 2009.

Browning, Robert. *The Poetical Works of Robert Browning*. Vol. 5, *Men and Women*. Edited by Ian Jack and Robert Inglesfield. Oxford: Clarendon Press, 1995.

Buchanan-Brown, John. *Early Victorian Illustrated Books: Britain, France and Germany, 1820–1860*. London: British Library; New Castle, DE: Oak Knoll Press, 2005.

Burkett, Andrew. "Photographing Byron's Hand." *European Romantic Review* 26, no. 2 (2015): 129–48.

Burnett, George. *Specimens of English Prose-Writers, from the Earliest Times to the Close of the Seventeenth Century*. London: Longman, 1807.

Burwick, Frederick, and Walter Pape, eds. *The Boydell Shakespeare Gallery*. Bottrop: Peter Pomp, 1996.

Butler, Marilyn. "Against Tradition: The Case for a Particularized Historical Method." In *Historical Studies and Literary Criticism*, edited by Jerome J. McGann, 25–47. Madison: University of Wisconsin Press, 1985.

———. *Jane Austen and the War of Ideas*. Oxford: Clarendon Press, 1975.

Byrne, Paula. *Perdita: The Life of Mary Robinson*. London: Harper Collins, 2004.

Byron, George Gordon Noel, Baron Byron. *Byron's Dream*. Illustrated by Mrs Lees. London: Dickinson and Co., 1849.

———. *Byron's Letters and Journals*. Edited by Leslie A. Marchand. 13 vols. London: John Murray, 1973–94.

———. *Byron's Poetry and Prose*. Edited by Alice Levine. New York: W. W. Norton, 2010.

———. *Childe Harold's Pilgrimage: Canto the Fourth*. London: John Murray, 1818.

———. *The Complete Poetical Works*. Edited by Jerome J. McGann. 7 vols. Oxford: Clarendon Press, 1980–93.

———. *The Illustrated Byron, with upwards of two hundred engravings from original drawings*. London: Henry Vizetelly, 1854–55.

———. *Lord Byron: The Major Works*. Edited by Jerome J. McGann. Oxford World's Classics. Oxford: Oxford University Press, 2000.

———. *Lord Byron: Selected Poems*. Edited by Susan Wolfson and Peter Manning. London: Penguin, 1996.

———. *Lord Byron's Don Juan: with Life and Original Notes by A. Cunningham Esq. and Many Illustrations on Steel*. London: Charles Daly, 1852.

————. *Lord Byron's Poetical Works, with Life and Notes by Allan Cunningham, Esq. Select Family Edition*. London: Charles Daly, [1850?].

————. *The Poetical Works of Lord Byron*. Edited by William Michael Rossetti. Illustrated by Ford Madox Brown. London: E. Moxon, Son and Co., 1870.

————. *Poetry of Byron*. Edited by Matthew Arnold. London: Macmillan, 1881.

————. *A Selection from the Works of Lord Byron*. Edited by Algernon Charles Swinburne. Moxon's Miniature Poets. London: Edward Moxon, 1866.

————. *The Works of Lord Byron*. 2nd ed. 5 vols. Leipzig: Bernhard Tauchnitz, 1866.

————. *The Works of Lord Byron*. Edited by E. H. Coleridge and Rowland E. Prothero. 13 vols. London: John Murray, 1898–1904.

————. *The Works of Lord Byron, with His Letters and Journals and His Life*. 17 vols. London: John Murray, 1832.

"Byron: The Answer." *Zion's Herald* (Boston) 3, no. 17 (27 April 1825): 2.

"The Byron Memorial." *The Times*. 17 July 1875: 9.

"The Byron Monument." *The Times*. 9 November 1876: 6.

"Byron's Contemporaries." *The Times*. 20 October 1874: 2.

"Byron's Grave." *The Times*. 22 April 1875: 7.

Cadell, Robert. "Notice to the *Waverley Novels*." Edinburgh: Robert Cadell, 1844.

Calè, Luisa. *Fuseli's Milton Gallery: Turning Readers into Spectators*. Oxford: Clarendon Press, 2006.

Canuel, Mark. *Religion, Toleration, and British Writing, 1790–1830*. Cambridge: Cambridge University Press, 2005.

Carey, D., ed. *Beauties of the Modern Poets in Selections from the Works of Byron, Moore, Scott &c.* London: Wightman and Cramp, 1826.

Carline, Richard. *Pictures in the Post: The Story of the Picture Postcard and Its Place in the History of Popular Art*. London: Gordon Fraser, 1971.

Carlyle, Thomas. *The Works of Thomas Carlyle: Centenary Edition*. Edited by H. D. Traill. 30 vols. New York: AMS Press, 1974.

Carpenter, Humphrey. *The Seven Lives of John Murray: The Story of a Publishing Dynasty*. London: John Murray, 2008.

Carpenter, Joseph Edwards, ed. *The Public School Speaker and Reader: A Selection of Prose and Verse, from Modern and Standard Authors*. London: Frederick Warne, 1869.

Certeau, Michel de. *The Practice of Everyday Life*. Translated by Steven Rendall. Berkeley: University of California Press, 1984.

Chancellor, Edwin Beresford. *Memorials of St. James's Street*. London: Grant Richards, 1922.

Chandler, James. *England in 1819: The Politics of Literary Culture and the Case of Romantic Historicism*. Chicago: University of Chicago Press, 1998.

Chartier, Roger. *The Order of Books: Readers, Authors and Libraries in Europe between the Fourteenth and the Eighteenth Centuries*. Translated by Lydia G. Cochrane. Cambridge: Polity, 1994.

Chaucer, Geoffrey. *Troilus and Criseyde: A Facsimile of Corpus Christi, Cambridge Library MS 61*. Introductions by M. B. Parkes and Elizabeth Salter. Cambridge: D.S. Brewer, 1978.

Cheeke, Stephen. *Byron and Place: History, Translation, Nostalgia*. Basingstoke: Palgrave, 2003.

Chew, Samuel. "The Byron Apocrypha." *Notes and Queries* 92 (1919): 113–15.

Chorley, Henry. *Memorials of Mrs Hemans: with Illustrations of her Literary Character from her Private Correspondence.* 2 vols. London: Saunders and Otley, 1836.

"Christmas Books." *Daily News.* 7 November 1863: 2.

Cianci, Giovanni, and Jason Harding. *T. S. Eliot and the Concept of Tradition.* Cambridge: Cambridge University Press, 2009.

Cole, Emily, ed. *Lived in London: Blue Plaques and the Stories behind Them.* London and New Haven, CT: Yale University Press, 2009.

Coleridge, Samuel Taylor. *Biographia Literaria: or, Biographical Sketches of My Literary Life and Opinions.* Edited by James Engell and W. Jackson Bate. 2 vols. Princeton, NJ: Princeton University Press, 1983.

———. *The Collected Letters of Samuel Taylor Coleridge.* Edited by E. L. Griggs. 6 vols. Oxford: Clarendon Press, 1956–71.

———. *Marginalia.* Edited by H. J. Jackson and George Whalley. 6 vols. Princeton, NJ: Princeton University Press, 1980–2001.

———. *The Rime of the Ancient Mariner.* Illustrated by Gustave Doré. London: Doré Gallery and Hamilton, Adams and Co., 1876.

[Coleridge, Samuel Taylor, and Robert Southey]. *Omniana.* 2 vols. London: Longman, Hurst, Rees, Orme and Brown, 1812.

Colley, Linda. *Britons: Forging the Nation, 1707–1837.* London: Vintage, 1996.

Collini, Stefan. *English Pasts: Essays in History and Culture.* Oxford: Oxford University Press, 1999.

Connell, Philip. "Death and the Author: Westminster Abbey and the Meanings of the Literary Monument." *Eighteenth-Century Studies* 38, no. 4 (2005): 557–85.

Conwell, Russell Herman. *The Life of Charles Haddon Spurgeon, the World's Great Preacher.* Philadelphia: Edgewood, 1892.

Copeland, Robert. *Parian: Copeland's Statuary Porcelain.* Woodbridge, Suffolk: Antique Collectors' Club, 2007.

Court, Franklin E. "The Social and Historical Significance of the First English Literature Professorship in England." *PMLA* 103, no. 5 (1988): 796–807.

Cowper, William. *The Poems of William Cowper.* Edited by John D. Baird and Charles Ryskamp. 3 vols. Oxford: Clarendon Press, 1980–95.

Cox, Philip. *Reading Adaptations: Novels and Verse Narratives on the Stage, 1790–1840.* Manchester: Manchester University Press, 2000.

Coysh, Arthur W. *The Dictionary of Picture Postcards in Britain, 1894–1939.* Woodbridge, Suffolk: Antique Collectors' Club, 1984.

Crary, Jonathan. *Techniques of the Observer: On Vision and Modernity in the Nineteenth Century.* Cambridge, MA: MIT Press, 1990.

Craske, Matthew. "Westminster Abbey 1720–70: A Public Pantheon Built Upon Private Interest." In *Pantheons: Transformations of a Monumental Idea,* edited by Richard Wrigley and Matthew Craske, 57–79. Aldershot: Ashgate, 2004.

Crawford, Robert. *Young Eliot: From St Louis to "The Waste Land."* London: Jonathan Cape, 2015.

Cronin, Richard. *Romantic Victorians: English Literature, 1824–1840.* Basingstoke: Palgrave, 2002.

Cruz, Consuelo. "Identity and Persuasion: How Nations Remember Their Pasts and Make Their Futures." *World Politics* 52 (2000): 275–312.

D'Andrea, Thomas D. *Tradition, Rationality, and Virtue: The Thought of Alasdair MacIntyre.* Aldershot: Ashgate, 2006.

Dane, Joseph A. *Blind Impressions: Methods and Mythologies in Book History.* Philadelphia: University of Pennsylvania Press, 2013.

Darrah, William C. *The World of Stereographs.* Gettysburg, PA: Darrah, 1977.

Dawson, Carl, ed. *Matthew Arnold: The Critical Heritage.* Vol. 2, *The Poetry.* London: Routledge/ Taylor and Francis, 2005.

Derrida, Jacques. *Of Grammatology.* Translated by Gayatri Chakravorty Spivak. Baltimore: Johns Hopkins University Press, 1998.

———. "Signature Event Context." *Glyph* 1 (1977): 172–97.

The Diadem; or, Poetical Scraps: Comprising a Selection of Lyric, Moral, Sentimental and Humorous Poetry, from the Most Admired Authors. Leith: Commercial List Office, 1830.

Dick, Thomas. *The Philosophy of a Future State.* New York: R. Schoyer, 1831.

Dimock, Wai Chee. "A Theory of Resonance." *PMLA* 112, no. 5 (1997): 1060–71.

Disraeli, Benjamin. *Sybil: or, The Two Nations.* In *The Bradenham Edition of the Novels and Tales of Benjamin Disraeli,* vol. 9. London: Peter Davies, 1927.

———. *Sybil: or The Two Nations.* Edited by Sheila M. Smith. Oxford: Oxford University Press, 1981.

———. *Venetia.* In *The Bradenham Edition of the Novels and Tales of Benjamin Disraeli,* vol. 7. London: Peter Davies, 1927.

Disraeli, Isaac. *Curiosities of Literature.* 13th ed. London: Edward Moxon, 1843.

Dobson, Austin. *The Civil Service Handbook of English Literature.* London: Lockwood, 1874.

Douglas-Fairhurst, Robert. *Victorian Afterlives: The Shaping of Influence in Nineteenth-Century Literature.* Oxford: Oxford University Press, 2002.

Driver, Henry Austen. *Byron and "The Abbey."* London: Longman, Orme, Brown, Green and Longmans, 1838.

Drummond, Lewis A. *Spurgeon: Prince of Preachers.* Grand Rapids, MI: Kregel Publications, 1992.

Dryden, John. *The Works of John Dryden: Now First Collected in Eighteen Volumes Illustrated with Notes, Historical, Critical, and Explanatory, and a Life of the Author, by Walter Scott, esq.* London: William Miller, 1808.

Duguid, Paul. "Material Matters: The Past and Futurology of the Book." In *The Future of the Book,* edited by Geoffrey Nunberg, 63–102. Berkeley: University of California Press, 1996.

Duncan, Ian. *Scott's Shadow: The Novel in Romantic Edinburgh.* Princeton, NJ: Princeton University Press, 2007.

Dunstan, Angela. "The Shelley Society, Literary Lectures, and the Global Circulation of English Literature and Scholarly Practice." *Modern Language Quarterly* 75, no. 2 (2014): 279–96.

Eagleton, Terry. *Literary Theory: An Introduction.* Oxford: Blackwell, 1983.

Eaves, Morris. "The Sister Arts in British Romanticism." In *The Cambridge Companion to British Romanticism,* edited by Stuart Curran, 236–69. Cambridge: Cambridge University Press, 1993.

Edgcumbe, Richard. "The Byron Memorial." *The Standard* (London). 20 April 1875: 3.

[———]. *Byron Memorial Loan Collection Catalogue.* 2nd ed. London: William Clowes and Sons, 1877.

Edgcumbe, Richard. *History of the Byron Memorial*. London: Effingham Wilson, 1883.

Egan, Gerald. "Radical Moral Authority and Desire: The Image of the Male Romantic Poet in Frontispiece Portraits of Byron and Shelley." *The Eighteenth Century: Theory and Interpretation* 50, no. 2–3 (2009): 185–205.

Elfenbein, Andrew. *Byron and the Victorians*. Cambridge: Cambridge University Press, 1995.

———. *Romanticism and the Rise of English*. Stanford, CA: Stanford University Press, 2009.

Eliot, George. *The George Eliot Letters*. Edited by Gordon S. Haight. 9 vols. New Haven, CT: Yale University Press, 1954–78.

Eliot, Simon. *Some Patterns and Trends in British Publishing, 1800–1919*. Occasional Papers of the Bibliographical Society 8. London: Bibliographical Society, 1994.

Eliot, T. S. *After Strange Gods: A Primer of Modern Heresy*. London: Faber and Faber, 1933.

———. *On Poetry and Poets*. London: Faber and Faber, 1957.

———. *The Poems of T. S. Eliot*. Edited by Christopher Ricks and Jim McCue. 2 vols. London: Faber and Faber, 2015.

———. "The Romantic Generation If It Existed." *Athenaeum* (18 July 1919): 616–17.

———. "Tradition and the Individual Talent." In *The Norton Anthology of Theory and Criticism*, edited by Vincent B. Leitch et al., 1092–98. New York: W. W. Norton, 2001.

———. *The Use of Poetry and the Use of Criticism*. London: Faber and Faber, 1964.

Ellis, David. *Byron in Geneva: That Summer of 1816*. Liverpool: Liverpool University Press, 2011.

Ellis, George. *Specimens of the Early English Poets*. London: Longman, 1790.

Ellison, Robert H. *The Victorian Pulpit: Spoken and Written Sermons in Nineteenth-Century Britain*. London: Associated University Presses, 1998.

Elwin, Malcolm. *Lord Byron's Family: Annabella, Ada and Augusta 1816–1824*. London: John Murray, 1975.

Engelberg, Karsten Klejs. *The Making of the Shelley Myth: An Annotated Bibliography of Criticism of Percy Bysshe Shelley, 1822–1860*. London: Mansell, 1988.

Erickson, Lee. *The Economy of Literary Form: English Literature and the Industrialization of Publishing, 1800–1850*. Baltimore: Johns Hopkins University Press, 1996.

The Excursionist's Guide to Cambridge. Cambridge: E. Johnson, [1865?].

Ezell, Margaret. *Writing Women's Literary History*. Baltimore: Johns Hopkins University Press, 1993.

Faflak, Joel, and Julia M. Wright, eds. *Nervous Reactions: Victorian Recollections of Romanticism*. Albany: SUNY Press, 2004.

Faÿ-Hallé, Antoinette, and Barbara Mundt. *Nineteenth-Century European Porcelain*. London: Trefoil Books, 1983.

Feldman, Paula R. Introduction to Felicia Hemans, *Records of Woman: With Other Poems*, edited by Paula R. Feldman, xi–xxix. Lexington: University Press of Kentucky, 1999.

———. "The Poet and the Profits: Felicia Hemans and the Literary Marketplace." *Keats-Shelley Journal* 46 (1997): 148–76.

Felski, Rita. *Uses of Literature*. Oxford: Blackwell, 2008.

Ferry, Anne. *Tradition and the Individual Poem: An Inquiry into Anthologies*. Stanford, CA: Stanford University Press, 2001.

Fido, Martin. "'From His Own Observation': Sources of Working Class Passages in Disraeli's *Sybil*." *Modern Language Review* 72 (1977): 267–84.

Finden, Edward, and William Finden. *Findens' Illustrations of the Life and Works of Lord Byron.* With notes by William Brockedon. 3 vols. London: John Murray and Charles Tilt, 1833–34.

Flanders, Judith. *Consuming Passions: Leisure and Pleasure in Victorian Britain.* London: Harper Press, 2006.

Flavin, Michael. *Benjamin Disraeli: The Novel as Political Discourse.* Brighton: Sussex Academic Press, 2005.

Flint, Kate. *The Victorians and the Visual Imagination.* Cambridge: Cambridge University Press, 2000.

Ford, George H. *Keats and the Victorians: A Study of His Influence and Rise to Fame, 1821–1895.* New Haven, CT: Yale University Press, 1945.

Fraser, Hilary. *The Victorians and Renaissance Italy.* Oxford: Blackwell, 1992.

Freeman, Michael. "Lady Llanover and the Welsh Costume Prints." *National Library of Wales Journal* 34, no. 2 (2007): 235–51.

Friedman, Winifred H. *Boydell's Shakespeare Gallery.* New York: Garland, 1976.

Fritzsche, Peter. *Stranded in the Present: Modern Time and the Melancholy of History.* Cambridge, MA: Harvard University Press, 2004.

Frow, John. *Cultural Studies and Cultural Value.* Oxford: Clarendon Press, 1995.

Fulford, Timothy. "Virtual Topography: Poets, Painters, Publishers and the Reproduction of the Landscape in the Early Nineteenth Century." *Romanticism and Victorianism on the Net* 57–58 (2010).

Fuller, Michael. *Making Sense of MacIntyre.* Aldershot: Ashgate, 1998.

Galperin, William. *The Return of the Visible in British Romanticism.* Baltimore: Johns Hopkins University Press, 1993.

Gamer, Michael. "A Matter of Turf: Romanticism, Hippodrama, and Satire." *Nineteenth-Century Contexts* 28, no. 4 (2006): 305–34.

———. *Romanticism, Self-Canonization, and the Business of Poetry.* Cambridge: Cambridge University Press, 2017.

Garber, Marjorie. *Quotation Marks.* London: Routledge, 2003.

Garval, Michael D. *"A Dream of Stone": Fame, Vision, and Monumentality in Nineteenth-Century French Literary Culture.* Newark: University of Delaware Press, 2004.

Geertz, Clifford. *The Interpretation of Cultures.* New York: Basic Books, 1973.

Genette, Gérard. *Paratexts: Thresholds of Interpretation.* Translated by Jane E. Lewin. Cambridge: Cambridge University Press, 1997.

Getsy, David J. *Body Doubles: Sculpture in Britain, 1877–1905.* New Haven, CT: Yale University Press, 2004.

Gibbon, Charles, ed. *The Casquet of Literature: Being a Selection in Poetry and Prose from the Works of the Most Admired Authors.* London; Glasgow: n.p., 1873.

Gilfillan, George. *Galleries of Literary Portraits.* 2 vols. London: R. Groombridge, 1856–57.

———. *A Gallery of Literary Portraits.* Edinburgh: William Tait, 1845.

———. *George Gilfillan: Letters and Journals, with Memoir.* Edited by Robert A. Watson and Elizabeth S. Watson. London: Hodder and Stoughton, 1892.

———. *The History of a Man.* London: Arthur Hall, Virtue and Co., 1856.

———. *A Third Gallery of Portraits.* Edinburgh: James Hogg, 1854.

Gill, Stephen. *William Wordsworth: A Life.* Oxford: Oxford University Press, 1990.

Gill, Stephen. *Wordsworth and the Victorians.* Oxford: Clarendon Press, 1998.

Gitelman, Lisa. *Always Already New: Media, History, and the Data of Culture.* Cambridge, MA: MIT Press, 2006.

Glaister, Geoffrey Ashall. *Glossary of the Book.* London: George Allen and Unwin, 1960.

Godwin, William. *Essay on Sepulchres.* In *Political and Philosophical Writings of William Godwin,* edited by Mark Philp, vol. 6, *Essays,* 1–30. London: Pickering and Chatto, 1993.

Golden, Catherine J. *Posting It: The Victorian Revolution in Letter Writing.* Gainesville: University Press of Florida, 2010.

Goldman, Paul. *Victorian Illustration: The Pre-Raphaelites, the Idyllic School and the High Victorians.* Burlington, VT: Lund Humphries, 2004.

Goode, Mike. "Blakespotting." *PMLA* 121, no. 3 (2006): 769–86.

Gordon, Catherine. "The Illustration of Sir Walter Scott: Nineteenth-Century Enthusiasm and Adaptation." *Journal of the Warburg and Courtauld Institutes* 34 (1971): 297–317.

Graham, William. *Last Links with Byron, Shelley, and Keats.* London: Leonard Smithers, 1898. "The Grave of Lord Byron." *The Times.* 23 April 1875: 11.

Graver, Bruce. "Wordsworth, Scott, and the Stereographic Picturesque." *Literature Compass* 6, no. 4 (2009): 896–926.

Gray, Erik. *Milton and the Victorians.* Ithaca, NY: Cornell University Press, 2009.

Gray, Michael, Arthur Ollman, and Carol McCusker. *First Photographs: William Henry Fox Talbot and the Birth of Photography.* New York: Powerhouse Books, in association with the Museum of Photographic Arts, San Diego, 2002.

Greenblatt, Stephen. *Shakespearean Negotiations: The Circulation of Social Energy in the Renaissance.* Berkeley: University of California Press, 1988.

Greg, W. W. "The Rationale of Copy-Text." *Studies in Bibliography* 3 (1950): 19–36. Reprinted in *Collected Papers,* ed. J. C. Maxwell, 374–91. Oxford: Clarendon Press, 1966.

Groth, Helen. *Victorian Photography and Literary Nostalgia.* Oxford: Oxford University Press, 2003.

Grytzell, Karl Gustav. *County of London: Population Changes, 1801–1901.* Lund, Sweden: Royal University of Lund, 1969.

Guillory, John. "Enlightening Mediation." In *This Is Enlightenment,* edited by Clifford Siskin and William Warner, 37–63. Chicago: University of Chicago Press, 2010.

———. "Genesis of the Media Concept." *Critical Inquiry* 36 (2010): 321–62.

Hales, J. W., ed. *Longer English Poems, with Notes, Philological and Explanatory, and an Introduction on the Teaching of English.* London: Macmillan, 1872.

Hall, S. C., ed. *The Book of Gems: The Modern Poets and Artists of Great Britain.* London: Whittaker and Co., 1842.

Hallam, Arthur Henry. *The Letters of Arthur Henry Hallam.* Edited by Jack Kolb. Columbus: Ohio State University Press, 1981.

Hamilton, Walter, ed. *Parodies of the Works of English and American Authors.* 6 vols. London: Reeves and Turner, 1884–89.

Harrison, Brian. "The Sunday Trade Riots of 1855." *Historical Journal* 8, no. 2 (1965): 219–45.

Hartog, François. *Regimes of Historicity: Presentism and Experiences of Time.* Trans. Saskia Brown. New York: Columbia University Press, 2015.

Harvey, John. *Men in Black.* London: Reaktion, 1995.

Hawkins, Ann R. "Evoking Byron from Manuscript to Print: Benjamin Disraeli's *Venetia*." *Papers of the Bibliographical Society of America* 98, no. 4 (2004): 449–76.

Hazlitt, William. *The Selected Writings of William Hazlitt*. Edited by Duncan Wu. 9 vols. London: Pickering and Chatto, 1998.

Hebron, Stephen, and Elizabeth C. Denlinger. *Shelley's Ghost: Reshaping the Image of a Literary Family*. Oxford: Bodleian Library, 2010.

Heffernan, James A. W. *Museum of Words: The Poetics of Ekphrasis from Homer to Ashbery*. Chicago: University of Chicago Press, 1993.

Hemans, Felicia. *Felicia Hemans: Selected Poems, Letters, Reception Materials*. Edited by Susan J. Wolfson. Princeton, NJ: Princeton University Press, 2000.

———. *Poems of Felicia Hemans*. Edinburgh: William Blackwood, 1865.

———. *Selected Poems, Prose and Letters*. Edited by Gary Kelly. Peterborough, ON: Broadview, 2002.

———. *The Works of Mrs Hemans, with a Memoir by her Sister*. 7 vols. Edinburgh: William Blackwood, 1839.

Henderson, Andrea K. "William Henry Fox Talbot: The Photograph as Memorial for Romanticism." *BRANCH: Britain, Representation and Nineteenth-Century History*, edited by Dino Franco Felluga. Extension of *Romanticism and Victorianism on the Net*. Accessed 30 May 2016.

Hill, Richard J. *Picturing Scotland through the Waverley Novels: Walter Scott and the Origins of the Victorian Illustrated Novel*. Farnham: Ashgate, 2010.

Hills, Richard L. *Papermaking in Britain, 1488–1988: A Short History*. London: Athlone Press, 1988.

Hilton, Boyd. *A Mad, Bad and Dangerous People? England, 1783–1846*. The New Oxford History of England. Oxford: Clarendon Press, 2006.

Hilton, Tim. *John Ruskin: The Early Years*. New Haven, CT: Yale University Press, 1985.

———. *John Ruskin: The Later Years*. New Haven, CT: Yale University Press, 2000.

Hippisley Coxe, Antony D. "Equestrian Drama and the Circus." In *Performance and Politics in Popular Drama: Aspects of Popular Entertainment in Theatre, Film and Television*, edited by David Bradby, Louis James, and Bernard Sharratt, 109–18. Cambridge: Cambridge University Press, 1980.

History of the Scott Monument, Edinburgh. Edinburgh: Printed for the Magistrates and Town Council, 1881.

Hobhouse, John Cam. *Imitations and Translations from the Ancient and Modern Classics, Together with Original Poems Never Before Published*. London: Longman, 1809.

[———]. *Remarks on the Exclusion of Lord Byron's Monument from Westminster Abbey*. London: the author, 1844.

Hobsbawm, Eric. "Introduction: Inventing Traditions." In *The Invention of Tradition*, edited by Eric Hobsbawm and Terence Ranger, 1–14. Cambridge: Cambridge University Press, 1983.

Hofkosh, Sonia. "Early Photography's Late Romanticism." *European Romantic Review* 22, no. 3 (2011): 293–304.

Holmes, Richard. *Shelley: The Pursuit*. London: Flamingo, 1995.

Holt, Tonie, and Valmai Holt. *Picture Postcards of the Golden Age: A Collector's Guide*. London: Granada, 1971.

"The Home and Grave of Byron." *Harper's New Monthly Magazine* 21 (1860): 606–10.

Hoock, Holger. "The British Military Pantheon in St Paul's Cathedral: The State, Cultural Patriotism, and the Politics of National Monuments, c.1790–1820." In *Pantheons: Transformations of a Monumental Idea*, edited by Richard Wrigley and Matthew Craske, 81–105. Aldershot: Ashgate, 2004.

Hood, Edwin Paxton. *Dark Sayings on a Harp: and Other Sermons on Some of the Dark Questions of Human Life*. London: Jackson, Walford, and Hodder, 1865.

Howsam, Leslie. *Cheap Bibles: Nineteenth-Century Publishing and the British and Foreign Bible Society*. Cambridge: Cambridge University Press, 2002.

Hueffer, Ford Madox [Ford Madox Ford]. *Ford Madox Brown: A Record of his Life and Work*. London: Longmans, Green, 1896.

Hunnisett, Basil. *Engraved on Steel: The History of Picture Production Using Steel Plates*. Aldershot: Ashgate, 1998.

Hunt, Leigh. "Canting Slander." *The Examiner* 778 (22 December 1822): 804–6.

[Iley, Matthew]. *The Life, Writings, Opinions and Times of [...] Lord Byron*. London: the author, 1825.

"Illustrated Books." *Journal of the Society of Arts*. 22 January 1864: 159.

"Illustrated Selections of Poetry." *Illustrated London News*. 29 December 1866: 11.

"Illustrated Works." *London Review* 22 (January 1859): 475.

"The Illustration Nuisance." *Pall Mall Gazette*. 28 December 1866: 12.

"In Memory of Mrs Hemans." *Aberdeen Weekly Journal*. 25 January 1899: 12.

Jacks, Lawrence Pearsall. *Life and Letters of Stopford Brooke*. 2 vols. London: John Murray, 1917.

Jackson, H. J. *Romantic Readers: The Evidence of Marginalia*. New Haven, CT: Yale University Press, 2005.

James, Henry. *The Aspern Papers*. London: J. M. Dent, 1994.

———. *The Complete Notebooks of Henry James*. Edited by Leon Edel and Lyall H. Powers. New York: Oxford University Press, 1987.

Jenkyns, Richard. *Westminster Abbey*. Cambridge, MA: Harvard University Press, 2004.

Jones, Howard Mumford. "The Author of Two Byron Apocrypha." *Modern Language Notes* 41, no. 2 (1926): 129–31.

Jonson, Ben. *The Complete Poems*. Edited by George Parfitt. London: Penguin, 1996.

Jordan, Hoover H. "A Photograph of Thomas Moore." *Keats-Shelley Journal* 28 (1979): 24–25.

Journals of the House of Lords. Vol. 75. 3rd series. London: Hansard, 1844.

Jump, John D., ed. *Tennyson: The Critical Heritage*. London: Routledge and Kegan Paul, 1967.

Kastan, David Scott. *Shakespeare and the Book*. Cambridge: Cambridge University Press, 2001.

Keats, John. *Letters of John Keats*. Edited by Robert Gittings. Oxford: Oxford University Press, 1970.

———. *The Poems of John Keats*. Edited by Jack Stillinger. London: Heinemann, 1978.

Kelly, Ronan. *Bard of Erin: The Life of Thomas Moore*. London: Penguin, 2008.

Kennedy, James. *Conversations on Religion, with Lord Byron and others, held in Cephalonia, a short time previous to His Lordship's Death*. London: John Murray, 1830.

Kermode, Frank. *The Classic: Literary Images of Permanence and Change*. Cambridge, MA: Harvard University Press, 1975.

———. *Romantic Image*. London: Routledge, 1957. Reprinted 2002. Page references are to the 2002 edition.

Kierkegaard, Søren. *Fear and Trembling*. Translated by Alastair Hannay. London: Penguin, 2005.

Kittler, Friedrich A. *Gramophone, Film, Typewriter*. Stanford, CA: Stanford University Press, 1999.

Korte, Barbara. *Flowers for the Picking: Anthologies of Poetry in (British) Literary and Cultural Studies*. Amsterdam: Rodopi, 2000.

Koselleck, Reinhart. *The Practice of Conceptual History: Timing History, Spacing Concepts*. Translated by Todd Samuel Presner et al. Stanford, CA: Stanford University Press, 2002.

Kruppa, Patricia Stallings. *Charles Haddon Spurgeon: A Preacher's Progress*. New York: Garland, 1982.

Lamb, Charles. *Specimens of English Dramatic Poets, Who Lived about the Time of Shakspeare*. London: Longman, 1808.

Landon, Richard G. "Small Profits Do Great Things: James Lackington and Eighteenth-Century Bookselling." *Studies in Eighteenth-Century Culture* 7 (1976): 387–99.

Lang, Timothy. *The Victorians and the Stuart Heritage: Interpretations of a Discordant Past*. Cambridge: Cambridge University Press, 1995.

Langan, Celeste, and Maureen N. McLane. "The Medium of Romantic Poetry." In *The Cambridge Companion to British Romantic Poetry*, edited by James Chandler and Maureen N. McLane, 239–62. Cambridge: Cambridge University Press, 2008.

Latané, David E. *Palgrave's Golden Treasury and Victorian Anthologies*. Morganton: West Virginia University Press, 1999.

Latour, Bruno. *Reassembling the Social: An Introduction to Actor-Network Theory*. Oxford: Oxford University Press, 2005.

Lee, Rev. James, ed. *Bible Illustrations*. Vol. 6. London: published by subscription, 1867.

Lethbridge, Stefanie. "Anthological Reading Habits in the Eighteenth Century: The Case of Thomson's *Seasons*." In *Anthologies of British Poetry: Critical Perspectives from Literary and Cultural Studies*, edited by Barbara Korte, Ralf Schneider, and Stefanie Lethbridge, 89–103. Amsterdam: Rodopi, 2000.

Levinson, Marjorie. *Wordsworth's Great Period Poems*. Cambridge: Cambridge University Press, 1986.

Levinson, Sanford. *Written in Stone: Public Monuments in Changing Societies*. Durham, NC: Duke University Press, 1998.

Lister, Raymond. *Prints and Printmaking: A Dictionary and Handbook of the Art in Nineteenth-Century Britain*. London: Methuen, 1984.

Liu, Alan. "The Power of Formalism: The New Historicism." *ELH* 56 (1989): 721–71. Reprinted in Alan Liu, *Local Transcendence: Essays on Postmodern Historicism and the Database*, 28–68. Chicago: University of Chicago Press, 2008.

———. "Wordsworth and Subversion, 1793–1804: Trying Cultural Criticism." *Yale Journal of Criticism* 2, no. 2 (1989): 55–100. Reprinted as "Trying Cultural Criticism: Wordsworth and Subversion," in Alan Liu, *Local Transcendence: Essays on Postmodern Historicism and the Database*, 71–108. Chicago: University of Chicago Press, 2008.

Lockhart, John Gibson. *Memoirs of the Life of Sir Walter Scott, Bart*. 10 vols. Toronto: George N. Morang, 1901.

[———?]. "Remarks on *Don Juan*." *Blackwood's Edinburgh Magazine* 5, no. 29 (August 1819): 512–18. Reprinted in *Blackwood's Magazine, 1817–25: Selections from Maga's Infancy*, 6 vols., gen. ed. Nicholas Mason, vol. 5, *Selected Criticism, 1817–19*, ed. Tom Mole, 315–22. London: Pickering and Chatto, 2006.

Lootens, Tricia A. *Lost Saints: Silence, Gender, and Victorian Literary Canonization*. Charlottesville: University of Virginia Press, 1996.

"Lord Byron." *Bury and Norwich Post* 5 (September 1832): 4.

"Lord Byron's Answer." *Christian Spectator* (New Haven, CT) 7, no. 9 (September 1825): 450–52.

"Lord Byron's Religious Opinions." *New-England Magazine* (Boston) 1 (August 1831): 112.

"Lord Byron's Statue." *Berrow's Worcester Journal*. 30 August 1838: 4.

"Lord Byron's Tomb." *The Times*. 6 October 1866: 9.

Lupton, Christina. *Knowing Books: The Consciousness of Mediation in Eighteenth-Century Britain*. Philadelphia: University of Pennsylvania Press, 2012.

Lynch, Deidre Shauna. *Loving Literature: A Cultural History*. Chicago: University of Chicago Press, 2015.

Lyrical Gems: A Selection of Moral, Sentimental, and Descriptive Poetry, from the Works of the Most Popular Modern Writers. Glasgow: Richard Griffin, 1825.

Macaulay, Thomas Babington. "Speech on Parliamentary Reform," delivered 2 March 1831. In *Selected Writings*, edited by John Clive and Thomas Pinney, 165–80. Chicago: University of Chicago Press, 1972.

MacIntyre, Alasdair. *After Virtue: A Study in Moral Theory*. 2nd ed. London: Duckworth, 1984.

———. *Three Rival Versions of Moral Enquiry: Encyclopaedia, Genealogy, Tradition*. Notre Dame, IN: University of Notre Dame Press, 1990.

———. *Whose Justice? Which Rationality?* Notre Dame, IN: University of Notre Dame Press, 1988.

Mackay, Charles, ed. *A Thousand and One Gems of English Poetry*. Illustrated by J. E. Millais, John Gilbert, and Birket Foster. London: George Routledge and Sons, 1867.

MacLeod, Christine. *Heroes of Invention: Technology, Liberalism and British Identity, 1750–1914*. Cambridge: Cambridge University Press, 2007.

Macleod, Donald. *New Cyclopaedia of Illustrative Anecdote, Religious and Moral*. London: E. Stock, 1872.

Mandell, Laura. "Putting Contents on the Table: The Disciplinary Anthology and the Field of Literary History." *Poetess Archive Journal* 1, no. 1 (2007).

Mannheim, Karl. *Essays on the Sociology of Knowledge*. London: Routledge and Kegan Paul, 1952.

Manning, Peter. "Wordsworth's 'Illustrated Books and Newspapers' and Media of the City." In *Romanticism and the City*, edited by Larry Peer, 223–40. New York: Palgrave Macmillan, 2011.

Marchand, Leslie A. *Byron: A Biography*. 3 vols. London: John Murray, 1957.

Marcus, Leah. *Puzzling Shakespeare: Local Reading and Its Discontents*. Berkeley: University of California Press, 1988.

Martindale, Charles. "Introduction: Thinking Through Reception." In *Classics and the Uses of Reception*, edited by Charles Martindale and Richard F. Thomas, 1–13. Oxford: Blackwell, 2006.

———. *Redeeming the Text: Latin Poetry and the Hermeneutics of Reception*. Cambridge: Cambridge University Press, 1993.

Matthews, Samantha. *Poetical Remains: Poets' Graves, Bodies, and Books in the Nineteenth Century*. Oxford: Oxford University Press, 2004.

Matthiessen, F. O. *The Achievement of T. S. Eliot*. London: Oxford University Press, 1935.

Maxwell, Richard, ed. *The Illustrated Victorian Book*. Charlottesville: University of Virginia Press, 2002.

McEwan, Ian. *Saturday*. London: Jonathan Cape, 2005.

McGann, Jerome J. *The Beauty of Inflections: Literary Investigations in Historical Method and Theory*. Oxford: Clarendon Press, 1988.

———. *Byron and Romanticism*. Edited by James Soderholm. Cambridge: Cambridge University Press, 2002.

———. *A Critique of Modern Textual Criticism*. Chicago: University of Chicago Press, 1983.

———. Introduction to the *New Oxford Book of Romantic Period Verse*, edited by Jerome J. McGann, xiv–xxvi. Oxford: Oxford University Press, 1993.

———. *Social Values and Poetic Acts: The Historical Judgment of Literary Work*. Cambridge, MA: Harvard University Press, 1988.

———. *The Textual Condition*. Princeton, NJ: Princeton University Press, 1991.

———. "Who's Carving Up the Nineteenth Century?" *PMLA* 116, no. 5 (2001): 1415–21.

McGill, Meredith L. *American Literature and the Culture of Reprinting, 1834–1853*. Philadelphia: University of Pennsylvania Press, 2002.

McGonagall, William. "An Address to the Rev. George Gilfillan." In *Collected Poems*, edited by Chris Hunt, 294–95. Edinburgh: Birlinn, 2006.

McKelvy, William R. *The English Cult of Literature: Devoted Readers, 1774–1880*. Charlottesville: University of Virginia Press, 2007.

McKenzie, D. F. "Printing and Publishing, 1557–1700: Constraints on the London Book Trades." In *The Cambridge History of the Book in Britain*, vol. 4, *1557–1695*, ed. John Barnard and D. F. McKenzie with the assistance of Maureen Bell, 553–67. Cambridge: Cambridge University Press, 2002.

McKerrow, R. B. *Prolegomena for the Oxford Shakespeare: A Study in Editorial Method*. Oxford: Clarendon Press, 1939.

McKitterick, David, ed. *The Making of the Wren Library, Trinity College, Cambridge*. Cambridge: Cambridge University Press, 1995.

McWilliam, Rohan. "The Theatricality of the Staffordshire Figure." *Journal of Victorian Culture* 10, no. 1 (2005): 107–14.

Meisel, Joseph S. *Public Speech and the Culture of Public Life in the Age of Gladstone*. New York: Columbia University Press, 2001.

"Memorial Tablets." *Journal of the Society of Arts*. 20 June 1866: 688.

"Memorial to Sir Walter Scott in Westminster Abbey." *The Times*. 20 April 1889: 4.

"Memorials of Eminent Men." *Journal of the Society of Arts*. 11 May 1866: 703.

Merriam, Harold G. *Edward Moxon, Publisher of Poets*. New York: Columbia University Press, 1939.

Michael, Ian. *The Teaching of English: From the Sixteenth Century to 1870*. Cambridge: Cambridge University Press, 1987.

Michalski, Sergiusz. *Public Monuments: Art in Political Bondage, 1870–1997*. London: Reaktion, 1998.

Milbank, Alison. *Dante and the Victorians*. Manchester: Manchester University Press, 1998.

Mill, John Stuart. *Collected Works of John Stuart Mill*. Edited by John M. Robson. 33 vols. Toronto: University of Toronto Press, 1963–91.

Miller, J. Hillis. *Illustration*. London: Reaktion, 1992.

Miller, Judith. *Miller's Antiques Handbook and Price Guide, 2012–13*. London: Mitchell Beazley, 2011.

Miller, Lucasta. "The Human Factor." Interview with Stephen Greenblatt. *The Guardian*. 26 February 2005. http://www.theguardian.com/books/2005/feb/26/biography.

Mitchell, W.J.T. *Iconology: Image, Text, Ideology*. Chicago: University of Chicago Press, 1986.

Mole, Tom. *Byron's Romantic Celebrity: Industrial Culture and the Hermeneutic of Intimacy.* Basingstoke: Palgrave, 2007.

———. "Impresarios of Byron's Afterlife." *Nineteenth-Century Contexts* 29, no. 1 (2007): 17–34.

———. "Lord Byron and the End of Fame." *International Journal of Cultural Studies* 11, no. 3 (2008): 343–61.

———. "Romantic Long Poems in Victorian Anthologies." In *Romanticism: Criticism and Debates,* edited by Mark Canuel, 625–34. London: Routledge, 2014.

———. "Romantic Memorials in the Victorian City: The Inauguration of the 'Blue Plaque' Scheme, 1868." *BRANCH: Britain, Representation and Nineteenth-Century History,* edited by Dino Franco Felluga. Extension of *Romanticism and Victorianism on the Net.* (2012).

———, ed. *Romanticism and Celebrity Culture, 1750–1850.* Cambridge: Cambridge University Press, 2009.

———. "Spurgeon, Byron, and the Contingencies of Mediation." *Romanticism and Victorianism on the Net* 58 (2010; pub. 2012).

"Monument for Sir Walter Scott." *Caledonian Mercury* (Edinburgh). 29 October 1832: 3.

Moore, Doris Langley. *The Late Lord Byron.* London: John Murray, 1961.

Moore, Thomas. *Letters and Journals of Lord Byron with Notices of His Life.* 2 vols. London: John Murray, 1830–31.

Moran, James. *The Printing Press: History and Development from the Fifteenth Century to Modern Times.* Berkeley: University of California Press, 1973.

Moretti, Franco. *Distant Reading.* London: Verso, 2013.

———. *Graphs, Maps, Trees: Abstract Models for Literary History.* London: Verso, 2005.

Morgan, Monique R. *Narrative Means, Lyric Ends: Temporality in the Nineteenth-Century British Long Poem.* Columbus: Ohio State University Press, 2009.

Morgan, Prys. "From a Death to a View: The Hunt for the Welsh Past in the Romantic Period." In *The Invention of Tradition,* edited by Eric Hobsbawm and Terence Ranger, 43–99. Cambridge: Cambridge University Press, 1983.

Morison, John. *Portraiture of Modern Scepticism; or, A Caveat Against Infidelity.* London: Frederick Westley and A. H. Davis, 1832.

"Mr Disraeli: His Character and Career." *Edinburgh Review* 97 (1853): 420–61.

Murray, Venetia. *High Society in the Regency Period: 1788–1830.* London: Penguin, 1999.

Najarian, James. *Victorian Keats: Manliness, Sexuality, and Desire.* New York: Palgrave, 2003.

"The National Byron Memorial." *The Times.* 21 January 1876: 8.

"New Illustrated Books." *Morning Post.* 8 December 1860: 2.

Newhall, Beaumont. Introduction to William Henry Fox Talbot, *The Pencil of Nature.* Edited by Beaumont Newhall. New York: Da Capo Press, 1969.

Nichol, John. *Byron.* London: Macmillan, 1880.

Nora, Pierre. "Between Memory and History: *Les Lieux de Mémoire.*" Translated by Marc Roudebush. *Representations* 26 (1989): 7–24.

———. "Generation." In *Realms of Memory: The Construction of the French Past,* edited by Pierre Nora, translated by Arthur Goldhammer, 3 vols., 1:499–531. New York: Columbia University Press, 1998.

Norman, Sylva. *Flight of the Skylark: The Development of Shelley's Reputation.* London: Max Reinhardt; Norman: University of Oklahoma Press, 1954.

Nowell-Smith, Simon. *International Copyright Law and the Publisher in the Reign of Queen Victoria*. Oxford: Clarendon Press, 1968.

"Observations on the Character, Opinions, and Writings of the Late Lord Byron." *Christian Observer* (Boston) 25, no. 2 (1 February 1825): 79.

O'Connell, Mary. *Byron and John Murray: A Poet and His Publisher*. Liverpool: Liverpool University Press, 2014.

Oldenburg, Claes, and Emmett Williams, eds. *Store Days: Documents from the Store (1961) and Ray Gun Theater (1962)*. New York: Something Else Press, 1967.

O'Neill, Michael. "'Trying to Make It as Good as I Can': Mary Shelley's Editing of Shelley's Poetry and Prose." In *Mary Shelley in Her Times*, edited by Betty T. Bennett and Stuart Curran, 185–97. Baltimore: Johns Hopkins University Press, 2000.

O'Neill, Michael, and Charles Mahoney, eds. *Romantic Poetry: An Annotated Anthology*. Oxford: Blackwell, 2008.

"Our Address." *Illustrated London News*. 14 May 1842: 1.

Ozouf, Mona. "The *Panthéon*: The École Normale of the Dead." In *Realms of Memory: The Construction of the French Past*, edited by Pierre Nora, translated by Arthur Goldhammer, 3 vols., 3:325–46. New York: Columbia University Press, 1998.

Palgrave, Francis Turner. *The Golden Treasury of the Best Songs and Lyrical Poems in the English Language: Selected and Arranged with Notes by Francis Turner Palgrave*. Edited by Christopher Ricks. London: Penguin, 1991.

———. "On Readers in 1760 and 1860." *Macmillan's Magazine* 1 (1859–60): 489.

Parrish, Stephen. "The Whig Interpretation of Literature." *TEXT* 4 (1988): 343–50.

Payne, Blanche. *The History of Costume*. New York: Harper Collins, 1992.

Peach, Annette. "Portraits of Byron." *The Walpole Society* 62 (2000): 1–144.

Pearsall, Derek. "The *Troilus* Frontispiece and Chaucer's Audience." *Yearbook of English Studies* 7 (1977): 68–74.

Pfau, Thomas. *Romantic Moods: Paranoia, Trauma, and Melancholy, 1790–1840*. Baltimore: Johns Hopkins University Press, 2005.

Phillips, Mark Salber. *Society and Sentiment: Genres of Historical Writing in Britain, 1740–1820*. Princeton, NJ: Princeton University Press, 2000.

The Pictorial Guide to Cambridge: Containing Descriptions of Its Colleges, Halls [. . .] Illustrated with [. . .] Engravings on Wood. Cambridge: T. King, 1847.

Piper, Andrew. *Dreaming in Books: The Making of the Bibliographic Imagination in the Romantic Age*. Chicago: University of Chicago Press, 2009.

Poe, Edgar Allan. *Selections from the Critical Writings of Edgar Allan Poe*. Edited by F. C. Prescott. New York: Gordian Press, 1981.

Poets of England and America; Being Selections from the Best Authors of Both Countries. London: Whittaker and Co., 1853.

Poole, Adrian. *Shakespeare and the Victorians*. London: Arden Shakespeare, 2004.

Porter, Jean. "Tradition in the Recent Work of Alasdair MacIntyre." In *Alasdair MacIntyre*, edited by Mark C. Murphy, 38–69. Cambridge: Cambridge University Press, 2003.

Postman, Neil. *Technopoly: The Surrender of Culture to Technology*. New York: Vintage, 1993.

"A Prayer for Lord Byron: To the Right Hon. Lord Byron, at Pisa." *Zion's Herald* (Boston) 3, no. 17 (27 April 1825): 2.

Price, Leah. *The Anthology and the Rise of the Novel: From Richardson to George Eliot.* Cambridge: Cambridge University Press, 2000.

———. *How to Do Things with Books in Victorian Britain.* Princeton, NJ: Princeton University Press, 2012.

"The Proposed Byron Memorial." *The Times.* 20 May 1875: 5.

Pugh, P. D. Gordon. *Staffordshire Portrait Figures.* New and revised ed. Woodbridge, Suffolk: Antique Collectors' Club, 1987.

Pyne, J. B. *Lake Scenery in England.* London: Day and Son, 1859.

Raven, James. *The Business of Books: Booksellers and the English Book Trade, 1450–1850.* New Haven, CT: Yale University Press, 2007.

Read, Benedict. *Victorian Sculpture.* New Haven, CT: Yale University Press, 1982.

Readings in Poetry: A Selection from the Best English Poets, from Spenser to the Present Times; and Specimens of Several American Poets of Deserved Reputation. London: John W. Parker, 1833.

Reiman, Donald, ed. *The Romantics Reviewed.* 9 vols. London: Garland, 1972.

A Review of the Character and Writings of Lord Byron. London: Sherwood, Gilbert and Piper, 1826.

Ricks, Christopher. "The Making of *The Golden Treasury.*" In *The Golden Treasury of the Best Songs and Lyrical Poems in the English Language: Selected and Arranged with Notes by Francis Turner Palgrave,* edited by Christopher Ricks, 437–50. London: Penguin, 1991.

Rigny, Ann. *The Afterlives of Walter Scott: Memory on the Move.* Oxford: Oxford University Press, 2012.

Roberts, M.J.D. *Making English Morals: Voluntary Association and Moral Reform in England, 1787–1866.* Cambridge: Cambridge University Press, 2004.

Robinson, John Martin. *Temples of Delight: Stowe Landscape Gardens.* London: National Trust, 1994.

Robson, Catherine. *Heart Beats: Everyday Life and the Memorized Poem.* Princeton, NJ: Princeton University Press, 2012.

Roe, Nicholas. *John Keats and the Culture of Dissent.* Oxford: Clarendon Press, 1997.

Rogers, Byron. "Byron the Rover Returns to the Abbey." *The Times.* 9 May 1969: 12.

Rogers, Samuel. *Italy: A Poem.* London: Edward Moxon, 1840.

Rorty, Richard. *Contingency, Irony, and Solidarity.* Cambridge: Cambridge University Press, 1989.

Rossetti, William Michael, ed. *Rossetti Papers, 1862–1870: A Compilation.* New York: Charles Scribner's Sons, 1903.

———. *Selected Letters of William Michael Rossetti.* Edited by Roger W. Peattie. University Park: Pennsylvania State University Press, 1986.

———. *Some Reminiscences of William Michael Rossetti.* 2 vols. New York: Charles Scribner's Sons, 1906.

Rovee, Christopher. *Imagining the Gallery: The Social Body of British Romanticism.* Stanford, CA: Stanford University Press, 2006.

Ruskin, John. *The Stones of Venice.* Edited by Jan Morris. Boston: Little, Brown, 1981.

Rutherford, Andrew, ed. *Byron: The Critical Heritage.* London: Routledge, 1970.

Rzepka, Charles J. "The Feel of Not to Feel It." *PMLA* 116, no. 5 (2001): 1422–31.

Salganik, M. J., and D. D. Heckathorn. "Sampling and Estimation in Hidden Populations Using Respondent-Driven Sampling." *Sociological Methodology* 34, no. 1 (2004): 193–239.

Samuel, Raphael. *Theatres of Memory: Past and Present in Contemporary Culture.* London: Verso, 1994.

Schaaf, Larry J. *Records of the Dawn of Photography: Talbot's Notebooks P & Q*. Cambridge: Cambridge University Press, 1996.

———. *William Henry Fox Talbot's The Pencil of Nature, Anniversary Facsimile: Introductory Volume*. New York: Hans P. Kraus, Jr., 1989.

Schivelbusch, Wolfgang. *The Railway Journey: Trains and Travel in the Nineteenth Century*. Translated by Anselm Hollo. Oxford: Blackwell, 1980.

Schwarzbach, F. S. "Twelve Ways of Looking at a Staffordshire Figurine: An Essay in Cultural Studies." *Victorians Institute Journal* 29 (2001): 6–60.

Scott, Walter. *The Letters of Sir Walter Scott*. Edited by H.J.C. Grierson. 12 vols. London: Constable, 1932–37.

———. *Readings for the Young, from the Works of Sir Walter Scott*. 2 vols. Edinburgh: Robert Cadell, 1848.

———. *Rob Roy*. Edited by Ian Duncan. Oxford World's Classics. Oxford: Oxford University Press, 1998.

———. *Waverley*. Edited by Claire Lamont. Oxford World's Classics. Oxford: Oxford University Press, 1986.

"Scott Memorial in Westminster Abbey." *The Times*. 22 May 1897: 16.

Seaton, A.V. "Cope's and the Promotion of Tobacco in Victorian England." *European Journal of Marketing* 20, no. 9 (1986): 5–26.

Sedgwick, Eve Kosofsky. *Between Men: English Literature and Male Homosocial Desire*. New York: Columbia University Press, 1985.

Sentilles, Renée M. *Performing Menken: Adah Isaacs Menken and the Birth of American Celebrity*. Cambridge: Cambridge University Press, 2003.

"Sermons of the Rev. C. H. Spurgeon." *North American Review* 86, no. 178 (1858): 275.

"Shall Byron Have a Statue?" *Punch*. 18 November 1876: 212.

"Shall Lord Byron Have a Statue?" *Punch*. 3 May 1879: 193.

Shelley, Mary. *The Last Man* (1826). Edited by Anne McWhir. Peterborough, ON: Broadview, 1996.

Shelley, Percy Bysshe. *The Complete Poetry of Percy Bysshe Shelley*. Edited by Donald H. Reiman and Neil Fraistat. 2 vols. to date. Baltimore: Johns Hopkins University Press, 2000–2004.

———. *The Letters of Percy Bysshe Shelley*. Edited by Frederick L. Jones. 2 vols. Oxford: Clarendon Press, 1964.

———. *Poems from Shelley*. Edited by Stopford A. Brooke. London: Macmillan, 1880.

———. *The Poems of Shelley*. Edited by Geoffrey Matthews, Kelvin Everest, Michael Rossington, and Jack Donovan. 4 vols. to date. London: Longman, Routledge, 1989–2014.

———. *Posthumous Poems of Percy Bysshe Shelley*. Edited by Mary Shelley. London: John and Henry L. Hunt, 1824.

———. *Shelley's Poetry and Prose*. Edited by Donald H. Reiman and Sharon B. Powers. New York: W. W. Norton, 1977.

Sheppard, John. *Thoughts Chiefly Designed as a Preparative or Persuasive to Private Devotion*. London: G. and B. Whittaker, 1824.

Shorter, Thomas, ed. *A Book of English Poetry; for the School, the Fireside, and the Country Ramble*. London: T. J. Allman, 1861.

Simonsen, Peter. *Wordsworth and the Word-Preserving Arts: Typographic Inscription, Ekphrasis and Posterity in the Later Work*. Basingstoke: Palgrave, 2007.

Sinclair, Fiona. *Scotstyle: 150 Years of Scottish Architecture*. Edinburgh: Royal Incorporation of Architects in Scotland, 1984.

Sinker, Robert. *The Library of Trinity College, Cambridge*. Cambridge: Deighton, Bell and Co., 1891.

"Sir Walter Scott Memorial." *The Times*. 3 July 1896: 8.

Siskin, Clifford, and William Warner, eds. *This Is Enlightenment*. Chicago: University of Chicago Press, 2010.

Smiles, Samuel. *A Publisher and His Friends: Memoir and Correspondence of the Late John Murray, with an Account of the Origin and Progress of the House, 1768–1843*. 2 vols. London: John Murray, 1891.

———. *Self-Help: With Illustrations of Character and Conduct*. London: John Murray, 1859.

Smith, Barbara Herrnstein. *Contingencies of Value: Alternative Perspectives for Critical Theory*. Cambridge, MA: Harvard University Press, 1988.

Smith, Graham. "William Henry Fox Talbot's Calotype Views of Loch Katrine." *Bulletin of the University of Michigan Museums of Art and Archaeology* 7 (1984–85): 49–77.

Smith, Paul. *Disraeli: A Brief Life*. Cambridge: Cambridge University Press, 1996.

Snow, Vernon. "The First Illustrated Book." *Times Literary Supplement* (23 December 1965): 1204.

"Some Account of the Art of Photogenic Drawing." *Edinburgh Review* 76 (1843): 309.

Sontag, Susan. *On Photography*. London: Penguin, 1977.

Southey, Robert. *Letters from England: by Don Manuel Alvarez Espriella. Translated from the Spanish*. Edited by Jack Simmons. London: Cresset, 1951.

———. *Specimens of the Later English Poets, with Preliminary Notices*. London: Longman, 1807.

Spurgeon, Charles Haddon. *The Autobiography of Charles H. Spurgeon, Compiled from his Diary, Letters, and Records by his Wife and his Private Secretary*. 3 vols. Chicago: F. H. Revell, 1898–1900.

———. *The Bible and the Newspaper*. London: Passmore and Alabaster, 1878.

———. *The Letters of Charles Haddon Spurgeon*. Edited by Charles Spurgeon. London: Marshall Bros., 1923.

———. *The Metropolitan Tabernacle Pulpit (including The New Park Street Pulpit)*. 63 vols. London: Passmore and Alabaster, 1855–1917.

———. *The Saint and his Saviour: the Progress of the Soul in the Knowledge of Jesus*. Nashville: Graves, Marks and Co., 1857.

———. *Sermons in Candles*. London: Passmore and Alabaster, 1890.

———. *The Treasury of David*. 7 vols. London: Passmore and Alabaster, 1882.

———. *Words of Wisdom for Daily Life*. London: Passmore and Alabaster, 1892.

Staff, Frank. *The Picture Postcard and Its Origins*. London: Lutterworth Press, 1966.

Standley, Fred L. *Stopford Brooke*. New York: Twayne, 1972.

Stanley, Arthur Penrhyn. *Historical Memorials of Westminster Abbey*. London: John Murray, 1868.

"The Statue of Byron in the Library of Trinity College Cambridge." *Notes and Queries*, 6th series, 4 (1881): 421–23.

St. Clair, William. *The Reading Nation in the Romantic Period*. Cambridge: Cambridge University Press, 2004.

Stein, Atara. *The Byronic Hero in Film, Fiction and Television*. Carbondale: Southern Illinois University Press, 2004.

Stevens, Christine. "Welsh Peasant Dress: Workwear or National Costume?" *Textile History* 33 (2002): 63–78.

Stillinger, Jack. "A Practical Theory of Versions." In *Coleridge and Textual Instability: The Multiple Versions of the Major Poems*, 118–40. Oxford: Oxford University Press, 1994.

———. "Textual Primitivism and the Editing of Wordsworth." *Studies in Romanticism* 28 (1989): 3–28.

Stillinger, Jack, and Deidre Lynch, eds. *The Norton Anthology of English Literature: The Romantic Period*. 8th ed. New York: W. W. Norton, 2006.

Sutherland, Kathryn. *Jane Austen's Textual Lives: From Aeschylus to Bollywood*. Oxford: Oxford University Press, 2007.

Swinburne, Algernon Charles. *The Complete Works of Algernon Charles Swinburne*. Edited by Sir Edmund Gosse and Thomas James Wise. 20 vols. New York: Russell and Russell, 1925. Reprinted 1968. Page references are to the 1968 edition.

Talbot, William Henry Fox. *The Pencil of Nature (Facsimile Edition)*. Chicago: KWS, 2011.

———. *William Henry Fox Talbot: Photographs from the J. Paul Getty Museum*. Los Angeles: J. Paul Getty Museum, 2002.

———. *William Henry Fox Talbot: Selected Texts and Bibliography*. Edited by Mike Weaver. Boston: G. K. Hall, 1993.

Tanselle, G. Thomas. "The Editorial Problem of Final Authorial Intention." *Studies in Bibliography* 29 (1976): 167–211. Reprinted in *Textual Criticism and Scholarly Editing*, 27–71. Charlottesville: University Press of Virginia, 1990.

———. *Literature and Artifacts*. Charlottesville: Bibliographical Society of the University of Virginia, 1998.

Taylor, Charles. *A Secular Age*. Cambridge, MA: Harvard University Press, 2007.

Tennyson, Alfred Lord. *The Poems of Tennyson*. Edited by Christopher Ricks. 2nd ed. 3 vols. Berkeley: University of California Press, 1987.

Tennyson, Hallam. *Alfred Lord Tennyson: A Memoir by his Son*. 2 vols. London: Macmillan, 1897.

———, ed. *Tennyson and his Friends*. London: Macmillan, 1911.

"Tennyson Illustrated by Doré." *The Times*. 29 December 1868: 10.

Thirty Illustrations of Childe Harold. London: Art Union, 1855.

Thomas, Julia. *Pictorial Victorians: The Inscription of Values in Word and Image*. Athens: Ohio University Press, 2004.

Thompson, Flora. *Lark Rise to Candleford*. London: Penguin, 2008.

Thomson, Andrew, W. Cunningham, Alexander Fraser, and D.T.K. Drummond. *Four Lectures to Young Men*. Edinburgh: William Innes, 1842.

Thomson, James. "Shelley." In *The Speedy Extinction of Evil and Misery: Selected Prose of James Thomson (B.V.)*, edited by William David Schaefer, 199–207. Berkeley: University of California Press, 1967.

Thorpe, James. *Principles of Textual Criticism*. San Marino, CA: Huntington Library, 1972.

Todd, John. *The Student's Manual*. Northampton: J. H. Butler, 1835.

Truths Illustrated by Great Authors. 4th ed. London: William White, 1855.

Turner, Bryan S., and June Edwards. *Generations, Culture and Society*. Buckingham: Open University Press, 2002.

Turner, Charles Tennyson. *Sonnets*. London: Macmillan, 1864.

Twyman, Michael. *Breaking the Mould: The First Hundred Years of Lithography*. London: British Library, 2001.

———. *The British Library Guide to Printing: History and Techniques*. London: British Library, 1998.

Tyrrell Alex, with Michael T. Davis. "Bearding the Tories: The Commemoration of the Scottish Political Martyrs of 1793–94." In *Contested Sites: Commemoration, Memorial and Popular Politics in Nineteenth-Century Britain*, edited by Paul A. Pickering and Alex Tyrrell, 25–56. Aldershot: Ashgate, 2004.

Wade, Thomas. *Mundis et Cordis*. London: John Miller, 1835.

Walker, Richard. *Regency Portraits*. 2 vols. London: National Portrait Gallery, 1985.

[Walter, John]. *Record of the Death-Bed of C.M.W.* London: Gilbert and Rivington, [1844].

Ward-Jackson, Philip. *Public Sculpture of the City of London*. Liverpool: Liverpool University Press, 2003.

Wark, McKenzie. *Telesthesia: Communication, Culture and Class*. Cambridge: Polity, 2012.

Watson, Nicola J. *The Literary Tourist: Readers and Places in Romantic and Victorian Britain*. Basingstoke: Palgrave, 2006.

Watson, William. "The Scott Monument, Princes Street, Edinburgh." In *The Collected Poems of William Watson*, 46. London: George G. Harrap, 1936.

Webb, Timothy. *Shelley: A Voice Not Understood*. Manchester: Manchester University Press, 1977.

Weber, Max. *The Protestant Ethic and the Spirit of Capitalism*. Translated by Talcott Parsons. London: Routledge, 2001.

Weinstein, Jack Russell. *On MacIntyre*. Toronto: Wadsworth/Thomson, 2003.

White, Daniel E. *Early Romanticism and Religious Dissent*. Cambridge: Cambridge University Press, 2010.

White, Hayden. Foreword to Reinhart Koselleck, *The Practice of Conceptual History: Timing History, Spacing Concepts*, translated by Todd Samuel Presner et al., ix–xiv. Stanford, CA: Stanford University Press, 2002.

White, Henry A. *Sir Walter Scott's Novels on the Stage*. New Haven, CT: Yale University Press, 1927.

Wilcox, R. Turner. *The Mode in Costumes*. New York: Charles Scribner, 1958.

Williams, Bernard. *Truth and Truthfulness: An Essay in Genealogy*. Princeton, NJ: Princeton University Press, 2002.

Williams, Charles William. "Byron's Grave." *The Times*. 25 April 1870: 11.

Williams, Howard, ed. *Anthologia Anglica: A New Selection from the English Poets from Spenser to Shelley*. London: n.p., 1873.

Williams, Jeffrey J. "The Statistical Turn in Literary Studies." In *How to Be an Intellectual: Essays on Criticism, Culture and the University*, 61–64. New York: Fordham University Press, 2014.

Williams, Raymond. *Keywords: A Vocabulary of Culture and Society*. Revised and expanded ed. London: Fontana, 1983.

———. *Resources of Hope*. London: Verso, 1989.

Wilson, Cheryl A. *Literature and Dance in Nineteenth-Century Britain: Jane Austen to the New Woman*. Cambridge: Cambridge University Press, 2009.

[Wilson, John]. "Small Talk." *Blackwood's Edinburgh Magazine*, 5, no. 30. September 1819: 686.

Wiltshire, John. *Recreating Jane Austen*. Cambridge: Cambridge University Press, 2001.

Wodehouse, P. G. *Piccadilly Jim*. London: Arrow, 2008.

Wolfson, Susan J. Introduction to *Felicia Hemans: Selected Poems, Letters, Reception Materials*, edited by Susan J. Wolfson, xiii–xxix. Princeton, NJ: Princeton University Press, 2000.

———. "Our Puny Boundaries: Why the Craving for Carving Up the Nineteenth Century?" *PMLA* 116, no. 5 (2001): 1432–41.

Wolfson, Susan, J., and Peter Manning, eds. *The Longman Anthology of British Literature: The Romantics and Their Contemporaries.* 4th ed. New York: Longman, 2010.

Wood, Gillen D'Arcy. *The Shock of the Real: Romanticism and Visual Culture, 1760–1860.* Basingstoke: Palgrave, 2001.

Wood, John. *The Scenic Daguerreotype: Romanticism and Early Photography.* Iowa City: University of Iowa Press, 1995.

Woof, Robert, ed. *Wordsworth: The Critical Heritage.* Vol. 1, *1793–1820.* London: Routledge, 2001.

Wootton, Sarah. *Consuming Keats: Nineteenth-Century Representations in Art and Literature.* Basingstoke: Palgrave, 2006.

Wordsworth, William. *The Fourteen-Book Prelude.* Edited by W.J.B. Owen. The Cornell Wordsworth. Ithaca, NY: Cornell University Press, 1985.

———. *Guide to the Lakes.* Edited by Ernest de Selincourt with a preface by Stephen Gill. London: Frances Lincoln, 2004.

———. *Last Poems, 1821–1850.* Edited by Jared Curtis. The Cornell Wordsworth. Ithaca, NY: Cornell University Press, 1999.

———. *Lyrical Ballads, and Other Poems, 1797–1800.* Edited James Butler and Karen Green. The Cornell Wordsworth. Ithaca, NY: Cornell University Press, 1992.

———. *Our English Lakes, Mountains and Waterfalls, as Seen by William Wordsworth, photographically illustrated* [by Thomas Ogle]. London: A. W. Bennett, 1864; 2nd ed. 1866.

———. *Poems, in Two Volumes, and Other Poems, 1800–1807.* Edited by Jared Curtis. The Cornell Wordsworth. Ithaca, NY: Cornell University Press, 1983.

———. *The Poems of William Wordsworth.* London: Edward Moxon, 1845.

———. *Poems of Wordsworth.* Chosen and edited by Matthew Arnold. London: Macmillan and Co., 1879.

———. *The Poetical Works of William Wordsworth.* Edited by William Michael Rossetti. Illustrated by Henry Dell. London: Edward Moxon, Son and Co., [1870].

———. *The Poetical Works of William Wordsworth.* Edited by William Michael Rossetti. Illustrated by Edwin Edwards. London: Edward Moxon, Son and Co., 1871.

———. *A Selection from the Works of William Wordsworth.* Edited by Francis Turner Palgrave. Moxon's Miniature Poets. London: Edward Moxon and Co., 1865.

———. *Selections from the Poems of William Wordsworth, Chiefly for the Use of Schools and Young Persons.* Edited by Joseph Hine. London: Edward Moxon, 1831.

Wu, Duncan, ed. *Romanticism: An Anthology.* 3rd ed. Oxford: Blackwell, 2006.

X.Y.Z. [Neal, John?] "American Writers." *Blackwood's Edinburgh Magazine* 17, no. 97 (February 1825): 186–207.

Yarrington, Alison. *The Commemoration of the Hero, 1800–1864: Monuments to the British Victors of the Napoleonic Wars.* New York: Garland, 1988.

———. "Popular and Imaginary Pantheons in Early Nineteenth-Century England." In *Pantheons: Transformations of a Monumental Idea,* edited by Richard Wrigley and Matthew Craske, 107–21. Aldershot: Ashgate, 2004.

Young, B. W. *The Victorian Eighteenth Century.* Oxford: Oxford University Press, 2007.

Zachs, William. *The First John Murray and the Late Eighteenth-Century London Book Trade.* Oxford: Published for the British Academy by Oxford University Press, 1998.

INDEX

Numbers in *italics* refer to illustrations

Pharand, Michel, 262n13

Phillips, Thomas, 264n53

Phillips, Willard, 254

Phiz (Hablot K. Browne), 48

photography, 156–57, 248n9, 267n39; as book illustration, 52–53, 267n49; of manuscripts, 157–58, 267n42; printing of, 17, 157. *See also* postcards

plaques, commemorative. *See* markers, commemorative

Playfair, William, 146

Pocklington, Joseph, 66–67, 249n29

Poe, Edgar Allan, 215

Poetical Works of Lord Byron, The (Rossetti), 77–81, 79, 252n25, 252n27

Poets' Corner, 174–75. *See also* Westminster Abbey

Political Martyrs' Monument (Edinburgh), 149–51, 158, 266nn16–17

postcards, 160–63, 160, 162, 268n52

Postman, Neil, 18, 237n56

Powles, Judy, 260n26

Prelude, The. See under Wordsworth, William

Price, Leah, 188, 189, 193, 220, 253n10

printing techniques, 17, 47–48, 236m49, 237n52, 245n10

printmaking. *See* illustration

Prometheus Unbound. See under Shelley, Percy Bysshe

Public School Speaker and Reader, The (Carpenter), 279n17

Pyne, J. B., 67, 249n30

Queen Mab. See under Shelley, Percy Bysshe

Rae, William, 148, 155

Ramsay, Allan, 147, 149

Raven, James, 191–92

Read, Benedict, 147

reception tradition: anthology, 189–90, 194, 273n14; contacts between types of, 3, 24, 25, 26–30, 90, 103–4, 119, 128–30, 152, 189–90, 194; critics and, 3, 4, 5–6, 21–28,

54, 89–90, 98, 99, 107–16; literary, 21–28, 53–54, 93, 94, 98, 109, 128–29, 261n52, 273n14; religious, 89–116, 118–19, 128–30, 253n12. *See also* historicism; tradition

recitation, 24, 28, 188, 202, 207, 214, 276n18

reform, political, 133–34, 148, 154, 165

Reiman, Donald, 23

religious belief, 12, 89, 91–92, 94–99, 101, 107, 109–11, 113–16, 180, 253n12

religious reception. *See under* reception tradition

remediation, definition of, 19. *See also* mediation

reprints and collected works. *See under* books

Ricks, Christopher, 273n9

Robertson, Edward, 75

Robertson, Frederick, 36

Robinson, Mary, 10–11, 234n9

Rob Roy. See under Scott, Walter

Robson, Catherine, 202

Roe, Nicholas, 22, 23

Rogers, Samuel, 40, 165–66

Romantics: in anthologies, 123–24, 185–224, 273n10, 277nn35–36; on illustration, 45–47, 51; in reception history, 24–25, 53, 89–130, 273n14; and the spirit of the age, 13, 193; in Victorian reprints, 45, 50–54, 75–85, 273n21

"Rosabelle." *See under* Scott, Walter

Rossetti, Dante Gabriel, 24, 77

Rossetti, William Michael, 77–78, 80, 81, 83, 169, 244n52

Rosslyn, Lord (Robert St. Clair-Erskine), 135, 169, 271n57

Roubiliac, Louis-François, 140, 144, 264n50

Royal Society of Arts. *See* Society of Arts

Ruskin, John, 30, 70, 119, 129, 152, 261n49

Sala, George, 171

Salvation Army, 96

Samuel, Raphael, 14–15

scalable reading, 194, 275n33

Schaaf, Larry, 157, 267n49

Scott, Walter, 10, 11, 15, 22–23, 39, 59, 77, 101,
135, 137, 138, 146, 169, 180, 234n1, 237n63,
247n1, 248n10, 266n16; in anthologies, 9,
211–12; as editor, 48–49, 189; illustrated
works of, 47, 48, 49; on illustrations, 46,
51; "The Lady of the Lake," 1–2; *Lay of
the Last Minstrel*, 211–12; "Marmion," 34;
portraits and statues of, 19, 20, 135, 137,
138, 139, 164, *178*, 179–80, 272n65; *Rob
Roy*, 38; "Rosabelle," 211–12; *Waverley*, 38.
See also Scott Monument
Scottish National Gallery, 139
Scottish National Portrait Gallery, 139
Scott Monument, 145–63, *149*, *156*, *159*, 164,
180; design and construction of, 30,
147–48, 151–55, 172–74, 176–77; funding
for, 136, 153–54; inauguration of, 136, 156,
171; in other media, 20, 156, *160–62*, *161–63*;
as photographic subject, 156–57, *158–59*
secularization, 95–97; and religious reception tradition, 95–96, 98–101, 105–7, 109,
115; Romanticism and, 74, 90, 98–101,
105–16, 130. *See also* religious belief
Sedgwick, Eve Kosofsky, 243n20
Selection from the Works of Lord Byron
(Swinburne), 78, 252n30
Senancour, Étienne Pivert de, 32
"Sensitive Plant, The." *See under* Shelley,
Percy Bysshe
sermons, 30, 90–91, 94, 103, 104, 114, 116,
118–20, 124–27, 129
Severn, Joseph, 40
Shakespeare, William, 103, 121, 122, 215,
279n15; in anthologies, 104, 194; illustrated editions of, 48, 54; portraits and
statues of, 73–74, *75*, 137, 140, 142, 166,
174–77, *175*, *178*
"She Walks in Beauty." *See under* Byron,
George Gordon
Shelley, Mary, 40, 200, 201, 209, 279n20
Shelley, Percy Bysshe, 9–10, 15, 23, 32,
36, 37, 39, 77, 94, 121, 128, 167,
200–203, 215, 225–28, 257n56, 276n6,
276nn10–11; *Alastor*, 199, 217, 218–19,

220; in anthologies, 187, 190–91, 194,
195, 199–202, 205, 208–10, 217–19, 224,
277n35; atheism of, 100–101, 105–6, 109,
128; *The Cenci*, 199, 217, 219–20; "The
Cloud," 199, 203, 277n35; feminization of,
205; literary portrayals of, 33–35, 41–42;
"Ozymandias," 200, 225–28, *226*; as poet
of sound, 101, 108, 257n43; portraits and
statues of, 112, *178*, 272n69; *Prometheus
Unbound*, 104, 106, 110, 200, 275n3; *Queen
Mab*, 106, 108, 199, 200, 217–18, 220, 224,
279n20; reimagined as Christian, 99–116;
"The Sensitive Plant," 199, 203, 208–9;
"To a Skylark," 199, 201–2, 203, 209–10,
276nn18–19, 277n35; Victorians' treat-
ment of controversy, 217–18, 220
Sheppard, John, 89, 90, 91, 93, 94, 254n21
Siege of Valencia, The. See under Hemans,
Felicia
Sinker, Robert, 144
Siskin, Clifford, 15, 16
Smiles, Samuel, 155
Smith, Alan, 249n29
Smith, Paul, 170
Smith, Sheila M. 233n2
Snow, Vernon, 267n49
societal divisions, as poetic theme, 206
Society of Arts (*also* Royal Society of Arts),
165–67
Sontag, Susan, 60
Southey, Robert, 40, 189, 213, 249n29,
275n30
Specimens of the Early English Poets (Ellis),
275n30
Spurgeon, Charles Haddon, 30, 99, 117–30,
258n4, 259n14, 259n24; career of, 118–20;
as mediator of Byron, 117–18, 121–30, 224;
publications of, 119, 122, 126; reading by,
118, 120–24, 127, 128–30, 260n27, 260n29,
260n33, 261n35, 261n41; and Ruskin, 119, 129,
261n49; sermons of, 118, 119–22, 125, 129–30
Spurgeon College, 123
Stanhope, Earl (Philip Henry Stanhope),
168, 170

Stanley, Arthur Penrhyn, 138

St. Clair, William, 51, 74, 190, 191–92, 272n5, 273n21, 274n25

St. Paul's Cathedral, 134, 139–40, 163

statues, 18, 135–47, 166, 169–80, 264n50, 265n6, 272n65

Steell, John, 148–49, 154, 172

Stein, Atara, 240n22

Stein, Gertrude, 244n48

Stewart, Dugald, 147

Stowe, Harriet Beecher, 77, 171

Sun Pictures in Scotland (Talbot), 156, 157–58

Swinburne, Algernon Charles, 24, 31–32, 38, 77, 78, 81, 130, 244n47, 252n30

Sybil. See under Disraeli, Benjamin

Talbot, William Henry Fox, 19, 52, 156, 157–59, 267n39, 267n49

Tanselle, G. Thomas, 53

Tauchnitz, Bernhard, 260n27

Taylor, Charles, 12, 95, 96

Taylor, Henry, 40

Tennyson, Alfred, 24, 32, 37–38, 103, 134, 169, 178; illustrated works by, 60; "To the Queen," 35–36

Thomas, Julia, 54

Thomson, James, 96, 111, 152, 257n43

Thornycroft, Thomas, 174–74, 175, 177

Thorpe, James, 238n10

Thorwaldsen, Bertel, 142–44, 143, 168, 169, 172, 177, 179, 180, 264n53, 265n59

Thousand and One Gems of English Poetry, A (Mackay), 186–87

Thucydides, 12

time, concepts of, 12, 25–26, 39, 60. *See also* historicism; history, concepts of

tissue guards. *See under* frontmatter

title pages. *See under* frontmatter

"To a Skylark." *See under* Shelley, Percy Bysshe

"To the Queen." *See under* Tennyson, Alfred

Todd, John, 9

tourism, 20, 24, 60–61, 65–68, 70–71, 120, 139–40, 143–44, 161, 162, 167, 175–76, 216, 250n44

tradition, 25–30, 241n34, 241nn36–37, 241n40, 241n46; high-art, 240n22, 240n31; invented, 65–66. *See also* reception tradition

Trelawny, Edward John, 40, 168, 169, 269n29

Trinity College Library (Cambridge), 117, 140–44, 141, 143, 145, 148, 264n50

Truths Illustrated by Great Authors (White), 124, 126, 127

Tuck & Sons, Raphael, 161–62

Turner, Charles Tennyson, 144

Turner, J.M.W., 48, 68

Venables, George, 36

Venetia. See under Disraeli, Benjamin

Victoria, Queen, 102, 153, 154, 174

Victoria and Albert Museum (*also* South Kensington Museum), 170, 270n41

Victorians, interests of, 49–50, 73, 160–61; religious habits of, 90–91, 253n7; views on Romanticism, 9–11, 13–16, 24–25, 31–42, 49–55

Virgil, 140, 142

visual culture. *See* culture, visual

Vizetelly, Henry, 50, 52

"Voice of Spring, The." *See under* Hemans, Felicia

Wade, Thomas, 101

Wales, invented traditions of, 65–66

Walter, Catherine, 267n49

Walter, John, 267n49

Wark, McKenzie, 236n40

Warner, William, 15, 16

The Waste Land (Eliot), 26–27

Watson, Nicola, 83, 269n23

Watson, William, 152–53

Waverley. See under Scott, Walter

Webb, Timothy, 209, 276n10

Weber, Max, 155

Weekes, Henry, 112, 264n50

Wellington, Duke of (Arthur Wellesley), 147, 149, 176–77, 178, 180, 271n63, 272n66

West, William, 75–76

A NOTE ON THE TYPE

THIS BOOK has been composed in Arno, an Old-style serif font in the classic Venetian tradition, designed by Robert Slimbach at Adobe.